REPRESENTING WOMEN

▼

POST-CONTEMPORARY INTERVENTIONS

Series Editors: Stanley Fish and Fredric Jameson

REPRESENTING WOMEN

Law, Literature, and Feminism

▼

SUSAN SAGE HEINZELMAN AND

ZIPPORAH BATSHAW WISEMAN,

EDITORS

Duke University Press   Durham and London   1994

DEDICATION

From Sue

To Kurt, Calum, and Clare—always loving,

always laughing

From Zipporah

To Fred, David, and Eric, without whom

I would rather not even imagine

© 1994 Duke University Press

All rights reserved

Printed in the United States of America on acid-free paper ∞

Designed by Cherie Holma Westmoreland

Typeset in Joanna by Tseng Information Systems, Inc.

Library of Congress Cataloging-in-Publication Data appear on

the last printed page of this book.

Anne B. Goldstein, "Representing the Lesbian in Law and

Literature," © Anne B. Goldstein, 1994.

CONTENTS

Preface   vii
Acknowledgments   xi

I LAW AND LITERATURE: BREAKING DOWN THE WALLS   1

From Class Actions to "Miss Saigon": The Concept of Representation
in the Law   *Martha Minow*   8

The Narrative and the Normative in Legal Scholarship
Kathryn Abrams   44

Commonalities: On Being Black and White, Different and
the Same   *Judy Scales-Trent*   57

Less than Pornography: The Power of Popular Fiction
Carol Sanger   75

II REPRESENTING POWER AND SHIFTING PERSPECTIVE   101

Race and Essentialism in Feminist Legal Theory
Angela P. Harris   106

Presence of Mind in the Absence of Body   *Linda Brodkey and
Michelle Fine*   147

Pornography and Canonicity: The Case of Yeats's "Leda and
the Swan"   *Elizabeth Butler Cullingford*   165

Sex at Work   *Susan B. Estrich*   189

III REVISING ANCIENT TALES   247

Why Women Can't Read: Medieval Hermeneutics, Statutory Law,
and the Lollard Heresy Trials   *Rita Copeland*   253

Voices of Record: Women as Witnesses and Defendants in the Old
Bailey Sessions Papers   *Margaret Anne Doody*   287

Guilty in Law, Implausible in Fiction: Jurisprudential and Literary
Narratives in the Case of Mary Blandy, Parricide, 1752
Susan Sage Heinzelman 309

Witnessing Women: Trial Testimony in Novels by Tonna, Gaskell,
and Eliot *Christine L. Krueger* 337

Representing the Lesbian in Law and Literature
Anne B. Goldstein 356

Notes on Editors and Contributors 385

PREFACE

▼

      This anthology is situated at the intersection of Anglo-American common law, literature, and feminism. We intend these essays to provoke commentary, disagreement, and assent; the essays do not insist upon a consistent political position, nor do they espouse a particular critical methodology. The collection, therefore, leaves itself open to criticism from those who might wish it to be more radical, more compromising, or, simply, more representative. We have tried to suggest the multiple and complex ways in which women talk about themselves and allow others to talk about them, ways that are sometimes liberating and sometimes incriminating, but always fraught with questions of personal and therefore political power. The essays in this anthology remind us that even in the last decade of the twentieth century there are many obstacles to women's assertion of their right to power; but the essays also remind us of the many possibilities for such assertions.

    The power of representation is not only inherently implied by the act of speaking and writing, not only implied by the content of that speech and text, but also by the way such speaking and writing confirms and fits in with a body of knowledge already recognized and valued in the world. It is for this latter reason—that individual stories are part of a larger narrative—that the organization of the anthology insists upon the importance of interdisciplinary thought. Interdisciplinarity requires that stories about how people live their lives, and the kind of values and systems of meaning that such living implies, are no longer kept separate within the confines of discipline-specific formations, like law and literature. A story about a woman's legal power is not separate from a story about her reproductive and productive power. It has been very much to the detriment of women's power in and through representation that these interdependent narratives have been confined within discipline-specific forms of knowledge, each with its apparently appropriate topics, subjects of study, and methodologies—what Foucault identifies as "discursive practices." These discursive practices determine what gets named as knowledge, how it gets named and by whom, how that knowledge gets generated, and by whom it is dispersed. Feminism is, of course, one of the more critically significant interdisciplinary methodologies that questions this traditional production of knowledge.

Feminism questions intellectual proprietorship: it cuts across disciplinary boundaries and asks what's at stake when those boundaries are broken down. It asks why those disciplines have been represented as impermeable, as if there were a clear line between what's inside the discipline and what's outside. We have resisted dividing the anthology into essays on "The Representation of Women in the Law" and "The Representation of Women in Literature" because it is precisely this reduction of the terms "Women" and "Law" or "Literature" into simple, uncomplicated categories of representation that disarms women when they try to tell their own stories. The organization of the anthology, we would hope, suggests the complex and interconnected power relationships between different forms, occasions, and narrators.

We have also tried to indicate how the same energy and conviction that women writers have employed covertly and overtly against a system that might otherwise silence them can be turned to speaking about women in ways that legal discourse can embrace. This means that authenticity (i.e., narrative authority) will no longer remain a "fictional" value when women address their representation and misrepresentation in legal contexts. We also hope that the interweaving of the fictional with the nonfictional that occurs in many of the essays might undo the seeming opposition between legal discourse, traditionally characterized by its claim to objective and rational epistemology, and literary discourse, characterized as subjective and imaginative (that is, unreal or irrational).

The question of what universe certain discourses construct and whether that universe is real or unreal is a question more properly undertaken in a collection on narrative and narratology. We have not attempted to engage all of the current debates on the nature and status of narrative or the text, nor have we attempted to survey the range of critical methodologies that might reasonably be invoked when describing "a speaking subject." Whichever kind of subject one chooses to identify with, however, a crucial question remains in a text that claims to be a representative collection on representation: For whom are we, as editors, speaking? We take to heart Elizabeth Spelman's observation that "[t]hose who produce the 'story' of women want to make sure they appear in it. The best way to ensure that is to be the storyteller and hence to be in a position to decide which of the many facts about women's lives ought to go into the story, which ought to be left out."[1] Or, in the case of this anthology, which of the many essays that characterize women's representation ought to go into the collection, which ought to be left out. By our selection, we claim a certain authority for our authors, but for whom do we claim our authors are speaking? Is the author speaking only for herself? Is she speaking for others in her particular class, racial, or ethnic group? And if not, what can be said about the representation of those who do not have access to any language—legal or literary—that claims attention? Is it enough for those unrepresented women that we can share some part of their experience through the suasive power of real stories, like those told in court, and also through the imaginative life that literature generates?

While these questions may have equivocal answers, there is no doubt that the capacity to tell one's own story brings power, and that the more culturally significant the forum in which the story is told and the more powerful the audience that listens to the story, the more likely it is that the story will have some practical effect in the world. But, as the essays in this anthology demonstrate, simply being able to tell the story is not enough: one has to be aware of how the story might be contained within certain disciplinary boundaries and thus restrained in its effects (Part I. Law and Literature: Breaking Down the Walls); one has to be aware of how the story might articulate and perpetuate an ideological agenda that will run counter to the best interests of the storyteller (Part II. Representing Power and Shifting Perspective); and one has also to be aware of the historical context of the story and its telling in order to comprehend the power of traditional representations (Part III. Revising Ancient Tales). We hope that this anthology will make the retelling of old stories compelling and the telling of new ones both necessary and possible.

Notes

1. Elizabeth V. Spelman, *Inessential Woman: Problems of Exclusion in Feminist Thought* 159 (1988).

ACKNOWLEDGMENTS

▼

An anthology is, by definition, the work of many hands, but the most important work is performed by the contributors. We begin, therefore, by thanking all those who have written for this collection and all those who have allowed their work to be reprinted here. Their patience with the process of publication and their willingness to make changes in their texts has made our task of editing this collection much easier than we were warned it would be.

This collection grew out of "cross-disciplinary" seminars we taught together at the University of Texas and conversations with Christine Krueger, which, in turn, led to our conceiving of the first symposium on women and the law at the University of Texas School of Law. Many of the articles in this anthology were part of that symposium. It was made possible by the support and encouragement of Dean Mark Yudof, the Will E. Orgain lectureship, and Professor Michael Tigar. Margaret Wolfe contributed her amazing administrative skills and taught us how an ideal conference should run. In addition to his administrative support, Mike Tigar also contributed his considerable culinary talents to the occasion.

Friends and colleagues contributed many varieties of support to this anthology. Anne B. Goldstein, Kurt Heinzelman, Christine Krueger, JoAnn Pavletich, and Majorie Curry Woods gave us the gift of their time and judgments. Kurt Heinzelman also gave us his steady counsel and his wonderful cuisine. Pamela McGraw was a manuscript editor extraordinaire. The Sunday morning aerobics-laugh-brunch club—John and Anna, Liz and Alan, and especially, Yvette, and its penumbra, Janis and Evan—gave us the requisite mental and physical health to carry this project through its long gestation period.

For all and to all we are grateful.

LAW AND LITERATURE:

BREAKING DOWN

THE WALLS

I

The essays in this section suggest both the complexities of discussing what constitutes "representation" and the many ways in which the comparative and contextualizing nature of interdisciplinary inquiry can challenge traditional representations of women. Representation is, typically, not representative, and interdisciplinary inquiry can reveal the particular ways in which representations constitute meaning: interdisciplinary inquiry requires us to examine both the representation itself and the historical and cultural means by which certain representations become embedded as stereotypes. In particular, examining women's representation across the disciplines of law and literature, two extremely powerful and culturally central bodies of knowledge, reveals how differently women's stories have been told, how variously women's voices have been heard. As Virginia Woolf remarked on surveying the representation of women in canonical English literature: "[I]f woman had no existence save in the fiction written by men, one would imagine her a person of utmost importance. . . . Imaginatively she is of the utmost significance; practically she is completely insignificant."[1] Virginia Woolf wrote that at the beginning of the twentieth century. As we approach the beginning of the twenty-first century, we still need to challenge that gap between what a woman is "imaginatively" and what she is "practically." And one critical way in which this can be done is to examine carefully the functions that representation serves in constructing our culture.

Such a task is precisely that undertaken by Martha Minow in her essay "From Class Actions to 'Miss Saigon': The Concept of Representation in the Law." Minow examines the complexities of representation—questions of merit and bias, of equity and equality, of difference and sameness, of community and individuality—by juxtaposing aesthetic and legal questions about "who may speak for someone else" and under what circumstances any representation is indeed representative. For Minow, as for Michael J. Shapiro, "representations do not imitate reality but are the practices through which things take on meaning and value"[2] and, as such, define the manner in which certain individuals and groups have come to be seen as able to speak for themselves, while others have been relegated to the category of those who must be spoken for, which, in turn, raises the issue of who, specifically, will do their talking.

Minow begins by juxtaposing two debates about representativeness: the first, the controversy over the casting of an English Caucasian actor in the 1990 Broadway production of "Miss Saigon," the hit London musical—Actors' Equity had refused to give permission to the actor, arguing that it could not "appear to condone the casting of a Caucasian in the role of a Eurasian"; the second, the controversy over hiring practices in law schools highlighted by Professor Derrick Bell's decision to take an unpaid leave from Harvard Law School until the school "hired for its tenure track a female law professor of color." Both debates, notes Minow, centered on the question of merit versus symbolism; in "both contexts, one side argued that there must be someone hired from the minority community while the other side maintained that hiring must be color-blind and merit-based." The debates "reflect arguments made on behalf of historically excluded groups that group membership serves as a proxy for shared experiences and especially common experiences as victims of societal prejudice. Opponents . . . resist such arguments because they undermine the commitment to treating individuals as individuals." Minow examines the contributions of philosopher Hanna Feinchel Pitkin; of theorists concerned with difference, like feminist and critical race theorists; and the contributions of a variety of scholars interested in validating empathy as a means to explore these complexities of representation.

Minow presents Professor Pitkin's four divergent definitions of representation: (1) formally, representation means "the authorized arrangement preceding and initiating the creation of a representative"; (2) representation refers to "the notion of likeness, mirror, map, or portrait. . . . Representing here depends . . . on the representative's characteristics and ability to 'stand for' those he represents"; (3) representation refers to "symbolic substitution: The flag stands for the nation"; (4) representation refers to "a range of analogies to roles through which an individual may provide, care, or speak for another." Professor Pitkin's definitions of representation—actor, trustee, deputy, agent, steward—reopen the central ambiguities of the concept of representation: Who is best qualified to "speak for another"? What determines the actions of the representative—the wishes of those she represents or her decision about what might be best for those she represents? What values and standards does the representative use in determining what is in the best interests of those he represents?

Minow situates these definitions of representation within two contemporary movements in academic circles: difference theory and the idea of empathy. In difference theory, she explains, critics question the use of "universal and abstract norms [that] may once have advanced a democratic and antihierarchical agenda, [but that] in current operation . . . often fail to reflect—fail to represent—the experiences, interests, and needs of the full variety of human beings." Difference theorists argue that "[s]peaking expresses power; it is empowering; and speaking for others depends on their trust." Difference theory raises the questions of how many differences need to be represented: how can any cohesive political action emerge from a caucus divided along the lines of racial, gender, sexual, and religious difference? A second view of the concept of representation is based on the assumption that, despite the traditional liberal belief that each individual has "distinct and conflicting ideas," people "(1) often want to care about the good of others (altruism) and (2) have the ability to understand and know the wants and needs of others (empathy)." What these empathy advocates suggest is an understanding of representation based on "reconstructing rules and institutions to expect and reinforce" people's capacity to care for others.

Minow applies these conflicting readings of representation to two specific legal contexts—to juries and class actions—indicating, once again, how fraught with contradictions and complexities is the claim to "speak for another." She concludes that "[b]eneath the clashing assertions of essential differences and meritocracy . . . are our common experiences: betrayal by those who claim to speak for us but do not understand, and connection with those who seem so different. Law, at its best, cannot resolve such deep conflicts. Law can only manage them, temporarily." Minow's essay, juxtaposing the worlds of theater and law, sets the stage for many of the explicit and implicit themes of this collection—who speaks, who will be heard, and under what circumstances.

Looking at how law does manage those "deep [cultural] conflicts," Kathryn Abrams concludes that one strategy that has become increasingly important to women is storytelling, specifically storytelling about their own lives. In her essay "The Narrative and the Normative in Legal Scholarship," Abrams argues that "[a]uthors use their own experiential stories, or those of others, to illuminate what unites and divides us across lines of gender, race, class, or sexual orientation." It is the role of this experiential storytelling in legal scholarship, and consequent proposals for legal change, that Abrams focuses on and that engages us, once again, with the question of just how representative—that is, inclusive—one woman's story can be. Abrams's account of the transformative nature of storytelling in legal scholarship also reminds us of the similar effect that women's experiential narratives have had on traditional literary criticism—not only in terms of methodology but also in terms of what texts become available for critical readings. Abrams's reading of the relationship between feminist narratives and the construction of the normative in legal scholarship is thus a formal account and indicates just how significant structural change is to the story of women's relationship to their legal and literary representations.

Abrams surveys the variety of feminist narrative scholarship—both in terms of its authorship and its form—and its effect upon mainstream legal scholars: "[m]ainstream scholars wonder if narrative can and does contribute to the prescriptions for legal change that are a primary focus of legal scholarship." These scholars doubt that general policy can be deduced from particular stories; they doubt that epistemologically sound reasons can be found for "translating stories into normative proposals." Their assumptions about what feminist narrative scholarship cannot do is, of course, based on their unquestioned assumptions about what traditional legal scholarship does do. "Many legal scholars strive for what Edward Rubin has called a 'unity of discourse' with the courts they address: they assume the same posture of distance from their subject, and employ the same specificity in legal formulation, and abstraction from the concrete details of claimants' lives, that characterize appellate opinions." Feminist narratives, needless to say, infrequently satisfy these criteria. What Abrams suggests is that a broader understanding of what constitutes the normative in legal scholarship needs to be adopted, and she begins this process by tracing the chronological emergence of feminist narrative in feminist scholarship and sketching the potential political effect such narratives might have on legal policy.

Abrams analyzes the different, and not mutually exclusive, forms that narrative scholarship can take: "excluded voices" narratives, a second generation of narratives termed "mid-course correction" narratives, and "paradigm-shifting" narratives. She argues that the manner in which such forms of narrative scholarship can transform, and already have transformed legal policy and decision-making suggests that it is not only "the abstract elegance of a proposed solution" that might be persuasive to decisionmakers. They might also be persuaded "by a particularized depiction of the lives of those affected by a legal rule."

Judy Scales-Trent's essay, or rather meditation, "Commonalities: On Being Black and White, Different and the Same," is precisely the kind of "excluded voices" narrative that Abrams suggests can effect legal change by correcting partial representations. Scales-Trent, who is a lawyer and a professor of law, is also a black woman who looks white. She wrote the journal notes, and the essay, as a way of coming to terms with these anomalies, as a way of existing at the boundaries of race and color. Her journal entries cover three years, from 1978 to 1981, and register the profound sense of alienation she experiences from her own identity and history, as a black child, and from the identity imposed upon her by a white world that sees her as a black person who is "really white." The journal traces Scales-Trent's journey from self-hatred and confusion to an acceptance of her identity: "I claim only myself, and define myself by my own name." Such self-definition allows Scales-Trent to understand her commonality with others, to "hear echoes of [her] song in the songs of others," in the songs of her Native American sisters, her Chinese-American sisters, and her lesbian sisters, and, indeed, in the stories of all those who, at a particular moment, find themselves on the outside, "who [feel their] difference and [their] exclusion so keenly."

For Carol Sanger, one way in which women share a common mode of representation is through the values and meanings attached to the maternal body. In her essay "Less Than Pornography: The Power of Popular Fiction," Sanger compares the limited representation of women as mothers in two popular novels, *Presumed Innocent* and *The Good Mother*, specifically addressing the conflict between representing woman as mother and representing woman as a sexual being. Pointing out that best-selling fiction influences public opinion by reinforcing prejudices, Sanger explores the continued insistence upon certain stereotypes of women's sexuality. In addition, she argues that popular fiction, particularly when laced with even the appearance of legal authority, "may reinforce familiar values with subtlety and ease." Looking at the treatment of women in popular legal fiction, she suggests, "tells not so much how society views lawyers . . . as it suggests perceptions about the power or influence of law for civilians."

Sanger notes that in *Presumed Innocent*, there are essentially only two women characters: Carolyn Polhemus, the promiscuous Barbie-doll, "a helluva lawyer," prosecuting attorney, and bad mother; and her foil, Barbara, loving mother, mathematics graduate student, loyal wife, and, sadly, killer of Carolyn. The plot hinges on the apparent rape of Carolyn, a rape that she appears to have invited by her sexually loose conduct, and the aggression of the suburban housewife preserving her family against her enemy, the vamp. *Presumed Innocent*, concludes Sanger, "works because it relies on exaggerated but hard-to-shake notions about good wives and vampy women" and because these stereotypes are sanctioned by the authenticity and "realities of a criminal prosecution."

In the second novel, *The Good Mother*, the tensions of the woman as a sexual being and mother are concentrated in one figure, that of Anna Dunlap, sexually active, single mother. What the fiction of the novel requires of both the protagonist and the reader is that she be made by the law to choose between being a good mother or a sexually active woman, since it is apparently not possible to be both. Such a dilemma is not atypical of many single mothers, who have lost custody of their children for sexual behavior that does not meet with the approval of legal decisionmakers.

Both novels tell stories that suggest that "community and law are slow to defend sexual women." (A 1992 case in Austin, Texas, where a grand jury initially refused to indict a man who had confessed to rape because his victim asked him to wear a condom, suggests that a woman's sexual knowledge risks harming her legally, rather than protecting her.) Moreover, both stories also suggest the essential opposition in our culture of the two images of women: the good mother and the sexual woman. Anna Dunlap and Carolyn Polhemus are feared, suggests Sanger, "because their single marital status carries a presumption not of innocence but of sexual availability." *Presumed Innocent* "seasons us to an essentially sexual conception and use of women. Such representations, whether best-sellers or other forms of popular fiction, invigorate sexist images by making them simple, commonplace, acceptable." *The Good Mother* instructs us about how sexist representations shore up existing systems of belief and what happens when women fail to take those representations seriously.

Notes

1. Virginia Woolf, *A Room of One's Own* 44–45 (Penguin, 1972) (1928).
2. Michael J. Shapiro, Preface to *Politics of Representation: Writing Practices in Biography, Photography, and Policy Analysis* xi (1988).

FROM CLASS ACTIONS TO

"MISS SAIGON"

The Concept of Representation in the Law

Martha Minow

▼

Setting the Stage

In August 1990, the producer of "Miss Saigon," the hit London musical, decided to cancel its Broadway production because the U.S.-based actors' union denied permission for the English lead actor to perform the play in New York.[1] Actors' Equity, the union, issued a statement that it could not "appear to condone the casting of a Caucasian in the role of a Eurasian."[2] The conflict between the union and the producer produced a cause célèbre debated in the theater community, in the press, and inside Actors' Equity itself. A week after its initial decision, the union reversed itself, saying it had "applied an honest and moral principle in an inappropriate manner."[3] After weeks of negotiations securing complete casting freedom to the producer, plans for the play revived, but the issue continued to produce controversy and wide media coverage for months thereafter.

The context of the controversy included advance ticket sales of $25 million;[4] the recent election of an African-American mayor concerned about both remedying discrimination and preserving the theater industry;[5] the political attack on controversial art by conservative American officials seeking to control the uses of federal subsidies;[6] an emerging public conflict over attention to "politically correct" claims about racism, sexism, and homophobia;[7] and the United States Supreme Court's repudiation of most public affirmative action programs.[8]

For me, there was one more context for the debate. As I read about the casting of "Miss Saigon," I could not help but draw connections to another "casting" debate, closer to my home.[9] The ongoing debate over why law school faculties remain largely white and male intensified with Professor Derrick Bell's decision to take a leave without pay until Harvard Law School hired for its tenure track a female law professor of color. Further intensifying the issue at Harvard, a group of law students sued the school and claimed that discriminatory hiring practices hindered their education.[10] Both "Miss Saigon" and Harvard Law School generated arguments about merit and about symbolism, about overcoming discrimination and about risks of new forms of discrimination, about fairness and about representation. In both contexts, one side argued that there must be someone hired from the minority community while the other side maintained that hiring must be color-blind and merit-based.[11]

Many arguments in the law school hiring context echo those generated by the "Miss Saigon" casting controversy; see if they sound familiar to you. Jonathan Pryce, the white English actor cast by the producer for the role, commented: "What is appropriate is that the best person for the job play the role and I think it's completely valid that I play the role."[12] Translated for law school hiring, this argument sounds like: "what is appropriate is that the best person for the job get the job; excellence must not be sacrificed for other purposes."

About "Miss Saigon," Frank Rich commented: "By refusing to permit a white actor to play a Eurasian role, Equity makes a mockery of the hard-won principles of nontraditional casting and practices a hypocritical reverse racism."[13] Similarly, though perhaps less vividly, professors have argued that demanding the appointment of a professor because of her sex and race contravenes hard-fought principles of equal opportunity and color-blindness.[14] Even more directly on point were arguments over a hiring controversy at Harvard a few years back: when white civil rights activists and black civil rights lawyers were invited as visitors to teach a course on civil rights, students protested the school's failure to hire a full-time faculty member of color for such a course. In its defense, the Harvard administration challenged the idea that a white person who had devoted his life to the subject could not teach about civil rights.[15]

In contrast, Ellen Holly, a black actress, commented about the "Miss Saigon" casting debate:

> Racism in America today is nothing so crass as mere hatred of a person's skin color. It is rather an affliction of so many centuries' duration that it permeates institutions to the point of becoming indivisible from them. Only when the darker races attempt to break out of the bind—and inconvenience

whites in the process—do whites even perceive racism as an issue. Only when a white is asked to vacate a role on racial grounds does the matter become a front-page issue.[16]

Analogously, in law school faculties around the country, individuals argue about institutionalized racism. Some observers argue that implicit preferences for people who are part of the "old-boy network" go unnoticed, while preferences for someone from a traditionally excluded group provoke an uproar. Advocates for change assert that only actual results in hiring should count as evidence that historic exclusions are being overcome.

From this point of view, what may look like a preference for a member of a racial minority is really an effort to counteract a preference for whites. But another argument for preferring members of racial minorities simply views them as people specially qualified for the job at hand. In the wake of the "Miss Saigon" controversy, the distinguished playwright August Wilson defended his demand for a black director for the film production of one of his plays as follows:

> We are an African people who have been here since the early 17th century. We have a different way of responding to the world. We have different ideas about religion, different manners of social intercourse. We have different ideas about style, about language. We have different esthetics. Someone who does not share the specifics of a culture remains an outsider, no matter how astute a student or how well-meaning their intentions. I declined a white director not on the basis of race but on the basis of culture. White directors are not qualified for the job.[17]

Similarly, a professor of color is needed, many argue, because that person will bring cultural perspectives otherwise missing from the law school community. That perspective will enrich the classroom, the scholarship, the counseling of students who share that background, and the counseling of students who do not share that background. In addition, some law school faculty members may conclude that their school should hire a Hispanic professor, because the increasing numbers of Hispanic students need the knowledge held by that person and because white, Asian, and African-American students need to see a Hispanic person in the respected position at the head of the class. Hence the slogan, "No education without representation."[18]

An additional argument arises in the law school hiring debate. Professors are role models, and only members of historically excluded groups can serve adequately as role models for students of those groups, goes this variation of the argument.[19] Some who support this position maintain somewhat differently that only a variety of role models can serve the needs of all students. Thus the special pedagogical needs of students who are members of minority groups are distinct from and yet complementary to the benefit for all students from diversity among the faculty. Further, in a distributive justice sense, the focus on race and sex in hiring should serve to shift resources, including the resource of academic attention, to new agendas for legal scholarship and teaching.[20] Finally, the presence of actors of color in a play can encourage young people of color to consider acting as a career just as professors of color can inspire nonwhite students to pursue academic careers.

Most striking to me is the parallel between those who find the entire framework of debate unacceptable, whether in the contexts of "Miss Saigon" casting or law school hiring. Playwright David Henry Hwang, one of the first to complain about the casting choice in "Miss Saigon," later said that he could not choose between minority casting and the producer's right to cast whom he wants because that is "like asking me to pick between my father and my mother; I can't. It's real hard for me to pick between artistic freedom on the one hand and discrimination on the other."[21] Similarly, some law professors argue that the choice cannot be between excellence and diversity because both are critical. In addition, many reject the implication that schools must trade or sacrifice some excellence in order to achieve diversity.

One person struggling with these tensions concluded that at least the debate over the casting in "Miss Saigon" brought the chronic difficulties facing actors of color to public attention. Shirley Sun, director, producer, and writer of the recent film "Iron and Silk," defended the public attention provoked by the stance of Actors' Equity toward "Miss Saigon." She wrote, "a minority group should not intentionally be excluded from [a Broadway play] with impunity . . . 'Artistic freedom' should not be used to exclude any group. If the stage is a sublime place where any actor can play any role, why can't an Asian or Asian-American play a Eurasian role?"[22] If theater offers the possibility that actors can entice audiences to suspend their disbelief and be transported by crafted illusions, why cannot more actors have this chance to transport the audience?[23] The casting decision in "Miss Saigon" then was not about matching the actor's race with the character's race, but about the magical creation of an illusion of reality by whichever actor gains the chance to play the role.[24] Some producers specifically endorse cross-racial casting not only to give the best candidate the chance with the role but also to enrich and challenge the plays with the different dimensions that such casting may afford.[25] Similar arguments are offered for entire cross-cultural productions, such as the Cleveland Play House presentation of "The Glass Menagerie" with a black cast.[26]

The debates over casting "Miss Saigon" and law school faculties reflect the prevalence of contemporary assumptions about group differences. They reflect arguments made on behalf of historically excluded groups that group membership serves as a proxy for shared experiences and especially common experiences as victims of societal prejudice. Opponents, styled as defenders of neutrality, resist such arguments because they undermine the commitment to treating individuals as individuals.[27] Some opponents further charge that the call for hiring members of racial minorities is incoherent if the advocates really want someone who holds a particular, "politically correct" view. Skin color is no determinant of such views, this argument continues, and political litmus tests for hiring violate academic freedom.

The volley between these sides is interminable and confusing. Certainly no one on one side convinces many on the other. Maybe we can understand the debates better by seeing connections to deeper confusions about the concept of representation throughout our society, made especially vivid in legal and political contexts. Let's see how confused we can get, or how confused we already are.

If treated as problems of representation, these issues must be examined in light of the questions: Who may speak for someone else? What is the difference between symbolizing or standing for another, on the one hand, and advancing the interests of another?[28] Which should a representative pursue? I will suggest that enduring confusion about these issues of representation pervades not only controversial hiring decisions but also a range of contemporary legal issues.

One example is elected representatives. Should the representative do just what the voters say they want, such as impose no new taxes, or instead pursue what the representative understands to be the voters' real and best interests? Should the representative look like the voters, eat pork rinds or blintzes or enchiladas, or are these efforts to mirror or resemble the represented irrelevant?[29]

Another example: Who should serve on a jury and who should be disqualified as biased or ill-equipped? Should all Spanish-speaking jurors be excluded from a case involving Spanish-speaking witnesses out of fear that these jurors will have special claims of expertise in the deliberations—or would such exclusion deny the parties and the society a full and fairly representative jury?[30] Who may act as a named representative in a class action: a typical member of the plaintiff group, a specially articulate member, or a member whose injuries are exemplary in the sense of displaying the full variety of those alleged by all the plaintiffs?[31]

When does the completion of a lawsuit preclude a new lawsuit on the same issue brought by different people—when do the parties in the first lawsuit adequately represent for subsequent possible parties? For example, should a suit by black firefighters suing a city for discriminatory hiring practices preclude a new suit by white firefighters dissatisfied with the resulting affirmative action remedy?[32] If the black firefighters cannot represent white firefighters, can the city defending its practices represent the whites? Or should the whites have a chance for a new day in court because their interests were not represented by either the city or the black plaintiffs?

When does a fiduciary fully represent the beneficiary and when should doubts be raised about this representation? The fiduciary may have concerns that differ from those of the beneficiary. This might be the case with investment managers in charge of pension funds intended to benefit some workers who have interests in the ongoing viability of the industry. Those workers may prefer investments in that industry rather than investments with the highest market return.[33] Does the fact that the fiduciary is not a member of the beneficiary group affect that investment judgment? Would a member of the group make a better, more representative judgment? Or is this kind of concern for membership irrelevant to investment decision-making, and properly so?

When should an attorney for tactical purposes have certain personal characteristics because these might benefit the client? Should a woman lawyer be willing to represent a man charged with rape, and a black attorney represent a white employer charged with race discrimination? When should an attorney's membership in the same group as the client matter to the client, or to a judge? Would it make a difference if an argument for gay rights is advanced by a lawyer who is "out"? Would it make a difference if an argument on behalf of a person with a hearing impairment is made by someone with a hearing impairment?[34] Should those group characteristics have an effect? Given that they do currently have an effect, what tactical choices should attorneys and clients make, and should any ethical concerns constrain those choices?

Finally, who can and who should speak for a child or a person physically or mentally unable to speak for herself? What if a child faces a choice between medical treatment and adherence to a religious belief? Who should speak for an elderly person who cannot express a view about whether to stay on a respirator?

These are hard issues. With the help of some philosophic debates I will suggest that we have long been confused about them. I will then argue that two specific developments in legal and political thought cast new confusion—but also new light—on the problem of representation. I look first to the contributions of people concerned with difference, such as feminists and critical race theorists, and then to the contributions of a variety of scholars interested in empathy. After exploring the genuine tension between these two emerging schools of thought, I will return to a few of the legal questions I have just mentioned about who can and who should represent another. And perhaps, I will also get a chance to return to theater before I am done.

Presenting Representation

To deal thoughtfully with confusion, I like to turn to philosophers, especially analytic philosophers. It is not that I understand them. It is that they are so clear about their confusion, so the rest of us can relax about ours. Thus, if an analytic philosopher applies the clarifying tools of careful study of words and their meanings, distinctions and their applications, and analogies and their limitations, and the subject still seems confusing, the reader may conclude with some confidence that the concept just is confusing. Such, I maintain, is the case with representation as a concept, and I proffer the elegant book on the subject by Hanna Feinchel Pitkin as evidence.[35] Many contrasting meanings gather in the crevices of the word "representation." Two contrasting consequences result. Efforts to pin down distinctive meanings may founder as the meanings shade into and evoke one another. Efforts to clarify the concept may instead convert ideal versions of representation into merely definitional notions. Pitkin's ambitious historical and analytic treatment of the concept helps to depict and describe these confusing dimensions of the notion, representation, as she runs circles around the concept and also shows that the concept is circular as used.

Professor Pitkin identifies the relatively modern use of the concept, and notes that the ancient Romans used a similar word to mean the literal bringing into presence of something previously absent, or the embodiment of an abstraction in an object.[36] She then distinguishes two dominant contemporary views of representation: the person who does what is best for those in his or her charge and the person who reflects accurately the wishes and opinions of those he or she is assigned to represent.[37] But beyond this conceptual distinction, Professor Pitkin demonstrates the inadequacy of any single definition for the concept.[38]

Pitkin specifies and contrasts four divergent definitions and she simultaneously explores their mutual influences and internal tensions. First, a formal definition looks to the authorized arrangement preceding and initiating the creation of a representative.[39] Pitkin criticizes this notion as circular; it lacks both any directive about the actual task to be performed and any measure of accountability for the performance of that task.[40] In a second definition, representation refers to the notion of likeness, mirror, map, or portrait. Representing here depends not on authority, accountability, or any kind of acting, but instead on the representative's characteristics and ability to "stand for" those he represents.[41] This definition has a measure of the representative's success: it is the verisimilitude or believability of the representation. Because it turns on the personal characteristics of the representative rather than any actions taken, this concept resembles the emphasis on appearance in the debates over hiring in "Miss Saigon" and law school faculties.[42]

The emphasis on accuracy in this second definition is problematic. A fully accurate depiction is probably impossible, even in art (where this may not even be the goal).[43] Because of this impossibility, other dimensions of representation may operate under the name of appearance or imitation. Professor Pitkin notes: "As soon as the correspondence is less than perfect, we must begin to question what sorts of features and characteristics are relevant to action, and how good the correspondence is with regard to just those features."[44] Choosing which traits to make relevant raises questions of authorization or substitution. Alongside the shortfall between ideal resemblance and limited resemblance is the gap between the ideal and the real representative in other senses. The use of one trait rather than others as a basis for resemblance further confuses the relation between ideal and real. "We tend to assume that people's characteristics are a guide to the actions they will take, and we are concerned with the characteristics of our legislators for just this reason. But it is no simple correlation; the best descriptive representative is not necessarily the best representative for activity or government."[45] As this statement by Pitkin suggests, there is something slippery and thus misleading in the use of a term like representation. One of its meanings slides into its other meanings without consistency or reliability. Similarly, talking about a representative in terms of a likeness may imply something that is typical. Yet, this too may be unsatisfactory, for the concept does not address along which lines the representative is to be typical. In asking for a representative poem, we may not mean a typical one but instead the best one, the best example. Similarly, people often choose representatives who are not typical of the class they represent.[46]

Besides the formal definition of authorized representation and the likeness definition, a third meaning of representation, as noted by Pitkin, refers to symbolic substitution: The flag stands for the nation; the symbol "x" stands for the unknown quantity of apples; π stands for plaintiff. This notion of a symbol, if freighted with meaning, may explain why a leader who is not accountable or typical is nonetheless sometimes described as a representative; that leader may in some respect be a symbol of the polity, the community, or the beliefs of those represented.[47] This definition, however, lacks any guide for what a representative is to do or how one could judge the performance of a representative.[48]

Pitkin's fourth definition actually is a range of analogies to roles through which an individual may provide, care, or speak for another. Actor, trustee, deputy, agent, steward—these are all notions with different shades of meaning pertinent to the idea of speaking for another.[49] But the selection of which of these terms to accept as an analogy replicates the central ambiguity within the notion of representation itself: should the representative do what the represented party wants or what the representative thinks is best?[50] Professor Pitkin notes how tilting to either extreme risks eliminating the very role of the representative. Doing entirely what the represented party wishes converts the representative into a mere conveyor of information, while doing only what the representative thinks is best risks eliminating any connection, obligation, or accountability to the represented party.[51] It is not enough, according to Professor Pitkin, for the representative to choose whether or not to pursue the client's wishes. To be a representative, it is necessary also that such choices be justifiable.[52] And yet this very notion of justification simply reopens the question, along with what values or standards to use in measuring representation.

Talk of the interests, even the objective interests of those represented, is tempting in evaluating a representative, but the ambiguities and assessment difficulties with this set of concepts are notorious.[53] In Professor Pitkin's analysis, different theories of interests reflect contrasting political conceptions of the good, justice, knowledge, and social class and social solidarity.[54] She concludes that

> [t]he more a writer sees interests, wants, and the like as definable only by the person who feels or has them, the more likely he is to require that a representative consult his constituents and act in response to what they ask of him. At the extreme, again, substantive acting for others becomes impossible, and a theorist must either fall back on other views of representation or declare the concept an illusion.[55]

Ultimately, the representative quality of given persons or institutions turns on their capacities to justify themselves to those who are allegedly represented or who otherwise care.[56] Again circularity of the concept appears: "representative" means what others are convinced it means. So if you and I are confused about how to measure or check whether someone is a good representative or whether a representative function is appropriate to a given role, we are in good company. Pitkin's work at least affords vocabulary for naming the possible meanings afloat amid the confusion.

Not just confusion but also conflict over the meaning of representation emerges now in the face of two recent movements in scholarly circles.

The first I will call *difference theory*; it has been pursued especially by feminists and critical race theorists. They have questioned the use of abstract universal terms or norms by showing how implicitly those terms or norms actually embrace the particular experiences or interests of those in positions of sufficient authority or dominance to govern. However much universal and abstract norms may once have advanced a democratic and antihierarchical agenda,[57] in current operation such ideas often fail to reflect—fail to represent—the experiences, interests, and needs of the full variety of human beings. Thus, traditional norms of equality and liberty may have well suited white Christian men without disabilities but often disadvantaged any who departed from that particular identity and experience. Freedom from the establishment of a religion, according to the Supreme Court, is not violated by public displays of a Christmas creche when combined with secular symbols.[58] For non-Christians, this "neutral" rule does not feel neutral. (Indeed, observant Christians, too, may be insulted by treatment of a significant religious holiday that renders both Santa and Jesus as simply shopping mall decorations.)[59]

Similarly, equal protection against discrimination on the basis of sex is not violated, again according to the Supreme Court, where an employer refuses to include pregnancy in its insurance coverage, because not only men but also some women are not pregnant at any given time.[60] Again, from the perspective of many women, this decision seems a bit peculiar and reflective of something other than women's experiences. A rule about what constitutes rape that requires a victim to fight back physically but does not take her verbal "no" as sufficient resistance reflects traditionally male rather than traditionally female understandings of sexuality and of self-defense.[61] Let me try one more: a rule guaranteeing freedom to enter into binding contracts may look neutral.[62] But if it lacks any prohibition against racially discriminatory treatment within those contracts, anyone in jeopardy of discrimination on the basis of race would view this as a perversely crabbed interpretation of freedom of contract. Nonetheless, this is the Supreme Court's present view.

Theorists of difference have taken such examples and explored how apparently neutral, abstract rules written without the perspective of some end up implementing the perspectives of others.[63] Advocates for persons with disabilities have been especially effective in this critique recently. They have demonstrated how historic efforts restraining the use of sign language so that profoundly deaf people could fit into the larger society actually denied those people meaningful language.[64] They have pointed out how buildings that are inaccessible to people who use wheelchairs are not neutral but disabling, and how mass transit systems that are hazardous to people with visual or hearing impairments are also not neutral but instead reflect the kinds of persons for whom they were clearly designed.[65]

If we think about people who feel excluded by such social institutions and rules, two cautionary rules emerge. First, claims to know what others want or need are suspect if made without the basis of shared experiences along the lines of the trait used for past exclusions. Translation: You don't know, and you get it wrong. This is what the excluded group is likely to say to those outside their group who claim to speak for them. Secondly, claims to speak for others by people not in the group are vulnerable on the grounds that participation itself is a value and the process of representing a viewpoint is an exercise of power that should be enjoyed by those on whose behalf the exercise is claimed. Perhaps no representative can be fully able to know the interests of everyone in the group. But as a political matter, the group may want to give the benefit of the doubt to a member of the group. It is a matter of trust. Translation: We speak for ourselves, and thus one of us should do the speaking. Speaking expresses power; it is empowering; and speaking for others depends upon their trust.

The difference critique is associated with what can be called "identity politics."[66] Some of its exponents call for proportional representation in the electoral context. Some of its opponents, and even some who sympathize, raise pointed objections. How many differences now need to be represented? Must the African-American caucus divide along gender lines and the gender caucus divide along racial lines, and all of them divide further along the lines of sexual orientation, disability, and religion? If so, how can any political movement emerge?[67] Others challenge the implicit claim that sociological traits of a person match interests or preferences, and still others worry about the conflicts between notions of identity as natural or fixed and notions of identity as personally chosen or socially constructed.[68]

But this is simply a glimpse of the debates internal to this movement. The difference critique endures and affords an angle on problems of representation. Indeed, the rules and practices about given forms of representation may be vulnerable to the criticism that they veil, in the guise of a false universalism, the particular views and interests of some. For those rules and practices, justifiable representation may call for attention to the two claims: (1) you don't know, and you get us wrong; and (2) we speak for ourselves.[69]

The Challenge of Empathy

A second and contrasting challenge to notions of representation questions the assumption that people *cannot* justifiably speak for others because they have sharply distinct and conflicting interests. That we each have distinct and conflicting interests is a familiar, liberal idea. The idea that we are each self-interested monads abounds, although it has not been powerful enough to preclude many models and forms of representation in law and politics. At least since Hobbes, the problem that representation was supposed to solve rested on a view that humans are separate and have conflicting wills.[70] Moreover, where theories of liberalism, democracy, and relativism dominate, as they have in recent American culture, people "tend to think that, in the last analysis, each man has the right to define his own good, and if he rejects something, no one has the right to insist that it is good for him."[71] Representation, in this view, is appropriate only for people who know their own interests and who can find an agent with no clashing interests.[72]

But maybe, just maybe, the idea that we are all basically self-interested is wrong. This is the kind of doubt posed by the second new development in scholarship that challenges rules of representation. Some feminists, some humanists, some self-styled communitarians join a variety of people who think it wrong or incomplete to think of people as simply separate, autonomous, and self-interested. I will call these people the *empathy* advocates. They argue that people (1) often want to care about the good of others (altruism) and (2) have the ability to understand and know the wants and needs of others (empathy).[73] The empathy advocates also argue that individuals act out of duty, love, and benevolence as well as self-interest, and that "people often take account of both other individuals' interests and the common good when they decide what constitutes a 'benefit' that they want to maximize."[74] Works by Amartya Sen in economics, J. G. A. Pocock in history, and Carol Gilligan in psychology indicate the variety of disciplines and specific points made by scholars advocating this view.[75]

These critics identify the power of altruism, the motivation and willingness to care for and give to others with no hope of gain for oneself.[76] They point out the power of group identity, or solidarity, that enhances cooperation without any expectation of future reciprocity or current rewards or punishments.[77] They also explain the malleability of human beings, and discuss how learning environments and social arrangements can reinforce either selfishness or sharing and altruism.[78] They have confidence in at least some cognitive and emotional capacities we each have to resonate and identify with others. Translation: (1) Don't be so sure I don't care to understand you or cannot understand you, and (2) give me a chance or else *you're* the one who ensures that we'll just all be selfish.

If these critics are onto something, they too provide a set of questions to test existing rules and practices about representation. If people already can take the perspective of others and care for them, then maybe people who are not like me can nonetheless represent me. And if people learn and grow more or less empathetic toward others depending upon the worlds and others they encounter, then maybe we should bet on rules predicated on empathy instead of rules presumed on narrow self-interest.[79]

Have you noticed that these questions point in quite different directions for the inquiry prompted by the difference critics?[80] The difference critics call for skepticism about the possibility of representation by people who are not themselves members of the represented group. They remind us that representatives often get it wrong. They remind us that participation itself is a value and should be enjoyed by members of the actual groups that have not been allowed to speak for themselves in the past. The empathy advocates in contrast urge greater confidence in people's capacity to care for others and also recommend reconstructing rules and institutions to expect and reinforce that capacity. They remind us of the possibility that people can be other-regarding, and the possibility that societal rules affect this very possibility. How about that for confusion! But maybe this is *good* confusion. Keeping in mind contrasting commitments may make things seem complicated but also genuine and honest.[81]

Keeping in mind the philosopher's confusions about representation, I now add the two contrasting set of inquiries as I turn to examine examples of current rules and practices about representation. Besides pursuing the questions prompted by each set of criticisms, I will also try to evaluate the probative power of each critique in light of which problem has been more severe in each context: a failure to acknowledge differences or a failure to consider human capacity for empathy.

Scrutinizing Rules of Representation

I will not have time to examine each of the legal contexts of representation I mentioned at the start. But here are two, and a mention of the others in hopes of prompting further discussion.

Juries and Group Representation

The Supreme Court recently considered "whether a prosecutor's proffered explanation that prospective Latino jurors were struck from the venire because he suspected they might not abide by official translations of Spanish language testimony constitutes an acceptable 'race neutral' explanation."[82] The lower court acknowledged in this case that the defendant had demonstrated a prima facie case of discrimination.[83] The question posed was whether the government provided an adequate explanation for using its peremptory challenges. The case presented two related problems. First, is the use of peremptory challenges that results in a jury with apparently no Hispanic members a violation of an equal protection? And, secondly, if these challenges do produce a jury lacking members of Spanish heritage, is that result a constitutional violation?[84]

Earlier cases questioned the apparent exclusion of racial and ethnic minorities and women[85] from juries and jury pools. Even when the legal doctrine at stake is equal protection,[86] the notion of representation is close at hand. The popular conception of the jury as a group of peers is rooted in the institution's origins.[87] In addition, for some period of time, English law demanded that a suit involving a foreigner be tried by a jury composed at least in part by foreigners.[88] Social class, country of origin, race, ethnicity, and gender thus each have had significance in assuring the representative fairness of a jury.

At stake in the composition of juries is a conception of that decision-making body as a representative cross section of the society.[89] Achieving at least symbolic community participation in justice, this cross-sectional appearance provides the "likeness" version of representation, the resemblance to the larger community.[90] It also helps promote the apparent legitimacy of the result. As one commentator put it, "the jury is not a scientific instrument but rather a body that, through its diversity, can be fair."[91]

Besides the appearance of fairness through representation, the cross-sectional jury also promises to give insights based on the range of particular experiences that different kinds of people have. The film "Twelve Angry Men," for example, suggests how a juror with the same kind of background as the defendant could bring knowledge about how street kids use switchblades.[92] Differences of gender, race, and ethnicity provide for different kinds of knowledge relevant to the tasks of a jury. In this conception, the dimension of representation that matters is not the formal authorization idea, nor the trusteeship, but the descriptive or portrait representation.[93] Although interests of the represented group may be germane as well, it is as much the interests of the whole, diverse community in being mirrored aptly that is here at work. Moreover, the deliberative process within a group of diverse members brings the community within the institution of justice. By this theory, the prosecutor improperly used peremptories to strike all Hispanic and Spanish-speaking jurors in *People v. Hernandez.*[94] Striking otherwise eligible jurors because of their special knowledge undermines the purposes of bringing that special knowledge into the process and also removes otherwise eligible jurors because of their ethnic identity.[95]

Yet the critics of difference and empathy would shed contrasting lights on this problem. Suspicion of abstract rules for favoring some groups over others supports a challenge to the prosecutor's allegedly neutral reasons for striking the Spanish-speaking jurors. Fears that those jurors would not limit themselves to the official translation or would attain special influence in the jury room sound neutral but have the effect of preferring Anglos and disfavoring Hispanics.[96] Any jury selection process, however neutrally defined, that produces juries excluding people who look like the defendant exposes the process to questions: how can these people judge someone unlike themselves, and isn't it time for members of the group to participate? These are the difference claims: how can you know, and we should speak for ourselves.

These questions cast some doubt on the very premise of the peremptory challenge. In contemporary practice, the ability of the prosecution and of the defense to excuse a number of jurors without stating a cause responds to a perceived need to screen out biased jurors.[97] One kind of presumed bias is that the juror has experiences like those of the defendant; the fear here is that the juror will be unable to judge objectively if he or she resembles the defendant. Critics respond: why is someone so different likely to be objective? Perhaps the very grounds of difference give rise to bias. If you exclude all women from a jury called to judge a woman charged with killing her husband, why assume that men on the jury are objective?[98] Moreover, even without bias, someone quite different from the defendant may simply fail to understand her experiences. Especially if the juror belongs to a group that in general dominates the political and social worlds, that jury may lack awareness of the perceptions and motivations of someone outside that group, and may even lack tools to understand someone so different.

The empathy inquiry may seem to cut in the opposite direction, but it, too, gives grounds for questioning any peremptory challenges. It suggests that people can and do act out of motives beyond their own self-interest, and that people have capacities to empathize with others. It is not clear how wide that capacity is, and whether it can reach across the kinds of differences that have come to matter in this society: race, ethnicity, gender, class. But why permit a rule about peremptory challenges that would presume that people *cannot* empathize across lines of difference? Not only could such a rule be untrue to human possibilities; it might also be a self-fulfilling prophecy.[99]

It remains fair to ask whether empathies run differently between people who share those traits compared with people who do not.[100] My tentative answer is: I don't know. That very answer supports an argument for preserving the fullest cross section possible and limiting or ending peremptory challenges. Only then can the full range of empathic and nonempathic possibilities be played out. If the jury is to be representative, it should represent this kind of social variety.

Class Action Representation

The civil procedure rule that allows a group to serve as a party presents the courts with the difficulty of representation: who can speak for the group and who can lead them or exemplify them before the court? The federal rule, and the rules of states that copy it, specifically require that the parties selected as representatives be typical of the group[101] and be able to demonstrate their ability adequately to represent the group.[102] This element often applies as much to the parties' ability to secure attorneys who can provide adequate representation for the class as it does to the named parties' own representative capacity.[103] Where the representation is adequate and the court certifies the class, a final judgment binds all its members, for they are deemed to have had a fair opportunity to be heard.[104]

The rule's demand that the class representative be typical seems to adopt one of Professor Pitkin's types of representing: the descriptive standing for another, the mirror providing a likeness or portrait of the others.[105] Yet with adequacy of representation, the rule seems to have opted for a definition more concerned with the kinds of action the representatives can and will take; what matters is not simply their characteristics but also their behavior as representatives—and their lawyers' ability and accountability in that regard.[106] The rule seems attuned to the difference critique; with adequacy of representation it seems to consider the empathy view that one may speak for others as members of a group with shared interests in the absence of conflicting interests.[107]

Yet perhaps most importantly, both terms show how the class action rule opts for *some* notion of representation. It is not enough for the representative simply to be able to enforce legal rights for others.[108] It is not enough merely to protect or advocate a legal interest. The representative also must be free from conflicting interests. And the representative in some way must stand for, symbolize, or depict the members of the class. As Professor Bryant Garth has noted, "A court presented only with arguments, not with the representatives of real constituencies, might ignore the interests and views of what might be a majority of a lawsuit's beneficiaries."[109] Part of the advocacy, part of the right to be heard seems to include the presentation and representation of actual people who in some important way *look like* those they represent. That resemblance may serve as a proxy or predictor for who is likely to share interests or have access to knowledge about the interests of the others. But that resemblance may be important separately for the symbolic effect in the represented community and in the forums where they perform their representative tasks.

I think that this dimension helps to explain some court decisions such as *Johnson v. Georgia Highway Express, Inc.*[110] There a black man who had been discharged from employment sought to represent a class of "all similarly situated Negroes seeking equal employment opportunities" in a case claiming that the employer discriminated on the basis of race not only in discharges, but also in hiring, promotion, and the operation of segregated facilities. The trial court rejected this broadly defined class and restricted the class to those persons discharged because of their race.

The appeals court reversed and allowed the broad class, reasoning that the allegations of racial discrimination throughout the employer's practices was sufficiently common to, and typical of, the claims of the broader class. It acknowledged that the named representative might not be adequate to speak for class members whose injury arose not from discharge but from other employment practices, but the reviewing court did not conclude that this factual and legal difference would render the discharged party an inadequate representative. The common trait of membership in the minority racial group apparently stood out in the court's mind as the salient factor justifying both the broad definition of the class and the possible representation by the discharged party. The trait of racial minority membership, I suggest, would allow that individual to stand for all others claiming discrimination, albeit a variety of discriminations, on the basis of race.[111] The Supreme Court has subsequently rejected this kind of "across-the-board" class,[112] and I wonder whether this reflects a failure to understand symbolic and depiction aspects of representation.

How would the "across-the-board" class, represented by someone who shared only the trait of minority race membership, survive the difference critique and the empathy inquiry? Many difference theorists are currently engaged in questioning whether shared racial membership alone represents a real and significant similarity, or whether talk of the perspective of blacks, or even the perspective of black women, obscures the "rich diversity" existing among people who can be identified that way.[113] Professor Patricia Hill Collins has defended the notion of a black feminist standpoint to encompass "the plurality of experiences" that nonetheless also include "a distinctive set of experiences that offers a different view of material reality than that available to other groups."[114] The fact of subordination is critical to her identification of a black feminist standpoint. She acknowledges social class variations that help explain why not all African-American women share the standpoint she articulates.[115] Nonetheless, membership in a racial minority stands as a symbol of historic subordination which, for some purposes, should count as a basis for adequate representation.[116] I think the same could be argued for sex, although the courts have often viewed racial differences among women as salient enough to deny class representative status to a black woman for a class of white and black women.[117]

What about the empathy inquiry?[118] The Supreme Court itself has permitted the certification of a class whose representative no longer has a live, viable claim to match the claims of the represented class.[119] In these cases, the Court emphasized not only that the class representative had no conflicting interest with the class,[120] but also that the representative could actually competently urge the interests of the class, even while lacking an actually identical claim.[121] In one case, the Court went further and characterized the named representative as a "private attorney general."[122] If the reference to "attorney general" means anything in this context, it includes the respect for someone entrusted with pursuing the legal rights of others even without needing to have an actual personal claim.[123] It also means the possibility of empathy, proper incentives, and resources.[124]

Yet, in each of these instances, the named representative had at one time been a member of the class or experienced the kind of injury alleged by the class as a whole. That historical experience may be irrecoverable, but still the individual can remain a class representative. Thus, one court approved as a class representative for a lawsuit challenging the employer's maternity policy a woman who had been sterilized.[125] She had once been able to become a mother: that was enough to allow her to serve as a representative of mothers. The possibility of empathy without a common historical experience is not regarded by the courts as adequate for representation. Thus, the Eleventh Circuit recently approved the district court's denial of class certification where the named plaintiff for the proposed class of Haitian citizens facing United States deportation or exclusion proceedings or seeking political asylum in the United States did not allege that he himself was a member of that class.[126] Instead, noted the appellate court, "He is an attorney who represents Haitians facing action by the INS."[127]

Thus, the difference and empathy critics converge in supporting the approval of class representatives who share social and historical characteristics of past experience with the class, even if the representative no longer has the same experience or same legal claim. This underscores the significance of the depiction and symbolic dimensions of representation, alongside evidence that the representative can, in fact, adequately advance the views and claims of the constituent group.[128] A representative looks sufficiently like the class if the representative actually once had experiences similar to those of the other class members.

With more time and space, I would now turn to more representation issues. Consider preclusion rules: when is someone adequately represented in one lawsuit and therefore barred from bringing a new lawsuit?[129]

When is someone an adequate fiduciary for a beneficiary? Is it helpful or harmful to share interests with or social experiences with the beneficiary in making, for example, investment decisions for a pension fund?[130]

How should we judge the representation of clients by professionals such as lawyers and doctors? How should we judge the tactics pursued by the client who wants a lawyer from his or her own "group"?[131] Is this a wise tactic or one that undermines professional representation? How about when the client seeks someone from a different group, such as when a man charged with rape seeks a woman defense attorney, or when a white employer charged with racial discrimination seeks a black or Hispanic attorney? Are these legitimate and wise tactics or, instead, efforts to take advantage of stereotypes and prejudice?

And what about employment itself? Is being hearing-impaired an important qualification for serving as the president of Gallaudet University, and if so why?[132] Does sharing a trait with one's students enable service as a role model, an expert, or a representative, and if so, in what sense?

Are parents in any sensible sense representatives of their children?[133] Or are parents people with interests separate from and conflicting with their children's interests and creating a need for independent representatives for the children? Before you start to chuckle at the idea of a child bringing her lawyer over to meet her parents, consider the problems posed when parents seek to commit their children to mental hospitals, order them to have an abortion, or seek to withhold medical treatment from them.

Intermission

Behind all the representation problems I have discussed, I see the distrust of difference and the hope of empathy. These lie even deeper than the concerns generated by "Miss Saigon" and law school hiring. Beneath the clashing assertions of essential differences and meritocracy, and the claims of reparations countered by hiring freedom, I believe, are our common experiences: betrayal by those who claim to speak for us but do not understand, and connection with those who often seem so different. Law, at its best, cannot resolve such deep conflicts. Law can only manage them, temporarily.

For something more insightful, we need art. I cannot help but think of another contemporary play: "M. Butterfly." Playwright David Henry Hwang read a *New York Times* account about an actual affair between a male French diplomat and a Chinese opera singer who appeared to be a woman but who was actually a man. According to the *New York Times* story, the actual gender identity of the opera singer remained unknown to the diplomat, and Hwang asked, how could this be?[134] In the news story, the diplomat said he had never seen his Chinese lover naked and thought "her" modesty reflected Chinese custom. Hwang explained his own brilliant chain of thought:

> I thought, wait a minute here, that's not a Chinese custom. I began to think, maybe the guy had not fallen in love with an actual person but with this sort of fantasy stereotype of the Orient. I was driving along one day, some-where, thinking, hey, the diplomat thought he had found Madame Butterfly! I pulled into a record store, bought Puccini's opera, looked at the libretto, and, right there, in the store, I began to structure the beginning of the play where the diplomat fantasizes that he's Pinkerton and has found Butterfly. He realizes—by the end—that he, himself, is, in fact, Butterfly. He's the one who has been sacrificed for love, exploited by his lover, who turns out to be a spy. Once I had all this, I knew I could start writing at the beginning and go through to the end.[135]

"M. Butterfly" teases the audience about the identity of the opera singer. The playbill lists only the actor's last name and first initial to keep the real person's sex a mystery. The play gradually, methodically, and fantastically explores the projection of fantasy on what we think is different; the pro-jection of gender difference on top of racial and national difference, in the midst of searching for human connection, and in the midst of the jeopardy of betrayal. It is critical to the play that the audience suspend disbelief about who is the opera singer, who is the diplomat, and ultimately, who are we all, struggling to know and be known. As this play opens possibilities for new understandings, it exemplifies representation: the re-presentation of human experience, present and absent from our consciousness. From "Miss Saigon," to class actions, to "M. Butterfly," representation is changing even as it changes us.

Notes

Originally published in 39.3 *Cleveland State Law Review* 269 (1991); reprinted by permis-sion.

    I would like to thank Joe Singer, Anita Allen, Jack Balkin, Larry Blum, Mary Ann

Glendon, Moshe Halbertal, Frank Michelman, Nell Minow, Avi Soifer, Elizabeth V. Spelman, Zipporah Wiseman, Peter Lefkowitz, David Pointer, and David Wiseman for their help with this essay.

1. Mervyn Rothstein, "Producer Cancels 'Miss Saigon': 140 Members Challenge Equity," N.Y. Times, Aug. 9, 1990, at C15. The union has authority over all performers appearing on Broadway, and actors from foreign countries need the union's approval unless they are British "stars." The union said it had not resolved the question whether the British actor was a "star" for these purposes. Michael Kuchwara, " 'Miss Saigon' Canceled Over Casting of White Actor," Boston Globe, Aug. 9, 1990, at 79.

2. Kuchwara, supra note 1.

3. Mervyn Rothstein, "Equity Council Approves Accord on 'Miss Saigon'," N.Y. Times, Sept. 18, 1990, at C14.

4. Mervyn Rothstein, "Dinkins Offers to Help in 'Miss Saigon' Dispute," N.Y. Times, Aug. 10, 1990, at C3. According to one observer, only the large advance sales explain the public controversy over Equity's initial objection to casting a Caucasian. See Robert Armin, "Miss Saigon: Not the Final Word," Theater Week, Sept. 10–16, 1990, at 37–38 ("If Miss Saigon did not have such a tremendous advance sale . . . , very few people outside of the theatrical profession would have batted an eye over Equity's decision.").

5. Mervyn Rothstein, "Equity Will Reconsider 'Miss Saigon' Decision," N.Y. Times, Aug. 10, 1990, at C3.

6. Frank Rich explicitly analogized the National Endowment for the Arts denial of funding to artists depicting homoerotic and sexually explicit images with the Actors' Equity decision in the "Miss Saigon" case. Frank Rich, "Jonathan Pryce, 'Miss Saigon' and Equity's Decision," N.Y. Times, Aug. 10, 1990, at C1.

7. See generally Louis Menand, "Illiberalisms," New Yorker, May 20, 1991, at 10 (reviewing Dinesh D'Souza, Illiberal Education: The Politics of Race and Sex on Campus (1991)); see also Virginia Durr, Outside the Magic Circle (Hollinger F. Bernard ed., 1985) (discussing racism in the United States).

8. See, e.g., City of Richmond v. J. A. Croson Co., 488 U.S. 469 (1989). But see Metro Broadcasting, Inc. v. FCC, 110 S. Ct. 2997 (1990).

9. Making a similar connection to underscore his own viewpoint, Robert Brustein, director of the American Repertory Theater, commented, "Everyone's in the casting business. You have to cast a black woman in a law school as a law professor. You have to cast Asians, homosexuals, everyone, in order to get sufficiently diverse multicultural representation. That is what Yeats called the 'mad intellect of democracy,' thinking that democracy means there has to be equal representation for everything that happens." Richard Bernstein, "The Arts Catch Up with a Society in Disarray," N.Y. Times, Sept. 2, 1990, § 2, at 12 (quoting Robert Brustein).

10. See Debbie Howlett, "Harvard Hit with Bias Suit," USA Today, Nov. 21, 1990, at 3A. The plaintiff, an unincorporated student organization, claimed that Harvard Law School's faculty hiring practices discriminate against minority groups and thus violate a state antidiscrimination statute and a state statute guaranteeing equal rights in the

context of contracts. The trial court granted the defendant's motion to dismiss the case. Memorandum of Decision and Orders on Defendant's Motion to Dismiss and Other Pending Motions, Harvard Law Sch. Coalition for Civil Rights v. The President and Fellows of Harv. College, No. 90-7904-B (Super. Ct., 1991). Curiously, in light of the thesis of this essay, the decision largely rested on conclusions that the students could not represent the interests of minority members who might be victims of employment discrimination by the law school. Thus, the court ruled that the plaintiff group lacked a legal capacity to sue; that it lacked standing to assert the claims of any person wrongfully denied employment by the school; and that it could not assert a breach of contract regarding existing contracts between the school and its faculty, nor a breach regarding nonexistent contracts with minority candidates. Id.

11. Two law professors have commented from contrasting perspectives on the analogy between the "Miss Saigon" controversy and minority preference policy in comparative licensing proceedings undertaken by the Federal Communications Commission. Compare Charles Fried, "Metro Broadcasting, Inc. v. FCC: Two Concepts of Equality," 104 Harv. L. Rev. 107, 121–122 n.82 (1990) with Patricia Williams, "Metro Broadcasting, Inc. v. FCC: Regrouping in Singular Times," 104 Harv. L. Rev. 525 (1990).

For a thorough and provocative treatment of the law school hiring issue, see Duncan Kennedy, "A Cultural Pluralist Case for Affirmative Action in Legal Academia," 1990 Duke L.J. 705.

12. Rothstein, supra note 1, at C15.

13. Rich, supra note 6, at C3 ("This is a policy that if applied with an even hand would bar Laurence Oliver's 'Othello,' Pearl Bailey's Dolly Levi, and the appearances of Morgan Freeman in 'The Taming of the Shrew' and Denzel Washington in 'Richard III.' "). Some warn that cross-race casting should proceed asymmetrically and allow historically excluded groups the chance to play the majority of existing roles without allowing historically privileged groups opportunities to play the relatively more scarce minority roles. See Ellen Holly, "Why the Furor Over 'Miss Saigon' Won't Fade," N.Y. Times, Aug. 26, 1990, § 2, at 7 (criticizing the casting of whites into the occasional roles calling for minorities).

Rich, and others, also argued that opposing the casting of one lead part in "Miss Saigon" was counterproductive because the production of the play would itself open 34 Asian, black, and Hispanic roles in the musical and not all, he claimed, would be minor roles. Rich, supra note 6, at C3. Shirley Sun responded to this argument: "One wonders if anyone would have advised black actors to be content with minor roles in the current Broadway production of August Wilson's 'Piano Lesson' if a Caucasian actor had been cast in the lead as Boy Willies." Shirley Sun, "For Asians Denied Asian Roles, 'Artistic Freedom' Is No Comfort," N.Y. Times, Aug. 26, 1990, § 2, at 7. Still a different response would query why Rich or anyone else thinks that the other roles depicting racial minorities are any more likely to be cast with nonwhite actors, or any more appropriately so, and if so, why.

14. See, e.g., Randall Kennedy, "Racial Critiques of Legal Academia," 102 Harv. L.

Rev. 1745 (1989); Abigail M. Thernstrom, "On the Scarcity of Black Professors," *Commentary* 22, 25 (July 1990). Cf. Kathleen Sullivan, Speech to the Harvard Law School Visiting Committee, Mar. 15, 1991 (discussing reporter Lisa Olsen's charge of sexual harassment in the men's locker room of the Patriot football team and acknowledging that some people don't think a woman reporter belongs in the men's locker room. Sullivan then noted that on that theory perhaps women would not belong at Harvard Law School, either.).

15. To round out the analogy, one could simultaneously have argued that, just as African Americans teach contracts and tax law, whites should be allowed to teach about race relations. Yet this argument has the awkward implication that teaching contracts and tax law are "white" roles and teaching about race relations is a "minority" role.

16. Holly, *supra* note 13, at 7, 27. Similar points appeared in testimony before the New York City Commission on Human Rights. Al Levine, a Hofstra University law professor, testified that "[a]n all-black cast of 'Oh, Kay!' does not eliminate a history of racial discrimination." *Reprinted in* Thomas Walsh, "NYC Hearings on Theater Discrimination Uncover Anger & Demands for Action," *Back Stage*, Dec. 14, 1990, at 1 (quoting Al Levine). Bernard Marsh, an actor, criticized the virtually all-white casts of contemporary Broadway productions and noted, "We're trained to believe an actor is an actor. We've found that it only applies when the actor is white." *Id.* (quoting Bernard Marsh).

17. August Wilson, "'I Want a Black Director,'" *N.Y. Times*, Sept. 26, 1990, at A25; August Wilson, "I Don't Want to Hire Nobody Just 'Cause They're Black," *Spin*, Oct. 1990, at 70–71.

18. Student posters, bulletin boards, Harvard Law School, 1990.

19. Anita Allen explores the role model arguments with attention to her personal experiences while identifying the persistence of merit even within role model claims. *See* Anita Allen, "On Being a Role Model," 6 *Berkeley Women's L.J.* 22 (1990/1991).

20. This may be more like notions of political representation in legislature, and the implicit idea here is that the representatives will redirect resources. *See* Duncan Kennedy, *supra* note 11, at 728–30.

21. Kevin Kelly, "M. Butterfly, Miss Saigon and Mr. Hwang," *Boston Globe*, Sept. 9, 1990, at B89 (commenting that Hwang "might be considered Confucian. 'The superior man,' Confucius says, '. . . does not set his mind for anything or against anything; what is right he will follow.'").

22. Sun, *supra* note 13, at 7. She concludes:

> While black actors have progressed to playing Shakespeare—current examples include Denzel Washington as Richard III and Morgan Freeman as Petruchio in "Taming of the Shrew" in this summer's Shakespeare in the Park program—it is erroneous to use the black example to generalize about Asian-Americans. Clearly, Asian-Americans have not yet reached the stage where they are taken seriously enough to be able to play themselves in leading roles. Much less do they have the opportunity to be cast in non-

Asian roles. Until Asian-American actors can play Hamlet or Richard III, it is ludicrous to talk about reverse racism.

Id. at 27.

Especially noteworthy here is the reminder that different groups of people of color have different experiences dealing with racism. At the same time, this comment elides the difference between the actors and the roles they play by characterizing playing Asian characters as playing "themselves." I was most struck on this front by an experimental reading of the transcript of a documentary film by Frederick Wiseman staged by actors of the American Repertory Theater in Cambridge, Mass., in 1988. The actors had never seen the movie, and they performed the scenes and then joined the audience in watching the scenes from the movie. Some uncanny resemblances occurred, as when one actress decided to play with a rubber band nervously and then turned to watch the film clip, which showed the actual woman who uttered the lines in real life was chewing gum nervously as she spoke. But more striking were the differences. One of the real characters had made some racist statements; in the film clip, he seemed demonic and worked up. The actor reading the lines chose instead to read them flat, with little affect. The audience agreed that this effort by the actor was believable and more chilling than the racist statements made by the actual person who had originated the lines.

Perhaps the point about "depicting ourselves" may be somewhat different if the question involves an actor with disabilities. Perhaps there is a kind of knowledge and ease that is enabled only by having the disability, or perhaps there is a possibility of believable portrayal that the actor with a disability uniquely has to offer. It is tempting to argue that so few have the chance to play any theatrical role or be taken seriously for any role of a character without a disability that when the few roles calling for a person with disabilities are given out to someone without those disabilities, the rare opportunity to perform is eclipsed, and prejudice or ignorance about persons with disabilities may be the reason for the decision not to cast or even audition an actor who has a disability. See Andrea Wolper, "Beyond Tradition: Ethnic and Disabled Actors Assess the Present, Plan for the Future," Back Stage, Feb. 23, 1990, at 1A, 29 (producers tell an actress who uses a wheelchair not to audition for the role of a person in a wheelchair because they fear she would not be strong or well enough). But this relative rarity of good roles resembles the situation for Asian, African-American, and Hispanic actors, and female actors over the age of 40.

23. One idealized view has the actor becoming the character: Hanna F. Pitkin, The Concept of Representation 26 (1967) ("Ordinarily the actor in a play does not claim or even pretend to be the authorized representative of anyone. He does not pretend to act on authority of Hamlet, but to be Hamlet. His entire manner and appearance are directed to creating the illusion that this is someone else, someone whom he is playing or, as we say, representing on the stage."). Even less romantic views of acting celebrate the opportunity to convince an audience of an imagined world or set of possibilities.

The relative scarcity of such opportunities to create illusions through acting may be especially painful when a member of one minority group is cast as a member of another minority group. "Seret Scott, a black actress, became emotional as she told of times when she'd agreed to play Latinos, Asian-Americans and Native Americans. By complying, she said, she took jobs away from actresses from those ethnic groups." Allan Wallach, "Casting Aside Color," Newsday, July 1, 1990, Part II, at 4–5.

24. Curiously, few people considered the possibility of casting a Eurasian actor for the role; both white and Asian commentators suggested that the Eurasian character would have to be played either as Asian or European. Thus, the white actor cast in the role, Jonathan Pryce, declared that "If the character is half Asian and half European, you've got to drop down on one side of the fence or the other, and I'm choosing to drop down on the European side." Rothstein, supra note 1, at C15.

No one, to my knowledge, took the next step and argued that it would be best to have people from a group unlike the one to which the character belongs play the roles in order to challenge stereotypes. This approach could broaden the range of actors and audience and break out of simply enacting actual lived experience. Yet analogous argument in a legal context is unattractive: consider the claim that members of a given group should not be allowed to sit as judges or jurors in cases involving members of that group because they lack the requisite objectivity. For strong reasons rejecting such arguments, see Blank v. Sullivan & Cromwell, 418 F. Supp. 1 (S.D.N.Y. 1975); Pennsylvania v. Local Union 542, Int'l Union of Operating Eng'rs, 388 F. Supp. 115 (E.D. Pa. 1974).

25. The Non-Traditional Casting Project defines four types of nontraditional casting: (1) societal, in which nonwhite and/or female actors are cast in roles of characters with their ethnicity or sex; (2) cross-cultural, which transposes an entire play to a different culture; (3) conceptual, which casts an ethnic, female, or disabled actor in a role to give it greater resonance; and (4) casting of the best actor for a role even if this departs from the script. See generally Andrea Wolper, "Non-Traditional Casting: Definitions & Guidelines, Backtions & Guidelines," Back Stage, Feb. 23, 1990, at 29.

Zelda Fichandler, producing director at the Arena Stage Theater in Washington, D.C., has maintained that theater's task, "while not stretching credulity to the breaking point, is to stretch it as far as we can." Zelda Fichandler, "A Theater Should Live on the Cutting Edge," Washington Post, Dec. 13, 1990, at A22. Under her leadership, that theater has pursued nontraditional casting: actors are cast to play roles not written for someone of their race or ethnicity. See generally Zelda Fichandler, "Casting For a Different Truth," American Theater, May 1988, at 18.

A multiracial cast in a performance of Thornton Wilder's "Our Town," directed by Douglas Wager at the Arena Stage, led one reviewer to comment:

> standing in a mass on the stage, the cast's racial mix has seemed utterly unexceptional, but as the actors begin to step into character, it's suddenly startling. Emily and George, the two young lovers who will court, marry, and experience tragedy together, have both been cast with white performers, but each has been given a black sibling. George's father is Hispanic and speaks with a pronounced accent. Nothing whatever is made of this. This mix is casual, but also crucial, because it serves to point up the

play's universality with the same understatement and lack of fuss that eliminating sets and artifice did in that original 1938 production [of "Our Town"]. By suggesting that the New England village be represented onstage by a non-specific void, Wilder made his play universal. By transforming New England into an idealized global village in microcosm, Wager is doing the same thing.

Bob Mondello, "Rival Revivals," *City Paper*, Nov. 30, 1990, at 30. *See generally* Dan Sullivan, "Colorblind Casting: It's Not Yet a Tradition: When Black Is White, Women Are Men, and the Theater Is Challenging," *L.A. Times*, Oct. 2, 1988, at 50, 52 ("If the first purpose of 'non-traditional' is to open up new jobs, the second is to open up new possibilities."). Some critics have attacked such multiracial casting as distracting and political while others suggest that nontraditional casting suits classic or universal dramas but interferes with plays written about a specific ethnic or cultural group. *See* Megen Rosenfeld, "Theater: 1990—The Year Casting Turned a Color-Blind Eye to the Stage," *Washington Post*, Dec. 30, 1990, at G7; Joanne Kaufman, "Acting's Not Just for Able-Bodied Whites," *Wall Street Journal*, Jan. 4, 1990, at A12 (discussing "The Diary of Anne Frank" and "Raisin in the Sun"). Still others emphasize that nontraditional casting is not intended to diminish opportunities for ethnic actors to play ethnic roles. *See* Lisa Yoftee, "Ethnic Casting Issues Get Soapbox Treatment," *American Theater*, Feb. 1991, at 34.

26. *See* Josephine R. Abandy, "A Message From the Artistic Director," in *Cleveland Play House, The Glass Menagerie* (Playbill, April 4–May 7, 1989) (announcing first professional all-black production of "The Glass Menagerie" as a response to the need to respect multiracial and multinational heritage). Abandy concludes, "I also hope that this new interpretation of Tennessee Williams's haunting play will offer different and illuminating insights to those of you who are familiar with it, and will open its wonders to new audiences who have never seen it before." *Id.* Reviewer Tony Mastroianni acknowledged that this all-black production reflected Abandy's effort to remedy past neglect of the black community by the Play House, but maintained that a better approach would be to produce "good new plays by black playwrights." Tony Mastroianni, "The Casting Cracks This Glass Menagerie," *Akron Beacon Journal*, Apr. 15, 1989, at B5.

27. *See* Fried, *supra* note 11.

28. *See* Pitkin, *supra* note 23.

29. *See* Chisom v. Roemer, 111 S. Ct. 2354 (1991) (deciding to apply the Federal Voting Rights Act to state judicial elections); Houston Lawyers' Ass'n v. Texas Attorney Gen., 111 S. Ct. 2376 (1991) (same). This prompted the *New York Times* to ask, "Are Judges Representatives?" *N.Y. Times*, June 21, 1991, at A13. This question recalls to mind Senator Roman Hruska's comment on one of President Nixon's nominees to the Supreme Court: "Even if he were mediocre, there are a lot of mediocre judges and people and lawyers. They are entitled to a little representation, aren't they and a little chance?" 28 *Cong. Q. Almanac* 159 (1970).

30. *See* Hernandez v. New York, 111 S. Ct. 1859 (1981) (Kennedy, J., plurality) (approving use of peremptory challenges to exclude all Spanish-speaking jurors). But

see Witherspoon v. Illinois, 391 U.S. 510 (1968) (rejecting exclusion from jury of all those expressing religious or moral scruples about the death penalty because such a jury would not fully represent the views of the community). *Witherspoon* was limited, however, by Adams v. Texas, 448 U.S. 38 (1980). *See generally* Stephen Gillers, "Proving the Prejudice of Death-Qualified Juries After *Adams v. Texas*," 47 U. Pitt. L. Rev. 219 (1985).

31. *See* Kimberlé Crenshaw, "Demarginalizing the Intersection of Race and Sex: A Black Feminist Critique of Antidiscrimination Doctrine, Feminist Theory and Anti-racist Politics," 1989 U. Chi. Legal Forum 139, 143–50 (discussing decisions denying black women as representatives of classes asserting sex discrimination).

32. Martin v. Wilks, 490 U.S. 755 (1989).

33. *See* Martha Minow & Nell Minow, "Franchise Republics: The Examples of Shareholder Voting and Women's Suffrage," 41 Fla. L. Rev. 639, 647 (1989).

34. When Michael Chatoff presented an oral argument to the Supreme Court in a case involving the educational rights of a deaf child, he became the first deaf attorney to appear in that Court. Barbara Rosewicz, "Court Hears Argument by Deaf Lawyer," UPI, Mar. 23, 1982, *available in* LEXIS, Nexis Library, UPI file. Chatoff persuaded the Court to grant him permission to use an electronic communications system that allowed him to read the questions spoken by the justices. Charles Babcock, "Deaf Attorney Argues Before High Court for Disabled Student," *Washington Post*, Mar. 24, 1982, at A2. Both this technological innovation and the appearance of a deaf attorney elicited public attention to the case and dramatized its issue, which concerned the scope of accommodations required by public schools obligated by federal law to educate students with disabilities. Id. Ultimately denying the request for a sign language interpreter for the student, the Supreme Court nonetheless ruled that federal law required some degree of accommodation by the public schools. Board of Educ. of the Henrick Hudson Cent. Sch. Dist. v. Rowley, 458 U.S. 176 (1982). The Court concluded that the federal statutory requirements would be satisfied if the state provided sufficient personalized instruction and support services so that the individual child would benefit educationally. Id.

35. Pitkin, *supra* note 23.

36. Id. at 3.

37. Id. at 4. A representative *could* fulfill both of these views if the client's wishes match up with the representative's views of the client's best interests. This observation need not merely reflect the banal effect of coincidence because, on occasion, the representative may conclude that the client's best interests call for expressing or deferring to the client's express views.

38. *See, e.g.*, id. at 10, 53, 75, 87, 90, 115, 142.

39. Id. at 11, 27.

40. Id. at 28, 35, 39, 49. For this reason, Pitkin finds the concept incomplete if not unworkable even by those, like Thomas Hobbes, who advocated the formalist definition. Id. at 28, 35. Hobbes wishes to use the concept of representation to resolve how people with separate and conflicting wills could live in peace. Id. at 35.

41. *Id.* at 61.

42. Yet the fact that a resemblance must be believed by others raises troubling questions about the role of attitudes and concepts in constructing what people think is real. A white actor may be "made up" to look Asian. A person who may appear white may instead be African-American. *See* Ken Johnson, "Being and Politics," *Art in America*, Sept. 1990, at 155. Johnson describes a video installation by Adrian Piper entitled "Cornered." The work begins by confronting viewers with a video of Piper, who

> does not appear to be black—she has neither the skin color nor the characteristic facial features of someone of obvious African descent. And so she begins by announcing, "I'm black." Then, in a coolly authoritarian tone she suggests, "Now let's deal with this social fact and the fact of my stating it together."

Id. at 155–56. This work of art includes philosophic arguments and suggests that the questions it raises might help viewers to alter their understandings of "reality." *See id.* at 156.

43. Pitkin, *supra* note 23, at 66–69, 87. And for depictions intended to be accurate "representations," such as a map or blueprint, the thing itself must be read and interpreted. *Id.* at 86. Some values and guides outside the representation itself become critical in assessing its usefulness. *See* Michael J. Shapiro, Preface to *Politics of Representation: Writing Practices in Biography, Photography, and Policy Analysis* xi (1988) ("representations do not imitate reality but are the practices through which things take on meaning and value").

44. Pitkin, *supra* note 23, at 88.

45. *Id.* at 89. Unfortunately, at this point Pitkin offers the example, from Griffiths, of a lunatic who may be the best descriptive representative of lunatics, but "one would not suggest that they be allowed to send some of their number to the legislature." *Id.* Since the mental patient rights movement suggests something like this, this passage seems at best outdated.

46. *Id.* at 75–80, 90.

47. *Id.* at 103–05.

48. *Id.* at 112–13.

49. *Id.* at 125–43. Edmund Burke's theory of representation, which Pitkin explores at length, emphasizes the judgment of the representative while pursuing the constituents' interests:

> it is our duty when we have the desires of the people before us, to pursue them, not in the spirit of literal obedience, which may militate with their very principle, much less to treat them with a peevish and contentious litigation, as if we were adverse parties in a suit. . . . I cannot indeed take upon me to say I have honour to follow the sense of the people. The truth is, *I met it on the way*, while I was pursuing their interest according to my own ideas."

3 Edmund Burke, *Works and Correspondence* 354 (London, Rivington, 1852) (emphasis in the original).

50. See Pitkin, supra note 23, at 145, 153 (calling this the mandate-independence controversy).

51. See id. at 153, 163–64.

> All of these elements—what is to be represented, whether it is objectively determinable, what the relative capacities of representative and constituents are, the nature of the issues to be decided, and so on—contribute to defining a theorist's position on the continuum between "taking care of" so complete that it is no longer represented, and "delivering their vote" so passive that it is at most a descriptive "standing for."

Id. at 214.

52. See id. at 164 (arguing that when the representative feels in conflict with the express orders of those represented, this fact calls for considering the reasons for the discrepancy and may call for a reconsideration of the representative's views).

53. See id. at 156–62.

54. Compare id. at 173–74 (discussing Burke) with id. at 195 (discussing Madison).

55. Id. at 210.

56. See id. at 240. Perhaps Pitkin herself became confused here, or tempted to blend the related but distinct questions of what it means to be a representative and what it means to be a good representative.

57. See Stephen Holmes, "The Secret History of Self-Interest," in Beyond Self Interest 267, 284 (Jane J. Mansbridge ed., 1990).

58. See Lynch v. Donnelly, 465 U.S. 668 (1984). In subsequent decisions, the Court further confused matters by rejecting as a violation of the establishment clause a display that lacked any secular figures, while approving a display that combined a Christmas tree with a Chanukah menorah. Allegheny v. ACLU, 492 U.S. 573 (1989).

59. See David Cobin, "Creches, Christmas Trees and Menorahs: Weeds Growing in Roger Williams' Garden," 1990 Wis. L. Rev. 1597, 1609–10.

60. Geduldig v. Aiello, 417 U.S. 484 (1974).

61. Susan Estrich, Real Rape 29–56 (1987).

62. See Patterson v. McLean Credit Union, 491 U.S. 164 (1989).

63. See Catharine MacKinnon, Feminism Unmodified 1–5 (1987); Martha Minow, Making All the Difference: Inclusion, Exclusion, and American Law (1990); Patricia Williams, "Alchemical Notes: Reconstructed Ideals from Deconstructed Rights," 22 Harv. C.R.-C.L. L. Rev. 401 (1987). Cf. Pierre Clastres, Society Against the State (1989) (criticizing anthropological accounts that treat as universal the particular cultural patterns of the anthropologist's own society).

64. See Oliver Sacks, Seeing Voices 25–26 (1989).

65. See Robert L. Burgdorf, Jr., "The Americans with Disabilities Act: Analysis of a Second Generation Civil Rights Statute," 26 Harv. C.R.-C.L. L. Rev. 413, 418–19, 460–63, 470–81 (1991).

66. See generally Iris Young, Justice and the Politics of Difference 156–91 (1990).

67. See Elizabeth V. Spelman, Inessential Woman: Problems of Exclusion in Feminist Thought

(1988) (providing an elegant exploration of these differences and a call for politics based on mutual consultation and struggle).

68. *See* Steven Epstein, "Gay Politics, Ethnic Identity: The Limits of Social Constructionism," 17 *Socialist Rev.* 10 (May–Aug. 1987) (identifying conflict between academic arguments that gay identity is fluid and socially constructed and political arguments that gay identity is natural and determined).

69. There could be additional claims: (3) You *do* know, and you do us wrong (deliberate racism, etc.); (4) it's our turn to *do* for ourselves (nationalism response); (5) only with a representative from our group can we each have the vicarious experience of speaking and being there. Thanks to Anita Allen and Moshe Halbertal for these points.

70. *See* Pitkin, *supra* note 23, at 35 (discussing Hobbes). Note: Hobbes expressly excluded wives and "property," which encompassed slaves.

71. *Id.* at 159 (noting further that children and others who are thought not to be able to know their own interests cannot be represented so much as taken care of) ("Representation enters the picture precisely where the person acted for is conceived as capable of acting and judging for himself; and of such a person we assume that he will want what is in his interest."). This does, however, lead to paradoxical ideas about who exactly is competent to know his own interests; for if someone wants something that others think is not in his interest, the others may conclude he is not competent to know his interests and thus to select a representative to advance them. *See* Martha Minow, "Why Ask Who Speaks for the Child: Review of Gaylin & Macklin, Who Speaks for the Child: The Problems of Proxy Consent," 53 *Harv. Ed. Rev.* 444 (1983).

72. For a thoughtful article challenging this view in the context of legal representation for children, see Stephen Wizner & Miriam Berkman, "Being a Lawyer for a Child Too Young to be a Client: A Clinical Study," 68 *Neb. L. Rev.* 330 (1989). The authors describe three complex cases in which they represented young children in custody and visitation cases following their parents' divorces, and develop a set of presumptions for guiding lawyers in such situations to assure children's protection in and from the litigation process itself. They further call for investigation by the lawyer into the child's actual interests and advocacy of those interests. In a sense, such lawyers not only represent but also enact or embody the interests of children; the lawyer for a child assures distinct attention to the person who might otherwise be neglected or used by adults.

73. *See* Lawrence A. Blum, *Friendship, Altruism, and Morality* (1980).

74. Jane J. Mansbridge, Preface to *Beyond Self Interest*, *supra* note 57, at ix, x (suggesting that this approach involves in part a return to premodern understandings while also preserving the insights of modern social science).

75. *See, e.g.,* Carol Gilligan, *In a Different Voice* (1982); J. G. A. Pocock, *The Machiavellian Moment* (1975); Amartya K. Sen, "Rational Fools: A Critique of the Behavioral Foundations of Economic Theory," in *Scientific Models and Men* 317, 317–44 (Henry Harris ed., 1978).

76. E.g., Alfie Kohn, *The Brighter Side of Human Nature: Altruism and Empathy in Everyday*

Life (1990); Virginia Held, "Mothering vs. Contract," in *Beyond Self Interest, supra* note 57, at 287, 294.

77. Robyn M. Dawes et al., "Cooperation for the Benefit of Us—Not Me, or My Conscience," in *Beyond Self Interest, supra* note 57, at 97, 99.

78. Kohn, *supra* note 76, at 118–204 (discussing social science research indicating that predispositions to share and to be selfish can be reinforced or snuffed out); Jane Mansbridge, "The Rise and Fall of Self-Interest in the Explanation of Political Life," in *Beyond Self Interest, supra* note 57, at 3, 20–21 (describing James Buchanan, who won the Nobel Prize in economics for applying to economics a rational-choice model based on self-interest and then "repudiated the single motive of self-interest in favor of looking at context" and interdependence between people and rules and institutions, concluding that "we should try to design institutions to encourage motivations we believe on normative grounds are either good in themselves or will lead to good and just outcomes").

79. Contemporary African-American theater often analogously challenges the assumption of a separation between audience and stage and seeks to use theater to create or reinvent cultural unity and militant nationalism. *See* Genevieve Fabre, *Drumbeats, Masks, and Metaphor: Contemporary Afro-American Theater* 104–05, 108, 218, 236–38 (1983).

80. These questions point in quite different directions in evaluating a theory of representation like Edmund Burke's. The difference critique might well raise suspicions about his claims that a representative's own judgment may be better in pursuing constituents' interests than their express views, while the empathy critique might provide renewed support for Burke. Yet the notion of empathy seems to refer to a more egalitarian relation between representative and constituent than Burke's elite, enlightened trustee, who may sympathize with others from a superior position. *See* Burke, *supra* note 49, at 354.

81. The contrasting commitments here arise along at least two dimensions. Thus, understanding human self-interest and altruism reflects one contrast; recognizing each individual as the important unit of analysis contrasts with a view of the group as the important unit of concern.

82. Hernandez v. New York, 111 S. Ct. 242 (1990) (granting cert. limited to this question and a question about the proper standard of review). The Court rejected the challenge. Hernandez v. New York, 111 S. Ct. 1859 (1991).

83. People v. Hernandez, 528 N.Y.S.2d 625 (N.Y. App.2d 1988) (citing Batson v. Kentucky, 476 U.S. 79 (1986)).

84. One prior related case is United States v. Alcantar, 897 F.2d 436 (9th Cir. 1990) (remanding for new trial in similar case because the process for testing the prosecutor's reasons for striking proposed jurors was inadequate). In *Alcantar,* the prosecutor objected to Spanish-speaking jurors because some of the evidence introduced would be tape recordings of the defendant discussing her crimes. *Id.* at 537. The prosecutor feared that Spanish-speaking jurors would attain the appearance of a special expertise in the jury deliberations and would then influence other jurors. *Id.*

85. Taylor v. Louisiana, 419 U.S. 522 (1975); Hoyt v. Florida, 368 U.S. 57 (1961); Strauder v. West Virginia, 100 U.S. 303 (1879).

86. *See* Castaneda v. Partida, 430 U.S. 482 (1977); Hernandez v. Texas, 347 U.S. 475 (1954). Other similar cases interpret the Sixth Amendment. Taylor v. Louisiana, 419 U.S. 522 (1975).

87. Charles Rembar, *The Law of the Land: The Evolution of Our Legal System*, 116–71 (1980).

88. *See* Marion Constable, The Jury 'De Medietate Linguae': Changing Conceptions of Citizenship, Law, and Knowledge (1989) (unpublished Ph.D. dissertation, University of California (Berkeley)).

89. Tracy L. Altman, Note, "Affirmative Selection: A New Response to Peremptory Challenge Abuse," 38 *Stan. L. Rev.* 781, 787–93 (1986).

90. *Id.*

91. *Id.* at 790–91.

92. *Id.* at 791 n.50. In a different way, "Silence of the Lambs," which depicts a serial killer who has insight into how another serial killer will behave, suggests how people may understand others like themselves. However, I am unsure that this calls for representation of serial killers on juries. Insight does not mean judgment.

93. *See id.* at 791 n.41 (discussing Pitkin). Thus the descriptive dimension is achieved as traits like race and ethnicity become proxies for the variety of persons and knowledge in the society.

94. 582 N.Y.S.2d 625 (N.Y. App.2d 1988). The basic doctrine in the field holds that the defendant's right to a fair and impartial jury does not guarantee "jury of any particular composition," but instead that the jury be drawn from "a source fairly representative of the community." Taylor v. Louisiana, 419 U.S. 522, 538 (1975). *But see* Batson v. Kentucky, 476 U.S. 79 (1986) (which added to the mix the requirement that the use of peremptory challenges not reflect racially or ethnically discriminatory purposes).

95. This was not the Supreme Court's conclusion. A plurality of the Court concluded that the prosecutor offered a sufficiently race-neutral explanation by noting that the Spanish-speaking jurors might have difficulty accepting the English translator's version of Spanish testimony. Hernandez v. New York, 111 S. Ct. 1859 (1991) (Kennedy, J., plurality opinion). None of the opinions in the case explored the complex and partial relationships between ethnicity and fluency in Spanish.

96. Another effect is to elevate the English translation—or representation—of the evidence over the Spanish version. The actual effect on the outcome if Hispanics participate in a criminal jury involving a Hispanic defendant is hardly obvious. Members of the same group may be tougher than others in judging criminal matters. Yet they may also better understand excusing circumstances or more critically evaluate the law enforcement practices. In addition, diversity within the group called Hispanics renders predictions about their voting patterns on a jury dubious.

97. Altman, *supra* note 89, at 795. Cf. Commonwealth v. Local Union 542, Int'l Union of Operating Eng'rs, 388 F. Supp. 115, 177 (E.D. Pa. 1974) (Higginbotham, J.)

("Black lawyers have litigated in federal courts almost exclusively before white judges, yet they have not urged the white judges should be disqualified on matters of race relations").

98. *See* Hoyt v. Florida, 368 U.S. 57 (1961). Historian Linda Kerber is exploring the historical context for the arguments in that case.

99. *See* Altman, *supra* note 89, at 800 (discussing possibility that people are more or less empathetic in relation to rules and institutional expectations).

100. Sharing a trait does not entail understanding one another even in light of that trait, and certainly not in relation to other traits that are not shared.

101. *Fed. R. Civ. P.* 23(a)(3).

102. *Fed. R. Civ. P.* 23(a)(4).

103. *See, e.g.,* Goodman v. Lukens Steel Co., 777 F.2d 113, 124 (3d Cir. 1985); Susman v. Lincoln Am. Corp. 561 F.2d 86, 90 (7th Cir. 1977), *cert. denied*, 445 U.S. 942 (1980). A special problem arises where an attorney who is a member of the class seeks to be its named representative as well as its counsel. *See* Kelly A. Freeman, Note, "Conflicts of Interest in Class Action Representation Vis-à-Vis Class Representative and Class Counsel," 33 *Wayne L. Rev.* 141 (1986). Cf. Oxendine v. Williams, 509 F.2d 1405 (4th Cir. 1975) (nonlawyer prisoner denied right to represent others in pro se class action, largely for questions of competence). *See generally* Derrick Bell, "Serving Two Masters: Integration Ideals and Client Interests in School Desegregation Litigation," 85 *Yale L.J.* 470 (1976) (exploring potential conflicts in goals between public interest lawyers and their clients).

104. *See* Deborah Rhode, "Class Conflicts in Class Actions," 34 *Stan. L. Rev.* 1183, 1192 (1982) (providing a comprehensive analysis of the special representation problems presented where a class includes potentially conflicting interests and of procedural mechanisms for dealing with the problem of discerning the views of a large class). *See* Note, "The Attorney-Client Privilege in Class Actions: Fashioning an Exception to Promote Adequacy of Representation," 97 *Harv. L. Rev.* 947 (1984) (proposing an exception to the attorney-client privilege to help absent class members enforce the representational obligations of named parties).

105. *See* Pitkin, *supra* note 23 (discussing theory of "standing for" as a descriptive representative).

106. *Id.* at 51–52 (accountability and action as dimensions of representation).

107. Especially for defendant classes, some have proposed that those shared interests should predate the litigation itself. *See* Scott P. Miller, Note, "Certification of Defendant Classes Under Rule 23(b)(2)," 84 *Colum. L. Rev.* 1371, 1395 (1984).

108. Bryant Garth, "Conflict and Dissent in Class Actions: A Suggested Perspective," 77 *Nw. U. L. Rev.* 492, 503 (1982). Even an argument for eliminating class representatives concludes by recommending a continued role for "exemplary class members." *See* Jean W. Burns, "Decorative Figureheads: Eliminating Class Representatives in Class Actions," 42 *Hastings L.J.* 165, 194–95 (1990).

109. Garth, *supra* note 108, at 520.

110. 417 F.2d 1122 (5th Cir. 1969).

111. But see General Tel. v. Falcon, 626 F.2d 369 (5th Cir. 1980), *vacated in part and remanded*, 457 U.S. 147 (1982) (rejecting class certified to represent both employees denied promotion and applicants denied employment). *See also* Watson v. Fort Worth Bank & Trust, 798 F.2d 791 (5th Cir. 1986) (approving splitting into two classes of employees and applications).

112. *See* George M. Strickler, Jr., "Protecting the Class: The Search for the Adequate Representative in Class Action Litigation," 34 *DePaul L. Rev.* 73, 133–36 (1984).

113. Patricia Hill Collins, "The Social Construction of Black Feminist Thought," 14 *Signs* 745, 747 n.8 (1989).

114. Id. at 747 & n.8.

115. Id.

116. Similarly, one court approved a woman as a representative in a sex discrimination class although the named representative also held a position as an officer in the defendant corporation, apparently on the grounds that the position was only honorary. Rossini v. Ogilvy & Mather, Inc., 798 F.2d 590 (2d. Cir. 1986). Perhaps the court approves the woman as a representative because sex is thicker than job titles.

117. May black women serve as class representatives in lawsuits asserting both race and sex discrimination? *See* Crenshaw, *supra* note 31. In applying the class action rule to refuse this class representative status to black women, several courts remain vulnerable to the difference critique.

118. Collins, *supra* note 113, at 398–99 (identifying the ethic of caring for others, including the capacity for empathy, as elements of an alternative, African-American feminist epistemology). This suggests that although tensions between difference critiques and empathy critiques exist, so do important points of specific connection. The development of a black feminist epistemology partly reflects a difference critique attacking feminism for assuming that all women share something as women. *See* Spelman, *supra* note 67 (noting how the commitment to caring is a point of convergence between white and black feminists). Yet, this point begins to raise questions about what exactly is the meaning of claims that "caring" is specific to the African-American feminist viewpoint.

119. *See* United States Parole Comm'n v. Geraghty, 445 U.S. 388 (1980) (named plaintiff allowed to appeal the denial of class certification even after his own claim had become moot); Sosna v. Iowa, 419 U.S. 393 (1975) (permitting class to proceed although the named plaintiff had already satisfied the residency requirement and obtained a divorce and so no longer had a live claim against the state one-year residency requirement for a divorce); McCoy v. Ithaca Housing Authority, 559 F. Supp. 1351 (N.D. N.Y. 1983) (class action can proceed even though part of named plaintiff's claim became moot). *See generally* C. Douglas Floyd, "Civil Rights Class Actions in the 1980's: The Burger Court's Pragmatic Approach to Problems of Adequate Representation and Justiciability," 1984 B.Y.U. L. Rev. 1, 31–44. Different concerns arise where the named plaintiff seeks only damages while the class seeks equitable relief, for a conflict of interest appears when the defendant offers a cash settlement or a settlement precluding further action by the class. *See* Williams v. Vukovoch, 720 F.2d 909 (6th Cir. 1983);

Franks v. Kroger, 649 F.2d 1216 (6th Cir. 1981); Robert P. Schuwerk, "Future Class Actions," 39 *Baylor L. Rev.* 63, 198 (1987).

120. Sosna v. Iowa, 419 U.S., at 403.

121. Id.

122. United States v. Parole Comm'n v. Geraghty, 445 U.S., at 403.

123. *See* Strickler, *supra* note 112, at 144–45.

124. Id. This notion is also compatible with the view of litigation as a form of expression and political action. *See* NAACP v. Button, 371 U.S. 415 (1963) (organization becomes involved in litigation that actually focuses on a smaller number of actual litigants); In re Primus, 436 U.S. 412 (1978) (same); Bell, *supra* note 103 (criticizing this particular dimension of school desegregation litigation). This criticism has prompted sustained debate since its publication.

125. Association of Flight Attendants v. Texas Int'l Airlines, 89 F.R.D. 52, 62 (S.D. Tex. 1981). The court did not consider whether this individual retained a live interest in the maternity policy should she adopt, nor whether the policy covered adoption.

126. Ray v. United States Dept. of Justice, Immigration and Naturalization Serv. and State Dept., 908 F.2d 1549, 1558 (11th Cir. 1990). The court did not therefore pursue an argument empathy advocates would advance: that empathy can arise even in the absence of an identical experience and they would defend as a representative someone who both wants to care and demonstrates understanding of those needing representation.

127. Id. at 1558.

128. Taking this point one step further, a distinguished civil rights lawyer has noted that the disparity in socioeconomic circumstance "between the average civil rights attorney and the average client or class member in a civil rights case" can "create problems in the relationship." Julius Chambers, "Class Action Litigation: Representing Divergent Interests of Class Members," 4 *U. Dayton L. Rev.* 353, 355 (1979) (suggesting not that these problems raise the level of challenging the adequacy of representation, which covers the lawyer as well as the named representative, but instead urging greater attention to this problem of distance by the legal profession generally).

129. *See* Martin v. Wilks, 490 U.S. 755 (1989); Hansberry v. Lee, 311 U.S. 32 (1940).

130. *See generally* Betty Krikorian, *Fiduciary Standards in Pension and Trust Management* (1989).

131. *See* Rosewicz, *supra* note 34 (discussing deaf lawyer who represented a deaf student in the Supreme Court).

132. *See* Sacks, *supra* note 64, at 127–63.

133. After longstanding tradition recognizing parents as representatives of their children for purposes of litigation, the Supreme Court denied a group of African-American parents standing to sue on behalf of their children who were denied admission to private, tax-exempt schools. The Court reasoned in part that any stigma due to racial discrimination could be challenged only by the individual who was personally injured. Allen v. Wright, 468 U.S. 737, 757 (1984).

134. Kelly, *supra* note 21, at B93. In this way, the play challenges the audience to

think not only about the gender of the character, but also the gender of the actor, and thus the possibilities of cross-gender casting. Cross-gender casting, while uncommon, is not without precedent. *See* Sullivan, *supra* note 25, at 50.

135. Kelly, *supra* note 21, at B93.

THE NARRATIVE AND THE NORMATIVE
IN LEGAL SCHOLARSHIP

Kathryn Abrams

▼

[W]e read well, and with pleasure, what we already know how to read; and what we know how to read is to a large extent dependent upon what we have already read . . . —Annette Kolodny[1]

The substantive contributions of feminist legal scholarship are frequently remarked, if not always fully understood or appreciated. But legal scholars are only beginning to acknowledge the extent to which feminist jurisprudence has also challenged the methodological norms of legal scholarship.[2] While some feminist scholars communicate their substantive insights in ways that reflect the authorial voice, organizational structure, and epistemological assumptions of mainstream legal scholarship, others have forged a path that attempts to create more of a correspondence between method and message. This is perhaps nowhere truer than in the growing body of feminist narrative scholarship. The valuation of experiential knowledge, the conviction that the exclusion of women's perspectives has distorted the development of legal rules, and a growing frustration with the abstraction and distance conventionally required of legal decisionmakers have produced a wave of women's storytelling. Authors use their own experiential stories, or those of others, to illuminate what unites and divides us across lines of gender, race, class, or sexual orientation. They offer these stories not only to illuminate the insights that have been excluded, but to help legal decisionmakers develop less partial, more broadly responsive legal solutions. In this essay, I will attempt to shed light on the complex and incompletely understood relationship between experiential narratives and proposals for legal change.

The term "narrative scholarship" encompasses a strikingly heterogeneous body of work. Not only do narrative scholars vary in their substantive focus[3]—they may address issues of gender, race, class, sexual orientation, or some conjunction thereof—but they employ contrasting voices and tones, and communicate their messages in a variety of styles. Stories from several recently published feminist narrative works may help convey a sense of this variety.

Some scholars offer narratives that provide a kind of inside report—an internal vantage point—on perspectives little heard in legal discussion. In "Legal Images of Battered Women," for example, Martha Mahoney offers narratives of lesbian battering to illustrate the greater complexity of images of battering relationships that have evolved outside the legal system:

> I look back and can see that there was something good. It didn't start with violence and ugliness. It started with summer nights, two women in their early 20's trying to find a way to see each other. Both lived in households where it wasn't possible to be open about the relationship. Meeting at movies and bars until early in the morning—until one finally left her home. Night of lovemaking, not enough sleep and feeling fine at work the next day—being relaxed and happy. I had found something that I never even knew existed . . .
>
> And who is the monster in the next room who did this? She's just a woman like you who is feeling as upset as you are and is temporarily full of remorse. She is the only friend you have, the only one who seems to care. The idea of leaving seems worse than if you try to stay and make it work and make sure it doesn't happen again. Bruises heal and resentment fades back into the routines of work, shopping, watching re-runs of All Creatures Great and Small, and driving her to church on Sunday morning.[4]

For other narrative scholars, the emphasis is not so much on factually particularized, insider reportage as on communicating the emotional resonance of a little-understood experience. In "The Obliging Shell," Patricia Williams captures a critical moment in her emerging self-awareness as a black woman:

> I remember with great clarity the moment I discovered that I was "colored." I was three. I already knew that I was a "negro"; my parents had told me to be proud of that. But "colored" was something else; it was the totemic evil I had heard my little white friends talking about for several weeks before I finally realized that I was one of them. I still remember the crash of that devastating moment of union, the union of my joyful body and the terrible power-life of that devouring symbol of negritude. I have spent the rest of my life recovering from the degradation of being divided against myself . . .[5]

Some narratives focus on corporeal experience, their blunt, visceral language offering a challenge to the conventionally established boundaries of the private. In "Zig-Zag Stitching and the Seamless Web," for example, Marie Ashe relates her experience of the humiliations imposed on women in doctor-supervised hospital births:

> I recognized the doctor's voice as he spoke to the nurses. Push whenever you feel the urge, the nurse said to me. I felt the urge, and I pushed. Can I raise myself up on my elbows, I asked them. That won't work on this table, the nurse said. Just push again, now, it won't be long. I pushed again, and uttered a long, low moan, lasting the duration of the push. There's no need for that kind of noise, he said. I felt humiliation and fury. Damn it, he said, she's not pushing hard enough. Get me a forceps.[6]

Still other narrative authors employ a more allusive style to convey the ambiguity of experience. In a poem taken from her essay "Commonalities," Judy Scales-Trent confronts the way that her mixed-race parentage and "white" appearance makes her both similar to and different from black and white women:

> There she stood in her pink organdy dress,
>> pink socks,
>> pink ribbons,
>> patent leather shoes.
> She had rich brown skin
> Hair pulled back in braids so tight
>> bright eyes
>> bright smile
> She was me when I was six
> getting ready for church on Sunday morning—
> organdy dress so starched
> it scratched,
> head tender from the curling iron
> Mommie wielded so fiercely:
> pressed hair for Jesus, Lord!
>> pink ribbons
>> pink socks
>> patent leather shoes.
> So I smiled at her,
> seeing myself
> And she hid behind her mother's legs
> and said
> "I'm skeered of white people."[7]

Beyond its almost inexhaustible variety, the most striking characteristic of narrative scholarship has been its capacity to generate controversy in the legal community. Mainstream legal scholars have been alternately perplexed and perturbed by this form of scholarship;[8] several factors animate this response. First, there is the problem of authorship: these stories are coming from white women, people of color, and others to whom many mainstream scholars are unaccustomed to listening. Second, there is the problem of form: many of these essays depart from the linear, deductive form of argumentation common in mainstream legal scholarship. Additionally, there is the problem of epistemological stance: these essays lack the conventional distance of legal scholars from their subject, and make claims to know on the basis of experience, which are unsettling to those schooled in the epistemology of scientific objectivity. But some of the most interesting objections, and those on which I will focus here, concern the relationship between narratives and the normative effort of which legal scholarship considers itself to be a part. Mainstream scholars wonder if narrative can and does contribute to the prescriptions for legal change that are a primary focus of legal scholarship.[9]

Many legal scholars believe that the point of their work is to offer analyses or prescriptions that will improve the functioning of the legal system. Feminist scholars may disagree with this premise in some respects,[10] yet they concur inasmuch as their scholarship is aimed at the normative goal of ending gender, and other forms of, oppression. Mainstream legal scholars, however, are less confident than their feminist counterparts that narrative scholarship can fulfill such normative aspirations.

First, many legal scholars doubt that it is legitimate, or even possible, to derive general prescriptions from particular, highly contextualized stories. They may be skeptical about the insight communicated by the story, or doubtful that a narrative that reflects the experience of one person can serve as the basis for a legal response that will govern the lives of many. Second, even if mainstream scholars are willing to accept the project as plausible, they do not see the analytic machinery capable of translating stories into normative proposals. When mainstream legal scholars read experiential narrative scholarship, they look for an abstract framework—a kind of feminist analogue to the Posnerian economic analysis of law—that transforms the raw data provided by experiential narratives into the specific legal rules or proposals. They do not always find what they are looking for.

What is noteworthy about both of these reservations is that they are based on a set of unstated assumptions about what kind of proposals function as "normative" in legal scholarship. These assumptions are shaped by the conventions of mainstream legal scholarship—the scholarship we "already know how to read"—which forcefully govern our expectations regarding the proper addressees of legal scholarship, kinds of legal proposals that are acceptable to offer, and the forms of discourse in which they should be couched. Legal scholarship, for example, is most frequently addressed to federal (appellate) judges or those clerks or lawyers who frame arguments for them.[11] Only occasionally is legal scholarship addressed to state judges, federal or state legislators, or other legal scholars. And only very rarely is it addressed to the victims of social or legal wrongs, political activists, or interested general readers. This means that the wrong to be remedied has almost always been diagnosed by social or political leaders as a social problem; and it has usually been consigned to some branch of the legal system for remediation. These facts have direct implications for other features of the normative in legal scholarship. They mean that a normative proposal is usually a proposal for a change in the way that judges (or occasionally legislatures) address a legal issue currently before them: a new legal standard, or a new balancing of the factors that comprise the current legal standard. The identity of the likely addressees also influences the discourse in which legal scholarship is framed. Many legal scholars strive for what Edward Rubin has called a "unity of discourse" with the courts they address:[12] they assume the same posture of distance from their subject, and employ the same specificity in legal formulation, and abstraction from the concrete details of claimants' lives, that characterize appellate opinions.

Sometimes narrative scholarship satisfies one or more of the conventions governing the normative in legal scholarship; often it doesn't. Determining whether or not narrative scholarship conforms to these criteria, however, is less important in this context than recognizing the force and the partiality of the criteria themselves. Grasping this point requires looking away from the familiar forms of scholarship, and asking about the role of the normative—how scholars envision making the transition from the ideal to the actual—in less conventional work. A brief look at the historical emergence and political functions of narrative in feminist scholarship will not only illuminate the varied relations that exist between narrative and legal change; it will also suggest the contours of a broader conception of the normative in legal scholarship.

The first feminist narratives to emerge, historically, might be described as "excluded voices" narratives. They offered the stories of women, usually victims of a gender-specific injury, whose voices had not been heard in discussion of the problem as a social matter, or analysis of the proper remedial response as a matter of law. These narratives were offered to serve a number of different goals. Sometimes they were offered to get a social problem on the map: early narrative accounts of date rape served this function.[13] Sometimes they were offered to get a social problem on the legal agenda. This was often done by challenging the "neutrality" of distinctions that had been used to keep these problems out of courts or off the legal agenda. Early narrative accounts of spousal abuse challenged the neutrality or plausibility of a public/private distinction that had made legal actors reluctant to intervene in these cases.[14] Other times narratives were offered to suggest that what was thought to be an acceptable legal approach to a social problem was perilously partial or incomplete. Rape narratives challenged the legislative imposition and judicial interpretation of requirements such as "force" or "consent" that made rape cases difficult to prosecute and highly intrusive and demeaning to the victim.[15]

On a practical level, these narratives enjoyed a limited success: they brought gender-related injuries into the light of day, and made at least contestable the "neutrality" of legal rules that rendered such injuries irremediable. In this respect it is difficult to deny their "normative" value. On a scholarly level, however, excluded-voices narratives have engendered a mixed response. Where they have been used in a comparatively direct way to support a change in a legal rule, they have met with fairly positive response. Susan Estrich, for example, used a narration of her own rape to develop a victim's perspective on rape that contrasts with the male or perpetrator perspective implicit in current elements of force and consent; she then employed this contrast to develop victim-centered proposals for change in judicial approach to these elements. While Estrich's first-person narrative was controversial in many legal circles, most mainstream readers agreed that she had employed that narrative to develop a normative, legal agenda for change. Mainstream readers have been less receptive where the excluded voice embodies contradiction or ambivalence that makes it more complicated to translate into a particular proposal, or where some voices in the excluded group sound different from others. Readers may construe the scholarship to present a more unitary portrait than it does, or, alternately, may despair over the possibility of accommodating the cacaphony of voices they claim it introduces.

Such readers err in distorting, or doubting, the normative contribution of more ambiguous or complex narratives.[16] These narratives may combat stigma by rendering, in all their complexity, the lives of persons who may conventionally be depicted by simplifying stereotypes. They may facilitate coalescence among groups by pointing out previously unperceived commonalities among them—as Judy Scales-Trent does when she likens certain aspects of her situation to those of her lesbian or Native American sisters.[17] They may also suggest the need to correct or supplement a legal approach that derives from too unitary an image—as Martha Mahoney does when she juxtaposes the often unheard voices of strong, capable women in battering relationships to the unitary image of "learned helplessness."[18] While the incorporation of complex images into usable legal standards may be a difficult undertaking, it need not lead to the confusion or remedial paralysis that critics sometimes suggest. Mahoney, for example, does not propose rejection of the learned-helplessness approach that has been so useful in battered women's self-defense; she suggests instead that learned helplessness be presented in context, as one part of a relational struggle for power and control that may exhibit more variety than has been previously suggested.[19]

While excluded-voices narratives continue to be offered to call attention to unacknowledged gender-related problems, our society and our legal system have begun to recognize the gender-specific injuries underscored by earlier narratives, and it has become necessary to use narratives for additional purposes. Thus a second generation of narratives has emerged—later both chronologically and in the process of political change—to address these challenges. One set of narratives within this group might be referred to as "mid-course correction" narratives. They help demonstrate that a legal approach that is basically headed in the right direction has taken a wrong turn. The best examples of this type of story are those sexual harassment narratives that have been offered to show that women's perceptions of allegedly harassing behavior are often different from men's. These narratives have been used to support the argument that the cause of action for hostile-environment sexual harassment—in itself a good thing—had taken a wrong turn when it was joined to a "reasonable person" test for determining whether a violation had occurred.[20] This form of narrative scholarship has encountered less difficulty with mainstream readers because it displays some of the conventional indices of the normative: it responds to an acknowledged social problem already consigned to the legal system for resolution; it features courts or legislatures as its primary addressees. But it has also been less frequently employed. Not only are there few areas of gender-related law whose flaws are sufficiently contained that they can be remedied by mid-course corrections, but there are comparatively few doctrinal adjustments whose acceptance requires the experiential epiphany that narrative characteristically provides. Examples such as the "reasonable person/reasonable woman" debate in sexual harassment law may be happy coincidences that will not frequently recur.

Far more prevalent within this second generation are stories that might be described as "paradigm-shifting" narratives. This category comprises the largest and most challenging group of narratives being offered today; but they are also the most controversial. These narratives are offered when, in the view of the author, the legal system has reached an impasse: the law has progressed to the limits of what it can accomplish, given an ingrained conception of a particular problem; before it can move again, it is necessary that some reconceptualization take place. This reconceptualization is what many feminist or critical race scholars attempt to effect through narrative. Some paradigm-shifting narrative scholars try to reconceptualize the *subject* of legal action: Martha Mahoney's narratives try to change our view of battered women from passive victims of learned helplessness to capable women caught in a two-way struggle for power and control.[21] Other paradigm-shifting storytellers try to reconceptualize the *discourse* used to frame the legal questions: Marie Ashe's visceral accounts of childbirth, miscarriage, and abortion seek to alter the abstraction from bodily experience that she believes has distorted discourse about reproductive rights.[22] Still other narrative scholars attempt to reconceptualize the *task of the legal decisionmaker*: Patricia Williams uses narratives to evoke a "multi-valent form of seeing," which takes the perspective not only of perpetrators of discrimination, but of victims, concerned observers, and many positions in between, in determining what constitutes discrimination.

Paradigm-shifting narratives in many ways reflect the development of this form of scholarship: they suggest the growing confidence of feminist scholars in the complexity of the message that can be communicated through narrative, and in their own ability to use it; they reflect a greater willingness on the part of feminists and critical race scholars to offer systematic criticism of both the substantive and the methodological premises of the law. Yet these narratives may be particularly unsettling to mainstream readers. Some readers may object because they contest the substantive assumptions of the author: they may view the impasse identified by a critical scholar as a proper angle of repose. If mothers in battering relationships lose custody of their children, the cause may be not the victimizing imagery of learned helplessness but the danger that "nonfunctional" women present to their children. If no one is entitled to a race- or gender-conscious remedy without a showing of intentional discrimination or individual harm, this may reflect not the triumph of a perpetrator perspective, but rather the estimable values of individuality and meritocracy. Even among those readers who recognize a legal impasse, paradigm-shifting narratives may not meet the criteria for normative scholarship.[23] Critics may argue that such efforts do not yield a "bottom line"—they do not give legal actors new frameworks or complete analyses to substitute for the rejected paradigms. In some respects this may be true: many of these narratives point out the kind of change that is needed, rather than deliver an entirely new approach. Yet these objections overlook the distinctive contributions of narratives that offer a conceptual ground for rejecting an existing legal framework and point the way, however provisionally, toward a new conception.

Paradigm-shifting narratives offer a systematic critique of a substantive legal approach, framed in a form of discourse not conventionally used by legal decisionmakers. Their comparative freedom from dominant substantive and methodological assumptions may enable their practitioners to formulate perspectives on particular legal impasses that are more fully independent of the assumptions that produced them. This independence may assist them in identifying the elements of extant legal analysis that contributed to the problem. Patricia Williams's use of "multi-valent" narratives to critique the Court's opinion in *Croson v. City of Richmond*[24] permits her to see the monovalence of the Court's vision as a problem—an insight that might not have been available to her had she developed her critique through a more conventional form of legal discourse. Moreoever, by challenging dominant assumptions methodologically as well as substantively, paradigm-shifting narratives may encourage change by helping readers to see how deep our commitments to dominant, problematic assumptions actually run. Readers—like myself—who question Marie Ashe's claim that medicolegal regulation has distanced women from their physical experience may think again when they witness their own distress at Ashe's pungent, visceral images of birth and death. Finally, by offering a broad vision, or conception, around which future remedial efforts can be organized, paradigm-shifting narratives can commence a process of discussion and exchange, from which more specific legal proposals can arise. This understanding contests the distinction sometimes made by legal scholars between broad "political" analyses of group-based injuries and specific, court-oriented "legal" solutions. It also contests a widely held, individualistic assumption that legal solutions are formulated at a single pass, by one scholar working in isolation. Legal solutions—particularly those that respond to unacknowledged injuries or problematic impasses—are also the result of collaboration, over time, among many contributors. Paradigm-shifting narratives offer an organizing insight, and issue a call, for beginning such collaboration. Martha Mahoney's effort to distinguish separation assault—with its roots in feminist analysis of battering as a relational struggle and its branches extending to numerous paths for future scholarship—is a perfect example of such a call. And Catharine MacKinnon's gradual progress from publicization of Linda Marchiano's narratives to formulation of statutes and ordinances regulating pornography makes clear that stagewise remedial efforts need not founder or trail off into indecision.[25]

Paradigm-shifting narratives, as well as other kinds of narratives, help alter our conception of the normative by offering a new image of what is necessary to effect legal change. This new image describes a wider temporal and substantive horizon: "legal problems" are not born when a judge issues a flawed decision. They often begin as unacknowedged injuries, gain recognition as social problems, win a place on the legal agenda, and become the object of legislative or judicial attention before such flaws can even be diagnosed. Moreover, the myopia that can prevent any of these steps from being taken cannot neatly be divided into "social" and "legal" varieties: social attitudes and assumptions—such as the view of domestic violence as a "private" problem—influence legal response; those who would effect legal solutions have necessarily to be interested in both. This new image also embodies a different view of the kinds of knowledge that move legal decisionmakers to undertake legal change. Conventional legal scholarship often proceeds as if all that separates the legal system from transformative change in the area of race or gender is the proper three-part standard.[26] Narrative scholars take the contrasting position that what persuades decisionmakers to embrace new legal rules is not, or not only, the abstract elegance of a proposed solution. They may also be moved to action by a more visceral response: a response animated by a particularized depiction of the lives of those affected by a legal rule.[27] Because of its pungency and particularity, its inflection with the emotional resonances and factual minutiae of life, narrative may elicit this visceral understanding in a way that more abstract propositions rarely can.

Reflecting on this extended, encompassing vision of legal change may help us to define more broadly the role that legal actors can play in ending group-based oppression. It may also help us to read with pleasure, and to read well, a promising new form of scholarship.

Notes

I would like to thank Isabel Marcus, who first suggested to me that the normative contribution of narratives had to be understood in a political and historical context; Jim Atleson, Lucinda Finley, Betty Mensch, and Robert Steinfeld, who braved a small blizzard to come discuss the paper from which this essay emerged. My appreciation also goes to Zipporah Wiseman, Susan Heinzelman, and Patricia Cain, who organized the wonderful conference at which this essay was first presented in something like its current form.

1. Annette Kolodny, "Dancing Through the Mind Field," 6 *Feminist Stud.* 144, *reprinted in The New Feminist Criticism* (Elaine Showalter ed., 1985).

2. This recognition has produced a small but burgeoning body of feminist legal scholarship oriented toward questions of method. *See, e.g.,* Katharine T. Bartlett, "Feminist Legal Methods," 103 *Harv. L. Rev.* 829 (1990); Martha Fineman, "Challenging Law, Establishing Differences: The Future of Feminist Legal Scholarship," 42 *Fla. L. Rev.* 25 (1990); Deborah L. Rhode, "Feminist Critical Theories," 42 *Stan. L. Rev.* 617 (1990); Ruth Colker, "Feminist Litigation—An Oxymoron: A Study of the Briefs Filed in *Webster v. Reproductive Health Services,*" 13 *Harv. Women's L.J.* 137 (1990); Kathryn Abrams, "Feminist Lawyering and Feminist Method," 16 *Law & Soc. Inq.* 373 (1991).

More recently, a body of scholarship has emerged that explicitly takes up the use of narrative in feminist, critical race and gay legal analysis. *See, e.g.,* William Eskridge,

"Gaylegal Narratives," *Stan. L. Rev.* (forthcoming 1994); Jane Barron, "Resistance to Stories," 67 *S. Cal. L. Rev.* 255 (1994); Dan Farber & Suzanna Sherry, "Telling Stories Out of School: An Essay on Legal Narratives," 45 *Stan. L. Rev.* 807 (1993); Richard Delgado, "The Inward Turn in Outsider Jurisprudence," 34 *Wm. & Mary L. Rev.* 741 (1993); Mark Tushnet, "The Degradation of Constitutional Discourse," 81 *Geo. L.J.* 251 (1992); Mark Fajer, "Can Two Real Men Eat Quiche Together? Storytelling, Gender-Role Stereotypes, and Legal Protection for Lesbians and Gay Men," 46 *U. Miami L. Rev.* 511 (1992); Mary Coombs, "Outsider Scholarship: The Law Review Stories," 63 *U. Colo. L. Rev.* 683 (1992); Kathryn Abrams, "Hearing the Call of Stories," 79 *Cal. L. Rev.* 971 (1991); Alex Johnson, Jr., "The New Voice of Color," 100 *Yale L. J.* 2007 (1991).

3. In legal scholarship, feminist narratives have emerged alongside and in confluence with the "outsider" or "opposition" narratives offered by scholars of color. *See, e.g.,* Derrick Bell, *And We Are Not Saved,* (1987); Richard Delgado, "Storytelling for Oppositionists and Others: A Plea for Narrative," 87 *Mich. L. Rev.* 2411 (1989); Mari J. Matsuda, "Looking to the Bottom: Critical Legal Studies and Reparations," 22 *Harv. C.R.-C.L. L. Rev.* 323 (1987). Scholars within the latter group have sometimes described their effort to develop a critique of extant (legal) arrangements from the standpoint of minority groups as "critical race theory." Because some feminist legal scholars are women of color (or vice versa), some of the stories I refer to as "feminist narratives" can also be described as opposition narratives or critical race narratives. The narratives of Patricia Williams and Judith Scales-Trent fall into this category.

4. Martha R. Mahoney, "Legal Images of Battered Women: Redefining the Issue of Separation," 90 *Mich. L. Rev.* 1, 51–52 (1991).

5. Patricia J. Williams, "The Obliging Shell: An Informal Essay on Formal Equal Opportunity," 87 *Mich. L. Rev.* 2128, 2140 (1989).

6. Marie Ashe, "Zig-Zag Stitching and the Seamless Web: Thoughts on Reproduction and the Law," 13 *Nova L. Rev.* 355, 360 (1989).

7. Judith Scales-Trent, "Commonalities: On Being Black and White, Different and the Same," *infra,* p. 64.

8. *See, e.g.,* Dan Farber & Suzanna Sherry, *supra* note 2.

9. Farber and Sherry may be voicing one version of this reservation, when they argue that narrative work unaccompanied by non-narrative "analysis" is not sufficient to satisfy the norms of legal scholarship. *See* Dan Farber & Suzanna Sherry, *supra* note 2, at 849–54. However, the discussion below responds less to their analysis, which was published after this essay was written, than to repeated objections raised in the context of appointments committee deliberations.

10. They may understand the crucial role that description serves in systematic critique; they may also understand the factors that lead some scholars to label work they dislike, or with whose normative conclusions they disagree, "descriptive."

11. *See* Edward L. Rubin, "The Practice and Discourse of Legal Scholarship," 86 *Mich. L. Rev.* 1835, 1859–60 (1988) (also discussing the drawbacks of this orientation).

12. *Id.* at 1859–60.

13. *See* Robin Warshaw, *I Never Called It Rape* (1988) (providing a later compilation and

analysis of date rape narratives). Ironically, Katie Roiphe has recently used the same approach to place a critique of "rape crisis feminism" on the agendas of university administrators, young women, and, arguably, the "anti-PC" right. See Katie Roiphe, *The Morning After: Sex, Fear and Feminism on Campus* (1993).

14. *See, e.g.,* Lenore Walker, *The Battered Woman* (1979).

15. *See generally* Susan Estrich, "Rape," 95 Yale L.J. 1087 (1986).

16. I discuss the normative contribution of complex narratives at greater length in Kathryn Abrams, "Narrative, Unity, and Law," 13 Studies in L., Pol. & Soc. 3 (1993).

17. *See* Scales-Trent, *supra* note 7.

18. *See* Mahoney, *supra* note 4.

19. *Id.* The reader will note that I describe Mahoney's work as incorporating both excluded-voices narratives and as attempting to achieve, through narrative, the kind of "paradigm shift" I describe *infra* at text accompanying note 21. Mahoney's is one of a group of narratives that serve multiple functions. By offering the excluded voices of intelligent, competent battered women, Mahoney creates a more complex image that facilitates the shift to a view of battering as a struggle for power and control.

20. *See* Kathryn Abrams, "Gender Discrimination and the Transformation of Workplace Norms," 42 Vand. L. Rev. 1183, 1197–1214 (1989) (using narratives from cases and empirical work to argue for adoption of modified "reasonable woman" standard); *see also* Wendy Pollack, "Sexual Harassment: Women's Experience v. Legal Definitions," 13 Harv. Women's L.J. 35 (1990) (using women's narratives to illuminate the distance between their perceptions of sexual harassment and those embodied in law).

21. *See* Mahoney, *supra* note 4. It is actually my view that Mahoney's narratives, like many complex feminist and race narratives, serve several of these purposes simultaneously.

22. *See* Ashe, *supra* note 6.

23. By describing a "mainstream" legal scholarly view of what constitutes "normativity" in legal scholarship, I do not mean to suggest that the notion of normativity in legal scholarship has not previously been contested. Such contestation is one of the central features of a body of postmodern legal scholarship concerned with "the politics of form." *See* Pierre Schlag, "The Problem of the Subject," 69 Tex. L. Rev. 1627 (1991); Pierre Schlag, "Normativity and the Politics of Form," 139 U. Pa. L. Rev. 801 (1991); Pierre Schlag, "Normative and Nowhere to Go," 43 Stan. L. Rev. 167 (1990). Although I have learned much from this body of scholarship, I would differentiate my position in the following (substantially simplified) way. At least within the area of gender (and possibly other types of group-based oppression), I do not share with scholars such as Pierre Schlag the belief that many of the preconditions for (useful) normative scholarship have ceased to exist. Rather, I believe that the way in which normative legal change has occurred in the area of gender suggests that the scope of the "normative"—that is, the range of ways in which legal scholars can contribute to legal change—is much broader than we had previously thought.

24. 109 S. Ct. 706 (1989).

25. Catharine MacKinnon, *Feminism Unmodified: Discourses on Life and Law* (1987) (tracing

MacKinnon's progress in addressing pornography's harms to women, first politically and then legally in the "Pornography" section).

26. I thank Jim Atleson for this insight.

27. *See* Martha Nussbaum, *Love's Knowledge: Essays on Philosophy and Literature* (1990) (making the related point that moral decision-making is not simply a matter of "rational" choice among abstract principles but is also influenced by the vivid perception of the particulars of a situation, which is informed by imagination and emotional response, and also arguing that stories, particularly the fictional stories contained in great works of literature, can be useful in highlighting and developing this latter component of moral perception and decision-making).

COMMONALITIES

On Being Black and White, Different and the Same

Judy Scales-Trent

▼

[Author's Note: Many in my family are various shades of brown, as is common in most black families. Many others of us, however, look white. I wrote these journal notes, and this essay, as a way of coming to terms with the dilemma of being black and looking white in a society that does not handle anomalies very well.]

It is only recently that I have realized that the work that I do is deeply connected with my struggle to live within this dilemma. I am a lawyer and a professor of law. I write about the intersection of race and sex in American law, focusing on the status of black women in the law, that is, on the group that stands at the intersection of the race category and the sex category. I used to define my work in that way. Now that I have written this essay, I see my work differently. In this essay, I struggle to combine two statuses that our society says cannot be combined: black cannot be white, and white cannot be black. In my earlier work on race and sex, I argued that it did not make sense to try to maintain two distinct categories of race and sex in the law, when that separation ignored the very real existence of black women. There again, I argued that the categories seen as so pure, were not pure; that the boundaries thought impermeable were not impermeable. Looking at all of my work, I now understand that I have been working at the intersection of race and sex because I exist at the intersection of race and color, and because I understand, in a very profound way, that in order for me to exist, I must transgress boundaries.

I think this makes people profoundly uncomfortable. Categories make the world appear understandable and safe. Nonetheless, in this essay I ask you to experience my vision of the world—a world where the categories do not clarify, but confuse; a world where one must question the very existence of those categories in order to survive.

Journal Entries: November 1978–December 1981 [1]

November 1978

> He sang out:
> What did I do
> to be so black and blue?
> And I wept:
> What did I do
> to be so black,
>   so white?

November 26, 1978

I wish I had a name to make my home in, to hide inside of. Maybe we should bring back the name "mulatto." For a woman, the French would say "mulatresse." An identity. A group to belong to. You say "mulatto," and it conjures up meaning: a person despised by dark-skinned brothers and sisters.

> ("Who does she think she is? She think she white, man."
> "Hey, you think you better than me, huh?!")

Cast out, cast out, always cast out from the only home, the only safe place, the only refuge in a terrifying, vicious land. Cast out, and alone.

> No home. No home.
> No place to belong.
> No place to rest a frightened and lonely heart.
> No place to hide.

White people would let me in, of course. They think that I belong with them. They smile at me. They welcome me. They think I'm their sister.

> ("Did you see the way that nigger drives? We shouldn't give them licenses!")

They think I'm on their team. And so I'm always waiting, waiting for them to say it. Please don't say it. Don't do that to me. Jesus God, cabbie, can't I even go across town in a cab without having my whole identity called into question? Always wary. Always fighting their silent thoughts, their safe assumptions. Fighting for control of who I am.

That's who I am.

Cast out of my house.

And fighting for control.

And crying.

Missing the safe warmth of my childhood, a colored girl growing up in the protection of a strong family in the segregated South. Surrounded by their love and their strength and their definition of me and of themselves. We moved to New York City when I was very young. One of my warmest memories is of traveling back to North Carolina from New York every summer on the Jim Crow train. We children belonged to all the black adults on the train. Everyone talked and shared food . . . fried chicken and white bread, pimiento cheese sandwiches, deviled eggs: our shoe-box lunch.

Yes, I can see that. What I'm missing is the protection of the family.

But I lost something more when I grew up and moved out of the segregated South, out of the safety of my childhood home. Because the Jim Crow laws gave me an identity and a protection I couldn't give myself.

Suddenly, the world was opened to me: streets, movies, schools, restaurants. I put one foot into the world of white-Jewish-liberal-intellectuals when I was in the fifth grade, and I've been straddling two worlds ever since.

What do you do if you're rejected by one world,

> ("Oh, let's have Judy sit at the table with the white couple when they get here. She acts so white.")

and are constantly rejecting the other. I am perceived by some as white, by some as black, by yet others, as a black person but "really white," so (a) you can trust her and (b) you can't trust her.

And yet I'm me all the time.

Jerked back and forth by other people's needs and fears 'til it gets hard for me to figure out who I am in all this.

I'm glad I've started this writing.

These are the notes of a white black woman.

("Mommy, which water fountain should I drink out of, white or colored?")

December 1, 1979

Sometimes I feel like I'm black, passing for white.

Sometimes I feel like I'm white, passing for black.

On a good day, I just live my life.

December 2, 1979

I went to hear a chamber music recital last night at the Kennedy Center. This is the kind of music that filled my childhood . . . chamber music at the WQXR studio, symphony music at Tanglewood or Lewisohn Stadium, the Saturday afternoon opera on the radio when we were not allowed to make a sound in the apartment.

White music.

We were also exposed to black music—spirituals, "boogie-woogie," and the "classical" black composers and musicians. But our father disapproved of the rhythm-and-blues records we brought home when we were teenagers. As an adult, I have spent a long time getting in touch with other kinds of black music. Bill introduced me to jazz. And I was almost thirty when I first heard the blues. I couldn't get over it then, and I still can't. It speaks so directly to me and for me. It pierces my heart with pain or joy, sometimes both. And gospel music I have loved since I was a child. I loved it when the men's choir at St. Catherine's AME Zion church went on summer vacation and took their tacky cantatas with them. For that's when the gospel choir came. And the church jumped and shook, and the music made you feel.

It is hard, but very important, to fit the black and white music pieces comfortably into who I am. I need to be able to accept the black and the white heritages with their own validity.

That is all true, and important. But getting a little too intellectual. A way of avoiding the anxiety of last night's chamber recital. For you see, color makes it all more complicated. The concert hall seats maybe eight hundred, a thousand people. It was almost full. And I didn't see anyone who was not white. I felt very anxious and frightened. I was losing control of my identity as a black person: it was slipping away. Wasn't this proof that I was white? By their perception, didn't I fit in just perfectly? And wasn't it obvious that I wouldn't have been there if I weren't white? (1. All people who go to hear chamber music are white. 2. I go to chamber music recitals. 3. Therefore, I am white.) But at intermission, I saw about half a dozen black people. The pendulum tilted back to center and I was steadied.

I must gain better control over who I am. I must learn to live squarely, steadily and surely in the middle of ambiguity, centered strongly in my own No-Name. I must define the No-Name and make it my home.

December 15, 1979

More and more, lately, I have been thinking of dating white men. I have been thinking I could now date white men. I just returned from a visit at

Julie's house. One of their friends stopped by. I was attracted by his looks, his openness and enthusiasm, his excitement in learning.

Sexy.

I think it would be difficult. But with some help, I could do my part. I think this means something good in terms of my defining and accepting who I am, a white black woman. My definition of who I am is much less at risk. And it also feels sad, terribly sad. For I am, after all, a black woman, deep down where it counts, and where it hurts.

December 19, 1979

I remember having a startling thought several months ago. Someone gave me a standard line about how she had always wished she were tall. I started my standard response of how I wished I were short—when I suddenly realized that that just wasn't true. I liked being tall and looking good tall. Then last week I saw "Death and the King's Horsemen," a play by the Nigerian playwright Wole Soyinka. I was watching the beautiful dark-skinned women dancing and started my standard thought of how I wished my skin were that color. But that thought was immediately replaced by: "That's not true. I like the way I look. I look just fine."

I was startled. Pleased.

Hopeful that the thought will return.

There is so much yet I have to tell you about.

About the silence, the lifelong silence of my family. Was it such a terrible secret that we dare not talk about it? What was the secret? And what would happen if we did reveal it?

And about the guilt of a survivor, always protected by a white-skin disguise.

> Is it a disguise?
> How am I to take the good things that come my way?
> Would that cabbie have stopped if he had known?
> Would the doctor be civil if . . . ?
> Would the clerk have been so helpful?
> Would the real estate agent have rented me the apartment?

How can I say "No, don't be nice to me; I'm black"?

How can I try to keep from passing when all I'm trying to do is catch a fucking cab?

There is no way around it. I am passing all the time as I walk through the world. I can only correct the perceptions of those persons I deal with on a more than casual basis. And I feel like a fraud. And I hate it. I hate myself for not being able to solve the dilemma. And I hate black people and white people for putting me out there.

Catching a cab is just as hard for a white black person as for a black black person.

Or maybe not.

Maybe it has to be made hard to punish myself for my clever disguise.

I heap ashes upon my head and beg for forgiveness.

Sackcloth and ashes.

If I am forgiven,

perhaps I will be allowed back into the fold.

Will someone forgive me?

January 24, 1981

I am beginning to understand what they have done to us. The anger. All of the anger we can't show. And all of the men depressed. And the women, abandoned, un-cherished, un-beautiful.

. . .

What will become of us? How can we save ourselves and each other? How do we raise the children? How do we protect the children? (another body found in Atlanta today). Tell me, how do I raise a black-man child? Why am I raising a free child who knows what he is feeling? Maybe black men need to be depressed to stay alive. Feelings released create energy and potency: what can a black man do with those?

I am free to feel my aliveness, to stretch as far as I can—because I'm a woman, because I look white. Today, as Pat was getting off the elevator, a white man grabbed her and pushed her back, saying, "No nigger is going to get off this elevator before me!" I am spared that craziness by looking white. I am not pushed, abused, humiliated on a daily basis. I have my own craziness from being white/black, but I am not damaged the same way. I get to meet the test of what is called "beautiful" because I look white.

And so I can be valued as a woman by black men. Because I am not so damaged by the racism that I hate them. Because, coming from a white/black family, my father was allowed to make a good living and give us so much—financial security, protection, an open door to the world. Because I can feel beautiful.

It is, I think, the ultimate betrayal, the ultimate irony. The crazy way that racism worked has allowed me to be free and potent. And it has kept the men I love locked in. And impotent. They are enraged at me for being able to take such joy in life and to feel the strength of being whole.

I feel enormous guilt at my wholeness, at feeling potent, at my joy in life.

Luckily, there is a built-in price I will have to pay. Being alone. I can't go back to being less than I am: I want to stand on my toes and reach my arms up as high as I can. But I haven't yet found a black man who can stand watching me do that.

I weep for their need.

But I weep for me also.

". . . some dreams just hang in the air
like smoke
touching everything."[2]

> Plenipotentiary
> And the world said: "Yes.
> You may have everything.
> But you will have to be alone."
> "Well then,
>   suppose I have a little less.
>   Suppose my mind doesn't work so well,
>   and my body too . . .
>   then may I have someone?"
> The answer is still out.

December 14, 1981

Oddly enough, the last chapter is the hardest to write . . . not because it is painful, but because there is no demon driving me. I am writing now not as part of the learning, the exorcism, but writing to record what I have learned. As I have moved into adulthood this year, as I have come to a strong sense of my own self-worth, I have learned to make my home within myself. My definition of who I am is steady, and is not shaken by the definition of others. I do not have to cut myself or stretch myself into one procrustean bed or another. I am content to be who I am, and leave to others the comfort of their own definitions. I claim only myself, and define myself by my own name.

This does not mean that there is not, will never be confusion or pain at being a white black woman. What it means is that it does not control me. It cannot claim me. It is a dilemma I live within. I center myself in myself, in the ambiguity of myself, and move on with life.

> Soy bi-lingue, bi-cultural,
> y orgulloso de mi raza!

The bright, bold poster says it for me:

I am bilingual, bicultural,
and proud of my people!

There have been signposts this year that marked the journey. I remember
reading the blatherings of a newspaper columnist who argued that his dark
skin entitled him to a special position as spokesperson for black people.
I remember being stunned, as I reread *Black Rage*[3] this year, at the authors'
angry description of "fair-skinned dilettantes" who take out their self-hatred
on those with darker skins. What I remember most is that it was immediately clear to me that the authors were not saying anything about me, but
were saying worlds about themselves. And I remember the day I made a
joke about the color of my skin. It was a good joke—free and cloudless! My
friend and I laughed and felt good together.

And I have learned from good teachers this year. I remember especially
Pauli Murray's autobiography, *Proud Shoes*,[4] where she tells of her struggle
to accept her white slaveholder ancestors as part of her family, where she
tells of her struggle to accept herself. And Joel Williamson's book *New People:
Miscegenation and Mulattoes*:[5] what a revelation. If there is a whole book on
the unspeakable, it can't be taboo, but an issue capable of exploration and
comprehension. Williamson described the history of a new group that has
been created through the fusion of Africans and Europeans. He gave me a
history, a context. He saw me and validated my new sense of being.

And I have learned from the poetry of Chinese women and Native American women . . . women who felt the anguish of losing their unique ethnic
identity, and who were determined not to lose it all, determined to fuse the
two worlds through their poetry. A determination to be all one is, and for
that "all" to be more and more, and not less and less. I will travel with Zora
Neale Hurston, who has taught me with her life. And who said: "But I am
not tragically colored . . . No, I do not weep at the world—I am too busy
sharpening my oyster knife."[6]

There is a phantom pain. It comes and goes. It will always come and go. But
the pull toward self-hood, toward whole-ness is stronger. By being, I fuse
the two worlds. I need do no more

> There she stood in her pink organdy dress,
> > pink socks,
> > pink ribbons,
> > patent leather shoes.
> She had rich brown skin
> Hair pulled back in braids so tight
> > bright eyes
> > bright smile.
> She was me when I was six

getting ready for church on Sunday morning—
organdy dress so starched
it scratched,
head tender from the curling iron
Mommie wielded so fiercely:
pressed hair for Jesus, Lord!
    pink ribbons
    pink socks
    patent leather shoes.
So I smiled at her,
seeing myself.
And she hid behind her mother's legs
looked up at me
and said
"I'm skeered of white people."

Reflections: July 1989

This is how the exploration started, with notes in a journal. It was time for exploring old wounds, a time for growth. I was newly divorced, a single-parent, head-of-household. And newly come to the world of therapy. It was a time for working on unfinished business. It was a time of rapid, often forced learning. I had been pushed out of one world—not a happy one, but a known one, and therefore, a safe one. And this must have pressed on the bruise of aloneness, of feeling pushed out and homeless because of being a white black woman.

I say unwanted, "forced learning," but clearly it was learning that I wanted, because I went out looking for it. It was a time when I began to open up to the world in a new way, and began to be able to see all the resources and gifts the world made available to me. I began to see that although perhaps I did not see on the table the food that I wanted, there was enough on the table for me not to starve. And, as time went on, I began to see that indeed there was a feast on the table, and that it only took opening up to the feast, reaching out to the richness of life.

It was about this time that I began to hear echoes of my song in the songs of others, that I began to realize that I was not out in the world, a stranger and alone.

It was then that I began to see the many similarities between my feelings of sadness and strangeness and what others felt. How then could I be so sad when I was so much less alone? I was finally able to hear the stories and songs of my sisters, and I heard them say:

We are like you.
You are our sister.
We are with you.
You are not alone.
We feel the same pain.
We sing the same songs.

Let me tell you who spoke to me, and what I heard. Let me tell you
how they answered my call. Let me tell you how we are the same in our
differences.
Listen to the song of my Indian sister Janet Campbell:

Desmet, Idaho, March 1969

At my father's wake
    The old people
    Knew me,
    Though I
    Knew them not,
And spoke to me
In our tribe's
Ancient tongue,
Ignoring
The fact
That I
Don't speak
The language,
And so,
I listened
As if I understood
What it was all about,
And,
Oh,
How it
Stirred me
To hear again
That strange,
    Softly
    Flowing
Native Tongue,
So
Familiar to
My childhood ear.[7]

How this song moved me! I heard then, and hear now, a deep and moving love for her people, a profound memory from childhood of belonging and being safe in the embrace of her family and her people. But I also hear a sadness at the not-belonging-anymore. The loss of her father, the loss of her language, the loss of her home.

I remember summers spent with our grandparents, aunts, uncles and cousins in North Carolina. We played all day long, as we roamed from family home to family home, enjoying the freedom from the city streets, enjoying the sunshine. We ran through the grape arbor quickly, in hopes that the bees would not be able to catch us. We wriggled our bare feet in the grass, as we played "Simon Says" until it was too dark to see anymore. And then, the wonderful dusky evenings, when we sat on the front porch with our mother and grandparents, swinging and fanning, trying to keep cool. Sometimes my grandmother would let me water the petunias in the urns on the front steps (did they like that night watering?). But most of all, I remember it as a quiet, coming-together time. And I remember, like Janet Campbell, the murmurings of the grown-ups as they talked about whatever they talked about. I don't remember what they said. But I do remember the dark and quiet stealing over us all on the porch, enveloping us in quiet and safety. And I remember being embraced and comforted by their murmurings, sounds that lulled us to quiet and to rest.

Now I return to the South to visit my parents. And once again, as I go with them into the black southern community—the church, the bridge club meetings, the college convocation—I am transported back to my childhood, to the safe embrace of family and community and church.

("Lord, child, I can sure see your Aunt Estelle in your face. I would know you anywhere!")

"And, Oh, How it Stir[s] me To hear again That strange, Softly Flowing Native Tongue So Familiar to My Childhood ear." And yet, and yet, I too have left home. And I hear the sounds of the language, but I am no longer of the language. One day, in church with my parents, I wept from the beauty and from sadness. Because although I was reminded of coming to church as a child, when I was safe in the embrace of my family, my church, my community, and my God, it was an embrace which I now returned to only rarely, and then, as an outsider. It was a borrowed embrace. And I wept at the loss of leaving home.

This is, of course, a loss all of us know. And we all try to recapture or re-create that embrace as best we know how as we grow older and leave home. But there is something about moving from the southern black community to the northern white community that adds to the sense of loss, of homelessness.

It makes me think of a story I heard about Dr. M., a resident in psychiatry. When I first met her, I felt her warmth and kindness. I noticed her quiet competence, and her quite visible pregnancy! I saw her as woman filled with life. When I mentioned her to a friend who was also a psychiatrist, he said, almost in passing, that he had not realized that she was an Indian until one evening, when they were both on duty at the emergency psychiatric clinic of a local hospital. At that time, an elderly Indian man was brought in for emergency treatment. I don't think he said why the man was there. What struck him was Dr. M.'s statement that this man had left the reservation. And that reservation Indians are particularly cruel to those who leave the reservation. I was immediately stunned by the thought that Dr. M. was talking not only about this man, but about herself. Had she also "left the reservation"? She was clearly successful in a white world. How much had she paid for that success? And it was clear also that she was talking about me. For there are so many reservations: geographical ones, cultural ones, and reservations of the mind. When one leaves to explore, to live in another world, are you leaving the reservation? How do those feel who don't leave the reservation? Do they want to leave? Are they afraid to move into a hostile world? Are they mad because the world off the reservation is more welcoming to me, a white black person? There is no doubt that the members of the white community in my northern home are more welcoming to me than are the members of the black community. How painful that has been. And I can't tell if it is because I am so bilingual and bicultural that they are not clear that I am black. Or because I have left the reservation and must be made to pay for it. But I am clear that I miss the sweet language of my childhood. And I miss my home. My Indian sisters have helped me see that more clearly.

And there was yet another poem which, years ago, led me to see my sameness in my difference. Listen to the song of my Chinese sister, Laureen Mar:

Chinatown I

Seattle, Washington
She boards the bus at Chinatown,
holding the brown paper shopping bag
with twine handles that comes from
San Francisco or Vancouver.
It is worn thin with creases.
An oil spot darkens one side
where juice dripped from warm
roast duck, another shopping trip.
Today there is fresh bok choy

wrapped in Chinese newspapers.
Grasping the rail with her right hand
she climbs the steps carefully,
smiling at the driver, looking down
to check her footing, glancing
at him again. She sways down the aisle
as if she still carried wood buckets
on a bamboo pole through the village,
from the well to her house.
Her gray silk pajamas are loose,
better than "pantsuits."
Sometimes there are two or three women,
chattering with the quick, sharp tongue
of the wren: dried mushrooms too
expensive, thirteen dollars a pound now.
She sits down and sets the bag between her knees.
Her shoulder is close to mine.
I want to touch it, tell her I can understand
Chinese. Instead, I stare at the silver
bar crossing her back, and hope she knows
this is an Express; it does not stop before Genesee.[8]

What do you see when you read this poem? I see generations of Chinese women stretching back, from the old woman climbing the bus steps so carefully, to her mother, who "carried wood buckets on a bamboo pole through the village, from the well to her house." But has the line of Chinese women stopped? The writer knows she is a Chinese woman. She knows Chinese. She wants to touch the old woman, to let her know that she knows Chinese, that she is family. But she is prudent. She does not do so. But tell me: if others do not know you "know Chinese," if others do not know that you are family, are you family? Are you Chinese? Who controls what is real: can you do it yourself, or do you need the corroboration of others? The writer wants to reach out, to help, to belong, but dares not. She is and is not family. She is the same, and not the same.

It reminds me of the girl in the pink organdy dress. I knew I was like her. I remembered being her. And I reached out with a smile. But she saw only the white part. And it frightened her. Her fear said, "No, you aren't my family. Go away." She didn't know that I "knew Chinese."

But my Chinese sister knows my song, and helps me see that I am not alone.

It is not all mournful work. Some of the lessons I have learned have been through rowdy laughter. I have had funny teachers. Let me tell you about Dianna. We worked at the appellate division together. And one of the strange things about that office is that it was comprised of about twenty attorneys all in various stages of avoiding writing a brief. One day, when I was in the "walk-the-hall" stage of avoidance, I dropped into Dianna's office and started complaining about the general run of men about town, and the general level of confusion and poverty in my life. "What I need," I said to her, "is to find a prosperous, slightly boring dentist to settle down with." "Oh, I know just what you mean," she declared emphatically. "And if you find one, ask him if he has a sister!" We burst out laughing. And that's how I learned that Dianna was a lesbian.

It wasn't until years later that I realized that gay people, like me, are faced with the problem of "coming out" to people. Dianna has to decide when she should come out to someone, and how. She has to worry about how that person will respond. And as long as she keeps meeting new people, she will have to keep dealing with those issues of self-identification and exposure. These are issues I deal with also: when do I tell someone that I am black? and how? and how will they respond? And if I don't tell people (the apartment rental agent, the cab driver), aren't I "passing"? But Lord knows there's no reason for me to get into self-revelation with someone who's paid to drive me from home to the car shop.

"And why?" I think. "Why should my lesbian sisters have to come out to people? why are they not allowed to keep their sexual life private? why do they have to say: 'This is who I am. I hope you can deal with it. Even if you can't, I need for you to know who I am. I am a member of a despised group. If we are to know each other, you must know this.'" As I write the words, I know why they must come out. They must be clear about who they are, and one way to do this is to force other people to see who they are. As I do. This is also why I "come out." And, with them, I brace myself for the flinch, the startled look, the anxious intake of breath, the wary eye. I come out to white people to say to them: "Beware. I am Other. Proceed with caution." And I come out to black people (how painful it is to have to do it . . .) to say: "I am family. You are safe with me. I am you." But, of course, if you have to *say* that you are black, if your skin doesn't say it for you, then how safe are you, really? how can you be family? And again, I brace myself for not so much the startled look (black people are used to white black people), but for the wary eye. For I am still Other. Coming out only proclaims how I am different, not that I am the same.

I think sometimes how similar are the problems my lesbian sisters and I pose when we come out. Does the person who hears me come out have to confront the notion of black being white? Does the person who hears my lesbian sister come out have to confront the notion of female being male (that is, if one who loves women is a male)? How unsettling it must be to have someone announce to you that black is white, that female is male. We are talking about "transgressed boundaries, potent fusions and dangerous possibilities."

My lesbian sisters have shown me that I am not the only one who has to struggle with coming out. Their courage gives me courage.

The last story I want to tell you is one that I am really not proud of. I like to think it would not have happened if we hadn't been so tired and jet-lagged. But we were. There were eighteen of us coming from all parts of the country for a two-day board meeting in Oakland. We were a group of feminist lawyers and activists, a group very self-consciously created to represent as many different kinds of women as possible. In general, we enjoyed getting together enough to travel thousands of miles for a grueling two-day session. It was a group of women who are smart, considerate, funny, and committed to women's issues. Our first meeting was scheduled for Friday night at eight o'clock. We decided to hold the meeting at a restaurant near the hotel.

Now you must remember that for some of us, meeting at eight in the evening was in reality meeting at eleven in the evening, after an exhausting day of travel. Nonetheless, we were all energized by being together, and off we went to search for a restaurant with a table large enough to accommodate us. What a relief it was to find one, only a few blocks away. There were about a dozen of us there, and we were seated around a large round table. Menus came out, along with pots of tea and cups for sipping tea. We started to relax, to look with relish at the menu, to talk about what we would order and how we would share the food. And it was then that Dai broke into the overtired, energetic talking and said, with a flat voice, "I think we should all consider leaving this restaurant." Dai travels through the world in a wheelchair. And it appeared that this restaurant *was* wheelchair-accessible, but only if you didn't mind going through the back door, past bags of smelly garbage, and through a dirty corridor. Dai was visibly wounded by that process, and although she was by now seated at the table with us, she thought we should leave in protest.

There was a long silence. And I don't remember exactly what happened next. But what I do remember is that, at first, no one wanted to leave. There was the suggestion that perhaps we could go ahead and eat, and write a letter of complaint to the management later. Dai was bitter, and angry at us. "You wouldn't stay here if there were an entrance for blacks only." I remember being torn by her analogy. Was she right? But surely not: the only reason she couldn't come in the front door was because she couldn't maneuver her wheelchair up the stairs, a physical, not political, problem. Not a problem of status and degradation. But what I remember most clearly was being angry at her for having to deal with her anger when all I wanted to do was to enjoy my all-too-late dinner after an all-too-long day.

Eventually, of course, we left the restaurant. Two of the group stayed behind to explain to the manager why we left. Another was given the task of writing the owner about his noncompliance with relevant regulations on accessibility. We decided to check the restaurant for compliance before including it in our material for conference attendees that spring. But what struck me the most was that instant when I recalled a conversation with another black woman academic returning from a conference composed predominantly of white feminists, one of whom stated that she was tired of dealing with the anger of black women. We were outraged by their "fatigue." But that evening in Oakland, I saw that I could be, no, *was*, like those white women who were tired of dealing with my anger. For I did not want to deal with Dai's anger. And because I was not in the wheelchair, I was the one who was empowered. I was the one who could listen or not, pay attention to her anger or not, understand or refuse to understand, let my hunger for my own comfort get in the way of recognizing her pain. Dai showed me that in some ways, and to some people, anybody who is not in a wheelchair— be they black, Chinese, Indian, gay—is the insider. And she is the outsider, beating on the door, crying for inclusion. Wanting to be seen, wanting to be known.

I have learned many things from my sisters about being different and being the same. Sometimes, like that time, I did not want to learn the lesson. But it was an important lesson. I learned that sometimes I am the one who gets to wave "the magic wand . . . of inclusion and exclusion."[9] I am like Dai, who feels her difference and her exclusion so keenly. But I am also the nondisabled one. And thus, I am the insider. I am like my white sister too.

There are many more stories I could tell, for once I was able to see the commonalities I see them everywhere. And yet there are more questions, so many more unanswered questions.

I have been wondering why difference is so hard to accept. I have been wondering why difference makes us all so anxious that we create categories, and then expend enormous amounts of energy to make sure people fit in them, and stay in them. And I have been wondering why the system of dualism is so important: what is there about a continuum that is unsatisfying? frightening? Why must life—and we—be seen in either "black" or "white," with no shades in between? For it is this system of rigid dualism that fosters so much anxiety when people don't fit into the categories neatly, when people "transgress boundaries."

And why is it that we look so hard for sameness, when we are, each and every one of us, so different from each other?

And why is it that we find it so hard to find sameness, when we are, in so many ways, so much the same?

But this is the work of another paper. For now, it must suffice that I have come a little way along this path. I have been engaged in my own struggle with being different, and I have found, along the way, the sameness, the connectedness I needed. I have been able to see the commonalities. And have found a home.

Age of Womanhood

Now is the time
to examine old scars
to minister unhealed wounds
and reflect on faded pain
Time
to pause along this road
and groom for the stretch
that lies ahead
I am entering
my age of womanhood
Now
is the time
to make blues into stew
bake woes into bread
steep tears into
an ancient medicinal brew
the weight of womanhood
gathers about
my hips and breasts
centers me in time
I wear new clothes for it
I look back
on my footsteps
gather myself
into myself
step firmly down the road [10]

Notes

Originally published in 2 *Yale Journal of Law and Feminism* 305 (1990); reprinted by permission of The Yale Journal of Law and Feminism, Inc.

1. These journal entries are essentially unchanged from the original. As I pulled this essay together in 1989, I reworked several sentences and added a few others for purposes of clarity.

2. The poem fragment is from Lucille Clifton's poem "some dreams in the air." It is so powerful and wonderful that it is worth more than a credit cite:

some dreams hang in the air
like smoke. some dreams
get all in your clothes and
be wearing them more than you do and
you be half the time trying to
hold them and half the time
trying to wave them away.
their smell be all over you and
they get to your eyes and
you cry. the fire be gone
and the wood but some dreams
hang in the air like smoke
touching everything.

Lucille Clifton, *Good Woman: Poems and a Memoir 1969–1980*, at 155 (1987).

3. William H. Grier & Price M. Cobbs, *Black Rage* (1979).

4. Pauli Murray, *Proud Shoes: The Story of an American Family* (1956).

5. Joel Williamson, *New People: Miscegenation and Mulattoes in the United States* (1980).

6. Zora N. Hurston, "How It Feels To Be Colored Me," in *I Love Myself When I Am Laughing* 153, 153 (1979).

7. *The Third Woman: Minority Women Writers of the United States* 107 (Dexter Fisher ed., 1980).

8. *Id.* at 522.

9. Patricia Williams, "Alchemical Notes: Reconstructing Ideals from Deconstructed Rights," 22 *Harv. C.R.-C.L. L. Rev.* 413, 431 (1987).

10. Sandra Jackson-Opoku, "Age of Womanhood," 14 *Essence* 146 (Feb. 1984).

LESS THAN PORNOGRAPHY

The Power of Popular Fiction

Carol Sanger

▼

In this essay I examine two best-selling novels of the 1980s—Presumed Innocent[1] and The Good Mother.[2] Both books are about law: Presumed Innocent is the tale of murder in the big city; The Good Mother is the story of a custody fight over a little girl. Both contain the crucial ingredient of a legal novel: an important trial at center stage. The murder trial in Presumed Innocent answers the plot's spiraling question of whodunit, or at least who didn't. In The Good Mother the custody trial isolates and resolves legal issues of parenting pulled from an intense personal thicket.

In addition to genre, the books share themes essential to the story line of each but not apparent from reviews, press releases, or jacket blurbs. Both books are about women who enjoy nonmarital sex and are punished for it: one becomes a murder victim; the other loses custody of her child. Both women are characterized as bad mothers, a status connected to sexual activity and, especially in The Good Mother, responsible for their losses.

In this essay I argue that through the powerful coincidence of popularity, genre, and theme, Presumed Innocent and The Good Mother reinforce notions about the relation between good sex and bad mothering, and advance serious, nonfiction messages for women about law and sex. Both books use sex—the steamy, best-selling kind—to rivet and then divert attention from less sexual, though still sex-based, issues of justice raised in the novels. I focus here on the portrayals of women as mothers, wives, and lovers and assess the accuracy of the fictional depictions as measured against real law. While I later suggest that the images of women in Presumed Innocent may fortify negative, wrong-headed attitudes, similar in kind though not intensity to reactions following exposure to pornography, this essay does not end with a proposed model ordinance banning subliminally sexist best-sellers. Nonetheless, we should be alert to how fictional representations that are less than pornography work on those who read them.

The Setting

While scholars looking at lawyers in fiction is nothing new, the pursuit has become more fashionable in recent years. The law and literature movement, "a conscious scholarly concern with the interrelations of law and literature," claims two central interests—the investigation of "the law-related content of literary work" and "the literary aspects of the law."[3] Most work therefore focuses on either traditional criticisms of literary works that deal with lawyers, courts, and legal doctrine, or on the interpretation of legal language using the techniques of literary criticism.[4] In purpose and method, then, law and literature is serious business; "the effete and the anecdotal [sic] are not within the discipline."[5]

The discipline is also marked by the quality of the texts and the readers.[6] As explained in one of the earliest symposia, "Great writers often speak as prophets of statutory and common law changes. To the extent that writers are in the vanguard of community conscience, lawyers, as legislators and policy-makers, should be attentive to their work."[7] However, not all novels are prophetic or measure the "unconscious strivings" of the society, as canonical works—Billy Budd, Bleak House, The Merchant of Venice—may;[8] popular novels, like Presumed Innocent and The Good Mother may reflect what ordinary readers feel most comfortable with, their existing values.[9] Readers of romance novels, for example, prefer books characterized by true love and happy endings because through such plots the readers can "affirm their adherence to traditional values."[10] To the extent that traditional values may differ from higher strivings, popular works, particularly when laced with even the appearance of legal authority, may reinforce familiar values with subtlety and ease.

Indeed, such popular works may have particular force because of their broad and uncomplicated presentations. In his compelling review of Primo Levi's The Drowned and the Saved, Clive James illustrates that it is not necessarily the artistic work of highest quality that influences public opinion the most. James observes that, of the several exceptionally affecting literary and cinematic works on Nazi death camps, it was the crude television miniseries "Holocaust" that had "direct, verifiable historic effect":

> Just before the miniseries was screened in West Germany, a statute of limitations on Nazi crimes was about to come into effect. After the miniseries was screened, the statute was rescinded. Public opinion had been decisive. . . .

[I]t couldn't be denied that a clumsy story had broken through barriers of unawareness that more sophisticated assaults had not penetrated.[11]

In James's example, insistence on memory, the goal of the more serious Holocaust literature, was achieved through the use of a popular medium, a simplified plot, and caricatured portrayals.[12] The miniseries influenced public opinion not because of the inevitable power of its subject, but because of the entertaining quality of the presentation.[13] Best-selling fiction—by definition broadly entertaining, heavy on "trance potential" [14]—also influences, though the influence may be as much to reinforce as to penetrate barriers of unawareness. The effect of racist images in early movies, for example, was to solidify prejudices already held by viewers.[15]

Because popular books, like television miniseries, are sometimes clumsy, investigation of their significance has been taken up not by law and literature, but by popular culture.[16] There is, quite reasonably, little academic interest in interpreting the language of Presumed Innocent; it's the guts of the book, not Turow's syntax, that keeps it on the bookstore shelves. Presumed Innocent and The Good Mother may be just the ticket, however, for analyzing the relationship of lawyers and law to "public attitudes and visions constructed through institutions of mass culture." [17] David Papke has suggested, for example, that a comparison of the lawyer-heroes in Presumed Innocent and Auchincloss's Diary of a Yuppie ("characters less inclined to seek justice in the courtroom than therapy on the couch" [18]) with earlier, more classically heroic fictional lawyers may indicate "a decline in the dominant culture's sense of lawyers as special social actors." [19] Because fiction, including legal novels, has social influence, people read, as well as bargain, in the shadow of the law. The shadows cast by legal fiction may be especially strong because of the "strikingly legalistic" character of American culture, where "legal terms, images and scenarios infuse . . . conversations and imaginations." [20] Thus, as litigants are sometimes influenced by knowledge of legal rules to order their relationships outside the legal process, readers too may be affected by the version of the law presented in fiction. Looking at the treatment of women in popular legal fiction tells not so much how society views lawyers—the interesting though somewhat narcissistic inquiry more traditionally undertaken by law people when dissecting literature—as it suggests perceptions about the power or influence of law for civilians. The treatment of women— particularly mothers—in Presumed Innocent and The Good Mother suggests that some greater feminist attention to civil defense is in order.

The Texts

The plot of *Presumed Innocent* is classic detective stuff: beautiful corpse, innocent defendant, a surfeit of suspects, and hairpin evidentiary turns leading to the hero's eleventh-hour vindication. The book's first half sets up the characters, motives, and conundrums. Carolyn Polhemus, a deputy prosecuting attorney ("A smart, sexy gal. A helluva lawyer"),[21] is found naked and dead—bound, raped, bashed on the head. The details of her murder are packed with clues, all of which are interpreted logically and incorrectly by the investigators and, I assume, by most readers. Early money is on the theory that some rapist Carolyn had prosecuted decided to get even. "I figure," says Detective Lipranzer, "that the way the ropes are tied, that he put himself between her legs and was trying to let his weight strangle her. It's all skip-knotted. I mean . . . that he was sort of trying to fuck her to death."[22]

But other evidence troubles a rape theory. No signs of forced entry into Carolyn's apartment. No struggle before she was bound. Most significantly, the sperm inside Carolyn are "blanks," detective-talk for nonviable. While first taken to mean that the murderer was sterile, the police pathologist soon identifies another substance in the vagina of Carolyn Polhemus: "Contraceptive jelly . . . Used with a diaphragm."[23] Here the plot thickens—the autopsy reveals no diaphragm in the victim. This revelation leads the police to a new theory: "This man who kills her is her lover. He comes over. Has drinks. This lady has intercourse with man, Okay? Real nice. But he's an angry guy. Picks up something, kills her, tries to make it look like rape. Ties her up. Pulls out diaphragm. That's what I think."[24] The theory leads within a few pages to the arrest of the narrator, deputy prosecuting attorney Rusty Sabich, who was not only Carolyn's colleague but her lover until she threw him over for their boss.

The novel's second half, Rusty's trial, particularly praised for its "utter authenticity" and "verisimilitude,"[25] jolts the reader into the realities of a criminal prosecution by opening with authentic pleadings of the murder charge. *Voir dire*, bench conferences, direct and cross examinations, evidentiary rulings, admonishments to counsel, and instructions to the jury follow. Circumstantial evidence linking Rusty to Carolyn mounts up, but the case against Rusty falls apart following the testimony of the county pathologist. The pathologist's own report shows that Carolyn, who lost favor as a rape victim because of the missing diaphragm, had a tubal ligation years earlier. As defense counsel puts it to the pathologist, "Sir, is it not absurd to believe that Carolyn Polhemus used a spermicide on the night of April first?"[26] Yes, but then how to explain the spermicide at all? Ah, the pathologist, either from negligence or ill motive, mixed up specimens taken during different autopsies. The judge then dismisses the case for lack of evidence, and the novel is almost over.

While the book offers much else to discuss (the politics of big-time prosecutions and the ethical conduct of bench and bar are but two issues), I focus here on the depictions of the women characters. Apart from office staff and witnesses,[27] there are two: Carolyn, Rusty's lover, and Barbara, Rusty's wife. Carolyn, as best I can tell, looked and dressed very much like a Barbie doll: "Torrents of blond hair, and almost no behind, and this very full bosom. And long red fingernails, too . . . ," a description that most clearly resembles Malibu Barbie.[28] Rusty, the narrator, is overcome by even the memory of Carolyn's jangling jewelry and her light perfume, her silk blouses, her red lipstick and painted nails, that large heaving bosom and her long legs, that splash of bright hair. . . ."[29]

Carolyn not only looked sexy—"[e]ven in death, she retain[ed] her erotic bearing"[30]—but she also had slept with half of northern Illinois. The list includes deputy prosecutor Sabich, chief prosecutor Horgan, and the judge presiding over Rusty's trial. We are told that "every copper [who saw her] would roll his eyes and make like he was jerking off,"[31] and that a headline reading, "Lady P.A., Prosecutor of Perverts, Fucks Defendant and Lives Out Forbidden Fantasy" would not be unreasonable.[32] Carolyn's teenage son asks Rusty, "Was she like your girlfriend, too?" In what appears an attempt at sensitivity, Rusty answers, "I'm afraid at one point she was my girlfriend, too. Late last year . . . Just a little while."[33] Rusty then describes the kid "shak[ing] his head with real disgust. He's waiting to meet somebody she didn't gull, and there is nobody here that can make that claim."[34]

"The kid" raises the issue of Carolyn as mother. We grasp from the outset she's not a very good mother because no one even knows she has a child: at the funeral "[t]he only unfamiliar figure is a boy in his late teens who is seated beside the mayor, directly at the foot of the bier."[35] Carolyn "took off" after her son's birth and when he later tried to reestablish contact with her, she didn't want much to do with him because, in his words, "there were a lot of times . . . I'd call . . . and I could tell somebody else was there" and "she was real busy. She had her career and all."[36] The son may not make the obvious and dismal connection between his mother's sex life and her professional success, but readers are not spared: Carolyn was a woman who "fucked her way to the top."[37] Indeed, the one hint that a motherly heart might lurk beneath that heaving bosom is quickly axed. One of Carolyn's claim-to-fame cases involved taking the testimony of a six-year-old boy whose mother had tortured him by placing his head in a vise. Rusty is overwhelmed by Carolyn's gentle rapport with the boy:

Whatever wild surging, libidinal rivers Carolyn undammed in me by her manner and appearance, there was something about the tender attention she showed this needy child that drew me over the brink, that gave my emotions a melting, yearning quality that I took to be far more significant than all my priapic heat." [38]

Rusty rhetorically asks the psychiatrist on the case if Carolyn's manner is not extraordinary. "But Mattingly took my comments instead as a clinical inquiry. . . . 'I've thought about that,' he said. . . . 'And I believe . . . that in some small way she must remind him of his mother.' " [39]

The foil to Carolyn is Rusty's wife. Barbara is, first and above all, a wonderful mother. Rusty describes the relationship between Barbara and their eight-year-old son: "they enjoy a special sympathy, communion, a dependence that goes deeper even than the unsounded depths of mother and child." [40] She is also a good homemaker, "a willing captive within the walls of her own home, flawlessly keeping our house, tending our child, and toiling endlessly with her formulae and computer algorithms." [41] Barbara is also no slouch physically ("her bustline still peaked; the waist notwithstanding pregnancy, still girlish"), [42] or sexually ("an imaginative, athletic lover; . . . [Rusty] cannot complain about hangups or fetishes or what Barbara will not do"). [43] And she stands by her man. Upon Rusty's confession of his affair with Carolyn, Barbara's angriest response is to call Carolyn a bimbo. And although Barbara is furious when Rusty is assigned to investigate the murder of his former lover—a fury revealed by her calling him an asshole—Rusty knows that "[s]ooner or later, . . . I will see a woman of good humor, of blazing intelligence, full of quirky insight and sly wit, who is keenly interested in me." [44]

Barbara's only flaw, it turns out, is that she killed Carolyn. Barbara hit her on the head with an iron gardening implement, tied her up, and stuffed her with defrosted sperm collected from Barbara's own diaphragm, which had been stored in the basement freezer. (I'm not sure where Barbara learned to tie the fancy slipknots. We are told that she read voraciously on arcane subjects, but my hunch is that she must have helped their son make a knot board in Cub Scouts.) We learn all this months after the trial as Rusty discovers blood and blonde hair on the crowbar he is using to remove backyard fence posts. Barbara sees Rusty scrubbing the crowbar clean and tells him she's taken a job at Wayne State. Rusty tells Barbara that he has always loved her, that he'll never tell, and that he understands that Barbara did it "[f]or the good of us." Despite the fact that Barbara is a murderer, Rusty warmly endorses her retaining custody of their son. "That's one thing I don't worry about." [45] Barbara is "in better shape with him. It pulls her back. Barbara needs someone around who really cares about her. And Nat does. I always knew I couldn't split them up—it would be the worst thing I could do to either of them." [46]

To sum up, of all the possible suspects in this complex political mystery, the killer turns out to be the victim's lover's wife, motivated by revenge and rejection. Carolyn is murdered, Barbara goes on tenure track, and Turow calls it a day. There is no sense of injustice at the end; rather, a troubled marriage is amicably ended. If anything, the ending suggests a restoration of justice, where justice represents the male writer's implicit celebration of traditional cultural norms. [47] That Carolyn—a promiscuous, home-wrecking, successful woman lawyer—becomes an unsolved murder statistic does not rankle. If Rusty isn't mad at Barbara, why should we be? He and Carolyn did Barbara wrong. [48] To the extent that murder may have been an overreaction on Barbara's part, she seems to fall within a tradition in which women, "vulnerable to impulsive criminal acts," have received more lenient and protective treatment from the criminal justice system. [49]

What troubles about the ending is not so much its improbability—ringers confessing at the last moment are common within the mystery genre—but rather the drearily sexist nature of the improbability. In her otherwise enthusiastic review of Presumed Innocent, Anne Rice concludes that Barbara as murderer is "too bizarre to be believed in any appropriate context." [50] While Rice is right in finding the ending unconvincing, I think she is wrong in finding that no appropriate foundation had been laid. In the character Carolyn, Turow revitalizes the harder-than-we-thought-to-trash stereotype of the sexually active, had-it-coming rape victim. [51] Rape has been the area of law that has most vigorously taken women's sexuality into account. [52] Pervasive criminal justice practices such as stringent requirements of corroboration and proof of resistance, special cautionary instructions to juries, admission of evidence regarding the victim's prior sexual history, and absolute spousal exemptions resulted in part from images of women as seductive and untrustworthy. [53] And despite legislative reforms officially removing some prejudicial practices, many police officers, prosecutors, judges, jurors, and newspaper editors continue to act on the basis of traditional assumptions. [54] Turow takes literary advantage of the cultural baggage encasing rape. Carolyn's body and background are used here as a signal not to jurors deciding a case, but to readers engaged in a plot. Her image as a woman who deserved it—even wanted it—is not diminished by our learning that it was only a mock rape and—guess what?—another woman did it.

Because the story is pitched as intrigue of political, not domestic, dimensions, readers are distracted from considering Barbara as a contender for killer. Our sense of her comes only through the narrator's controlling, self-centered perspective. [55] The portrayal of Barbara appears to be clever because

81   The Power of Popular Fiction

at the novel's end she turns out to be something other than the pained but loyal wife we thought we had come to know. But the "other" is simply a less passive version of wife, one who is willing and quite able—using ordinary household items—to take on her fictional opposite, the vamp. Turow has, in turn, made Carolyn-as-vamp particularly threatening through the combination of her singleness, heaving bosom, and law degree. But although women attorneys may be less trusted, respected, paid, and rewarded than men attorneys,[56] there is no evidence that they are particularly promiscuous. Nor are wives so spectacularly vengeful as Turow's Barbara; while extramarital affairs usually create marital crises, murder is rarely the resolution.[57] In fact, women seldom kill, and when they do murder husbands or lovers, it is usually in response to physical violence, not jealousy.[58] Nevertheless, *Presumed Innocent* works because it relies on exaggerated but hard-to-shake notions about good wives and vampy women. When these two duke it out, a singular brand of suburban justice is applied, and wives win.

Wives win in another way in *The Good Mother*, a second novel in which the law fails a sexually active, single mother. Anna Dunlap, the narrator, and her attorney husband, Brian, divorce. By agreement, their small daughter Molly lives with Anna, who has arranged for the first time in her life a spare but satisfying and self-sufficient existence. Anna gives piano lessons to untalented students, works part-time in a university rat lab, puts Molly in day care, and meets Leo. Anna is careful to integrate Leo slowly into her household. Leo and Anna sleep together at night, but "he got up faithfully each morning he slept over and was out of the house before [Molly] emerged from her room."[59]

Things couldn't be going better—except that once when drying off after a shower, Leo lets Molly touch his penis. Molly had asked if she could and, in the interests of modern parenting, he said yes, unfortunately getting an erection in the touching process. When Molly mentions this to her father while visiting him for the weekend, Brian refuses to return Molly to Anna and sues for custody. During the custody trial, rendered with Turow-like verisimilitude, Anna agrees never to permit Leo near Molly again. Despite her pledge, the judge awards custody to Brian and his new wife, Brenda. Anna then rearranges her life. She gives up her apartment, jobs, and Leo and moves from Boston to Washington, D.C., to see as much of Molly as she is allowed. When Brian and Brenda move back to Boston, Anna follows them back. That is the story.

Like Turow's book, *The Good Mother* has its share of stereotyped characters. Leo, rather like the Alan Bates character in the film, *An Unmarried Woman*, is too good to be true: a handsome, verbal, sexual, nonsmoking, successful, single artist.[60] Molly is too cute. Brian wasn't a good lover, which is all right in itself, but he need not have been made a minister's son in apparent explanation. A hard question arises, however, with regard to the characterization of Anna. Is the portrayal of the mother stereotypical or, as may be more accurate and troubling, only typical? What are the indicia of good motherhood these days?

At the trial, Anna's sexual conduct is taken as the primary measure of her ability to mother well, and she has made two mistakes. The first, the shower encounter between Leo and Molly, approaches a near-perfect dilemma. What should a parent, reader, or court make of the event? Anna and her lawyer do not attempt to defend what happened or to instruct the court on psychological theories on sexual openness within the home. Their strategy is to concede Anna's mistake in negligently supervising Molly but to isolate the episode as a single, reparable error in judgment. For although it was Leo who acted, Anna takes legal and personal responsibility for having let it happen. She was the bad mother.

Paralleling the arrest of Rusty in Presumed Innocent, The Good Mother's first half slams shut with Leo's surprising admission. But while the shower episode is used more dramatically in the plot, Anna's second and more subtle mistake is just as damaging. One night Molly, half asleep, climbs into bed with Anna and Leo who have just finished having intercourse but are not yet physically separated. Anna describes the harmony she feels in holding at once the two she loves: "I can remember feeling a sense of completion, as though I had finally found a way to have everything. We seemed fused, the three of us, all the boundaries between us dissolved; and I felt the medium for that."[61] At the trial this moment becomes fatal evidence that "for the entire duration of her mother's relationship with [Leo], the child was exposed to a high degree of sexual activity."[62] Thus, despite the recommendation by the court-appointed psychiatrist that Molly should live with her mother, Anna loses.

Critics and publicists have concentrated on the tension between Anna as sexual woman and as mother, some recognizing the evocative connection between the names and dilemmas of Anna Dunlap and Anna Karenina.[63] The paperback cover brags that the book is "A Searing Novel of Woman's Life as Two Fierce Hungers—Erotic and Maternal—Compete and Collide."[64] Yet in several respects, the suggested tension between Anna's sexual and maternal inclinations seems a false conflict. First, Anna herself is not in conflict. If she must choose between Leo and Molly, Anna's choice is clear; she wants Molly. For this choice the character has been much criticized as evidence of an antifeminist backlash: "Maternalism retains primacy, despite its truncated form, and the novel offers no hint that Anna will seek adult erotic love ever again."[65] This prediction seems a bit drastic, although it plays into general dissatisfaction with the character of Anna as feminist wimp. But Anna likes her life domestic, understands the benefits of her dead-end job, and defends herself well against criticism from none other than Leo, who wants her to want more for herself. If one acknowledges Anna's competence to make choices, and certainly there is general audience approval for her decision to leave Brian, to take up with Leo, and to stand up to her grandfather, one must also accept her decision to pine over, adjust to, and even rationalize the loss of Molly.

The second shaky aspect to the maternal/erotic conflict is that for Anna and Leo, no choice was necessary. They could have continued in heightened sexuality forever so long as they kept Molly out of it. As a psychologist observed,

> With the flood of adults now making known that they were sexually used by relatives as children, might there be even a hint of the need to lock doors to make certain that children would not walk in? Not to do so, of course, should not result in the loss of custody. But it is a blissful state that does not know the nearness of the law.[66]

Content with her life and ignorant of the law, Anna presumed an innocence about her child's potential exposure to adult sexuality not shared by court or, it seems, by community. Self-identified New Left feminists have trouble with the three in bed: "How can we judge Anna, especially when we must have assented to, envied even, the depth of her awakening passion? . . . Yet can we assent fully to including a child of four in this moment of intimacy between her mother and her mother's lover?"[67]

After the court awards custody to Brian, Anna's lawyer explains that it was just the luck of the draw: Judge Sullivan was strict about sexual issues. But it is not just the fictitious Judge Sullivan who is strict about sexual issues. Real mothers have lost custody of real children because of sexual behavior less questionable than Anna's. Maternal cohabitation—whether long-term, occasional, or monogamous—still results in adverse custody decisions.[68] And as in *The Good Mother*, the decisions are sometimes based on the trial judge's disapproval of the mother's conduct rather than his application of statutory standards.[69] One critic described the movie version of *The Good Mother* as a pretentious film packed with "quirky issues and atypical characters."[70] Viewers and readers may find Anna to be a good, good enough, bad, or dreadful mother, but she is not atypical.

In their thoughtful review of *The Good Mother* and other "post feminist texts," Rosenfelt and Stacey conclude that because the novel contains "competing voices," like the psychiatrist who suggests to Anna that the trial's outcome is not all her fault, the book should not be read "as a didactic morality play, a warning to mothers to behave or pay the price."[71] Still, Anna loses Molly because Anna did not understand that she and a Massachusetts family court judge had different notions about child-rearing. The book rightly suggests, if not warns, that single mothers remain at risk if unaware of the legal rules and their application.

As important as awareness of the law's content is a recognition of its reach. Anna did not understand that even nonsexual personal choices about the management of her life, child, and household could have legal consequences. For while the book emphasizes and is organized around Anna's sexual awakening, a second, slower dawning is also underway. In starting her new unmarried life Anna makes decisions consonant with her new sense of self: "I had a sense, a drunken irresponsible sense, of being about to begin my life, of moving beyond the claims of my own family, of Brian, into a passionate experiment, a claim on myself." [72] As an example, she accepts child support for Molly but nothing for herself. It turns out not to be enough: "More than once I'd thought of calling Brian, of telling him that I'd been foolish to think I could manage on what we'd agreed on, that I needed more money from him . . . But each time I'd talk myself out of it. At the day-care center I knew mothers who managed school and jobs and childcare entirely on their own . . . It seemed shameful to me that I couldn't do it." [73] Anna then takes two part-time jobs, necessitating Molly's full-time enrollment in day care. Anna is taking care of herself, at one level a good thing. But at the trial to decide who gets Molly, Brian's lawyer characterizes Anna's life differently: "So you work forty hours a week away from your daughter, and then still have all the work and maintenance involved in the home to do also . . . As well as your social life, isn't that the case?" [74] Yes, says Anna.

This quick exchange between Brian's lawyer and Anna regarding work hours underscores a third "false conflict" or, more accurately, false emphasis, in the novel. Centering the trial around Anna's sex life obscures the harder, less sexy issues now arising in custody determinations. Anna's case is more typical, and therefore instructive, not because of her relationship with Leo, but because of the nonsexual economic aspects of her life. Statistics abound supporting the authenticity and prevalence of women like Anna, the newly marginalized woman following divorce: her standard of living has been greatly reduced; she has a job, not a career; her child is necessarily in day care; and her remarried husband is in superior economic and domestic circumstances.[75] Single mothers are less wealthy, less rested, less married. Thus even if there had been no "sexual irregularities," Anna might have had a hard time keeping custody of Molly. During the trial Anna saw an alternative picture of parents emerge: "Brian and Brenda, who'd done things the right way, who kept their pajamas on, whose life was ordered, productive." [76] Such factors—the stability and status of job, residence, marriage— count in real life, especially in states where no preference is given to the parent who has been the child's primary caretaker prior to the divorce, so that contesting parents appear before the court on equal equitable footing.[77]

In *The Good Mother* sexual satisfaction, the thematic center of Anna's new adulthood, is used to show the tension and complexity between personal and legal responsibilities. Miller makes her case well regarding Anna's confusion of sexual headiness and actual power. But the emphasis on maternal sexual conduct may skew readers' sense of other significant factors, such as comparative economic status, professional predictions about a child's well-being, and judicial biases that are more frequently at work when courts are choosing parents.

The Point

The stories told in *Presumed Innocent* and *The Good Mother* suggest that community and law are slow to defend sexual women. Most readers are conditioned not to expect much for Carolyn, an airbrushed caricature of a professional woman. But even monogamous Anna, a mascara-free user of laundromats, is severely penalized as a result of a sexual relationship. In both novels sexual activity is used to temper sympathy for women who might otherwise get some reader support—a rape victim and a pretty good mother. The law appears particularly strict when the woman's sexuality is perceived as interfering with her responsibilities as a mother. Anna, who has "conciously chosen to make motherhood her priority, and an unambitious competence her mode"[78] in order to be a better, more available, less-stressed mother, still loses her child, largely in consequence of becoming a sexual person. Sexy Carolyn's bad mothering seems gratuitously tossed in, accepted social shorthand for the proposition that Carolyn is not good, in case readers had somehow missed the point.

Why motherhood is regarded as inconsistent with sexuality is a confounding issue, largely outside the scope of this essay, if not a life's work. The starting point seems to be that "[m]aternal sexuality is a topic that makes virtually everyone anxious."[79] Explanations—religious, economic, political, and psychoanalytical—are available, plausible, and likely interrelated.[80] Elizabeth Janeway offers an excellent crash course on the psychological underpinnings of the two images of woman-as-sexual-being that Western society seems able to master: the good and chaste mother (the generic Mary) versus the bad and sexual insatiate (Eve).[81]

The essential incompatibility of the two images within American culture has remained constant, though historically adaptable. I offer examples from three centuries. The goodness of wives and mothers in pre-colonial New England was reflected in their very title—Goodwife or Goody;[82] in the penalty for adultery—death;[83] in the status connected to maternal fertility;[84] and in a perceived link between the witches and bad mothering.[85]

Nineteenth-century Victorian America transformed the Christian model of Mary into the ideal and nonsexual mother, while Eve became the tempting and nonmaternal prostitute.[86] Sex was either procreative (at menstruation girls were instructed on the care of their maternal organs),[87] pathological (mid-nineteenth-century hysteria was perceived as an inherently sexual disease),[88] or wicked.[89]

If "[n]ineteenth century American society provided but one socially respectable, nondeviant role for women—that of loving wife and mother,"[90] the post–Nineteenth Amendment, post-Freudian twentieth century brought some changes. Single women could have careers[91] and wives were permitted to enjoy sex within their marriages.[92] But, as Janeway points out,

> Eve is still with us. Tricked out in polyester, her doll-sized simulacrum presents herself as the *Cosmopolitan* girl. Other diminished versions of Eve appear in popular novels, movies, and of course on television. Charlie's fallen angels. It would be pleasant to think that these superficial puppets could operate as a kind of killed vaccine which would immune [sic] patriarchal society against the mythic terror of Eve and the revenge it invites, but I am afraid that is overly optimistic. Since Eve is the projection of masculine emotions onto the outside world, her influence is not easily affected. . . .
>
> [H]er real status derives from her ability to attract males even though she must combine this with work for pay. . . .[93]

Tom Wolfe provides a final, literary example of the contemporary incompatibility of motherhood with a particular form of sexuality, the glamorous. In *The Bonfire of the Vanities*, a novel of late-twentieth-century urban manners and criminal justice, he describes the only two categories of women apparent within fashionable society: the skinny and young (dates and second wives) and the skinny and forty (original wives). In one scene, Wolfe observes,

> What was missing from [the dinner party] was that manner of women who is neither very young nor very old, who has laid in a lining of subcutaneous fat, who glows with plumpness and a rosy face that speaks, without a word, of home and hearth and hot food ready at six and stories read aloud at night and conversations while seated at the edge of the bed, just before the Sandman comes. In short, no one ever invited . . . Mother.[94]

The connection between bad mothers and good sex in *Presumed Innocent* and *The Good Mother* may reflect current fondness and rhetorical support for traditional family values expressed in media as varying as political campaigns, television programming, and romance novels.[95] Recent legal scholarship has also articulated the benefits of marriage and traditional family life.[96] Sex outside marriage, like women's work outside the home,[97] threatens the family.[98] Divorced, and therefore potentially sexually active, women may be perceived as an assault on the suburbs and its underlying system of values more serious than the threat presented by earlier, less populated, and less permanent categories of unmarried women, such as the spinsters and "career girls." Comparing unmarried women in the novels of Charlotte Brontë and Barbara Pym, Ezell points out the abundance of single women in both Victorian times and the 1950s. She observes, "In all of Pym's novels, the spinsters find themselves in conflict with married women in the community. In spite of the respectability of the modern woman's financial independence, the motives behind the tensions are basically the same . . . jealousy, contempt, and envy."[99] Divorced women in the 1980s may be replacing spinsters in this regard. Anna and Carolyn are feared because their single marital status carries a presumption not of innocence but of sexual availability. Their sexuality endangers existing marriages and causes them to be bad mothers to boot.

While both Presumed Innocent and The Good Mother connect sex to motherhood, the books differ greatly in their uses of the characters' sexuality. In Presumed Innocent the women are paper dolls. Perhaps as a preemptive strike against anticipated feminist criticism, Turow gives these cutouts academic credentials—and from traditionally masculine disciplines—but this is faux feminism at its worst. Carolyn's J.D. only makes her an educated slut and Barbara's algorithms don't stem her murderous jealousy.[100] Turow pretends women are important, just as Rusty's lawyer Stern does by including Barbara in courtroom conferences during the trial. But when Barbara expresses appreciation for this, Rusty corrects her naive sense of participation: "Stern again wants all the jurors to see at the outset that my wife is still on my side and that we, in this modern age, defer to the opinions of women."[101] The women in Presumed Innocent are not asked for opinions; instead they are given straightforward tasks—to have intercourse, to commit murder—and neither Carolyn nor Barbara is very believable.[102] Turow uses Carolyn to tease not just Rusty and the rest of the office, but the reader as well. From the outset, the book, essentially a macho detective story, invites the reader to indulge for a couple hundred pages in a little sexist fun made more tolerably respectable by the legal context. Reading Presumed Innocent isn't like sneaking into one's neighborhood Pussy Cat Theatre; it's on the checkstands, it's recommended by colleagues as a "good read."

The Good Mother, on the other hand, is not as much fun. Though there are many steamy scenes, nicely depicted from a woman's perspective, they occur between descriptions of a piano recital, a family reunion, a child's bath. This seems to me much of the point. Sex is part of Anna's life, even one of her favorite parts. But in addition to being sexual, Anna also works, shops, and kids around. In The Good Mother sex is something women learn, think, and make decisions about. But it is not all they do. For many, *The Good Mother* may be not so much a good read as an instructive one.

Presumed Innocent, on the other hand, is glossy, fast-pitched sexism, used here to mean "the presentation of images of women as less than and inferior to men, existing to titillate and service men."[103] I suspect Turow's book works on readers in much the same way as pornography, by increasing tolerance for what is observed. Mock jury experiments, for example, show that subjects who have watched films depicting aggressive sexual acts against women are less likely to perceive real harm when later evaluating rape evidence.[104] When the victim has been portrayed as enjoying the aggression, as we glean Carolyn usually did, there is even less likelihood of the subject finding that the victim was harmed.[105] Recognizing the methodological and predictive limitations of these studies,[106] there is still little dispute that violent pornography, like other forms of violence, inures viewers of both sexes to the cruelty and reality of subsequent depictions of sexual violence. One simply gets used to it. As explained in testimony on the Minneapolis antipornography ordinance by a woman who engaged in increasingly violent levels of sexual activity at the request of her husband, "I could see how I was being seasoned to the use of pornography. . . ."[107]

Presumed Innocent is less than pornography. Nevertheless, the book seasons us to an essentially sexual conception and use of women. Such representations, whether best-sellers or other forms of popular fiction, invigorate sexist images by making them simple, commonplace, acceptable. As with pornography, the material takes hold because it offers "cues," both sexist and legal, which provoke responses to "systems of belief" already within the reader. Sexist beliefs may be unconscious, but as Charles Lawrence carefully explains in the context of unconscious racism, it doesn't matter: such beliefs are "part of the individual's rational ordering of her perceptions of the world."[108] The cleverness of *Presumed Innocent* is that it shores up sexist "barriers of unawareness" by plaiting acceptable cues—law, politics, police— with those that would otherwise be too locker-room to buy into. Less than pornography, *Presumed Innocent* is also more than just a good read. It is influential fiction that uses law to obscure, legitimize, and sell its near absurd misogyny.

Less absurd is the book's rueful grounding in real law. The rape-murder in *Presumed Innocent* and the custody determination in *The Good Mother* are only two areas of the law where cultural perceptions about women's sexual behavior have influenced the content and application of legal rules. Self-defense for men who kill unfaithful partners,[109] construction of wills against designing women beneficiaries,[110] nonintervention in domestic abuse cases,[111] the criminalization of prostitution but not its customers,[112] judicial reluctance to find or enforce cohabitation agreements as contracts,[113] and the slow recognition of sexual harassment as legal injury[114] are other examples of the law's patriarchy. In each of these areas women who are even perceived as engaging in sex for nonmarital purposes (fun or profit) have been, and to a dismaying extent remain, unprotected by the legal system.[115] American law has accepted two categories of women: good and bad. Membership in one or the other category is governed not just by the volume or circumstance of sexual availability or motivation—a smile, fingernail polish, marital status. Once categorized, the determination shades, sometimes substitutes for, standards such as intent, involvement, and innocence traditionally used to measure the legal consequences of individual conduct. Realism is acclaimed in *The Good Mother* and *Presumed Innocent* not only because Miller and Turow write well, but because in their role as cartographers, each has taken accurate notes of the terrain on which women and law meet.

Defending the point and method of minimalist writing, Frederick Barthelme explains that "here's this breeze coming in with this smell that isn't lilac, but it's something. . . . So I guess that's mostly what's going on with this new fiction—people rolling down the windows, trying to get a good whiff of what's out there."[116] Neither *Presumed Innocent* nor *The Good Mother* is accused of minimalism; they do, however, provide a whiff of what's out there for women interacting with law. And what makes these fictional whiffs matter is that they catch and carry the scent of the real.

Notes

An earlier version of this essay was published in 87 *Michigan Law Review* 1338 (1989).

1. Scott Turow, *Presumed Innocent* (1987).

2. Sue Miller, *The Good Mother* (1986).

3. David Papke, "Neo-Marxists, Nietzscheans, and New Critics: The Voices of the Contemporary Law and Literature Discourse," 1985 *Am. B. Found. Res. J.* 883, 884–85 (reviewing James B. White, *When Words Lose Their Meaning* (1984)). Law schools, bar associations, and judicial organizations offer courses, publish symposia, and hold conferences to consider the relationships among law and justice, texts and fiction. The published symposia include "Law and Literature: A Symposium," 29 *Rutgers L. Rev.* 223 (1976); "Symposium: Law and Literature," 32 *Rutgers L. Rev.* 603 (1979); "Symposium: Law and Literature," 60 *Tex. L. Rev.* 373 (1982); 6 *A.L.S.A. Forum* 125 (1982) (special issue on law and literature); "Symposium: Terror in the Modern Age: The Vision of Literature, The Response of Law," 5 *Hum. Rts. Q.* 109 (1983); "The Law and Southern Literature Symposium," 4 *Miss. C. L. Rev.* 165 (1984); *see also* David Papke, "Law and Literature: A Comment and Bibliography of Secondary Works," 73 *Law Libr. J.* 421 (1980) (listing individual articles). Concern that the law and literature movement has become an enterprise may now extend beyond law schools as enterprise and litera-

ture become a movement. *See* Richard Weisberg, "The Law-Literature Enterprise," 1 *Yale J.L. & Humanities* 1 (1988); "Students Seek Literary Insights into Management," *N.Y. Times*, Apr. 10, 1989 (The Living Arts), at 16.

4. William Page & Richard Weisberg, "Foreword: The Law and Southern Literature," 4 *Miss. C. L. Rev.* 165, 165–66 (1984) (also suggesting a third area of concern: the study of values and human rights from literary perspectives). There is, of course, no finite list of what law and literature is about. Legal scholars use literature, literary criticism, and literary techniques—such as storytelling—to address a range of personal, pedagogical, institutional, and cultural concerns. *See* James B. White, "What Can a Lawyer Learn from Literature?" 102 *Harv. L. Rev.* 2014, 2023–25 (1989) (review essay) (reviewing "inexhaustible" range of literary texts and their uses by legal scholars).

5. J. Allen Smith & John P. Laughlin, "Afterword: Law, Literature and Ethics," 4 *Miss. C. L. Rev.* 327, 328 (1984).

6. Victor Nell, *Lost in a Book: The Psychology of Reading for Pleasure* 4–5 (1988). In his thorough, curiously scientific study (*see, e.g.*, id., Figure 9.2 "Translucent Goggles in Place," at 185) of those who read for pleasure, or "ludic readers," Victor Nell risks substituting "a populist fallacy for an elitist error" and maintains that the two classes of readers (highbrow and lowbrow) "do not exist . . . [W]ithin every elite reader lurks a vestigial and fully formed lumpenprole, so that both classes are contained in one." *See generally* Lawrence Levine, *Highbrow/Lowbrow: The Emergence of Cultural Hierarchy in America* (1988).

7. J. Allen Smith, "Law and the Humanities: A Preface," 29 *Rutgers L. Rev.* 223, 223 (1976).

8. *Id.* at 225.

9. Smith, *supra* note 5, at 225.

10. Janice Radway, *Reading the Romance: Women, Patriarchy, and Popular Literature* 67, 118 (1984).

11. Clive James, "Last Will and Testament," *The New Yorker*, May 23, 1988, at 86, 90–91 (reviewing Primo Levi, *The Drowned and the Saved* (1988)) (accommodating his concern that crude works may diminish their subject matter by arguing that "if the wider public is to be reached the message has to be popularized").

12. Saul Bellow, *More Die of Heartbreak* (1987) (making the point from the consumer's perspective). The character of Uncle Benn has several times shown his nephew a favored and poignant Charles Addams cartoon about love and unhappiness and apologizes for doing so. The nephew responds:

> "Taking your situation into account, I can sympathize. Other people's obsessions don't turn me on. I can weather this one for a while—but if it's satire or caricature you want, why not Daumier or Goya, one of the masters?"
> "You don't always have a choice," Uncle Benn replies. "And I haven't got your culture. In the Midwest, minds are slower. I can see that Addams isn't in a class with the greats, but he makes a contemporary statement. . ."

Id. at 10.

13. A recent example of the influence of popular television programming on

viewer behavior in the United States is the suggested relation between the glamorous television series "L.A. Law" and an unexpected increase in law school applications. "Applications Up: Who Are These People?" 88-2 *Law Services Report, Newsletter of the Law School Admission Council* 1, 13 Apr.–May 1988.

14. NELL, *supra* note 4, at 146–47 (explaining that readers choose books based on subjective judgments regarding their literary merit, difficulty, and most important, their "trance potential," or "the perceived capacity of the book to exercise dominion and superiority . . . Though the term trance potential is new, the construct is not; it parallels the quality so avidly sought by nineteenth century publishers, the creation of a pleasant atmosphere for the reader.").

15. Garth Jowett, Film: *The Democratic Art* 220–24 (1976) (describing the 1933 Payne Fund studies on the influence of film upon children); *see also* Kristen Drotner, "School-girls, Madcaps, and Air Aces: English Girls and Their Magazine Reading Between the Wars," 9 *Feminist Stud.* 33, 49 (1983) (exploring the impact of popular periodicals on girls who grew up to be "the quiescent mother of the 1950's").

16. Scholarly inquiries are not necessarily limited to one or another level of liter-ary work. Anne T. Margolis, "Book Reviews," 9 *Signs* 493, 495 (1984) (reviewing Nina Auerbach, *Woman and the Demon: The Life of a Victorian Myth* (1982)) (stating that Auer-bach "mov[es] back and forth between 'serious' literature and popular culture, . . . forc[ing] us to confront the submerged analogies between [the] central paradigms of womanhood as they appear not only in 'classics' by Dickens, Thackeray, Mill, Elliot, and Freud but also in best-sellers such as *Trilby*, *She*, and *Dracula*.").

17. Anthony Chase, "Toward a Legal Theory of Popular Culture," 1986 *Wis. L. Rev.* 527, 535 (1988); *see also* Richard Posner, "Law and Literature: A Relation Reargued," 72 *Va. L. Rev.* 1351, 1356 (1986) ("There are better places to learn about law than novels—except perhaps to learn about how laymen react to law and lawyers.").

18. David Papke, "The Advocate's Malaise: Contemporary American Lawyer Novels," 38 *J. Legal Educ.* 413, 421 (1988).

19. *Id.* at 413.

20. *Id. See* Robert Mnookin and Louis Kornhauser, "Bargaining in the Shadow of the Law: The Case of Divorce," 88 *Yale L.J.* 950 (1979).

21. Turow, *supra* note 1, at 8.

22. *Id.* at 22.

23. *Id.* at 93.

24. *Id.*

25. Review quotes inside paperback edition.

26. Turow, *supra* note 1, at 336.

27. There is Rusty's secretary, an eavesdropper who lies on the stand. Mac, a deputy administrator who "beams up from her wheelchair, everybody's favorite smart-ass, brassy and irreverent," also has a few lines. *Id.* at 53. Sydney Pollack, director of the film version, observed to Turow, "You have three women in the story, and the only one who is not tainted is a paraplegic." Jeff Shear, "A Lawyer Courts Best-Sellerdom," N.Y. *Times*, June 7, 1987, at 79. Finally, there is Mrs. Krapotnik, a tenant in Carolyn's

building who is asked to point out anyone in the courtroom she has seen entering the victim's building. When she points to the judge and prosecutor, laughter breaks out in the courtroom at her preposterous identifications. Of course we later learn that all these guys did in fact visit Carolyn.

28. Turow, *supra* note 1, at 29.

29. *Id.* at 33. The burlesque portrayal of a sex-crazed woman attorney with red fingernails and lipstick is particularly annoying because it appears in a novel praised by Wallace Stegner for "a cast of characters who are dismayingly credible." *Id.* at inside cover. I might well be dismayed if I could but find such women attorneys. They do not show up at bar association or faculty meetings I attend.

30. *Id.* at 28.

31. *Id.* at 30.

32. *Id.* at 28.

33. *Id.* at 70.

34. *Id.*

35. *Id.* at 16.

36. *Id.* at 67–68.

37. *Id.* at 288.

38. *Id.* at 60.

39. *Id.* at 60–61.

40. *Id.* at 209.

41. The notion of mothers as captives also appears in Molly Haskell's description of "the women's film": "The circumscribed world of the housewife corresponds to the state of woman in general, confronted by a range of options so limited she might as well inhabit a cell. The persistent irony is that she is dependent for her well-being and 'fulfillment' on institutions—marriage, motherhood—that by translating the words 'woman' into 'wife' and 'mother,' end her independent identity. She then feels bound to adhere to a morality which demands that she stifle her own 'illicit' creative or sexual urges in support of a social code that tolerates considerably more deviation on the part of her husband." Molly Haskell, "The Women's Film," in *Film Theory and Criticism* 505, 510 (Gerald Mast & Marshall Cohen eds., 2d ed. 1979).

42. Turow, *supra* note 1, at 184.

43. *Id.* at 183.

44. *Id.* at 121.

45. *Id.* at 415.

46. *Id.* While parents who commit murder shouldn't necessarily lose custody of their children, it is a factor to consider. *See* Maria Chambers, "Accused in Wife's Murder, He Keeps Kids," *Nat'l L.J.*, June 27, 1988, at 13–14.

47. I thank Robert A. Ferguson for suggesting this.

48. Luckily Barbara doesn't know how wrong; apparently Rusty never revealed that Carolyn would taunt him by asking, in concert with their more daring sexual acts, "[D]oes Barbara do this for you?" Turow, *supra* note 1, at 110. It seems that Rusty also never told Carolyn that Barbara did. *Id.* at 183.

49. Carolyn G. Heilbrun & Alfred B. Heilbrun, "The Treatment of Women Within the Criminal Justice System: An Inquiry Into the Social Impact of the Women's Rights Movement," 10 Psychol. Women Q. 240, 241 (1986) (suggesting, with many qualifications, that since the 1970s women have received sentences more similar to those received by men for the same crimes).

50. Anne Rice, "She Knew Too Many, Too Well" N.Y. Times, June 28, 1987, at 29 (reviewing Turow, supra note 1).

51. See, e.g., Gary LaFree et al., "Jurors' Responses to Victims' Behavior and Legal Issues in Sexual Assault Trials," 32 Soc. Probs. 389, 397 (1985) (jurors less likely to believe defendant guilty when victim had reportedly engaged in sex outside of marriage).

52. See, e.g., Wallace Loh, "The Impact of Common Law and Rape Reform Statutes on Prosecution: An Empirical Study," 55 Wash. L. Rev. 543, 582 (1980) (rape cases are the only ones in which the prosecutor interviews the victim before charging).

53. Ronald J. Berger et al., "The Dimensions of Rape Reform Legislation," 22 Law & Soc. Rev. 329, 330, 333, 335, 339 (1988).

54. Id. at 334.

55. See Judith Baughman, "Literary Perspectives on Murder," 6 A.L.S.A. Forum 210 (1982) (comparing Truman Capote, In Cold Blood (1966) and Judith Rossner, Looking for Mr. Goodbar (1975) and discussing ways in which an author's point of view may influence readers' judgments about murder and justice).

56. See, e.g., Stuart V. N. Hodgson & Burt Pryor, "Sex Discrimination in the Court-room: Attorney Gender and Credibility," 71 Women's L.J. 7 (1985) (women rated female attorneys significantly less intelligent, less friendly, less capable, less expert, and less experienced than male attorneys).

57. Sonya Rhodes, "Extramarital Affairs: Clinical Issues in Therapy," 65 Soc. Casework 541 (1984).

58. Comment, "Provoked Reason in Men and Women: Heat-of-Passion Manslaughter and Imperfect Self-Defense," 33 U.C.L.A. L. Rev. 1679, 1723 (1986).

59. Miller, supra note 2, at 122.

60. Interestingly, Leo exhibits the top three qualities that readers of romance novels desire most in their heroes—intelligence, tenderness, and a sense of humor. Radway, supra note 10, at 81–83.

61. Miller, supra note 2, at 124.

62. Id. at 269.

63. Linda Wolfe, "Men, Women, and Children First," N.Y. Times, Apr. 27, 1986, at 1 (reviewing Miller, supra note 2). Not much can be said about the name Rusty Sabich, except to note that, consistent with Turow's general misogyny, his hero's name could be read as "Say, bitch." Such an interpretation would, of course, rival Alvy Singer's interpretation in the movie Annie Hall of a quickly spoken "Did you eat?" as "Jew eat?"

64. Sue Miller, The Good Mother (Dell pb. ed., 1987).

65. Deborah Rosenfelt & Jackie Stacey, "Second Thoughts on the Second Wave," 13 Feminist Stud. 341, 353 (1987).

66. Letter from Verneice D. Thompson to Carol Sanger (Aug. 1, 1988).

67. Rosenfelt & Stacey, *supra* note 65, at 357. The film version of the book has received similar criticism: "[*The Good Mother*] is about a woman without the good sense to carry her sleeping child out of her bed." Clive James, "Lately, Seeing Isn't Believing," *N.Y. Times*, Nov. 20, 1988, at H-18.

68. *See, e.g.*, Jarrett v. Jarrett, 400 N.E. 2d 421 (Ill. 1979) (mother's open cohabitation is grounds for losing custody, despite no showing of harm to children); Robert L. Gottsfield, "Custody Litigation: Private Lives, Public Issues," *Fam. Advoc.* 36 (Spring 1984); Nora Lauerman, "Nonmarital Sexual Conduct and Child Custody," 46 U. Cin. L. Rev. 647 (1977); "Mom Takes in Lover, Loses Custody; Lawyer Vows Appeal to High Court," *Nat'l L.J.*, Jan. 7, 1980, at 3. The risks of losing custody are particularly great if the mother's lover is a woman. *See, e.g.*, Newsome v. Newsome, 256 S.E.2d 849 (1979) (though gay mother is found to be "a loving mother who cares for and is interested in the well-being of [her child]," custody is awarded to father and his parents); *see also* Nan Hunter & Nancy Polikoff, "Custody Rights of Lesbian Mothers: Legal Theory and Litigation Strategy," 25 *Buffalo L. Rev.* 691 (1976). Homosexual fathers have also lost custody as a result of living with their partners. *See, e.g.*, Comment, "Burdens on Gay Litigants and Bias in the Court System: Homosexual Panic, Child Custody, and Anonymous Parties," 19 *Harv. C.R.-C.L. L. Rev.* 497 (1984).

69. *See, e.g.*, In re Marriage of Wellman, 104 Cal. Rptr. 148 (1980) (overturning trial court's *sua sponte* order forbidding custodial mother "overnight visitations" from members of the opposite sex). *But see* "Court Limits Woman's Rights to Male Guests," N.Y. Times, Mar. 12, 1989, at A-27 (Rhode Island Supreme court upholds lower court order prohibiting divorced mother " 'taking good care' of her three children" from having an unrelated man stay overnight in her home).

70. James, *supra* note 67.

71. Rosenfelt & Stacey, *supra* note 65, at 355.

72. Miller, *supra* note 2, at 10.

73. *Id.* at 88.

74. *Id.* at 265.

75. *See generally* Lenore J. Weitzman, *The Divorce Revolution: The Unexpected Social and Economic Consequences for Women and Children in America* (1985).

76. Miller, *supra* note 2, at 246.

77. *See* Richard Neely, "The Primary Caretaker Parent Rule: Child Custody and the Dynamics of Greed," 3 *Yale L. & Pol'y Rev.* 168 (1984); Nancy Polikoff, "Why Are Mothers Losing: A Brief Analysis of Criteria Used in Child Custody Determinations," 7 *Women's Rts. L. Rep.* 235 (1982).

78. Rosenfelt & Stacey, *supra* note 65, at 354.

79. Susan (Contratto) Weisskopf, "Maternal Sexuality and Asexual Motherhood," 5 *Signs* 766, 767–68 (1980) (confronting and exploring the "pervasive ideology of asexual motherhood" in the context of erotic feelings between mother and child during and after pregnancy).

80. *See* Thomas C. Grey, "Eros, Civilization and the Burger Court," 43 *Law & Contemp. Probs.* 83, 91–94 (1980) (offering a streamlined review of the perceived necessity

of sexual repression from Freudian, Weberian, and Marxist perspectives); *see also* John D'Emilio, *Intimate Matters: A History of Sexuality in America* (1988). A special issue on motherhood and sexuality in vol. 1, no. 2, of *Hypatia* contains a series of articles concerning philosophical, psychoanalytic, and political critiques of this subject. 1 (2) *Hypatia* (1986).

81. Elizabeth Janeway, "Who is Sylvia? On the Loss of Sexual Paradisms," 5 *Signs* 573, 574–79 (1980).

82. Laurel Ulrich, *Good Wives: Image and Reality in the Lives of Women in Northern New England 1650–1750*, at xiii (1982).

83. *Id.* at 94.

84. *Id.* at 159.

85. *Id.* at 158 ("If a witch was by definition a bad neighbor, she was also a bad mother. Instead of nursing babies, she gave suck to familiar spirits or to the Devil himself.").

86. Nancy Cott, "Passionlessness: An Interpretation of Victorian Sexual Ideology, 1790–1850," in *A Heritage of Her Own* 162 (Nancy Cott & Elizabeth Pleck eds. 1979) (tracing cultural development of women's lack of sexual passion). A task of motherhood throughout the nineteenth century was the reduction of licentiousness through both example and the moral upbringing of children, particularly sons, considered more at risk by virtue of their having sexual desires. Nancy Cott, *The Bonds of Womanhood: "Woman's Sphere" in New England, 1780–1835*, at 149–53 (1977); Carroll Smith-Rosenberg, *Disorderly Conduct: Visions of Gender in Victorian America* 119 (1985).

87. Smith-Rosenberg, *supra* note 86, at 187–88.

88. *Id.* at 206–07 (stating that masturbation or sexual excess, even within marriage, were two medically diagnosed causes).

89. Bram Dijkstra, *Idols of Perversity: Fantasies of Feminine Evil in Fin-de-Siècle Culture* (1986) (organizing visual representations of these sexual alternatives in this study of turn-of-the-century art, a "veritable iconography of misogyny"). Mothers were inducted into "The Cult of the Household Nun," where images of wife as Madonna, angel, and garden flower prevailed. Because marital sex was to be tolerated only for its procreative rewards, sexual pleasure (possibly obtained through "solitary vice") was regarded as sexual excess resulting in physical listlessness and mental degeneration. Thus collapsing, floating women became a popular subject for late nineteenth-century painters who, supported by scientific theory, "had a veritable field day exploring the autoerotic ramifications of the representations of the sleeping woman." *Id.* at 78. More prevalent than domestic garden angels or floating Madonnas, however, was the portrayal of women as sexually powerful and vengeful. Dijkstra catalogues the truly scary images of the sexual woman: virgin whores, daughters of Dracula, Judiths and Salomes, Sirens, and worse. *See also id.* at 272–332 (for worse portrayals).

90. Smith-Rosenberg, *supra* note 86, at 213.

91. *See* Frank Stricker, "Cook Books and Law Books: The Hidden History of Career Women in Twentieth Century America," in *A Heritage of Her Own, supra* note 86, at 476. Twentieth-century hostility to married women working remained pervasive.

Nancy Cott, *The Grounding of Modern Feminism* 175–211 (1987).

92. During the 1920s a new marital ideal emerged, the "companionate marriage," in which marital harmony was measured by the sexual satisfaction of both partners. Cott, *supra* note 91, at 156–57. Not surprisingly, "[a] new cultural apparatus formed around the revelation that sexual expression was a source of vitality and personality (not a drain on energy as nineteenth-century moralists had warned) and that female sexual desire was there to be exploited and satisfied." *Id.* at 150.

93. Janeway, *supra* note 81, at 584, 586.

94. Tom Wolfe, *The Bonfire of the Vanities* 333–34 (1987). But Wolfe too forgets the invitation. The only such mother he portrays is an assistant prosecuting attorney's wife who has just given birth to their first child. The sight of this new mother, dumpy in a bathrobe, causes the husband to fall more deeply in love with a pretty juror wearing brown lipstick. The curse of motherhood has come full circle; what horrifies the husband about his wife's appearance is that she was "[o]nly twenty-nine, and already she looked just like her mother." *Id.* at 29.

95. Women who regularly read romance novels list "bed-hopping" or promiscuity most frequently as something that should never be included in a romance. Radway, *supra* note 10, at 67, 74.

96. *See, e.g.,* Bruce C. Hafen, "The Constitutional Status of Marriage, Kinship, and Sexual Privacy—Balancing the Individual and Social Interests," 81 Mich. L. Rev. 463, 463–84 (1983) (including among the benefits provided by "formal families" the well-being of children, the transmission of cultural values, and a mediating structure between individual and state).

97. Carolyn and Anna demonstrate that working outside the home, in either blue or white collar, interferes with family life. Carolyn, a lawyer, is too busy for her child. Anna, a lab technician, is too poor. She cannot afford to hire a substitute mother like the nanny Brian and Brenda have employed to care for Molly. But work alone, without more, does not do mothers in. Compare Carolyn and Barbara, Anna and Brenda. Carolyn has chosen a high-pressure legal career as an alternative to motherhood. Turow is clear that her success is quite related to sexual relationships at work. Barbara, Rusty's wife, doesn't work. Anna works low-key jobs with no on-site sex. Brenda, the wife of Anna's former husband, is a lawyer and became involved with Brian at their firm. And who gets custody? A chart helps:

	Marital Status	Career Status	Sex on Job	Custody
Anna	Single	Technician	Platonic	Loses Molly
Brenda	Married	Lawyer	Fools around with Brian	Keeps Molly
Carolyn	Single	Lawyer	Fools around with everyone	Abandons son
Barbara	Married	Full-time mother	n/a	Keeps son

It appears that having a job in combination with single marital status and sexual activity creates the fatal combination.

98. Kristin Luker makes similar observations in the context of abortion. In analyzing the participation of political activists in the abortion movement, Luker found that "because pro-life [antiabortion] women are traditional women, their primary resource for marriage is the promise of a stable home, with everything it implies: children, regular sex, a 'haven in a heartless world.'" The availability of casual, nonprocreative sex therefore "undercuts pro-life women in two ways: it limits their ability to get into a marriage in the first place, and it undermines the social value placed on their presence once within a marriage." Kristin Luker, *Abortion and the Politics of Motherhood* 209 (1984). *See generally id.* at 192–215.

If such views are held more widely, then Miller and Turow may be signaling readers not only by their characters' sexual activities but through their use of birth control as well. Anna, for example, has an abortion during her relationship with Leo. Miller describes the decision to abort, the abortion clinic, and the procedure with matter-of-fact detail in a scene I had always thought unnecessary. But while it may not serve the plot, Anna's abortion may contribute significantly to reader assessment of her as a character. If, as Luker describes, pro-life people generally oppose the use of artificial contraception because it demeans the procreative purpose of sex, and pro-choice people tend to view contraceptives as "something like taking care of one's teeth—a sensible routine, a good health habit," then Anna's failed use of birth control and subsequent abortion prompt different moral judgments about her depending on readers' broader views of the relationship between sex and motherhood. *Id.* at 178. Similarly, in *Presumed Innocent*, where the entire plot hinges on a birth control device, Carolyn is doubly locked into reproductive symbolism. We think she was using a diaphragm, only to learn later that she didn't need one; she'd already been sterilized.

99. Margaret Ezell, "'What Shall We Do With Our Old Maids': Barbara Pym and the 'Woman Question,'" 7 *Int'l J. Women's Stud.* 450, 461 (1984). In *Crampton Hodnet*, for example, residents of North Oxford discuss with whom Mr. Latimer, the new curate, might lodge:

> ". . . Don't you remember Willie Bell?" [the vicar's wife] added, referring to a former curate who had lodged with a widow and eventually married her.
> The vicar looked rather embarrassed. "I hardly think that this is the same sort of thing," he said hastily. ". . . There are no widows in Leamington Lodge . . ."
> "But there are two spinsters," whispered Anthea to Miss Morrow. "Surely that's just as dangerous?

Barbara Pym, *Crampton Hodnet* 18 (1985). *See generally* Sheila Jeffrey, *The Spinster and Her Enemies: Feminism and Sexuality 1880–1930* (1985).

100. Nothing in the psychological profiles of women math majors reveals a susceptibility to murder. Sherry Blackman, "The Masculinity-Femininity of Women Who Study College Mathematics," 15 *Sex Roles* 33 (1986).

101. Turow, *supra* note 1, at 230.

102. Several friends have pointed out that the men in *Presumed Innocent* don't come

off very well either. I'm not sure I agree. While most of the male characters are unscrupulous (the lawyers) or cruel (a bad cop), in the hero Rusty and his faithful sidekick Detective Kipranzer, Turow has created a male friendship marked by conduct resembling a personal code of honor. See Anthony Chase, "An Obscure Scandal of Consciousness," 1 Yale J.L. & Human. 105, at 123 (the Lipranzer–Rusty relationship "constitutes the romance at the heart of Turow's book. . . . a story of male bonding, the endless struggle of heterosexual American men against loneliness, anxiety, women, and death"). Certainly Rusty is less heroic than earlier fictional lawyers. Papke, supra note 18, at 413–26. Nevertheless, while not loyal in every thought, word, or deed, Rusty has some decent qualities; Carolyn had none. Moreover, whether or not one likes Rusty, he is believable to readers, unlike any of the women in the book.

103. Lynee Segal, Is the Future Female? 114 (1987).

104. See Steven D. Penrod & Edward Donnerstein, "The Attorney General's Commission on Pornography: The Gaps Between 'Findings' and Facts," 1987 Am. B. Found. Res. J. 713.

105. Neil Malamuth et al., "A Longitudinal Content Analysis of Sexual Violence in the Best-Selling Erotic Magazines," 16 J. Sex Res. 226 (1980).

106. See Penrod & Donnerstein, supra note 104; Nadine Strossen, "The Convergence of Feminist and Civil Liberties Principles in the Pornography Debate," 62 N.Y.U.L. Rev. 201, 227–33 (1987).

107. Paul Brest & Ann Vandenberg, "Politics, Feminism, and the Constitution: The Anti-Pornography Movement in Minneapolis," 39 Stan. L. Rev. 607, 608 (1987).

108. Charles Lawrence, "The Id, the Ego, and Equal Protection: Reckoning with Unconscious Racism," 39 Stan. L. Rev. 317, 323 (1987); see also Deborah Rhode, "Perspectives on Professional Women," 40 Stan. L. Rev. 1163, 1187–92 (1988) (discussing the nature and effect of unconscious gender biases on the hiring and performance of professional women).

109. Comment, supra note 58, at 1723.

110. See, e.g., In re Estate of Reddaway, 329 P.2d 886 (Or. 1958); In re Dilios' Will, 167 A.2d 571 (Me. 1960).

111. See generally Lenore Walker, The Battered Woman (1979); Isabel Marcus, "Conjugal Violence: The Law of Force and the Force of Law," 69 Cal. L. Rev. 1657 (1981); see also Linda Gordon, Heroes of Their Own Lives 250–88 (1988) (presenting the history of battered women in Boston in cultural and political context).

112. See generally Rosemarie Tong, Women, Sex, and the Law (1984).

113. See Clare Dalton, "An Essay in the Deconstruction of Contract Doctrine," 94 Yale L.J. 997, 1095–1113 (1985) (pointing out that in cohabitation cases women are regarded either as loving "angels" whose services are given with no thought of personal gain or as immoral "whores" who lure men into promises with sexual bait).

114. See generally Catharine MacKinnon, Sexual Harassment of Working Women: A Case of Sex Discrimination (1979); Robin West, "The Difference in Women's Hedonic Lives: A Phenomenological Critique of Feminist Legal Theory," 3 Wis. Women's L.J. 81, 106–08 (1987).

115. Women who decline to engage in sex for marital purposes (husband wants to) have also been unprotected by the legal system through such law as the spousal exception to rape. *See generally* Note, "The Marital Rape Exception," 52 N.Y.U. L. Rev. 306 (1977).

116. Frederick Barthelme, "On Being Wrong: Convicted Minimalist Spills Bean," N.Y. Times, Apr. 3, 1988 (book review), at 1, 27.

REPRESENTING POWER AND

SHIFTING PERSPECTIVE

II

The essays in this section question the normative constraints that blind us to the difference between a woman's and a man's perspective on certain behaviors, like sexual harassment, as well as to the differences between women of different classes, races, or sexual orientations. These constraints are the product of specific individual biases and of institutional perspectives that together normalize behaviors, standards, and sentiments that might otherwise be called into question, such as the apparently "neutral" aesthetic standards that protect canonical texts from criticism.

One way we might begin to question what constitutes our experience of difference is to examine the categories of analysis that organize that experience. Those categories, which begin as temporary strategies for making sense out of our lives, tend to solidify into fixed, stable, and unchallengeable categories of knowledge. Such a shift from strategy to institution, to paraphrase Cynthia Ozick, occurs so imperceptibly that we accept as natural and culturally inherent that which we have ourselves constructed. What these essays do is to recontextualize those familiar categories, with their attendant value systems, so that the differences that were obscured by familiarity are reconstituted as differences that matter.

Angela Harris's essay, "Race and Essentialism in Feminist Legal Theory," confronts directly the cost of unifying all women's experience, in an attempt to build a feminist coalition that would answer the patriarchy, under the simplifying category of "women's experience." As Martha Minow points out, such categories help organize experience, but only at the "cost of denying some of it." The question Harris asks is: "Whose experience is going to be denied? Whose experience counts for less?" And in answer Harris argues that "the experience of black women is too often ignored, both in feminist theory and in legal theory, and gender essentialism in feminist legal theory does nothing to address this problem."

Harris's essay seeks to destabilize and subvert the apparent unity and universality of this essentialist perspective "by introducing the voices of black women, especially as represented in literature." In so doing, Harris contends with the essentialism of feminists like Catharine MacKinnon, whose "dominance theory" argues that "black women are white women, only more so." Harris insists that Pecola Breedlove, whose longing for the signs of white female beauty is traced in Toni Morrison's The Bluest Eye, is not merely another (albeit black) version of the woman oppressed by the patriarchy. Pecola's suffering is not a more intense version of a white woman's suffering; her pain is also of a different kind, one that traditional (white) feminism has not been able to accommodate.

Harris also points to the work of Robin West, where a more explicit gender essentialism obscures the erasure of the black woman's identity. West's argument assumes that "everyone has a deep, unitary 'self' that is relatively stable and unchanging" and that this self "differs significantly between men and women but is the same for all women . . . despite differences of class, race, and sexual orientation." Clearly, West assumes a self that is pre-socially gendered, and a self for which gender trumps all other conditions. First a woman; then a black woman, or a lesbian. The problems that such a construction of selfhood creates for those women whose race, class, or sexual orientation is not that of the dominant discourse are obvious.

To counter these essentialist narratives, Harris argues, we should turn to the voices of black women who can articulate what it means to have "multiple and contradictory selves, selves that contain the oppressor as well as the oppressed," and who can thereby insist on identity as a relational concept, rather than an inherent and stable unity. The focus of feminist theorizing must be shifted from essences to relationships, from a unified sense of the woman to a strategic and contingent sense of many women. And, further, to be "fully subversive, the methodology of feminist legal theory should challenge not only law's content but its tendency to privilege the abstract and unitary voice," which has traditionally been represented as the voice of the white, middle-class citizen.

While Harris turns to literary narratives that represent black women's voices to destabilize essentialist readings of women's experiences, Brodkey and Fine employ autobiographical narratives as a way of interrogating institutional constraints on women's voicing of their experiences. Focusing specifically on narratives of sexual harassment, Brodkey and Fine locate these personal stories in their historical and institutional context, insisting that "the transformative potential of the narratives cannot be understood apart from the context in which they were written and read." The narratives were written by undergraduate and graduate women at the University of Pennsylvania, in response to a survey about sexual harassment. The survey was undertaken before nationally televised hearings before the Senate Judiciary Committee underscored the differences in the ways stories about sexuality are told—harassment is located "at the nexus of gender, power, and sexuality in the academy—as it [is] in all institutions," and thus provides a case study of the way in which the current generation of young women, inheritors of feminist activism and agendas, have taken advantage of their inheritance.

Sadly, Brodkey and Fine are forced to conclude that despite their powerful sense of entitlement as women in the academy, these undergraduate and graduate women can reconcile their expectations of a professional relationship with their experiences of sexual harassment only by "severing mind from body and then privileging the 'mind's' dispassionate, even clinical explanation of events." The students' understanding of their experiences withdraws them from a position of empowerment, rather than inserting them into a conversation about the effects of gender and power in the academy. Students offered "rational" justifications for the behavior of their harassers, reinscribing into their own stories about what had happened the very victimization that was practiced on them in the original event: "personal knowledge does not necessarily become the grounds for political action." What can become the grounds for political action, however, is a feminist pedagogy that would "transform . . . wasted individual energy into a collective desire to identify and examine the institutional practices that succor sexual harassment and begin to institute counterpractices that do not."

Elizabeth Cullingford's essay on Yeats's "Leda and the Swan" is one of those "counterpractices," an example of how feminist pedagogy can interrogate the traditional, aesthetic assumptions of canonical literature. Cullingford recontextualizes the poem within its historical context to question the accepted oppositions between high art and low culture, between art and politics, that continue to shape the representation of women as subject to male power.

Cullingford demonstrates how "Yeats deliberately chose to situate the poem in the public arena in order to arouse controversy and flout censorship." By restoring the poem to the context of its original publication, she finds "its transgressive intent is readily apparent." While transgressing certain political and aesthetic boundaries fast becoming institutionalized in post-Treaty Ireland, the poem nevertheless represents a woman "violently attacked and raped by an animal." Thus, in reading the poem, Cullingford argues, we must both take account of its original context and also acknowledge the contemporary radical feminist critique of pornography and obscenity. And while "pornography" may seem an extreme term to apply to "Leda and the Swan," such a shift in perspective generates a whole new set of questions about the relationship between canonicity, women's sexuality, and the poem's textual and generic history. Cullingford's essay demonstrates "what happens when a writer cares more about using sexuality as a strategy for tilting at establishment authority than with the implications of that strategy for women, who are both the subjects of and subject to the power of his imagination." It also demonstrates how difficult it is for feminists to situate themselves, politically and aesthetically, in relationship to the canonical traditions of Western art.

Rather than tracing the way in which aesthetic and political power misrepresent women's sexuality, the last essay in this section examines the ways in which different stories about women's sexuality are being told by the courts—ways that reflect and reinforce the disempowering of women. Susan Estrich's essay "Sex at Work" is a work of feminist criticism and jurisprudence revealing how the new legal cause of action for sexual harassment, whose creation was a triumph for women, is being interpreted to reflect and reinforce the inequalities between men and woman. As the recent Senate hearings have made painfully clear, testifying about rape or sexual harassment is not the same thing, for a woman, as testifying about nonsexual behavior. Legislative reform, argues Estrich, cannot solve the problems of a society where "male power [is] most jealously preserved, and female power most jealously limited in the area of sex . . . even forced sex." For example, rape prosecutions are governed by rules, unique in criminal law, that impose extraordinary obligations on the victim, rules imposed on no victim of any other crime.

Through a detailed examination of the first Supreme Court case on sexual harassment as discrimination because of sex under Title VII, Estrich establishes that the rules and prejudices operating in sexual harassment cases "have been borrowed wholesale from traditional rape law." At the same time, she points out that where recent feminist attempts to reform rape law might have provided a model for sexual harassment law benefiting female victims, sexual harassment cases have instead adopted the doctrines "embrac[ing] female stereotypes that women cannot meet." What Estrich demonstrates is that, once again, it is women's responsibility to insist upon policy changes and legislative reforms that would allow them to distinguish their own experiences of sexual harassment and rape from the narratives of their sexuality told by the law. In the words of Christine Littleton, women must learn to take their own stories about themselves seriously "even when (or perhaps especially when) it has little or no relationship to what has been or is being said *about* us." [1] Moreover, women must also learn how to render those differences in their stories—so that the woman, like Anita Hill, who suffers sexual harassment can begin to convey her own reality. And once that retelling of the stories has been accomplished, then those stories must be transformed into legal policies that reflect the many different versions of sexual exploitation that women endure in this culture.

Notes

1. Christine A. Littleton, "Feminist Jurisprudence: The Difference Method Makes," 41 *Stan. L. Rev.* 751, 754 (1989).

RACE AND ESSENTIALISM
IN FEMINIST LEGAL THEORY

Angela P. Harris

▼

bein alive & bein a woman & bein colored is a metaphysical dilemma—
Ntozake Shange, *For Colored Girls Who Have Considered Suicide/When the Rainbow is Enuf*[1]

Prologue: The Voices in Which We Speak
Funes the Memorious

In "Funes the Memorious,"[2] Borges tells of Ireneo Funes, who was a rather ordinary young man (notable only for his precise sense of time) until the age of nineteen, when he was thrown by a half-tamed horse and left paralyzed but possessed of perfect perception and a perfect memory. After his transformation, Funes

> knew by heart the forms of the southern clouds at dawn on the 30th of April, 1882, and could compare them in his memory with the mottled streaks on a book in Spanish binding he had only once seen and with the outlines of the foam raised by an oar in the Rio Negro the night before the Quebracho uprising. These memories were not simple ones; each visual image was linked to muscular sensations, thermal sensations, etc. He could reconstruct all his dreams, all his half-dreams. Two or three times he had reconstructed a whole day; he never hesitated, but each reconstruction had required a whole day.[3]

Funes tells the narrator that after his transformation he invented his own numbering system. "In place of seven thousand thirteen, he would say (for example) *Maximo Perez*; in place of seven thousand fourteen, *The Railroad*; other numbers were Luis Melian Lafinur, Olimar, sulphur, the reins, the whale, the gas, the caldron, Napoleon, Agustin de Vedia."[4] The narrator tries to explain to Funes "that this rhapsody of incoherent terms was precisely the opposite of a system of numbers. I told him that saying 365 meant saying three hundreds, six tens, five ones, an analysis which is not found in the 'numbers' *The Negro Timoteo* or *meat blanket*. Funes did not understand me or refused to understand me."[5]

In his conversation with Funes, the narrator realizes that Funes's life of infinite unique experiences leaves Funes no ability to categorize: "With no effort, he had learned English, French, Portuguese and Latin. I suspect, however, that he was not very capable of thought. To think is to forget differences, generalize, make abstractions. In the teeming world of Funes, there were only details, almost immediate in their presence."[6] For Funes, language is only a unique and private system of classification, elegant and solipsistic. The notion that language, made abstract, can serve to create and reinforce a community is incomprehensible to him.

"We the People"

Describing the voice that speaks the first sentence of the Declaration of Independence, James Boyd White remarks:

> It is not a person's voice, not even that of a committee, but the "unanimous" voice of "thirteen united States" and of their "people." It addresses a universal audience—nothing less than "mankind" itself, located neither in space nor in time—and the voice is universal too, for it purports to know about the "Course of human events" (all human events?) and to be able to discern what "becomes necessary" as a result of changing circumstances.[7]

The Preamble of the United States Constitution, White argues, can also be heard to speak in this unified and universal voice. This voice claims to speak

> for an entire and united nation and to do so directly and personally, not in the third person or by merely delegated authority. . . . The instrument thus appears to issue from a single imaginary author, consisting of all the people of the United States, including the reader, merged into a single identity in this act of self-constitution. "The People" are at once the author and the audience of this instrument.[8]

Despite its claims, however, this voice does not speak for everyone, but for a political faction trying to constitute itself as a unit of many disparate voices; its power lasts only as long as the contradictory voices remain silenced.

In a sense, the "I" of Funes, who knows only particulars, and the "we" of "We the People," who know only generalities, are the same. Both voices are monologues; both depend on the silence of others. The difference is only that the first voice knows of no others, while the second has silenced them.

Law and Literature

The first voice, the voice of Funes, is the voice toward which literature might sometimes seem driven. In an essay, Cynthia Ozick describes a comment she once overheard at a party: "For me, the Holocaust and a corncob are the same."[9] Ozick understands this comment to mean that for a writer, all experience is equal. This is not to say that literature has no moral content, that it exists purely in the domain of the imagination, a place where only aesthetics matter. However, a poet may find in her imagination images of the Holocaust or images of a corncob, just as Funes finds with Maximo Perez to refer to the number "7013."

Law, however, has not been much tempted by the sound of the first voice. Lawyers are all too aware that "legal interpretive acts signal and occasion the imposition of violence upon others."[10] In their concern to avoid what they sometimes perceive as the social irresponsibility of the first voice, legal thinkers have veered in the opposite direction, toward the safety of the second voice, which speaks from the position of "objectivity" rather than "subjectivity," "neutrality" rather than "bias." This voice, like the voice of "We the People," is ultimately authoritarian and coercive in its attempt to speak for everyone.[11]

In both law and literature there are theorists who struggle against their discipline's grain. Literary theorists such as Henry Louis Gates, Jr., Gayatri Spivak, and Abdul JanMohamed are attempting to "read specific verbal and visual texts against complex cultural codes of power, assertion, and domination which these texts both reflect and, indeed, reinforce."[12] Legal theorists such as Mari Matsuda, Pat Williams, and Derrick Bell juxtapose the voice that "allows theorists to discuss liberty, property, and rights in the aspirational mode of liberalism with no connection to what those concepts mean in real people's lives"[13] with the voices of people whose voices are rarely heard in law. In neither law nor literature, however, is the goal merely to replace one voice with its opposite. Rather, the aim is to understand both legal and literary discourse as the complex struggle and unending dialogue between these voices.

The metaphor of "voice" implies a speaker. I want to suggest, however, that both the voices I have described come from the same source, a source I term "multiple consciousness." It is a premise of this article that we are not born with a "self," but rather are composed of a welter of partial, sometimes contradictory, or even antithetical "selves." A unified identity, if such can ever exist, is a product of will, not a common destiny or natural birthright. Thus, consciousness is "never fixed, never attained once and for all";[14] it is not a final outcome or a biological given, but a process, a constant contradictory state of becoming, in which both social institutions and individual wills are deeply implicated. A multiple consciousness is home to both the first and the second voices, and all the voices in between.

As I use the phrase, "multiple consciousness" as reflected in legal or literary discourse is not a golden mean or static equilibrium between two extremes, but rather a process in which propositions are constantly put forth, challenged, and subverted. Cynthia Ozick argues that "a redemptive literature, a literature that interprets and decodes the world, beaten out for the sake of humanity, must wrestle with its own body, with its own flesh and blood, with its own life."[15] Similarly, Mari Matsuda, while arguing that in the legal realm "[h]olding on to a multiple consciousness will allow us to operate both within the abstractions of standard jurisprudential discourse, and within the details of our own special knowledge,"[16] acknowledges that "this constant shifting of consciousness produces sometimes madness, sometimes genius, sometimes both."[17]

1. Introduction

In this essay, I discuss some of the writings of feminist legal theorists Catharine MacKinnon and Robin West. I argue that their work, though powerful and brilliant in many ways, relies on what I call gender essentialism—the notion that a unitary, "essential" women's experience can be isolated and described independently of race, class, sexual orientation, and other realities of experience. The result of this tendency toward gender essentialism, I argue, is not only that some voices are silenced in order to privilege others (for this is an inevitable result of categorization, which is necessary both for human communication and political movement), but that the voices that are silenced turn out to be the same voices silenced by the mainstream legal voice of "We the People"— among them, the voices of black women.

This result troubles me for two reasons. First, the obvious one: As a black woman, in my opinion the experience of black women is too often ignored both in feminist theory and in legal theory, and gender essentialism in feminist legal theory does nothing to address this problem. A second and less obvious reason for my criticism of gender essentialism is that, in my view, contemporary legal theory needs less abstraction and not simply a different sort of abstraction. To be fully subversive, the methodology of feminist legal theory should challenge not only law's content but its tendency to privilege the abstract and unitary voice, and this gender essentialism also fails to do.

In accordance with my belief that legal theory, including feminist legal theory, is in need of less abstraction, in this article I destabilize and subvert the unity of MacKinnon's and West's "woman" by introducing the voices of black women, especially as represented in literature. Before I begin, however, I want to make three cautionary points to the reader. First, my argument should not be read to accuse either MacKinnon or West of "racism" in the sense of personal antipathy to black people. Both writers are steadfastly antiracist, which in a sense is my point. Just as law itself, in trying to speak for all persons, ends up silencing those without power, feminist legal theory is in danger of silencing those who have traditionally been kept from speaking, or who have been ignored when they spoke, including black women. The first step toward avoiding this danger is to give up the dream of gender essentialism.

Second, in using a racial critique to attack gender essentialism in feminist legal theory, my aim is not to establish a new essentialism in its place based on the essential experience of black women. Nor should my focus on black women be taken to mean that other women are not silenced either by the mainstream culture or by feminist legal theory. Accordingly, I invite the critique and subversion of my own generalizations.

Third and finally, I do not mean in this article to suggest that either feminism or legal theory should adopt the voice of Funes the Memorious, for whom every experience is unique and no categories or generalizations exist at all. Even a jurisprudence based on multiple consciousness must categorize; without categorization each individual is as isolated as Funes, and there can be no moral responsibility or social change. My suggestion is only that we make our categories explicitly tentative, relational, and unstable, and that to do so is all the more important in a discipline like law, where abstraction and "frozen" categories are the norm.

Feminist Legal Theory

As a Black lesbian feminist comfortable with the many different ingredients of my identity, and a woman committed to racial and sexual freedom from oppression, I find I am constantly being encouraged to pluck out some one aspect of myself and present this as the meaningful whole, eclipsing or denying the other parts of self.—Audre Lorde, *Sister Outsider* [18]

The need for multiple consciousness in the feminist movement—a social movement encompassing law, literature, and everything in between—has long been apparent. Since the beginning of the feminist movement in the United States, black women have been arguing that their experience calls into question the notion of a unitary "women's experience." [19] In the first wave of the feminist movement, black women's [20] realization that the white leaders of the suffrage movement intended to take neither issues of racial oppression nor black women themselves seriously was instrumental in destroying or preventing political alliances between black and white women within the movement. [21] In the second wave, black women are again speaking loudly and persistently, [22] and at many levels our voices have begun to be heard. Feminists have adopted the notion of multiple consciousness as appropriate to describe a world in which people are not oppressed only or primarily on the basis of gender, but on the bases of race, class, sexual orientation, and other categories in inextricable webs. [23] Moreover, multiple consciousness is implicit in the precepts of feminism itself. In Christine Littleton's words, "[f]eminist method starts with the very radical act of taking women seriously, believing that what we say about ourselves and our experience is important and valid, even when (or perhaps especially when) it has little or no relationship to what has been or is being said *about* us." [24] If a unitary "women's experience" or "feminism" must be distilled, feminists must ignore many women's voices. [25]

In feminist legal theory, however, the move away from univocal toward multivocal theories of women's experience and feminism has been slower than in other areas. In feminist legal theory, the pull of the second voice, the voice of abstract categorization, is still powerfully strong: "We the People" seems in danger of being replaced by "We the Women." And in feminist legal theory, as in the dominant culture, it is mostly white, straight, and socioeconomically privileged people who claim to speak for all of us. [26] Not surprisingly, the story they tell about "women," despite its claim to universality, seems to black women to be peculiar to women who are white, straight, and socioeconomically privileged—a phenomenon Adrienne Rich terms "white solipsism." [27]

Elizabeth Spelman notes:

[T]he real problem has been how feminist theory has confused the condition of one group of women with the condition of all. . . . A measure of the depth of white middle-class privilege is that the apparently straightforward and logical points and axioms at the heart of much of feminist theory guarantee the direction of its attention to the concerns of white middle-class women.[28]

The notion that there is a monolithic "women's experience" that can be described independent of other facets of experience like race, class, and sexual orientation is one I refer to in this essay as "gender essentialism."[29] A corollary to gender essentialism is "racial essentialism"—the belief that there is a monolithic "Black Experience," or "Chicano Experience." The source of gender and racial essentialism (and all other essentialisms, for the list of categories could be infinitely multiplied) is the second voice, the voice that claims to speak for all. The result of essentialism is to reduce the lives of people who experience multiple forms of oppression to addition problems: "racism + sexism = straight black women's experience," or "racism + sexism + homophobia = black lesbian experience."[30] Thus, in an essentialist world, black women's experience will always be forcibly fragmented before being subjected to analysis, as those who are "only interested in race" and those who are "only interested in gender" take their separate slices of our lives.

Moreover, feminist essentialism paves the way for unconscious racism. Spelman puts it this way:

> [T]hose who produce the "story of woman" want to make sure they appear in it. The best way to ensure that is to be the storyteller and hence to be in a position to decide which of all the many facts about women's lives ought to go into the story, which ought to be left out. Essentialism works well in behalf of these aims, aims that subvert the very process by which women might come to see where and how they wish to make common cause. For essentialism invites me to take what I understand to be true of me "as a woman" for some golden nugget of womanness all women have as women; and it makes the participation of other women inessential to the production of the story. How lovely: the many turn out to be one, and the one that they are is me.[31]

In a racist society like this one, the storytellers are usually white, and so "woman" turns out to be "white woman."

Why, in the face of challenges from "different" women and from feminist method itself, is feminist essentialism so persistent and pervasive? I think the reasons are several. Essentialism is intellectually convenient, and to a certain extent cognitively ingrained. Essentialism also carries with it important emotional and political payoffs. Finally, essentialism often appears (especially to white women) as the only alternative to chaos, mindless pluralism (the Funes trap), and the end of the feminist movement. In my view, however, as long as feminists, like theorists in the dominant culture, continue to search for gender and racial essences, black women will never be anything more than a crossroads between two kinds of domination, or at the bottom of a hierarchy of oppressions; we will always be required to choose pieces of ourselves to present as wholeness.[32]

Part 2 of this essay examines some of Catharine MacKinnon's writings, the ways in which the voices of black women in those works are suppressed in the name of commonality, and the damage this process does to MacKinnon's analysis of male domination.[33, 34] Part 3 examines the underpinnings of Robin West's more explicit essentialism and argues that here, as well, the experience of white women is used to define the experience of all women. Part 4 discusses some of the reasons why feminist essentialism, despite its violation of feminist method, is so attractive. Part 5 offers no answers, but suggests that the experience of black women can be important in moving beyond essentialism and toward a jurisprudence of multiple consciousness, and that storytelling is the right way to begin the process.

2. Modified Women and Unmodified Feminism: Black Women in Dominance Theory

Catharine MacKinnon describes her "dominance theory," like the Marxism with which she likes to compare it, as "total": "[T]hey are both theories of the totality, of the whole thing, theories of a fundamental and critical underpinning of the whole they envision."[35] Both her dominance theory (which she identifies as simply "feminism") and Marxism "focus on that which is most one's own, that which most makes one the being the theory addresses, as that which is most taken away by what the theory criticizes. In each theory you are made who you are by that which is taken away from you by the social relations the theory criticizes."[36] In Marxism, the "that" is work; in feminism, it is sexuality.

MacKinnon defines sexuality as "that social process which creates, organizes, expresses, and directs desire, creating the social beings we know as women and men, as their relations create society."[37] Moreover, "the organized expropriation of the sexuality of some for the use of others defines the sex, woman. Heterosexuality is its structure, gender and family its congealed forms, sex roles its qualities generalized to social persona, reproduction a consequence, and control its issue."[38] Dominance theory, the analysis of this organized expropriation, is a theory of power and its unequal distribution.

In MacKinnon's view, "[t]he idea of gender difference helps keep the reality of male dominance in place."[39] That is, the concept of gender difference is an ideology that masks the fact that genders are socially constructed, not natural, and coercively enforced, not freely consented to. Moreover, "the social relation between the sexes is organized so that men may dominate and women must submit and this relation is sexual—in fact, is sex."[40]

For MacKinnon, male dominance is not only "perhaps the most pervasive and tenacious system of power in history, but . . . it is metaphysically nearly perfect."[41] The masculine point of view is point-of-viewlessness; the force of male dominance "is exercised as consent, its authority as participation, its supremacy as the paradigm of order, its control as the definition of legitimacy."[42] In such a world, the very existence of feminism is something of a paradox. "Feminism claims the voice of women's silence, the sexuality of our eroticized desexualization, the fullness of 'lack,' the centrality of our marginality and exclusion, the public nature of privacy, the presence of our absence."[43] The wonder is how feminism can exist in the face of its theoretical impossibility.

In MacKinnon's view, men have their foot on women's necks,[44] regardless of race or class, or of mode of production: "Feminists do not argue that it means the same to women to be on the bottom in a feudal regime, a capitalist regime, and a socialist regime; the commonality argued is that, despite real changes, bottom is bottom."[45] As a political matter, moreover, MacKinnon is quick to insist that there is only one "true," "unmodified" feminism: that which analyzes women *as women*, not as subsets of some other group and not as gender-neutral beings.[46]

Despite its power, MacKinnon's dominance theory is flawed by its essentialism. MacKinnon assumes, as does the dominant culture, that there is an essential "woman" beneath the realities of differences between women[47] —that in describing the experiences of "women," issues of race, class, and sexual orientation can therefore be safely ignored, or relegated to footnotes.[48] In her search for what is essential womanhood, however, MacKinnon rediscovers white womanhood and introduces it as universal truth. In dominance theory, black women are white women, only more so.

Essentialism in feminist theory has two characteristics that ensure that black women's voices will be ignored. First, in the pursuit of the essential feminine, Woman leached of all color and irrelevant social circumstance, issues of race are bracketed as belonging to a separate and distinct discourse—a process that leaves black women's selves fragmented beyond recognition. Second, feminist essentialists find that in removing issues of "race" they have actually only managed to remove black women—meaning that white women now stand as the epitome of Woman. Both processes can be seen at work in dominance theory.

MacKinnon begins "Feminism, Marxism, Method, and the State: An Agenda for Theory" (hereinafter *Signs* I) promisingly enough: She says she will render "Black" in uppercase, because she does not regard

Black as merely a color of skin pigmentation, but specifically stigmatic and/
or glorious and/or ordinary under specific social conditions. It is as much
socially created as, and at least in the American context no less specifically
meaningful or definitive than, any linguistic, tribal, or religious ethnicity,
all of which are conventionally recognized by capitalization.[49]

By the time she has finished elaborating her theory, however, black women
have completely vanished; remaining are only white women with an additional burden.

Dominance Theory and the Bracketing of Race

MacKinnon repeatedly seems to recognize the inadequacy of theories that
deal with gender while ignoring race, but having recognized the problem,
she repeatedly shies away from its implications. Thus, she at times justifies
her essentialism by pointing to the essentialism of the dominant discourse:
"My suggestion is that what we have in common is not that our conditions
have no particularity in ways that matter. But we are all measured by a male
standard for women, a standard that is not ours."[50] At other times she deals
with the challenge of black women by placing it in footnotes. For example,
she places in a footnote without further comment the suggestive, if cryptic,
observation that a definition of feminism "of coalesced interest and resistance" has tended both to exclude and to make invisible "the diverse ways
that many women—notably Blacks and working-class women—have moved
against their determinants."[51] In another footnote generally addressed to
the problem of relating Marxism to issues of gender and race, she notes that
"[a]ny relationship between sex and race tends to be left entirely out of account,
since they are considered parallel 'strata,'"[52] but this thought simply trails
off into a string of citations to black feminist and social feminist writings.

Finally, MacKinnon postpones the demand of black women until the
arrival of a "general theory of social inequality";[53] recognizing that "gender
in this country appears partly to comprise the meaning of, as well as bi-
sect, race and class, even as race and class specificities make up, as well as
cross-cut, gender,"[54] she nevertheless is prepared to maintain her "color-
blind" approach to women's experience until that general theory arrives
(presumably that is someone else's work).

The results of MacKinnon's refusal to move beyond essentialism are
apparent in "Whose Culture? A Case Note on *Martinez v. Santa Clara Pueblo*."[55]
Julia Martinez sued her Native American tribe, the Santa Clara Pueblo, in
federal court, arguing that a tribal ordinance was invalid under a provision
of the Indian Civil Rights Act guaranteeing equal protection of the laws. The

ordinance provided that if women married outside the Pueblo, the children of that union were not full tribal members, but if men married outside the tribe, their children were full tribal members. Martinez married a Navajo man, and her children were not allowed to vote or inherit her rights in communal land. The United States Supreme Court held that this question was a matter of Indian sovereignty to be resolved by the tribe.[56]

MacKinnon starts her discussion with an admission: "I find Martinez a difficult case on a lot of levels, and I don't usually find cases difficult."[57] She concludes that the Pueblo ordinance was wrong, because it "did nothing to address or counteract the reasons why Native women were vulnerable to white male land imperialism through marriage—it gave in to them, by punishing the woman, the Native person."[58] Yet she reaches her conclusion, as she admits, without knowledge other than "word of mouth" of the history of the ordinance and its place in Santa Clara Pueblo culture.

MacKinnon has Julia Martinez ask her tribe, "Why do you make me choose between my equality as woman and my cultural identity?"[59] But she, no less than the tribe, eventually requires Martinez to choose; and the correct choice is, of course, that Martinez's female identity is more important than her tribal identity. MacKinnon states:

> [T]he aspiration of women to be no less than men—not to be punished where a man is glorified, not to be considered damaged or disloyal where a man is rewarded or left in peace, not to lead a derivative life, but to do everything and be anybody at all—is an aspiration indigenous to women across place and across time.[60]

What MacKinnon does not recognize, however, is that though the aspiration may be everywhere the same, its expression must depend on the social historical circumstances. In this case, should Julia Martinez be content with struggling for change from within,[61] or should the white government have stepped in "on her behalf"? What was the meaning of the ordinance within Pueblo discourse, as opposed to a transhistorical and transcultural feminist discourse? How did it come about and under what circumstances? What was the status of women within the tribe, both historically and at the time of the ordinance and at the present time, and was Martinez's claim heard and understood by the tribal authorities or simply ignored or derided? What were the Pueblo traditions about children of mixed parentage,[62] and how were those traditions changing? In a jurisprudence based on multiple consciousness, rather than the unitary consciousness of MacKinnon's dominance theory, these questions would have to be answered before the ordinance could be considered on its merits and even before the Court's decision to stay out could be evaluated.[63] MacKinnon does not answer these questions, but leaves the essay hanging with the idea that the male supremacist ideology of some Native American tribes may be adopted from white culture and therefore is invalid.[64] MacKinnon's tentativeness may be due to not wanting to appear a white cultural imperialist, speaking for a Native American tribe, but to take up Julia Martinez's claim at all is to take that risk. Without a theory that can shift focus from gender to race and other facets of identity and back again, MacKinnon's essay is ultimately crippled. Martinez is made to choose her gender over her race, and her experience is distorted in the process.[65]

Dominance Theory and White Women as All Women

The second consequence of feminist essentialism is that the racism that was acknowledged only in brackets quietly emerges in the feminist theory itself—both a cause and an effect of creating "Woman" from white woman. In MacKinnon's work, the result is that black women become white women, only more so.

In a passage in Signs I, MacKinnon borrows from Toni Cade Bambara, describing a black woman with too many children and no means with which to care for them as "grown ugly and dangerous from being nobody for so long." MacKinnon then explains:

> By using her phrase in altered context, I do not want to distort her mean-
> ing but to extend it. Throughout this essay, I have tried to see if women's
> condition is shared, even when contexts or magnitudes differ. (Thus, it is
> very different to be "nobody" as a Black woman than as a white lady, but
> neither is "somebody" by male standards.) This is the approach to race and
> ethnicity attempted throughout. I aspire to include all women in the term
> "women" in some way, without violating the particularity of any woman's
> experience. Whenever this fails, the statement is simply wrong and will
> have to be qualified or the aspiration (or the theory) abandoned.[66]

I call this the "nuance theory" approach to the problem of essentialism:[67] by being sensitive to the notion that different women have different experiences, generalizations can be offered about "all women" while qualifying statements, often in footnotes, supplement the general account with the subtle nuances of experience that "different" women add to the mix. Nuance theory thus assumes the commonality of all women—differences are a matter of "context" or "magnitude"; that is, nuance.

The problem with nuance theory is that by defining black women as "different," white women quietly become the norm, or pure, essential woman.[68] Just as MacKinnon would argue that being female is more than a "context" or a "magnitude" of human experience,[69] being black is more than a context or magnitude of all (white) women's experience. But not in dominance theory.

For instance, MacKinnon describes how a system of male supremacy has constructed "woman":

> Contemporary industrial society's version of her is docile, soft, passive, nurturant, vulnerable, weak, narcissistic, childlike, incompetent, masochistic, and domestic, made for child care, home care, and husband care. . . . Women who resist or fail, including those who never did fit—for example, black and lower-class women who cannot survive if they are soft and weak and incompetent, assertively self-respecting women, women with ambitions of male dimensions—are considered less female, lesser women.[70]

In a peculiar symmetry with this ideology, in which black women are something less than women, in MacKinnon's work black women become something more than women. In MacKinnon's writing, the word "black," applied to women, is an intensifier: If things are bad for everybody (meaning white women), then they're even worse for black women. Silent and suffering, we are trotted onto the page (mostly in footnotes) as the ultimate example of how bad things are.[71]

Thus, in speaking of the beauty standards set for (white) women, MacKinnon remarks, "Black women are further from being able concretely to achieve the standard that no woman can ever achieve, or it would lose its point."[72] The frustration of black women at being unable to look like an "All-American" woman is in this way just a more dramatic example of all (white) women's frustration and oppression. When a black woman speaks on this subject, however, it becomes clear that a black woman's pain at not being considered fully feminine is different qualitatively, not merely quantitatively, from the pain MacKinnon describes. It is qualitatively different because the ideology of beauty concerns not only gender but race. Consider Toni Morrison's analysis of the influence of standards of white beauty on black people in The Bluest Eye.[73] Claudia MacTeer, a young black girl, muses, "Adults, older girls, shops, magazines, newspapers, window signs—all the world had agreed that a blue-eyed, yellow-haired, pink-skinned doll was what every girl child treasured."[74] Similarly, in the black community, "high yellow" folks represent the closest black people can come to beauty, and darker people are always "lesser. Nicer, brighter, but still lesser."[75] Beauty is whiteness itself; and middle-class black girls

> go to land-grant colleges, normal schools, and learn how to do the white man's work with refinement: home economics to prepare his food; teacher education to instruct black children in obedience; music to soothe the weary master and entertain his blunted soul. Here they learn the rest of the lesson begun in those soft houses with porch swings and pots of bleeding

heart: how to behave. The careful development of thrift, patience, high morals, and good manners. In short, how to get rid of the funkiness. The dreadful funkiness of passion, the funkiness of nature, the funkiness of the wide range of human emotions. Wherever it erupts, this Funk, they wipe it away; where it crusts, they dissolve it; wherever it drips, flowers, or clings, they find it and fight it until it dies. They fight this battle all the way to the grave. The laugh that is a little too loud; the enunciation a little too round; the gesture a little too generous. They hold their behind in for fear of a sway too free; when they wear lipstick, they never cover the entire mouth for fear of lips too thick, and they worry, worry, worry about the edges of their hair.[76]

Thus, Pecola Breedlove, born black and ugly, spends her lonely and abused childhood praying for blue eyes.[77] Her story ends in despair and the fragmentation of her mind into two isolated speaking voices, not because she's even further away from ideal beauty than white women are, but because Beauty *itself* is white, and she is not and can never be, despite the pair of blue eyes she eventually believes she has. There is a difference between the hope that the next makeup kit or haircut or diet will bring you salvation and the knowledge that nothing can. The relation of black women to the ideal of white beauty is not a more intense form of white women's frustration: It is something other, a complex mingling of racial and gender hatred from without, self-hatred from within.

MacKinnon's essentialist, "color-blind" approach also distorts the analysis of rape that constitutes the heart of "Feminism, Marxism, Method, and the State: Toward Feminist Jurisprudence." By ignoring the voices of black female theoreticians of rape, she produces an ahistorical account that fails to capture the experience of black women. MacKinnon sees sexuality as "a social sphere of male power of which forced sex is paradigmatic."[78] As with beauty standards, black women are victimized by rape just like white women, only more so: "Racism in the United States, by singling out Black men for allegations of rape of white women, has helped obscure the fact that it is men who rape women, disproportionately women of color."[79] In this peculiar fashion MacKinnon simultaneously recognizes and shelves racism, finally reaffirming that the divide between men and women is more fundamental and that women of color are simply "women plus." MacKinnon goes on to develop a powerful analysis of rape as the subordination of women to men, with only one more mention of color: "[R]ape comes to mean a strange (read Black) man knowing a woman does not want sex and going ahead anyway."[80]

This analysis, though rhetorically powerful, is an analysis of what rape means to white women masquerading as a general account; it has nothing to do with the experience of black women.[81] For black women, rape is a far more complex experience, and an experience as deeply rooted in color as in gender.

For example, the paradigm experience of rape for black women has historically involved the white employer in the kitchen or bedroom as much as the strange black man in the bushes. During slavery, the sexual abuse of black women by white men was commonplace.[82] Even after emancipation, the majority of working black women were domestic servants for white families, a job that made them uniquely vulnerable to sexual harassment and rape.[83] Moreover, as a legal matter, the experience of rape did not even exist for black women. During slavery, the rape of a black woman by any man, white or black, was simply not a crime.[84] Even after the Civil War, rape laws were seldom used to protect black women against either white or black men, since black women were considered promiscuous by nature.[85] In contrast to the partial or at least formal protection white women had against sexual brutalization, black women frequently had no legal protection whatsoever. "Rape," in this sense, was something that only happened to white women; what happened to black women was simply life.

Finally, for black people, male and female, "rape" signified the terrorism of black men by white men, aided and abetted, passively (by silence) or actively (by "crying rape"), by white women. Black women have recognized this aspect of rape since the nineteenth century. For example, social activist Ida B. Wells analyzed rape as an example of the inseparability of race and gender oppression in *Southern Horrors: Lynch Law in All Its Phases*, published in 1892. Wells saw that both the law of rape and Southern miscegenation laws were part of a patriarchal system through which white men maintained their control over the bodies of all black people: "[W]hite men used their ownership of the body of the white female as a terrain on which to lynch the black male."[86] Moreover, Wells argued, though many white women encouraged interracial sexual relationships, white women, protected by the patriarchal idealization of white womanhood, were able to remain silent, unhappily or not, as black men were murdered by mobs.[87] Similarly, Anna Julia Cooper, another nineteenth-century theorist, "saw that the manipulative power of the South was embodied in the southern patriarch, but she describes its concern with 'blood,' inheritance, and heritage in entirely female terms and as a preoccupation that was transmitted from the South to the North and perpetuated by white women."[88]

Nor has this aspect of rape become purely a historical curiosity. Susan Estrich reports that between 1930 and 1967, 89 percent of the men executed for rape in the United States were black;[89] a 1968 study of rape sentencing in Maryland showed that in all 55 cases where the death penalty was imposed the victim had been white, and that between 1960 and 1967, 47 percent of all black men convicted of criminal assaults on black women were immediately released on probation.[90] The case of Joann Little is testimony to the continuing sensitivity of black women to this aspect of rape. As Angela Davis tells the story:

> Brought to trial on murder charges, the young Black woman was accused of killing a white guard in a North Carolina jail where she was the only woman inmate. When Joann Little took the stand, she told how the guard had raped her in her cell and how she had killed him in self-defense with the ice pick he had used to threaten her. Throughout the country, her cause was passionately supported by individuals and organizations in the Black community and within the young women's movement, and her acquittal was hailed as an important victory made possible by this mass campaign. In the immediate aftermath of her acquittal, Ms. Little issued several moving appeals on behalf of a Black man named Delbert Tibbs, who awaited execution in Florida because he had been falsely convicted of raping a white woman.
>
> Many Black women answered Joann Little's appeal to support the cause of Delbert Tibbs. But few white women—and certainly few organized groups within the antirape movement—followed her suggestion that they agitate for the freedom of this Black man who had been blatantly victimized by Southern racism.[91]

The rift between white and black women over the issue of rape is high-lighted by the contemporary feminist analyses of rape that have explicitly relied on racist ideology to minimize white women's complicity in racial terrorism.[92]

Thus, the experience of rape for black women includes not only a vulnerability to rape and a lack of legal protection radically different from that experienced by white women, but also a unique ambivalence. Black women have simultaneously acknowledged their own victimization and the victimization of black men by a system that has consistently ignored violence against women while perpetrating it against men.[93] The complexity and depth of this experience is not captured, or even acknowledged, by MacKinnon's account.

MacKinnon's essentialist approach recreates the paradigmatic woman in the image of the white woman, in the name of "unmodified feminism." As in the dominant discourse, black women are relegated to the margins, ignored or extolled as "just like us, only more so." But, as Barbara Omolade points out, "Black women are not white women with color."[94] Moreover, feminist essentialism represents not just an insult to black women, but a broken promise—the promise to listen to women's stories, the promise of feminist method.

3. Robin West's "Essential Woman"

While MacKinnon's essentialism is pervasive but covert, Robin West expressly declares her essentialism. In the last section of "The Difference in Women's Hedonic Lives: A Phenomenological Critique of Feminist Legal Theory,"[95] West argues:

> Both the liberal and the radical legalist have accepted the Kantian assumption that *to be human* is to be in some sense autonomous—meaning, minimally, to be differentiated, or individuated, from the rest of social life.
>
> Underlying and underscoring the poor fit between the proxies for subjective well-being endorsed by liberals and radicals—choice and power—and women's subjective, hedonic lives is the simple fact that women's lives—*because of our biological, reproductive role*—are drastically at odds with this fundamental vision of human life. Women's lives are *not* autonomous, they are profoundly relational.[96]

In West's view, women are ontologically distinct from men, because "Women, and *only* women, and *most* women, transcend *physically* the differentiation or individuation of biological self from the rest of human life trumpeted as the norm by the entire Kantian tradition."[97] That is, because only women can bear children, and because women have the social responsibility for raising children, our selves are profoundly different from male selves. "To the considerable degree that our potentiality for motherhood defines ourselves, women's lives are relational, not autonomous. As mothers we nurture the weak and we depend upon the strong. More than do men, we live in an interdependent and hierarchical natural web with others of varying degrees of strength."[98]

This claim about women's essential connectedness to the world becomes the centerpiece of "Jurisprudence and Gender."[99] West begins the article with the question, "What is a human being?" She then asserts that "perhaps the central insight of feminist theory of the last decade has been that wom[e]n are 'essentially connected,' not 'essentially separate,' from the rest of human life, both materially, through pregnancy, intercourse, and breast-feeding, and existentially, through the moral and practical life."[100] For West, this means that "all of our modern legal theory—by which I mean 'liberal legalism' and 'critical legal theory' collectively—is essentially and irretrievably masculine."[101] This is so because modern legal theory relies on the "separation thesis," the claim that human beings are distinct individuals first and form relationships later.[102]

Black women are entirely absent from West's work, in contrast to MacKinnon's; issues of race do not appear even in guilty footnotes. However, just as in MacKinnon's work, the bracketing of issues of race leads to the installation of white women on the throne of essential womanhood.

West's claims are clearly questionable on their face insofar as the experience of some women—"mothers"—is asserted to stand for the experience of all women. As with MacKinnon's theory, West's theory necessitates the stilling of some voices—namely, the voices of women who have rejected their biological, reproductive role—in order to privilege others. One might also question the degree to which motherhood, or our potential for it, defines us.[103] For purposes of this article, however, I am more interested in the conception of self that underlies West's account of "women's experience."

West argues that the biological and social implications of motherhood shape the selfhood of all, or at least most, women. This claim involves at least two assumptions.[104] First, West assumes (as does the liberal social theory she criticizes) that everyone has a deep, unitary "self" that is relatively stable and unchanging. Second, West assumes that this "self" differs significantly between men and women but is the same for all women and for all men despite differences of class, race, and sexual orientation: that is, that this self is deeply and primarily gendered. In a later part of this essay I will argue that black women can bring the experience of a multiple rather than a unitary self to feminist theory.[105] Here I want to argue that the notion that the gender difference is primary to an individual's selfhood is one that privileges white women's experience over the experience of black women.

The essays and poems in *This Bridge Called My Back* [106] describe experiences of women of color that differ radically from one another. Some contributors are lesbians; some are straight; some are class-privileged, and others are not. What links all the writings, however, is the sense that the self of a woman of color is not primarily a female self or a colored self but a both-and self. In her essay "Brownness," [107] Andrea Canaan describes both-and experience:

> The fact is I am brown and female, and my growth and development are tied to the entire community. I must nurture and develop brown self, woman, man, and child. I must address the issues of my own oppression and survival. When I separate them, isolate them, and ignore them, I separate, isolate, and ignore myself. I am a unit. A part of brownness.[108]

A personal story may also help to illustrate the point. At a 1988 meeting of the West Coast "fem-crits," Pat Cain and Trina Grillo asked all the women present to pick out two or three words to describe who they were. None of the white women mentioned their race; all of the women of color did.

In this society, it is only white people who have the luxury of "having no color"; only white people have been able to imagine that sexism and racism are separate experiences.[109] Far more for black women than for white women, the experience of self is precisely that of being unable to disentangle the web of race and gender—of being enmeshed always in multiple, often contradictory, discourses of sexuality and color. The challenge to black women has been the need to weave the fragments, our many selves, into an integral, though always changing and shifting, whole: a self that is neither "female" nor "black," but both-and.[110] West's insistence that every self is deeply and primarily gendered, then, with its corollary that gender is more important to personal identity than race, is finally another example of white solipsism. By suggesting that gender is more deeply embedded in self than race, her theory privileges the experience of white people over all others,[111] and thus serves to reproduce relations of domination in the larger culture.[112] Like MacKinnon's essential woman, West's essential woman turns out to be white.

4. The Attractions of Gender Essentialism

"Strategies become institutions."—Cynthia Ozick, Art and Ardor [113]

If gender essentialism is such a terrible thing, why do two smart and politically committed feminists like Catharine MacKinnon and Robin West rely on it? In this section I want to briefly sketch some of the attractions of essentialism. First, as a matter of intellectual convenience, essentialism is easy. Particularly for white feminists—and most of the people doing academic feminist theory in this country at this time are white—essentialism means not having to do as much work, not having to try and learn about the lives of black women, with all the risks and discomfort that that effort entails.[114] Essentialism is also intellectually easy because the dominant culture is essentialist—because it is difficult to find materials on the lives of black women, because there is as yet no academic infrastructure of work by and/or about black women or black feminist theory.[115]

Second, and more important, essentialism represents emotional safety. Especially for women who have relinquished privilege or had it taken away from them in their struggle against gender oppression, the feminist movement comes to be an emotional and spiritual home, a place to feel safe, a place that must be kept harmonious and free of difference. In an essay, Minnie Bruce Pratt describes her early involvement in the women's movement after having lost her children in a custody fight for being a lesbian, and her reluctance to look for or recognize struggle and difference within the movement itself:

> We were doing "outreach," that disastrous method of organizing; we had gone forward to a new place, women together, and now were throwing back safety lines to other women, to pull them in as if they were drowning, to save them. I understood then how important it was for me to have this new place; it was going to be my home, to replace the one I had lost. I needed desperately to have a place that was mine with other women, where I felt hopeful. But because of my need, I did not push myself to look at what might separate me from other women. I relied on the hopefulness of all women together: what I felt, deep down, was hope that they would join me in my place, which would be the way I wanted it. I didn't want to have to limit myself.
>
> I didn't understand what a limited, narrow space, and how short lasting it would be if only my imagination and knowledge and abilities were to go into the making and extending of it. I didn't understand how much I was still inside the restrictions of my culture, in my vision of how the world could be. I, and the other women I worked with, limited the effectiveness of our struggle for that place by our own racism and anti-Semitism.[116]

Many women, perhaps especially white women who have rejected or been rejected by their homes of origin, hope and expect that the women's movement will be a new home and home is a place of comfort, not conflict.

Third, feminist essentialism offers women not only intellectual and emotional comfort, but the opportunity to play all-too-familiar power games both among themselves and with men. Feminist essentialism provides multiple arenas for power struggle, which crosscut one another in complex ways. The gameswomanship is palpable at any reasonably diverse gathering of feminists with a political agenda. The participants are busy constructing hierarchies of oppression, using their own suffering (and consequent innocence) to win the right to define "women's experience" or to demand particular political concession for their interest group. White women stress women's commonality, which enables them to control the group's agenda; black women make reference to 200 years of slavery and argue that their needs should come first. Eventually, as the group seems ready to splinter into mutually suspicious and self-righteous factions, someone reminds the group that after all, women are women and we are all oppressed by men, and solidarity reappears through the threat of a common enemy.[117] These are the strategies of zero-sum games; and feminist essentialism, by purveying the notion that there is only one "women's experience," perpetuates these games.

Finally, as Martha Minow has pointed out, "Cognitively, we need simplifying categories, and the unifying category of 'woman' helps to organize experience, even at the cost of denying some of it."[118] Abandoning mental categories completely would leave us as autistic as Funes the Memorious, terrorized by the sheer weight and particularity of experience.[119] No categories at all, moreover, would leave nothing of a women's movement, save perhaps a tepid kind of "I've got my oppression, you've got yours" approach.[120] As Elizabeth Spelman has put the problem:

> At the heart of anything that can coherently be called a "women's movement" is the shared experience of being oppressed as women. The movement is, as it has to be, grounded in and justified by the fact of this shared experience: without it there would be neither the impulse nor the rationale for the political movement (whatever else is true of the movement). That is, unless in some important sense women speak in a single voice, the voice each has as a woman, there are no solid grounds for a "women's movement." [121]

The problem of avoiding essentialism while preserving "women" as a meaningful political and practical concept has thus often been posed as a dilemma.[122] The argument sometimes seems to be that we must choose: use the traditional categories or none at all.[123]

5. Beyond Essentialism: Black Women and Feminist Theory

> [O]ur future is predicated upon our ability to relate within equality. As women, we must root out internalized patterns of oppression within ourselves if we are to move beyond the most superficial aspects of social change. Now we must recognize differences among women who are our equals, neither inferior nor superior, and devise ways to use each others' difference to enrich our visions and our joint struggles.—Audre Lorde, *Sister Outsider* [124]

In this part of the essay, I want to talk about what black women can bring to feminist theory to help us move beyond essentialism and toward multiple consciousness as feminist and jurisprudential method. In my view, there are at least three major contributions that black women have to offer post-essentialist feminist theory: the recognition of a self that is multiplicitous, not unitary; the recognition that differences are always relational rather than inherent; and the recognition that wholeness and commonality are acts of will and creativity, rather than passive discovery.

The Abandonment of Innocence

Black women experience not a single inner self (much less one that is essentially gendered), but many selves. This sense of a multiplicitous self is not unique to black women, but black women have expressed this sense in ways that are striking, poignant, and potentially useful to feminist theory. Writer bell hooks describes her experience in a creative writing program at a predominantly white college, where she was encouraged to find "her voice," as frustrating to her sense of multiplicity.

> It seemed that many black students found our situations problematic precisely because our sense of self, and by definition our voice, was not unilateral, monologist, or static but rather multi-dimensional. We were as at home in dialect as we were in standard English. Individuals who speak languages other than English, who speak patois as well as standard English, find it a necessary aspect of self-affirmation not to feel compelled to choose one voice over another, not to claim one as more authentic, but rather to construct social realities that celebrate, acknowledge, and affirm differences, variety.[125]

This experience of multiplicity is also a sense of self-contradiction, of containing the oppressor within oneself. In her article "On Being the Object of Property,"[126] Patricia Williams writes about herself writing about her great-great-grandmother, "picking through the ruins for my roots."[127] What she finds is a paradox: She must claim for herself "a heritage the weft of whose genesis is [her] own disinheritance."[128] Williams's great-great-grandmother, Sophie, was a slave, and at the age of about eleven was impregnated by her owner, a white lawyer named Austin Miller. Their daughter Mary, Williams's great-grandmother, was taken away from Sophie and raised as a house servant.

When Williams went to law school, her mother told her, "The Millers were lawyers, so you have it in your blood."[129] Williams analyzes this statement as asking her to acknowledge contradictory selves:

> [S]he meant that no one should make me feel inferior because someone else's father was a judge. She wanted me to reclaim that part of my heritage from which I had been disinherited, and she wanted me to use it as a source of strength and self-confidence. At the same time, she was asking me to claim a part of myself that was the dispossessor of another part of myself; she was asking me to deny that disenfranchised little black girl of myself that felt powerless, vulnerable and, moreover, rightly felt so.[130]

The theory of black slavery, Williams notes, was based on the notion that black people are beings without will or personality, defined by "irrationality, lack of control, and ugliness." [131] In contrast, "wisdom, control, and aesthetic beauty signify the whole white personality in slave law." [132] In accepting her white self, her lawyer self, Williams must accept a legacy of not only a disinheritance but a negation of her black self: To the Millers, her forebears, the Williamses, her forebears, did not even have selves as such.

Williams's choice ultimately is not to deny either self, but to recognize them both, and in so doing to acknowledge guilt as well as innocence. She ends the piece by invoking "the presence of polar bears" [133]—bears that mauled a child to death at the Brooklyn Zoo and were subsequently killed themselves, bears judged in public debate as simultaneously "innocent, naturally territorial, unfairly imprisoned, and guilty." [134]

This complex resolution rejects the easy innocence of supposing oneself to be an essential black self with a legacy of oppression by the guilty white Other. With such multilayered analyses, black women can bring to feminist theory stories of how it is to have multiple and contradictory selves, selves that contain the oppressor as well as the oppressed. [135]

Strategic Identities and "Difference"

A post-essentialist feminism can benefit not only from the abandonment of the quest for a unitary self, but also from Martha Minow's realization that difference—and therefore identity—is always relational, not inherent. [136] Zora Neale Hurston's work is a good illustration of this notion. In an essay written for a white audience, "How It Feels to Be Colored Me," [137] Hurston argues that her color is not an inherent part of her being, but a response to her surroundings. She recalls the day she "became colored—the day she left her home in an all-black community to go to school: "I left Eatonville, the town of the oleanders, as Zora. When I disembarked from the river-boat at Jacksonville, she was no more. It seemed that I had suffered a sea change. I was not Zora of Orange County any more, I was now a little colored girl." [138] But even as an adult, Hurston insists, her colored self is always situational: "I do not always feel colored. Even now I often achieve the unconscious Zora of Eatonville before the Hegira. I feel most colored when I am thrown against a sharp white background." [139]

As an example, Hurston describes the experience of listening to music in a jazz club with a white male friend:

My pulse is throbbing like a war drum. I want to slaughter something—give pain, give death to what, I do not know. But the piece ends. The men of the orchestra wipe their lips and rest their fingers. I creep back slowly to the veneer we call civilization with the last tone and find the white friend sitting motionless in his seat, smoking calmly.

"Good music they have here," he remarks, drumming the table with his fingertips.

Music. The great blobs of purple and red emotion have not touched him. He has only heard what I felt. He is far away and I see him but dimly across the ocean and the continent that have fallen between us. He is so pale with his whiteness then and I am so colored.[140]

In reaction to the presence of whites—both her white companion and the white readers of her essay—Hurston invokes and uses the traditional stereotype of black people as tied to the jungle, "living in the jungle way."[141] Yet in a later essay for a black audience, "What White Publishers Won't Print,"[142] she criticizes the white "folklore of 'reversion to type'":

This curious doctrine has such wide acceptance that it is tragic. One has only to examine the huge literature on it to be convinced. No matter how high we may *seem* to climb, put us under strain and we revert to type, that is, to the bush. Under a superficial layer of western culture, the jungle drums throb in our veins.[143]

The difference between the first essay, in which Hurston revels in the trope of black person as primitive, and the second essay, in which she deplores it, lies in the distinction between an identity that is contingent, temporary, and relational, and an identity that is fixed, inherent, and essential. Zora as jungle woman is fine as an argument, a reaction to her white friend's experience; what is abhorrent is the notion that Zora can always and only be a jungle woman.[144] One image is in flux, "inspired" by a relationship with another;[145] the other is static, unchanging, and ultimately reductive and sterile rather than creative.

Thus, "how it feels to be colored Zora" depends on the answer to these questions: "'Compared to what? As of when? Who is asking? In what context? For what purpose? With what interests and presuppositions?' What Hurston rigorously shows is that questions of difference and identity are always functions of a specific interlocutionary situation—and the answers, matters of strategy rather than truth."[146] Any "essential self" is always an invention; the evil is in denying its artificiality.[147]

To be compatible with this conception of the self, feminist theorizing about "women" must similarly be strategic and contingent, focusing on relationships, not essences. One result will be that men will cease to be a faceless Other and reappear as potential allies in political struggle.[148] Another will be that women will be able to acknowledge their differences without threatening feminism itself. In the process, as feminists begin to attack racism and classism and homophobia, feminism will change from being only about "women as women" (modified women need not apply), to being about all kinds of oppression based on seemingly inherent and unalterable characteristics.[149] We need not wait for a unified theory of oppression;[150] that theory can be feminism.

Integrity as Will and Idea

> Because each had discovered years before that they were neither white nor male, and that all freedom and triumph was forbidden to them, they had set about creating something else to be.—Toni Morrison, *Sula*[151]

Finally, black women can help the feminist movement move beyond its fascination with essentialism through the recognition that wholeness of the self and commonality with others are asserted (if never completely achieved) through creative action, not realized in shared victimization. Feminist theory at present, especially feminist legal theory, tends to focus on women as passive victims. For example, for MacKinnon, women have been so objectified by men that the miracle is how they are able to exist at all. Women are the victims, the acted-upon, the helpless, until by radical enlightenment they are somehow empowered to act for themselves.[152] Similarly, for West, the "fundamental fact" of women's lives is pain—"the violence, the danger, the boredom, the ennui, the non-productivity, the poverty, the fear, the numbness, the frigidity, the isolation, the low self-esteem, and the pathetic attempts to assimilate."[153]

This story of woman as victim is meant to encourage solidarity by emphasizing women's shared oppression, thus denying or minimizing difference, and to further the notion of an essential woman—she who is victimized. But as bell hooks has succinctly noted, the notion that women's commonality lies in their shared victimization by men "directly reflects male supremacist thinking. Sexist ideology teaches women that to be female is to be a victim."[154] Moreover, the story of woman as passive victim denies the ability of women to shape their own lives, whether for better or worse. It also may thwart their abilities. Like Minnie Bruce Pratt, reluctant to look farther than commonality for fear of jeopardizing the comfort of shared experience, women who rely on their victimization to define themselves may be reluctant to let it go and create their own self-definitions.

At the individual level, black women have had to learn to construct themselves in a society that denied them full selves. Again, Zora Neale Hurston's writings are suggestive. Though Hurston plays with being her "colored self" and again with being "the eternal feminine with its string of beads,"[155] she ends "How It Feels to Be Colored Me" with an image of herself as neither essentially black nor essentially female, but simply a brown bag of miscellany propped against a wall.

> [Against a wall in] company with other bags, white, red and yellow. Pour out the contents, and there is discovered a jumble of small things priceless and worthless. A first-water diamond, an empty spool, bits of broken glass, lengths of string, a key to a door long since crumbled away, a rusty knife-blade, old shoes saved for a road that never was and never will be, a nail bent under the weight of things too heavy for any nail, a dried flower or two still fragrant. In your hand is the brown bag. On the ground before you is the jumble it held—so much like the jumble in the bags, could they be emptied, that all might be dumped in a single heap and the bags refilled without altering the content of any greatly. A bit of colored glass more or less would not matter. Perhaps that is how the Great Stuffer of Bags filled them in the first place—who knows?[156]

Hurston thus insists on a conception of identity as a construction, not an essence—something made of fragments of experience, not discovered in one's body or unveiled after male domination is eliminated.

This insistence on the importance of will and creativity seems to threaten feminism at one level, because it gives strength back to the concept of autonomy, making possible the recognition of the element of consent in relations of domination,[157] and attributes to women the power that makes culpable the many ways in which white women have actively used their race privilege against their sisters of color.[158] Although feminists are correct to recognize the powerful force of sheer physical coercion in ensuring compliance with patriarchal hegemony,[159] we must also "come to terms with the ways in which women's culture has served to enlist women's support in perpetuating existing power relations."[160]

However, at another level, the recognition of the role of creativity and will in shaping our lives is liberating, for it allows us to acknowledge and celebrate the creativity and joy with which many women have survived and turned existing relations of domination to their own ends. Works of black literature like Beloved, The Color Purple, and Song of Solomon, among others, do not linger on black women's victimization and misery; though they recognize our pain, they ultimately celebrate our transcendence.[161]

Finally, on a collective level this emphasis on will and creativity reminds us that bridges between women are built, not found. The discovery of shared suffering is a connection more illusory than real; what will truly bring and keep us together is the use of effort and imagination to root out and examine our differences, for only the recognition of women's differences can ultimately bring the feminist movement to strength. This is hard work, and painful work;[162] but it is also radical work, real work. As Barbara Smith has said, "What I really feel is radical is trying to make coalitions with people who are different from you. I feel it is radical to be dealing with race and sex and class and sexual identity all at one time. I think that is really radical because it has never been done before."[163]

Epilogue: Multiple Consciousness

I have argued in this essay that gender essentialism is dangerous to feminist legal theory because in the attempt to extract an essential female self and voice from the diversity of women's experience, the experiences of women perceived as "different" are ignored or treated as variations on the (white) norm. Now I want to return to an earlier point: that legal theory, including feminist legal theory, has been entranced for too long and to too great an extent by the voice of "We the People." In order to energize legal theory, we need to subvert it with narratives and stories, accounts of the particular, the different, and the hitherto silenced.

Whether by chance or not, many of the legal theorists telling stories these days are women of color. Mari Matsuda calls for "multiple consciousness as jurisprudential method";[164] Patricia Williams shows the way with her multilayered stories and meditations.[165] These writings are healthy for feminist legal theory as well as legal theory more generally. In acknowledging "the complexity of messages implied in our being,"[166] they begin the task of energizing legal theory with the creative struggle between Funes and We the People: the creative struggle that reflects a multiple consciousness.

Notes

Originally published in 42 Stanford Law Review 581 (1990). © 1990 by the Board of Trustees of the Leland Stanford Junior University; reprinted by permission.

An earlier version of this essay was presented at the first annual Conference on Critical Race Theory, sponsored by the University of Wisconsin Institute for Legal Studies, July 7–12, 1989; my indescribable gratitude to all the participants in that conference, but especially to Derrick Bell, Teri Miller, and Ginger Patterson. Thanks also to the many other people who provided insightful comments and criticism, including Herma Hill Kay, Kristin Luker, Robert Post, and Deborah Rhode.

1. Ntozake Shange, "no more love poems #4," in For Colored Girls Who Have Considered Suicide/When the Rainbow is Enuf 45 (1977) (The poem in part reads: "bein alive & bein a

woman & bein colored is a metaphysical dilemma / i havent conquered yet / do you see the point / my spirit is too ancient to understand the separation of soul & gender / my love is too delicate to have thrown back on my face.")

2. Jorge Luis Borges, Labyrinths: Selected Stories and Other Writings 59 (D. Yates & J. Irby eds., 1964).

3. Id. at 63–64.

4. Id. at 64.

5. Id. at 65.

6. Id. at 66.

7. James Boyd White, When Words Lose Their Meaning 232 (1984).

8. Id. at 240.

9. Cynthia Ozick, "Innovation and Redemption: What Literature Means," in Art and Ardor 238, 244 (1983).

10. Robert M. Cover, "Violence and the Word," 95 Yale L.J. 1601, 1601 (1986); see also Robert Weisberg, "The Law-Literature Enterprise," 1 Yale J.L. & Human. 1, 45 (1988) (describing how students of legal interpretation are initially drawn to literary interpretation because of its greater freedom, and then almost immediately search for a way to reintroduce constraints).

11. See Peter Goodrich, "Historical Aspects of Legal Interpretation," 61 Ind. L.J. 331, 333 (1986) (arguing that legal interpretation is theological in derivation and "unjustifiably authoritarian in its practice").

12. Henry Louis Gates, Jr., "Editor's Introduction: Writing 'Race' and the Difference It Makes," in "Race," Writing, and Difference, 1, 16 (H. L. Gates, Jr. ed. 1986).

13. Mari J. Matsuda, "When the First Quail Calls: Multiple Consciousness as Jurisprudential Method," 11 Women's Rts. L. Rep. 7, 9 (1989).

14. Teresa de Lauretis, "Feminist Studies/Critical Studies: Issues, Terms, and Contexts," in Feminist Studies/Critical Studies 1, 8 (T. de Lauretis ed. 1986).

15. Ozick, supra note 9, at 247.

16. Matsuda, supra note 13, at 9.

17. Id. at 8.

18. Audre Lorde, "Age, Race, Class, and Sex: Women Redefining Difference," in Sister Outsider 114, 120 (1984).

19. For example, in 1851, Sojourner Truth told the audience at the woman's rights convention in Akron, Ohio:

> That man over there says women need to be helped into carriages and lifted over ditches, and to have the best place everywhere. Nobody ever helps me into carriages, or over mud-puddles or gives me any best place! And ain't I a woman? Look at me! Look at my arm! I have ploughed, and planted, and gathered into barns, and no man could head me! And ain't I a woman? I could work as much and eat as much as a man—when I could get it—and bear the lash as well! And ain't I a woman? I have borne thirteen children, and seen them most all sold off to slavery, and when I cried out with my mother's grief, none but Jesus heard me! And ain't I a woman?

Address by Sojourner Truth (1851), reprinted in *Black Women in Nineteenth-century American Life: Their Words, Their Thoughts, Their Feelings* 234, 235 (B.J. Loewenberg & R. Bogin eds. 1976).

20. I use "black" rather than "African-American" because some people of color who do not have African heritage and/or are not American nevertheless identify themselves as black, and in this essay I am more interested in stressing issues of culture than of nationality or genetics. I use "black" rather than "Black" because it is my contention in this essay that race and gender issues are inextricably intertwined, and to capitalize "Black" and not "Woman" would imply a privileging of race with which I do not agree.

21. For a discussion of white racism in the suffrage movement, see Angela Y. Davis, *Women, Race and Class* 110–26 (1981); Paul Giddings, *When and Where I Enter: The Impact of Black Women on Race and Sex in America* 159–70 (1984). *See also* Giddings, *supra*, at 46–55 (white racism in the abolitionist movement).

22. *See, e.g.*, Davis, *supra* note 21; bell hooks, *Ain't I a Woman? Black Women and Feminism* (1981) [hereinafter hooks, *Ain't I a Woman?*]; bell hooks, *Feminist Theory: From Margin to Center* (1984) [hereinafter hooks, *Feminist Theory*]; bell hooks, *Talking Back: Thinking Feminist, Thinking Black* (1989) [hereinafter hooks, *Talking Back*]; Gloria I. Joseph & Jill Lewis, *Common Differences: Conflicts in Black and White Feminist Perspectives* (1981); *This Bridge Called My Back: Writings by Radical Women of Color* (C. Moraga & G. Anzaldua eds., 1983) [hereinafter *This Bridge Called My Back*]; Hazel V. Carby, "White Woman Listen! Black Feminism and the Boundaries of Sisterhood," in *The Empire Strikes Back: Race and Racism in 70s Britain* 212 (Centre for Contemporary Cultural Studies ed., 1982); Maria C. Lugones & Elizabeth V. Spelman, "Have We Got a Theory for You! Feminist Theory, Cultural Imperialism and the Demand for 'The Woman's Voice,'" 6 *Women's Stud. Int'l F.* 573 (1983).

23. *See, e.g.*, de Lauretis, *supra* note 14, at 9 (characterizing the feminist identity as "multiple, shifting, and often self-contradictory").

24. Christine A. Littleton, "Feminist Jurisprudence: The Difference Method Makes," 41 *Stan. L. Rev.* 751, 764 (1989). MacKinnon's definition of feminist method is the practice of "believing women's accounts of sexual use and abuse by men." Catharine A. MacKinnon, "Introduction: The Art of the Impossible," in *Feminism Unmodified* 1, 5 (1987). Littleton argues that MacKinnon's major contribution to feminist jurisprudence has been "more methodological than programmatic." Littleton, *supra* at 753–54. In Littleton's view, "the essence of MacKinnon's view on feminism comes down to a single choice: feminist method or not." *Id.* at 752–53.

25. *See* Jane Flax, "Postmodernism and Gender Relations in Feminist Theory," 12 *Signs* 621, 633 (1987): "[W]ithin feminist theory a search for a defining theme of the whole or a feminist viewpoint may require the suppression of the important and discomforting voices of persons with experiences unlike our own. The suppression of these voices seems to be a necessary condition for the (apparent) authority, coherence, and universality of our own."

Elizabeth Spelman sees this as "the paradox at the heart of feminism: Any attempt to talk about all women in terms of something we have in common undermines attempts to talk about the differences among us, and vice versa." Elizabeth V. Spelman, *Inessential Woman: Problems of Exclusion in Feminist Thought* 3 (1988).

26. *See, e.g.,* Catherine A. MacKinnon, "On Collaboration," in *Feminism Unmodified, supra* note 24, at 198, 204 ("I am here to speak for those, particularly women and children, upon whose silence the law, including the law of the First Amendment, has been built").

27. Adrienne Rich, "Disloyal to Civilization: Feminism, Racism, Gynephobia," in *On Lies, Secrets, and Silence* 275, 299 (1979) (defining white solipsism as the tendency to "think, imagine, and speak as if whiteness described the world").

28. Spelman, *supra* note 25, at 4.

29. Elizabeth Spelman lists five propositions which I consider to be associated with gender essentialism:

1. Women can be talked about "as women."
2. Women are oppressed "as women."
3. Gender can be isolated from other elements of identity that bear one's social, economic, and political position such as race, class, ethnicity; hence sexism can be isolated from racism, classism, etc.
4. Women's situation can be contrasted to men's.
5. Relations between men and women can be compared to relations between other oppressor/oppressed groups (whites and Blacks, Christians and Jews, rich and poor, etc.), and hence it is possible to compare the situation of women to the situation of Blacks, Jews, the poor, etc.

Id. at 165.

30. *See* Deborah K. King, "Multiple Jeopardy, Multiple Consciousness: The Context of a Black Feminist Ideology," 14 *Signs* 42, 51 (1988) ("To reduce this complex of negotiations to an addition problem (racism + sexism = black women's experience) is to define the issues, and indeed black womanhood itself, within the structural terms developed by Europeans and especialy white males to privilege their race and their sex unilaterally"); *see also* Spelman, *supra* note 25, at 114–32 (chapter entitled "Gender & Race: The Ampersand Problem in Feminist Thought"); Barbara Smith, "Notes for Yet Another Paper on Black Feminism, or Will the Real Enemy Please Stand Up?," 5 *Conditions* 123, 123 (1979) (the effect of multiple oppression is "not merely arithmetic").

31. Spelman, *supra* note 25, at 159.

32. Audre Lorde writes: "As a Black lesbian feminist comfortable with the many different ingredients of my identity, and a woman committed to racial and sexual freedom from oppression, I find I am constantly being encouraged to pluck out some one aspect of myself and present this as the meaningful whole, eclipsing or denying the other parts of self." Lorde, *supra* note 18, at 120.

33. In my discussion I focus on Catharine A. MacKinnon, "Feminism, Marxism, Method, and the State: An Agenda for Theory," 7 *Signs* 515 (1982) [hereinafter Mac-

Kinnon, *Signs* I], and Catharine A. MacKinnon, "Feminism, Marxism, Method, and the State: Toward Feminist Jurisprudence," 8 *Signs* 635 (1983) [hereinafter MacKinnon, *Signs* II], but I make reference to the essays in MacKinnon, *Feminism Unmodified, supra* note 24, as well.

34. *See also* Marlee Kline, "Race, Racism, and Feminist Legal Theory," 12 *Harv. Women's L.J.* 115 (1989) (containing a similar—and thus to my mind, remarkably insightful—critique of MacKinnon's work; I recommend Kline's article to all interested in the challenge women of color pose to MacKinnon's theory).

35. MacKinnon, "Desire and Power," in *Feminism Unmodified, supra* note 24, at 46, 49.

36. *Id.* at 48.

37. MacKinnon, *Signs* I, *supra* note 33, at 516 (footnote omitted).

38. *Id.*

39. MacKinnon, *supra* note 24, at 3.

40. *Id.* Thus, MacKinnon disagrees both with feminists who argue that women and men are really the same and should therefore be treated the same under the law, and with feminists who argue that the law should take into account women's differences. Feminists who argue that men and women are "the same" fail to take into account the unequal power relations that underlie the very construction of the two genders. Feminists who want the law to recognize the "differences" between the genders buy into the account of women's "natural difference," and therefore (inadvertently) perpetuate dominance under the name of inherent difference. *See id.* at 32–40, 71–77.

41. MacKinnon, *Signs* II, *supra* note 33, at 638.

42. *Id.* at 639.

43. *Id.*

44. *See* MacKinnon, "Difference and Dominance: On Sex Discrimination," in *Feminism Unmodified, supra* note 24, at 32, 45.

45. MacKinnon, *Signs* I, *supra* note 33, at 523.

46. *See* MacKinnon, *supra* note 24, at 16.

47. Although MacKinnon's explicit position is that until women are free from male domination, we simply don't know what we might be like, as Katharine Bartlett notes, in *Feminism Unmodified* MacKinnon "speaks of 'women's point of view,' 'woman's voice,' woman's 'distinctive contribution,' of standards that are 'not ours,' of empowering women 'on our own terms,' and of what we 'really want.' These references all suggest a reality beyond social construct that women will discover once freed from the bonds of oppression." Katherine T. Bartlett, "MacKinnon's Feminism: Power on Whose Terms?" (Book Review), 75 *Cal. L. Rev.* 1559, 1566 (1987) (citations omitted).

48. *See, e.g.,* MacKinnon, *Signs* II, *supra* note 33, at 39 n.8 ("This feminism seeks to define and pursue women's interest as the fate of all women bound together. It seeks to extract the truth of women's commonalities out of the lie that all women are the same.").

49. MacKinnon, *Signs* I, *supra* note 33, at 516 n.*

50. MacKinnon, "On Exceptionality: Women as Women in Law," in *Feminism Unmodified, supra* note 24, at 70, 76.

51. MacKinnon, *Signs I*, supra note 33, at 518 & n.3.

52. Id. at 537 n.54.

53. MacKinnon, supra note 24, at 3.

54. Id. at 2.

55. MacKinnon, "Whose Culture? A Case Note on *Martinez v. Santa Clara Pueblo*," in *Feminism Unmodified*, supra note 24, at 63.

56. Martinez v. Santa Clara Pueblo, 436 U.S. 49, 71–72 (1978).

57. MacKinnon, supra note 55, at 66.

58. Id. at 68.

59. Id. at 67.

60. Id. at 68.

61. As she did. *See* Martinez v. Santa Clara Pueblo, 402 F. Supp. 5, 11 (D.N.M. 1975), rev'd, 540 F.2d 1039 (10th Cir. 1976), rev'd 436 U.S. 49 (1978).

62. The district court hints that such questions were decided on a case-by-case basis. Id. at 16. Why was an ordinance thought necessary?

63. In her article "Dependent Sovereigns: Indian Tribes, States, and the Federal Courts," 56 U. Chi. L. Rev. 671 (1989), Judith Resnik begins to address some of these issues.

64. MacKinnon, supra note 55, at 69.

65. Elsewhere, MacKinnon explicitly asserts that gender oppression is more significant than racial oppression. *See* Catharine A. MacKinnon, "Francis Biddle's Sister: Pornography, Civil Rights, and Speech," in *Feminism Unmodified*, supra note 24, at 163, 166–68.

66. MacKinnon, *Signs I*, supra note 33, at 520 n.7.

67. The reference is to an article titled "Feminism: 'The Black Nuance,'" *Newsweek*, Dec. 17, 1973, at 89–90; cf. Spelman, supra note 25, at 114–15 (describing article in the *New York Times* in which the women are white and the blacks are men).

68. MacKinnon recognizes a similar process in Marxism, whereby gender oppression becomes merely a variant form of class oppression. *See* MacKinnon, *Signs I*, supra note 33, at 524–27. What MacKinnon misses is that her own theory reduces racial oppression to a mere intensifier of gender oppression.

69. *See, e.g.*, MacKinnon, supra note 65, at 169 ("Defining feminism in a way that connects epistemology with power as the politics of women's point of view, [the discovery of feminism] can be summed up by saying that women live in another world: specifically, a world of *not* equality, a world of inequality.").

70. MacKinnon, *Signs I*, supra note 33, at 530. Yet, having acknowledged that black women have never been "women," MacKinnon continues in the article to discuss "women," making it plain that the "women" she is discussing are white.

71. Applied to men, however, the word "black" ameliorates: MacKinnon concedes that black men are not quite as bad as white men, although they are still bad, being men. For instance, in a footnote she qualifies her statement that "[P]ower to create the world from one's point of view is power in its male form," id. at 537, with the recognition that black men have "less" power: "But to the extent that they cannot create the world

from their point of view, they find themselves unmanned, castrated, literally or figuratively." Id. at 537 n.54. The last clause of this statement appears, puzzlingly, to be a reference to lynching; but it was not for *failing* to create the world but for the more radical sin of *making the attempt* that black men were "literally castrated."

72. Id. at 540 n.59. Similarly, in *Feminism Unmodified*, MacKinnon reminds us that the risk of death and mutilation in the course of a botched abortion is disproportionately borne by women of color, but only in the context of asserting that "[n]one of us can afford this risk." MacKinnon, "Not by Law Alone: From a Debate with Phyllis Schlafy," in *Feminism Unmodified*, supra note 24, at 21, 25.

73. Toni Morrison, *The Bluest Eye* (1970).

74. Id. at 14.

75. Id. at 57.

76. Id. at 64.

77. Id. at 34 ("It had occurred to Pecola some time ago that if her eyes, those eyes that held the pictures, and knew the sights—if those eyes of hers were different, that is to say, beautiful, she herself would be different. Her teeth were good, and at least her nose was not big and flat like some of those who were thought so cute. If she looked different, beautiful, maybe [her father] would be different, and Mrs. Breedlove too. Maybe they'd say, 'Why, look at pretty-eyed Pecola. We mustn't do bad things in front of those pretty eyes.'").

78. MacKinnon, *Signs II*, supra note 33, at 646.

79. Id. at 646 n.22; *see also* MacKinnon, "A Rally Against Rape," in *Feminism Unmodified*, supra note 24, at 81, 82 (black women are raped four times as often as white women); Diana Russell, *Sexual Exploitation* 185 (1984) (black women, who comprise 10 percent of all women, accounted for 60 percent of rapes reported in 1967).

Describing Susan Brownmiller, *Against Our Will: Men, Women and Rape* (1976), MacKinnon writes, "Brownmiller examines rape in riots, wars, pogroms, and revolutions; rape by police, parents, prison guards; and rape motivated by racism—seldom rape in normal circumstances, in everyday life, in ordinary relationships, by men as men." MacKinnon, *Signs II*, supra note 33, at 646.

80. MacKinnon, *Signs II*, supra note 33, at 653; cf. Susan Estrich, *Real Rape* 3 (1987) (remarking, while telling the story of her own rape, "His being black, I fear, probably makes my account more believable to some people, as it certainly did with the police"). Indeed. Estrich hastens to assure us, though, that "the most important thing is that he was a stranger." Id.

81. *See* Alice Walker, "Advancing Luna—and Ida B. Wells," in *You Can't Keep a Good Woman Down* 93 (1981) ("Who knows what the black woman thinks of rape? Who has asked her? Who cares?").

82. As Barbara Omolade notes:

> To [the white slave holder the black woman slave] was a fragmented commodity whose feelings and choices were rarely considered: her head and her heart were separated from her back and her hands and divided from her womb and vagina. Her back and muscle were pressed into field labor where she was forced to work with men and

work like men. Her hands were demanded to nurse and nurture the white man and his family as domestic servant whether she was technically enslaved or legally free. Her vagina, used for his sexual pleasure, was the gateway to the womb, which was his place of capital investment—the capital investment being the sex act and the resulting child the accumulated surplus, worth money on the slave market.

Barbara Omolade, "Hearts of Darkness," in *Powers of Desire: The Politics of Sexuality* 354 (A. Snitow, C. Stansell & S. Thompson eds., 1983).

83. See Jacqueline Jones, *Labor of Love, Labor of Sorrow* 150 (1985). In *Beloved*, Toni Morrison tells the story of Ella, whose "puberty was spent in a house where she was shared by father and son, whom she called 'the lowest yet.' It was 'the lowest yet' who gave her a disgust for sex and against whom she measured all atrocities." Toni Morrison, *Beloved* 256 (1987) (Ella knew "[t]hat anybody white could take your whole self for anything that came to mind. Not just work, kill, or maim you, but dirty you. Dirty you so bad you couldn't like yourself anymore. Dirty you so bad you forgot who you were and couldn't think it up."). Sethe, one of the protagonists in *Beloved*, kills her own baby daughter rather than relinquish her to such a life. Cf. Omolade, *supra* note 82, at 355 (" 'Testimony seems to be quite widespread to the fact that many if not most southern boys begin their sexual experiences with Negro girls' " (quoting John Dollard, *Caste and Class in a Southern Town* 139 (rev. ed. 1949))).

84. See Jennifer Wriggins, "Rape, Racism, and the Law," 6 *Harv. Women's L.J.* 103, 118 (1983).

85. Susan Estrich gives an example: When a black man raped a white woman, the death penalty was held to be justified by the Virginia Supreme Court; but when a black man raped a black woman, his conviction was reversed, on the grounds that the defendant's behavior, "though extremely reprehensible, and deserving of punishment, does not involve him in the crime which this statute was designed to punish." Christian v. Commonwealth, 64 Va. (23 Gratt.) 954, 959 (1873), *quoted in* Estrich, *supra* note 80, at 35–36. On the intertwining of gender and race oppression in the law of rape and its connection to lynching, see Jacquelyn Dowd Hall, " 'The Mind That Burns in Each Body': Women, Rape, and Racial Violence," in *Powers of Desire: The Politics of Sexuality*, *supra* note 82, at 328; Wriggins, *supra* note 84, at 103. On the intertwining of gender and race oppression in the miscegenation laws, see Karen A. Getman, "Sexual Control in the Slaveholding South: The Implementation and Maintenance of a Racial Caste System," 7 *Harv. Women's L.J.* 115 (1984). *See generally* Paul A. Lombardo, "Miscegenation, Eugenics, and Racism: Historical Footnotes to *Loving v. Virginia*," 21 *U.C. Davis L. Rev.* 421 (1988).

86. Hazel V. Carby, "On the Threshold of Woman's Era: Lynching, Empire, and Sexuality in Black Feminist Theory," in *"Race," Writing, and Difference*, *supra* note 12, at 301, 309.

87. Carby notes, "those that remained silent while disapproving of lynching were condemned by Wells for being as guilty as the actual perpetrators of lynching." Id. at 308.

Of course, courageous white women have spoken out against lynching and even about the white women's complicity in its occurrence by choosing to remain silent. See Davis, supra note 21, at 194–96; Hall, supra note 85, at 337–40 (discussing the work of Jessie Daniel Ames and the Association of Southern Women for the Prevention of Lynching in the 1930s). However, as Davis also points out, such forms of intervention were sadly belated. Davis, supra note 21, at 195.

88. Carby, supra note 86, at 306 (discussing Anna Julia Cooper, A Voice from the South (1892)) ("By linking imperialism to internal colonization, Cooper thus provided black women intellectuals with the basis for an analysis of how patriarchal power establishes and sustains gendered and racialized social formations. White women were implicated in the maintenance of this wider system of oppression because they challenged only the parameters of their domestic confinement; by failing to reconstitute their class and caste interests, they reinforced the provincialism of their movement.").

89. Estrich, supra note 80, at 107 n.2.

90. Wriggins, supra note 84, at 121 n.113 (finding that "the average sentence received by Black men, exclusive of cases involving life imprisonment or death, was 4.2 years if the victim was Black, 16.4 years if the victim was white"). I do not know whether a white man has ever been sentenced to death for the rape of a black woman, although I could make an educated guess as to the answer.

91. Davis, supra note 21, at 174.

92. For example, Susan Brownmiller describes the black defendants in publicized Southern rape trials as "pathetic, semiliterate fellows," Brownmiller, supra note 79, at 237, and the white female accusers as innocent pawns of white men, see, e.g., id. at 233 ("confused and fearful, they fell into line"). See also Davis, supra note 21, at 196–99.

93. See Carby, supra note 86, at 307 (citing Ida B. Wells, "Southern Horrors" (1892), reprinted in Ida B. Wells, On Lynchings 5–6 (1969)) (miscegenation laws, directed at preventing sexual relations between white women and black men, "pretended to offer 'protection' to white women but left black women the victims of rape by white men and simultaneously granted to these same men the power to terrorize black men as a potential threat to the virtue of 'white womanhood').

94. Barbara Omolade, "Black Women and Feminism," in The Future of Difference, 247, 248 (H. Eisenstein & A. Jardine eds., 1980).

95. Robin West, "The Difference in Women's Hedonic Lives: A Phenomenological Critique of Feminist Legal Theory," 3 Wis. Women's L.J. 81 (1987).

96. Id. at 140.

97. Id.

98. Id. at 141.

99. Robin West, "Jurisprudence and Gender," 55 U. Chi. L. Rev. 1 (1988).

100. Id. at 3. West further posits a "fundamental contradiction" in women's experience equivalent to the "fundamental contradiction" posited by some critical legal scholars between autonomy and connection; whereas men experience a fundamental contradiction between autonomy and connection, women experience a fundamental contradiction between invasion and intimacy. See id. at 53–58.

101. Id. at 2.

102. *Id.*

103. The danger of such a theory is that, like some French feminist scholarship, it threatens to reembrace the old belief, used against women for so long, that anatomy is destiny: "A good deal of French feminist scholarship has been concerned with specifying the nature of the feminine. . . . This principle of femininity is sought in the female body, sometimes understood as the preoedipal mother and other times understood naturalistically as a pantheistic principle that requires its own kind of language for expression. In these cases, gender is not constituted, but is considered an essential aspect of bodily life, and we come very near the equation of biology and destiny, that conflation of fact and value, which Beauvoir spent her life trying to refute." Judith Butler, "Variations on Sex and Gender: Beauvoir, Wittig and Foucault," in *Feminism as Critique: Essays on the Politics of Gender* 128, 140 (S. Benhabib & D. Cornell eds., 1987).

Curiously, MacKinnon's dominance theory, which claims to be "total," says very little about motherhood at all. *See* Littleton, *supra* note 24, at 762 n.54.

104. I have taken this analysis from Nancy Fraser and Linda Nicholson's analysis of Nancy Chodorow's work. Nancy Fraser & Linda Nicholson, "Social Criticism without Philosophy: An Encounter Between Feminism and Postmodernism," in *Universal Abandon? The Politics of Postmodernism* 83, 96 (A. Ross ed., 1988). *See generally* Nancy Chodorow, *The Reproduction of Mothering: Psychoanalysis and the Sociology of Gender* (1978).

105. *See* text accompanying notes 125–135 *infra.*

106. *This Bridge Called My Back, supra* note 22.

107. *Id.* at 232.

108. *Id.* at 234.

109. Cf. Spelman, *supra* note 25, at 167 (describing the phrase "as a woman" as "the Trojan horse of feminist ethnocentrism, for its use typically makes it look as if one can neatly isolate one's gender from one's race or class").

110. *See, e.g.,* Zora Neale Hurston, *Their Eyes Were Watching God* (1937) (protagonist Janie slowly creates herself out of the oppressions of gender and race); Toni Morrison, *Song of Solomon* (1977) (one of the strongest characters is a woman with no navel—a woman who has literally created herself); Shange, *supra* note 1, at 31, 34 (the "lady in red" daily creates herself as a bold, wild, sexy woman, then, in the morning, sends the man she's attracted home and becomes an "ordinary / brown / braided woman / with big legs & full lips / reglar"); Alice Walker, *The Color Purple* (1982) (two sisters, Celie and Nettie, construct healthy selves out of the potentially killing circumstance of being abused young black girls from a "broken home").

111. Feminist essentialism also strengthens the wall between the genders. The binary character of essentialism tends to make men into enemies, rather than beings who are also crippled by the dominant discourse, though in different ways. Cf. Joan C. Williams, "Deconstructing Gender," 87 Mich. L. Rev. 797, 841 (1989) "To break free of traditional gender ideology, we need at the simplest level to see how men nurture people and relationships and how women are competitive and powerful.").

112. In this sense, my point about feminist essentialism is analogous to the point

Joan Williams has made about the ideology of domesticity, a Victorian notion that some feminists have used to argue that women are "more nurturing than men ('focused on relationships'), less tied to the questionable virtues of capitalism, and ultimately more moral than men." Id. at 807 (note the resemblance to West's picture of the essential woman). Williams argues powerfully that this critique, though attractive because it seems less "strident" than traditional radical arguments, in the end leaves women open to the same old patterns of discrimination, only now justified by "choice." Id. at 801, 820–21.

113. Cynthia Ozick, "Literature and the Politics of Sex: A Dissent," in *Art & Ardor* 287 (1983).

114. At an international conference on women's history in 1986, a white feminist, in response to questions about why Western women's history is still white women's history, answered, "We have enough of a burden trying to get a feminist viewpoint across, why do we have to take on this extra burden?" Spelman, *supra* note 25, at 8.

115. Moreover, essentialism is built into the structure of academia. There are "black studies" and "women's studies" departments, but no departments of "gender and ethnicity" or "race and gender studies."

116. Minnie Bruce Pratt, "Identity: Skin Blood Heart," in Elly Bulkin, Minnie Bruce Pratt & Barbara Smith, *Yours in Struggle: Three Feminist Perspectives on Anti-Semitism and Racism* 9, 30 (1984).

117. But this peace is only temporary, for the divisions between women remain real even when suppressed: "The idea of 'common oppression' was a false and corrupt platform disguising and mystifying the true nature of women's varied and complex social reality. Women are divided by sexist attitudes, racism, class privilege, and a host of other prejudices. Sustained woman bonding can occur only when these divisions are confronted and the necessary steps are taken to eliminate them. Divisions will not be eliminated by wishful thinking or romantic reverie about common oppression despite the value of highlighting experiences all women share." hooks, Feminist Theory, *supra* note 22, at 44.

118. Martha Minow, "Feminist Reason: Getting It and Losing It," 38 J. *Legal Educ.* 47, 51 (1988); *see also* Martha Minow, "The Supreme Court 1986 Term—Foreword: Justice Engendered," 101 *Harv. L. Rev.* 10, 64–66 (1987) [hereinafter Minow, "Justice Engendered"]. Minow also suggests that gender essentialism is part of our early childhood experience and thus is built into our psyches. Her reference on this point, however, is to Chodorow's work, which, as Minow concedes, "underplays the significance of early formation of racial, religious, and national identities, which are layered into the psychodynamic process of individuation with perhaps as much power as gender identities." Minow, "Feminist Reason: Getting It and Losing It," *supra*, at 52 n.23.

119. *See* Spelman, *supra* note 25, at 2 (footnote omitted) (using the metaphor of the multiplicity of pebbles on a beach).

120. *See, e.g.,* Littleton, *supra* note 24, at 753 n.11 (rejecting "uncritical pluralism"); *see also* Elly Bulkin, "Hard Ground: Jewish Identity, Racism, and Anti-Semitism," in

Bulkin, Pratt & Smith, *supra* note 116, at 89, 99 (noting the danger of " 'hunkering down in one's oppression,' refusing to look beyond one's identity as an oppressed person").

121. Spelman, *supra* note 25, at 15.

122. *See* id.; Seyla Benhabib & Drucilla Cornell, "Introduction: Beyond the Politics of Gender," in *Feminism as Critique, supra* note 103, at 1, 13; Fraser & Nicholson, *supra* note 104, at 97; Mary E. Hawkesworth, "Knowers, Knowing, Known: Feminist Theory and Claims of Truth," 14 *Signs* 533, 537 (1989).

123. *See* J. M. Balkin, "Deconstructive Practice and Legal Theory," 96 *Yale L.J.* 743, 753 (1987) ("The history of ideas, then, is not the history of individual conceptions, but of favored conceptions held in opposition to disfavored conceptions."); *see also* George Lakoff & Mark Johnson, *Metaphors We Live By* 14–19 (1980) (discussing the concepts underlying binary spatial metaphors such as "good is up" and "bad is down"); Lorde, *supra* note 18, at 114 ("Much of Western European history conditions us to see human differences in simplistic opposition to each other: dominant/subordinate, good/bad, up/down, superior/inferior.").

124. Lorde, *supra* note 18, at 122.

125. Hooks, *Talking Back, supra* note 22, at 11–12.

126. Patricia Williams, "On Being the Object of Property," 14 *Signs* 5 (1988).

127. Id. at 5.

128. Id. at 6–7.

129. Id. at 6.

130. Id.

131. Id. at 11.

132. Id. at 10.

133. Id. at 24.

134. Id. at 22.

135. Donna Haraway, "A Manifesto for Cyborgs: Science, Technology, and Socialist Feminism in the 1980s," 15 *Socialist Rev.* 65 (1985) (arguing that postmodernist theorists [who reject the idea of a "self" altogether, preferring to speak instead of multiple "subject positions"] offer feminists the chance to abandon the dream of a common language and the power games of guilt and innocence in favor of "a powerful infidel heteroglossia"). Haraway's symbol for this alternate path is the cyborg, a being that transgresses the familiar boundaries of nature vs. culture, animate vs. inanimate, and born vs. made. She suggests that " 'women of color' might be understood as a cyborg identity, a potent subjectivity synthesized from fusions of outsider identities," and that the writings of women of color are a tool for subverting Western culture without falling under its spell. Id. at 93–94.

136. Minow, "Justice Engendered," *supra* note 118, at 34–38.

137. Zora Neale Hurston, "How It Feels to Be Colored Me," in *I Love Myself When I Am Laughing . . . And Then Again When I Am Looking Mean and Impressive* 152 (Alice Walker ed., 1979).

138. Id. at 153.

139. *Id.* at 154.

140. *Id.*

141. *Id.*

142. Zora Hurston, "What White Publishers Won't Print," in *I Love Myself When I Am Laughing . . . And Then Again When I Am Looking Mean and Impressive, supra* note 137, at 169.

143. *Id.* at 72.

144. As Barbara Johnson perceptively notes:

> In the first [essay], Hurston can proclaim "I am this"; but when the image is repeated as "you are that," it changes completely. The content of the image may be the same, but its interpersonal use is different. The study of Afro-American literature as a whole poses a similar problem of address: any attempt to lift out of a text an image or essence of blackness is bound to violate the interlocutionary strategy of its formulation.

Barbara Johnson, "Thresholds of Difference: Structures of Address in Zora Neale Hurston," in *"Race," Writing, and Difference, supra* note 12, at 322–23.

145. *See* Barbara Smith & Beverly Smith, "Across the Kichen Table: A Sister-to-Sister Dialogue," in *This Bridge Called My Back, supra* note 22, at 113, 119 (two sisters discuss the black selves they miss when they are with white women: "Because the way you act with Black people is because they inspire the behavior. And I *do* mean inspire.").

146. Johnson, *supra* note 144, at 323–24.

147. bell hooks makes a related point about the self's relationality:

> Discarding the notion that the self exists in opposition to an other that must be destroyed, annihilated (for when I left the segregated world of home and moved in and among white people, and their ways of knowing, I learned this way of understanding the social construction of self), I evoked the way of knowing I had learned from unschooled southern black folks. We learned that the self existed in relation, was dependent for its very being on the lives and experiences of everyone, the self not as signifier of one "I" but the coming together of many "I"s, the self as embodying collective reality past and present, family and community.

hooks, *Talking Back, supra* note 22, at 30–31.

148. Thus Joan Williams argues that feminism must move away from "the destructive battle between 'sameness' and 'difference' toward a deeper understanding of gender as a system of power relations." Williams, *supra* note 111, at 836. In her view, gender must be "deconstructed." *See id.* at 841, quoted in note 111, *supra*. The deconstruction approach would make clear the payoff of feminism for men as well as women. This change will also encourage women of color to identify themselves as feminists. *See* hooks, *Feminist Theory, supra* note 22, at 70 ("Many black women refused participation in the feminist movement because they felt an anti-male stance was not a sound basis for action.").

149. *See* hooks, *Feminist Theory, supra* note 22, at 31 ("Focus on social equality with men as a definition of feminism led to an emphasis on discrimination, male attitudes, and legalistic reforms. Feminism as a movement to end sexist oppression directs our

attention to systems of domination and the inter-relatedness of sex, race, and class oppression").

Elizabeth Spelman suggests that feminism be expanded by conceiving of not just two genders, but many—a function of race and class as well as sex. Spelman, *supra* note 25, at 174–77.

150. *See* note 53 *supra* and accompanying text.

151. Toni Morrison, *Sula* 52 (1974).

152. As Andrew Ross has noted, even the female "collaborators" MacKinnon attacks with fury are seen as stupid, not as wrong or evil. Andrew Ross, "Without Pleasure," 1 *Yale J.L. & Human.* 193, 200 (1989).

153. West *supra* note 95, at 143.

154. hooks, *Feminist Theory, supra* note 22, at 45.

155. Hurston, *supra* note 137, at 155.

156. *Id.*

157. As Gramsci points out, hegemony consists of two strands: "1. the 'spontaneous' consent given by the great masses of the population [and] 2. the apparatus of state coercive power which 'legally' enforces discipline on those groups who do not 'consent' either actively or passively." Antonio Gramsci, *Selections from the Prison Notebooks* 12 (Q. Hoare & G. Smith trans., 1971). Consent, however, is not liberal consent, freely given, but "a 'contradictory consciousness' mixing approbation and apathy, resistance and resignation." T. J. Jackson Lears, "The Concept of Cultural Hegemony: Problems and Possibilities," 90 *Am. Hist. Rev.* 567, 570 (1985).

158. For example, during slavery,

> [w]hite women performed acts of violence against Black slave women with whom their husbands had sexual relations. Often these racist acts were shaped by feelings of sexual jealousy rooted in and sustained by sexism: for such jealousy is a function of the sexism that makes the "proper" attention of her husband a condition of a woman's sense of self-worth.

Spelman, *supra* note 25, at 106 (footnotes omitted); *see also* hooks, *Feminist Theory, supra* note 22, at 49 ("Historically, many black women experienced white women as the white supremacist group who most directly exercised power over them, often in a manner far more brutal and dehumanizing than that of racist white men.").

159. MacKinnon, for example, points out that her dominance approach is based on a reality that includes

> not only the extent and intractability of sex segregation into poverty, which has been known before, but the range of issues termed violence against women, which has not been. It combines women's material desperation, through being relegated to categories of jobs that pay nil, with the massive amount of rape and attempted rape—44 percent of all women—about which virtually nothing is done; the sexual assault of children—38 percent of girls and 10 percent of boys—which is apparently endemic to the patriarchal family; the battery of women that is systematic in one quarter to one third of our homes; prostitution, women's fundamental economic condition, what

we do when all else fails, and for many women in this country, all else fails often; and pornography, an industry that traffics in female flesh, making sex inequality into sex to the tune of eight billion dollars a year in profits largely to organized crime.

MacKinnon, *supra* note 44, at 41 (footnotes omitted).

160. Williams, *supra* note 111, at 829 (analyzing how women use women's culture against themselves, "as they do every time a woman 'chooses' to subordinate her career for the good of the family and congratulates herself on that choice as a mature assessment of her own 'priorities'").

Black women have often actively embraced patriarchal stereotypes in the name of racial solidarity. *See* Giddings, *supra* note 21, at 322–23 (discussing women's concessions to male chauvinism in the civil rights movement of the 1960s); Lorde, *supra* note 18, at 119–21 (discussing refusal to confront sexism and homophobia within the black community).

161. *See* Morrison, *supra* note 83, at 273 ("[M]e and you, we got more yesterday than anybody. We need some kind of tomorrow.").

162. As Bernice Johnson Reagon has written:

> Coalition work is not work done in your home. Coalition work has to be done in the streets. And it is some of the most dangerous work you can do. And you shouldn't look for comfort. Some people will come to a coalition and they rate the success of the coalition on whether or not they feel good when they get there. They're not looking for a coalition; they're looking for a home! They're looking for a bottle with some milk in it and a nipple, which does not happen in a coalition. You don't get a lot of food in a coalition. You don't get fed in a coalition. In a coalition you have to give, and it is different from your home. You can't stay there all the time. You go to the coalition for a few hours and then you go back and take your bottle wherever it is, and then you go back and coalesce some more.

Bernice Johnson Reagon, "Coalition Politics: Turning the Century," in *Home Girls: A Black Feminist Anthology* 359 (B. Smith ed., 1983).

163. Smith & Smith, *supra* note 145, at 126.

164. Matsuda, *supra* note 13, at 9.

165. *See, e.g.*, Patricia J. Williams, "Alchemical Notes: Reconstructing Ideals From Deconstructed Rights," 22 *Harv. C.R.-C.L. L. Rev.* 401 (1987); Williams, *supra* note 126, at 5.

166. Williams, *supra* note 126, at 24.

PRESENCE OF MIND IN THE ABSENCE
OF BODY

Linda Brodkey and Michelle Fine

▼

We commonly tell stories about what happens to us and what we make of our experience. In a sense, then, the stories documenting our lives tell what we find worth remembering and contemplating and sharing with others. It is of course the "others" who complicate the telling of stories, for stories are not usually told to ourselves alone, but to those we hope will understand our construction of events. The stories included in this essay concern the sexual harassment of students by professors. We have tried to reconstruct the historical and institutional circumstances of telling along with the stories told because the transformative potential of the narratives cannot be understood apart from the context in which they were written and read.[1] The sexual harassment narratives were written by undergraduate and graduate women at the University of Pennsylvania in response to an open-ended question on the Penn Harassment Survey.[2]

These students are of the generation of women for many of whom, as Annette Kolodny recently put it, "feminism is either outdated—because of the naive belief that 'there aren't any problems any more'—or a distorted melange of media images and Reagan-era backlash."[3] For some of them, Kolodny adds, "feminism is both personal and problematic" because their mothers "tried to reject traditional family roles in a society that offered their offspring no compensating structures and amid a movement too new to prepare us all for the consequences of such radical change."[4] Yet the women who wrote these narratives know what sexual harassment is. Their narratives confirm the findings of survey research on college and university campuses: women students are routinely harassed; postsecondary institutions have been egregiously hesitant to address harassment (much less write, publish, and enforce sexual harassment policies); and remedies for reporting and grieving sexual harassment favor, if not harassers, their institutions.[5] After reading and reflecting on these narratives, we have come to believe that the future of academic feminism is activism and that activism begins in pedagogy.

The narratives clarify the findings of the Penn survey, namely, that women are reluctant to report sexual harassment and reticent when they do tell because they suspect that institutional indifference will lead to reprisals of one sort or another. We think their fears are justified and in turn warrant feminist curriculum intervention. What we have learned from women's narratives of their experiences of harassment, however, suggests that we will need to encourage all students and women in particular to explore not so much the fact but the complexities of harassment. After all, harassment sits at the nexus of gender, power, and sexuality in the academy—as it does in all institutions. Exploring it will take the students and us far outside the boundaries of legal definitions and institutional remedies. It will even take us outside of current feminist analyses of gender and sexuality, for most women students judge sexual harassment to be beyond the reach of law and feminism.

To teach this new generation is to try to understand that they encounter sexual harassment as women whose civil rights have been guaranteed since birth, and hence as women who have believed themselves to be protected by those laws and have only recently found that they are not. And to work with these women is also to realize that even as their narratives reveal the partiality of their visions of gender and sexuality, they critique the partiality of our more seasoned feminist analyses of gender inequity and sexual violence. We are arguing for feminist pedagogies to accompany what Donna Haraway calls "situated and embodied knowledges," the partiality and plurality of which contest "various forms of unlocatable, and so irresponsible, knowledge claims."[6] Partial perspectives exert a sobering influence on feminist pedagogies, privileging self-conscious acts of critical vision and imagination that are openly hostile to the already established vantage points of either relativism or totalization, which Haraway sees as "promising vision from everywhere and nowhere."[7] Yet she is also suspicious of all "innocent" positions, including what can be seen from the vantage points of subjugation, and offers positioning as a responsible political and epistemological feminist practice for continuing the conversation on gender already in progress in the academy. The pedagogical and political project then is to interrogate the ways in which the sexual harassment narratives undermine the transformative potential of narration by effectively withdrawing their narrators from the conversation we had hoped they would enter.

Telling It Like It Is/Was and Like It Isn't/Wasn't

Given that the Penn Harassment Survey focused primarily on sexual harassment, and given the demographics of students at Penn, the narratives written by undergraduate and graduate women raise almost exclusively the concerns of white women from the middle and upper social classes. Yet their narratives confirm the findings of other campus surveys and hence frustrate any hopes we may have had that knowledge of civil rights defends women against their harassers. Of particular concern here are the narratives written in response to Question 21:

> It would be helpful to us if you would describe this experience in detail. Please do so omitting any incriminating information (e.g., names, courses, etc.). You may include a separate piece of paper if necessary.

Ignoring for the moment the likelihood that the proviso to omit incriminating information may have also discouraged many women students from including details of any kind and the fact that the quarter-inch allotted for response was inadequate, we offer the narrative below as typical, inasmuch as the woman provides a markedly attenuated description of the event itself relative to the elaborate explanation of both her professor's behavior and her decision not to report him.

> When the incident happened, his attention lasted about one month. It did not occur to me that it was "sexual harassment" per se because I don't tend to think in terms of deviant behavior.
>
> I perceived a troubled man experiencing a mid-life crisis—and more important—a colleague with whom I genuinely shared intellectual commitments and interests. Unfortunately he saw a young, bright cutsie who could help him with his work and who could potentially serve as an escape route from his unsatisfactory marriage. Basically, all I had to do was make my "No" repetitive and very clear, but the situation was so muddied and in many ways, not so cut and dried as "sexual harassment." Things occurred on a very subtle level and are not reported for this reason. All professors have to say is "She's unstable, paranoid, imagining things or lying, etc." Graduate women don't have a leg to stand on.[8]

Many statements in this account warrant commentary. She refers to "the incident" but never describes what her professor actually did. We're not then certain if she considers the "attentions that lasted about one month" sexual harassment and hence "deviant behavior" or if, as she later asserts, "the situation was so muddied and in many ways, not so cut and dried as 'sexual harassment.'" She contrasts her complex view of him ("I perceived a troubled man experiencing a mid-life crisis—and more important—a colleague with whom I genuinely shared intellectual commitments and interests") with his simple view of her ("Unfortunately, he saw a young, bright cutsie who could help him with his work"). Here lies her conflict. And it matters because she has located the danger in his gendering of her, that is, in being turned into a woman. For she goes on to explain that his professional abuse is but a preface to an attempt to transform her into a woman whose body "could potentially serve as an escape route from his unsatisfactory marriage." She tells us that she dealt with her harasser as one might a perverse child—"Basically, all I had to do was make my 'No' repetitive and very clear"—and then explains that she and all the others have no other recourse, since "all professors have to say is 'She's unstable, paranoid, imagining things or lying, etc.'" And her last words, "Graduate women don't have a leg to stand on," summarize both her own situation and her position on the gendering of women by their male professors.

Leaving Your Body to Science

We have a good deal of sympathy for this graduate woman's rendering of the academic world she inhabits, where her experience of gender has been reduced to slut and madwoman. While we delight in her refusal to take her professor's extracurricular forced-choice exam, we are, nonetheless, troubled by the argument that she and other women students use to represent their strategies for resisting harassers, for it certainly looks as if their practice is to transcend their bodies and deny that women students are women. We say this because of the stunning regularity with which women students position themselves in their narratives as disinterested bystanders who have witnessed rather than experienced sexual harassment and who have been asked not to describe what happened to them, but to explain why professors harass their women students.

> This behavior increases when his wife leaves town, if we are in a situation involving liquor or if we are in the presence of other individuals who find this behavior entertaining.[9]

> Male faculty in a department in which I conduct research make suggestive comments, joke and tease most of the time. There are no female faculty members of the department and my assumption has always been that they were simply unaware of how their behavior was affecting the females who are associated in this department.[10]

> He was drunk which I'm sure contributed to the problem.[11]

What troubles us about the women's explanations of the extenuating circumstances surrounding acts of harassment is the extent to which each has positioned herself as a narrator who, because she has personally transcended the experience, is "free" to evaluate her harasser's behavior from the vantage point of an expert witness. She does this by assuming a clinical posture with respect to sexual harassment, treating the event as a mere symptom of a disease she must diagnose. Instead of a personal narrative recounting her own anger, sorrow, pain, or even pleasure, she impersonally catalogues his motives: he drinks; his wife is out of town; his colleagues egg him on; he's socially maladroit; he's old; he doesn't know any better. She's taking good care of him. That wouldn't concern us all that much except that the narrative positions women assign themselves suggest that they understand their own survival to depend on the ability to cleave their minds from their bodies. This mind/body split reproduces in each of them the very cultural ideology that has historically been used to distinguish men from women and justify gender oppression. By severing mind from body and then privileging the "mind's" dispassionate, even clinical, explanation of events, each woman materially reproduces in her narrative the very discursive dichotomies that have historically been used to define a seemingly endless string of culturally positive terms (male/mind/reason/culture) in contrast to a negative string (female/body/intuition/nature) [12]

We take such representations of self as mind by women students as pleas to be seen by professors as not women. In poststructural terms, the women attempt to achieve unity and coherence as writers in an academic discourse, often called science, that has in recent history offered a few privileged white males the comforting belief that they and they alone legislate reality. These men reside in a world in which "mind over matter" means that what counts is what each individual man can know, understand, and represent as empirical. While poststructural theories argue convincingly that the unity afforded our divided sense of ourselves as discursive subjects is an illusion,[13] we are presumably most attracted to discourses that promise to represent us to ourselves and others as empowered subjects—as the agents who speak the discourse rather than the objectified subjects of which it speaks. For many faculty and students, scientific discourse regulates academic speech and writing. And we think the women students are trying to reproduce a version of scientific discourse by positioning themselves as narrators who, having transcended their bodies, are then entitled to use their dispassionate observations as the bases of their clinical explanations of men's motives and cynical speculations on institutional reprisals. What happened to their bodies (sexual harassment) is not problematic and hence plays little part in the narratives; why it happened (his motives) and what would happen (reprisals), however, remain problematic long after the event and hence the narratives tell the story of a torturous struggle to represent themselves as genderless.

We see each woman student as offering to pay an exorbitant, not to mention impossible, price for the coherent self represented in her narrative. In exchange for her "mind," she leaves her body to science. Such a strategy for resisting harassment, however, uncritically accepts the illusory coherence of scientific discourse and presumes that human subjectivity is essentially rather than multiply determined (overdetermined) in democratic societies. Yet there is overwhelming evidence in theory, research, and practice that mind, body, gender, and sexuality are not facts we must live with but social constructions we have learned to live by.

Learning to Stand Together

Our goal in this essay is to discern the potential for a liberatory pedagogy of political analysis in the sexual harassment narratives. We understand such inquiry to be transformative, that is, intellectual work in which students and teachers think in terms of both epistemology (ways of knowing the world) and activism (ways of acting in the world). To this end, we have found it useful to review the narratives first in light of feminist standpoint theory,[14] and then in light of critical pedagogy[15] calling for educational projects of possibility that pose teachers and students as intellectual and political agents.

In Money, Sex, and Power, Nancy Hartsock argues that because women experience themselves as continuous with the world and men experience themselves as discontinuous with the world, they stand in materially different relationships with themselves, other people, and the world of objects. Thus, women and men view the world from entirely different and indeed opposing standpoints. Hartsock traces the construction of these opposing and gendered epistemologies to early childhood experiences of body and boundary as described in the work of Nancy Chodorow, reasoning that girls, "because of female parenting, are less differentiated from others than boys, more continuous with and related to the external object world."[16] Such a division of labor in parenting, argues Hartsock, means that "girls can identify with a concrete example present in daily life" while "boys must identify with an abstract set of maxims only occasionally present in the form of the father."[17] Relationality is particularly useful in explaining how women reason from experience. And it is plausible to conclude, as Hartsock has, that designating women as the primary caretakers of children results in gender-differentiated epistemologies, in which even harassed women would tend to see, create, and value relationality.

While Hartsock's notions inform us about what women might have been trying to do in their narratives, the idea that a single feminist standpoint could account for all women is not plausible. It obscures the complexity and diminishes the importance of differences, such as race and class, in women's lives. Further, the theory does not address the extent to which personal development through "object relations" is confounded by the cultural hegemony that affects the way women think about, talk about, and organize against harassment in the academy. In other words, the struggle toward standpoint cannot be abstracted from the struggle against the distractions and attractions of dominant ideology.[18] It is, after all, inside an academic hierarchy of asymmetrical relations between students and teachers that women students answered Question 21 like "good" students, thereby representing their personal experience of sexual harassment in the same disinterested terminology used in the survey.

Saturating standpoint theory with the understanding that cultural hegemony is also determining, we are better able to understand how women students might have independently arrived at similar political stances in their narratives of sexual harassment. Instead of describing what happened, their narratives try to explain what happened by imagining what might have motivated their harassers and what might have happened had they reported the harassment. A standpoint of relationality may account for the formal structure of the narratives, but the contents spell hegemony. The transcendent narrator is a standpoint from which a writer can relate the concerns of harasser and harassed alike. But the motives and reprisals women name come out of that dreary stockpile of conclusions/premises/arguments that individualism and proceduralism commonly use to explain why "you can't fight city hall" and why men can't be held accountable for harassment. The political potential of the standpoint of relationality as an activist epistemology is severely tested by the content of the sexual harassment narratives, inasmuch as it becomes clear that when women link the incident to men's motives and institutional reprisals, they are left standing alone and wishing they were not women. Their analysis of motives and reprisals leads them to believe that since men harass women for untold reasons, women who report harassment will be subjected to more of the same arbitrary treatment from the institution.

The dispassionate language in which graduate women speculate on institutional reprisals is academic and this strikes us as all the more eerie not only because it reproduces the mind/body split, but because their fears are far from academic. Consider, for instance, the way in which this student juxtaposes form and content in the following passage:

> I think female graduate students *probably* bear the brunt of sexual harassment at the University. Most of the guys who harass you or *just make life difficult* are your teachers and dissertation committee members. Graduate students here have no power. We're dependent on our departments for financial aid, and are afraid that these professors *could* black-ball us in our future careers. (emphasis ours) [19]

Because sexual harassment is woven into the very fabric of faculty-student relations, women do not as a matter of course appeal to legal remedies; institutional procedures only further jeopardize their professional lives. Student complaints about sexual harassment are not likely to be taken as seriously by their institution as allegations of capricious grading or irregular office hours. While the modulated phrasing may mean that women students are confronting irrational behavior from their professors by responding rationally, and relationally, this very act of using their heads effectively preempts these women's taking an activist stance.

Hartsock understands the epistemology of standpoint as liberatory: "Because of its achieved character and its liberatory potential, I use the term 'feminist' rather than 'women's standpoint.' Like the experiences of the proletariat, 'women's experience' and activity as a dominated group contains both negative and positive aspects. A feminist standpoint picks out and amplifies the liberatory possibilities contained in that experience." [20] We do not see relationality in the sexual harassment narratives as liberatory or even potentially so and think it could only become so if feminist educators were willing to work with students to imagine liberatory possibilities not raised when analysis fetishizes individual men's motives and institutional reprisals. In other words, we see relationality as an epistemology that helps to explain the reasoning of women students who experience inequity, bypass their outrage, and rationalize that the way it is is all there is.

A subjugated standpoint does not necessarily facilitate collective activism on behalf of women who, in the absence of support, have individually devised ad hoc strategies for deflecting harassment. With such strategies, a particular woman may be able to prevent or protect herself against individual acts of harassment. Such strategies, however, neither interrupt nor disrupt the material and ideological gender asymmetries organizing the academy. Such strategies do not call public attention to sexual harassment as simply the most overt and explicit of those practices reminding women that we are not card-carrying members (pun intended) of the academic club (and again).

What we've learned from reading these narratives is that if the women appear not to have said "what really happened," that was because we were only listening for the legal categories that "count" as sexual harassment:

that is, evidence of social transgressions that are specified by the Equal Employment Opportunity Commission (EEOC) guidelines and that can be documented empirically in terms that the court understands. The voices of women students in the sexual harassment narratives speak of a pervasive, routinized, and institutionalized sexual intimidation calling for a far more radical institutional project than heretofore suggested by either adversarial law or positioned feminism.

The violent behaviors that feminism and law bracket as sexual harassment and that institutions then treat as exceptional practices do not begin to capture the sense of danger lurking in the women's narratives. The unspoken oppression strikes us as all the more egregious when, as in the example below, her use of the language suggests she may also be a foreign student and thus even more vulnerable:

> I went to private office to visit this person. He greeted me at the door, closed the door and locked it. He leaned over me, standing very close and started unbuttoning my overcoat. I fumbled with coat buttons trying to make light of/ignore his behavior, and trying to dissipate his sexual attention. He helped me remove my hat, coat, scarf and hang them up. He took my hand and led me over to couch in office. We had often sat in that part of the office before to chat, with him on couch (often lounging) and me on chair facing him. He sat down on couch and pulled me by my hand to sit next to him. I pulled to try to sit in chair as per usual; he would not let go. He lay down on couch and pulled me down to sit next to him on edge of couch, near his hip level. He released my hand and I moved back to far end of couch. There were no chairs nearby. I could not move to sit elsewhere without drawing tremendous attention to my action: 1) I would be overtly rejecting him if he was seriously pursuing me sexually; 2) I would be quite rude if he then decided to pretend he had no sexual intentions. My first thought was not to provoke him since the door was locked and the office quite soundproof. He kept urging me to sit closer to him and I declined. He finally took my hand and pulled me, I resisted but moved closer as a last resort before an outright struggle and possible scream. He kept holding my hand. He then tried to pull me down on top of him, coaxing me verbally. I refused. I stayed upright and using as much strength as necessary and shook my head no, looking him straight in the eye. Luckily he wanted to seduce me, not assault me violently.[21]

Her narrative reminds us that even though legal categories account for his behavior, she appeals not to law but popular psychology to explain her professor's motives: "I felt that this incident was due more to an ego attack of older man (mid-60s) rather than the machinations of a sexual psychopath." If a stranger had attacked her on the street, no doubt she could have seen it as an assault. But she casts her professor's "strange" behavior in the most benign light possible—by comparing him to a psychopath—presumably so that she can imagine completing her studies:

> We have resumed our usual interactions. In this case, there was enough of a personal friendship to use as a basis to deal with the incident on a person-to-person way. Had that not been the case, however, I would have risked losing the support of an internationally renowned scholar with impressive professional contacts and influence. That's quite a bit of leverage to have over someone, isn't it? [22]

This narrative is unusual because its extensive analysis is grounded in a description of the event itself. To be sure, she offers the usual explanations of motives, but she elaborates the harassing incident in tandem with her many modes of resistance before stating her ambivalence about the institutional vulnerability of graduate student women.

When oppression is normalized, privatized, and rooted in a powerful and pervasive institutional ambivalence toward the oppressed, a woman student is more likely to pose and resolve the conflict in her narrative by glossing over the incident and concentrating on explanations:

> A mutual sexual attraction grew between myself and a professor. It was in part physical—in many settings and to people at large, the professor projects his sexuality—but was also based upon the discovery of shared values. This bond struck a chord with me, as I felt very lonely and isolated, for the usual—and institutionalized—reasons that graduate students feel this way. [23]

Her seeming calm is soon belied, however, by a catalogue of fears iterated in many of the narratives: "I shortly grew alarmed both at the power of my own feelings and the increasing power of the professor's feelings"; "Although I did not feel physically threatened—that seemed unlikely—I became afraid that he would begin to manipulate me by using the power of my own feelings and my need for him"; "This fear arose as I learned how he was irrationally competitive with us (graduate students)"; "I felt that I had lost both his respect and his important professional support"; "I knew if needed he would not 'go to bat' for me in the personally influential ways that professors have to work for their students." [24] In a later, more sustained passage, she explains why the fears that simmer internally are not to be expressed formally:

> It seemed impossible to resolve the situation by talking it over with him— the relationship always had an unspoken nature about it, and he very likely would have stonewalled me, making me feel totally responsible for what had happened. I did not feel that it would be helpful to speak to any other

faculty members given my own involvement and the provocative and controversial nature of a sexual and political relationship which is not even supposed to exist. I also feared discrediting myself and I felt that the faculty's personal loyalties rested with this professor.[25]

The women who wrote the narratives know they've been treated unfairly by their professors. And while they do not blame themselves, their reluctance to insist that professors are responsible leaves women students recognizing harassment but transfixed rather than transformed by their knowledge of oppression.[26] The fact that personal knowledge does not necessarily become grounds for political action is clear not only from the narratives, but from the survey. Even though 45 percent of graduate and professional women students reported some sexual harassment over the past five years, more than 80 percent handled it "by ignoring or going along with it or by avoiding contact with the offender." And, indeed, only between 0 percent and 6 percent of graduate students (depending on the type of harassment) report filing a formal grievance in response to an incident of harassment.[27]

Feminist interpretation means reading these stories as true but partial accounts of sexual harassment. But feminist pedagogy strives to recover the intellectual and creative energy dispersed when women try to transcend their bodies and find themselves standing alone against their harassers. This is a pedagogy that would transform that wasted individual energy into a collective desire to identify and examine the institutional practices that succor sexual harassment and begin to institute counterpractices that do not. The possibilities for pedagogy in the next section arise out of our analysis of the narratives and pose a feminist project in terms of transforming the scene of institutional harassment so that women in the academy are free to study and teach with our bodies and minds intact.

Learning How to Speak in the Academy

In this section we set out to amplify in pedagogy some political projects that we now think may have been attenuated in the sexual harassment narratives. We do this realizing that the survey itself may have encouraged harassed women to resolve prematurely the tensions and complexities their narratives posed. The designers of the survey had hoped that open-ended questions would offer women students an opportunity for both critique and empowerment. Instead, women respondents commonly took this opportunity to consolidate experiences about which they were seemingly quite ambivalent and effectively returned all responsibility for advocacy to the committee. At least this is how we have come to understand the lengths some women went to in thanking the committee:

> Thanks for your concern over this issue. I realize that I was less than responsible to my fellow students for not pursuing a formal "complaint" but I'm glad to help with the survey.[28]

> I do appreciate being able to tell someone about this who will take this information seriously.[29]

> I thank you for conducting this questionnaire. I hope you publish the results and information on the procedure for reporting situations.[30]

> Thanks for listening![31]

We take seriously Giroux's reminder that "oppositional political projects should be the object of constant debate and analysis."[32] We recommend basing the curriculum on a negative critique of these and/or other individualistic and futile attempts to interrogate or interrupt forms of institutional oppression organized around gender, race, and social class. Central to this project is the demystification of institutional policies and practices that cloak social inequities. We need to engage young women and men in exploring how our analyses of the causes and consequences of social inequities construct not only our understandings of the present, but our images of what is possible in the near or far future. Unable to imagine institutional change, the women who wrote the usual harassment narratives default to reworking relationships with faculty, or, even more consequentially, to reworking or denying their bodies.

Feminist pedagogy begins by animating the policies and procedures that contribute to harassment. The faceless image of authority sustains the illusion that institutions are immutable and hence oppression inevitable. This is the illusion feminists must first seek to dispel if we hope to enable young women and men to see oppression as mutable through critical and collective reflection and action. A pedagogy intentionally remote from political activism incidentally fosters the very alienation, individualism, and cynicism we confronted in these narratives. We were heartened to find young women who grew up in the wake of civil rights legislation and witnessed the victories and losses of the feminism movement in the courts and state legislatures struggling against harassment. Their collective narrative, however, is a story of despair, for each woman encounters the lechery of professors alone, with little hope that law can, or that the institution will, intercede on her behalf. And so she tries to rise above the scene of harassment in narratives reminding us that the halls of academe are littered with the bodies women students leave hostage in their flight from professorial treachery.

We could set an intellectual and political process in motion by asking students to imagine how a series of university representatives might respond to the narratives. What would the university counsel, the lawyer whose job it is to subvert grievances and suits against the institution, make of a narrative about the institutional threat of violence rather than an actual act of violence? How might the director of the Women's Center respond? Or a feminist professor? A nonfeminist professor? A faculty member who has been or thinks he may be named in a sexual harassment suit? The editor of the student newspaper or the alumni magazine? And what about the dean of the school? The man or woman chairing the department? The president of the university? The president of student government or the faculty senate? The counseling staff? What changes if we know that the narrator is white, black, straight, gay? The harasser white, black, straight, gay? While the list is far from complete, it points out that since institutions speak not one but several "languages," students need to apprise themselves of the range of "dialects" represented in their university.

At any given moment in its history, the representatives of a university will be unevenly committed to preserving the status quo, which means that the possibilities for political change are always contingent on revealing heterogeneity within what only appears to be a single voice to outsiders. While it is nearly always the case that the university lawyer will not hear such a narrative, the other representatives are not nearly so predictable in their responses. The related narrative task suggested by the first is, of course, revision. Having imagined what university representatives might do with the narrative as written, how might a particular narrative be rewritten to secure a hearing from each of the representatives? We are not suggesting an exercise in writing for audiences, but recommending that students do this kind of imaginative work before they meet and interview representatives concerning their jobs and their positions on harassment of women and minority constituencies on campus. This collaborative work requires students to take careful notes, report back to peers and faculty, and compare findings and impressions; they should do this before making any decisions about who and what to write, and before making plans for more sustained collective action. We see what can be learned from representatives of the institution as a first lesson in understanding how power is or is not dispersed locally and as a first step toward interrupting the illusion that institutional authority is literally anonymous.

What happens next is of course contingent on what students and teachers are willing to deem appropriate under the circumstances. Students might go on to write a white paper on the status of women students on their campus, a series of articles for the student or a city newspaper, a pamphlet for entering students and their parents, a broadside for students, faculty, and staff. Or they might decide that their preliminary research warrants additional studies of the institution and its relations with students on a number of issues that include but are not bounded by sexual harassment. The point is that it would be pedagogically irresponsible to set up an intellectual exploration such as we are suggesting and assume that students will have succeeded only if they reproduce familiar feminist analyses, that is, execute what we have already conceptualized. There is no feminist standpoint they must find. There is instead a feminist project, struggling to find the crevices in the institutional facade that glosses over oppression of students, staff, and faculty across lines of race, class, and gender.

The unevenness of institutional commitment to the status quo does not mean that any particular strategy meant to engage university representatives in a conversation will result in desired/desirable political change. We have only to review the recent political successes of the New Right in the academy and elsewhere to realize that heterogeneity is itself no guarantee that discussions will move administrations to more progressive policies. While speaking is certainly a form of action, institutional representatives often understand talk as a way of appeasing and defusing student, faculty, and staff activists. Students as well as educators need to bear in mind that talking and writing to representatives may not be enough unless they are also willing to enlist support from institutions that are (or have representatives who are) interested in their university. Included among the possibilities are: the press, professional organizations, legislators, community activists committed to gender and race equity, alumni, well-known political "radicals" willing to visit campus and speak out for students, and parents who thought that education would support, not undermine, their children. While political networking is as difficult to learn as to maintain, such a network is critical both as a lever for starting conversation inside the institution and as an alternative if or once a conversation breaks down. Outside the boundaries arbitrarily set by the academy, moreover, young women and men are sometimes better positioned to notice and interrupt the institution's version of reality and protectionism, and so better positioned to represent themselves as informed and critical agents of change.

Learning What to Do When Talk Is Just Talk

Women have been known to contemplate and even commit outrageous acts when conversation fails. The most dramatic example we know of happened at the University of Pennsylvania in the early 1980s. Once a week, with great regularity, the campus was secretly decorated with photographs of prominent male faculty, whose pictures were captioned "Wanted for Crimes Against Women" and signed by "The Women's Army." Along with others, we presumed this to be the work of a small group of undergraduate women, who, distressed that conversation with the provost, university government, and individual faculty failed to draw sufficient attention to problems of sexual harassment, resorted to extraordinary methods for naming the problem.

University officials and many faculty were alarmed that the "Women's Army" was irresponsibly accusing men. Which it was. Yet we also read these actions as evidence of the women's despair over adamant institutional refusal to listen and act. At the time Penn had an elaborate set of mechanisms for voicing student dissent, but "listening" was revealed as a way to appropriate such dissent, that is, to appease "angry young women." We have heard that at some other institutions, young women on campus welcome parents on Parents Day with the gruesome statistics of the likelihood that their daughter will be harassed and/or raped during her four years at college.

We are not recommending these strategies. They are not attempts to alter the conditions of women's lives. They are the voices of despair that institutional indifference provokes. People have been known, however, to throw caution to the wind when institutions refuse to talk, or when they intentionally set out to confound by offering talk in lieu of action. Women are particularly vulnerable once engaged in conversation, since the willingness to talk is considered the most important evidence of growing trust and cooperation. And most of us, needless to say, find it excruciatingly difficult to "go public" even when it becomes evident that the official conversation is fruitless.

While the work of the "Women's Army" and their sisters elsewhere does not provide models of political projects aimed toward transformation, the outrageous is nonetheless of untold pedagogical value. Worst-case scenarios stretch the sense of possibility even as they terrorize the imagination. Images of the "irrational strategies" we may want to avoid help us to imagine how to insist that institutions take seriously their conversations with women.

Feminist Archives for Intellectual Activism

The analysis suggests the need for an archive of feminist intellectual activism to chronicle the varied ways of identifying, analyzing, interrupting, and, under exceptionally perverse circumstances, disrupting gender-based power asymmetries in the academy. Feminist activism must reposition itself inside a larger politics of solidarity with "other self-conscious political projects,"[33] which at the very least would also include struggles around race/ethnicity, class, disability, and sexual orientation. Such an archive could already be stocked with: reports of the reemergence of women's consciousness-raising groups on campus; core curricula that mainstream feminist, African-Americanist, and Third World scholarship (and organized efforts to marginalize or eliminate them); charters for establishing women's centers; arguments for developing gay men's and lesbian women's studies programs; policies of professional organizations that monitor the use of sexist language in presentations and publications (Conference on College Composition and Communication); or the presence of African-American studies and women's studies courses within accredited programs (American Psychological Association). As impressive as we find this list, the narratives caution us that far more is needed. This new generation of women is equipped with a striking sense of entitlement and yet beset by fears that their female bodies are liabilities, their minds male, their professors likely to corrupt their intellectual relationships, and their legal rights hollow. We can't anticipate what they will contribute to either the archive or the struggle, but social history assures us that it will not be precisely what we contributed. After all, they inherited rather than advocated for the gains of the 1970s, yet they share the threat of stunning disappointments in the 1980s and 1990s.

Perhaps the lesson we most need to learn is that it is as important for students as it is for teachers to become researchers—students as well as teachers are intellectuals and need to see themselves as informed political agents. We have learned that teachers and students need to collaborate critically across generations, histories, life circumstances, and politics to create curricula and pedagogies that seek to transform institutions not by reproducing or resisting the practices of oppression, but by confronting the institution on intellectual grounds. Only thus can we imagine a context in which every woman's story could realize its full liberatory potential, and no woman would decline to tell her story because "Any information would be incriminating."[34]

Notes

Originally published in 170.3 *Journal of Education* 3 (1988); reprinted by permission.

1. We take this opportunity to thank the Quad Women's Group, the undergraduate women at Penn who in the four years we met with them weekly surprised and delighted us with stories of their lives as students, daughters, lovers, and friends. This essay is infused with dreams, desires, and fears that materialized in those sessions and

emerge here in our own academic dream of a story in which women stand together in their struggle to reclaim the bodies that accompany their minds.

2. John de Cani et al., "Report of the Committee to Survey Harassment at the University of Pennsylvania," 32 *Almanac*, Sept. 24, 1985, ii–xii. The Penn Harassment Survey was sent to students, faculty, and staff in March of 1985. The committee reported that 1,065 of the 2,251 usable questionnaires included answers to open-ended questions. Concerning undergraduate and graduate women's responses to the open-ended question asking them to describe an experience of harassment, 37 of the 66 undergraduate responses reported harassment by either professors or teaching assistants, and 44 of the 68 graduate responses concerned professors. While we did not include their narratives in this essay, readers will be interested to learn that of the 36 untenured women faculty at Penn who wrote about harassment, 17 reported being harassed by faculty (13 of whom were senior) and 1 by her dean; that 12 of 20 responses from tenured women faculty definitely concerned another faculty member (including 2 department chairs); and that 18 of the 32 women staff who responded reported being harassed by either their supervisors or faculty. Id. at ix–x. That any woman at Penn is potentially subject to harassment, regardless of status, reminds us that some men violate women's civil rights as a matter of course and that they do so with relative impunity inside the academy.

3. Annette Kolodny, "Dancing Between Left and Right: Feminism and the Academic Minefield in the 1980s," 14 *Feminist Studies* 453, 461 (1988).

4. Id.

5. Claire Robertson et al., "Campus Harassment: Sexual Harassment Policies and Procedures at Institutions of Higher Learning," 13 *Signs* 792 (1988).

6. Donna Haraway, "Situated Knowledges: The Science Question in Feminism and the Privilege of Partial Perspective," 14 *Feminist Studies* 575, 583 (1988).

7. Id. at 584.

8. de Cani et al., *supra* note 2, at File 403-31.

9. Id. at File 947-81.

10. Id. at File 431-61.

11. Id. at File 344-51.

12. *See, e.g.,* Cora Kaplan, *Sea Changes: Essays on Culture and Feminism* (1986).

13. *E.g.,* Catherine Belsey, *Critical Practice* (1980); Linda Brodkey, "On the Subjects of Class and Gender in 'The Literacy Letters,'" in 51(2) *College English* 125, 125–41 (1989).

14. *E.g.,* Nancy Hartsock, *Money, Sex, and Power: Toward a Feminist Historical Materialism* (1985).

15. *E.g.,* Henry A. Giroux, *Schooling and the Struggle for Public Life: Critical Pedagogy in the Modern Age* (1988).

16. Nancy Chodorow, *The Reproduction of Mothering: Psychoanalysis and the Sociology of Gender*, 238 (1978).

17. Id.

18. Antonio Gramsci, *Selections from the Prison Notebooks of Antonio Gramsci* (1971).

19. de Cani et al., *supra* note 2, at File 344-51.

20. Hartsock, *supra* note 14, at 232.

21. de Cani et al., *supra* note 2, at File 1974-31.

22. Id.

23. Id. at File 1851-31.

24. Id.

25. Id.

26. Michelle Fine, "Contextualizing the Study of Social Injustice," in 3 *Advances in Applied Social Psychology* 403, 403–31 (M. Saxe & L. Saxe eds., 1986).

27. de Cani et al., *supra* note 2, at viii.

28. Id., at 1799-11.

29. Id. at File 1841-31.

30. Id. at File 1486-11.

31. Id. at File 1418-31.

32. Giroux, *supra* note 15, at 69.

33. Sandra G. Harding, *The Science Question in Feminism* 163 (1988).

34. de Cani et al., *supra* note 2, at File 2174-C31.

PORNOGRAPHY AND CANONICITY

The Case of Yeats's "Leda and the Swan"

Elizabeth Butler Cullingford

∇

Leda and the Swan

A sudden blow: the great wings beating still
Above the staggering girl, her thighs caressed
By the dark webs, her nape caught in his bill,
He holds her helpless breast upon his breast.

How can those terrified vague fingers push
The feathered glory from her loosening thighs?
And how can body, laid in that white rush,
But feel the strange heart beating where it lies?

A shudder in the loins engenders there
The broken wall, the burning roof and tower
And Agamemnon dead.

       Being so caught up,
So mastered by the brute blood of the air,
Did she put on his knowledge with his power
Before the indifferent beak could let her drop?
—W. B. Yeats (1923)

       The representation (or nonrepresentation) of bodies and sexuality in Irish culture is conditioned by the social power of the Catholic church. St. Paul's antifeminism and valorization of the spiritual over the physical were especially influential in Ireland, because the

Figure 1. Bas-relief of "Leda and the Swan," from Elie Faure, *History of Art* (1921), vol. 1, facing page 3. Reproduced by permission of the National Museum, Athens, Greece.

generally positive role played by the Catholic clergy in the national struggle against England gave them moral authority. Nancy Scheper-Hughes cites sociological analyses of Irish Catholicism as "monastic, ascetic, Augustinian, Jansenist, and puritanical,"[1] while Adrian Frazier suggests that "Irish Jansenism [amounts] to something like a mass neurosis."[2] Penitential Catholicism intensified by residual Victorian prudery, however, is only part of the story. Although Cheryl Herr has recently offered a disturbingly essentialist account of Irish sexual paralysis,[3] Scheper-Hughes explores the social and economic etiology of rural schizophrenia to explain why the "Irish body image unconsciously reflects and reinforces sexual repression."[4] Economic conditions resulting from colonial exploitation and the Great Famine played a major part in producing late marriages, a high rate of celibacy, and a concomitant need to control the body and its desires in the Irish countryside.[5] Unregulated eroticism was sacrificed to the need to pass on the meager landholding undivided to the chosen male heir: the survival of the family in perilous economic circumstances dictated sexual choice. When small farmers moved to the towns, they brought their ethic with them despite the fact that it was no longer economically relevant, and their sexual conservatism continued to be reinforced by the ideals of a celibate clergy.

In 1922 the establishment of an Irish nation transformed the politically rebellious but virginal Kathleen Ni Houlihan, symbol of Ireland, into a home-bound pious housewife. The conservative and petty-bourgeois government of the Free State enforced by law and later enshrined in the Constitution its version of Irish identity as Gaelic, Catholic, and sexually pure. The dominance of Catholicism in the South was reinforced by the colonial legacy of Partition, which reified the confessional division between North and South. Because decolonization failed to change the way Southern Ireland was administered, the new government, backed by the clergy, emphasized the Irish language and the Catholic ethical code as the defining marks of independence.[6] Mary Douglas argues that fetishization of purity is characteristic of threatened minorities, whose concern with political boundaries is displaced into an obsession with bodily orifices and secretions.[7] Ireland's boundaries were compromised from without by continued British presence in the Treaty Ports and from within by Partition and the bitter legacy of civil war: the revolution was unfinished. Anxiety about political unity was partially displaced into an obsession with sexuality, defined as "dirt" and identified as "foreign" in origin. In their 1924 Lenten Pastorals, which Yeats condemned as "rancid, course [sic] and vague,"[8] the Bishops lambasted "women's immodest fashions in dress, indecent dances, unwholesome theatrical performances and cinema exhibitions, evil literature and drink."[9] Their continual condemnations of licentious behavior suggest that Ireland was experiencing a mild version of the sexual revolution of the Twenties: "The pity of it, that our Catholic girls . . . should follow the mode of pagan England by appearing semi-nude."[10] Was it for this, runs the subtext of many such effusions, that all that blood was shed?

In response to the perceived threat of national demoralization, Catholic morality was enacted into law. Film censorship was instituted in 1923; the censorship of literature and the press, preceded by the establishment of a Committee on Evil Literature in 1926, became law in 1929. The Bishops forced Cosgrave to revoke the legal right to divorce inherited by the Free State from the English parliament.[11] Although the importation and sale of contraceptives was not formally outlawed until 1935, advertisements for birth control devices were banned by the Censors. At the same time, illegitimacy conferred an overwhelming social and legal stigma. Both the main political parties and the majority of the population accepted the sexual purity legislation, since it accorded with their own prejudices, and the only systematic opposition to the policy of giving Catholic moral standards the backing of the State came from Yeats and his allies.[12]

Yeats began by opposing the Censorship of Films Bill (1923). He did not take refuge in the Audenesque claim that "poetry makes nothing happen," but argued that the appeal of the arts to "our imitative faculties" was counterbalanced by their statistically incalculable good effects.[13] The Bill, however, passed, and cleanliness was legally established as next to godliness. As Douglas points out, "holiness requires that different classes of things shall not be confused," so "hybrids and other confusions are abominated."[14] The horror inspired by the hybrid/bird underlies the Catholic reaction to Yeats's "Leda and the Swan," a poem representing the violent rape of a woman by a god disguised as a member of the lower species. Yeats deliberately chose to site the poem in the public arena in order to arouse controversy and flout censorship. Restored to the context of its publication in the monthly paper To-morrow,[15] its transgressive intent is readily apparent.

According to Yeats, the poem was inspired by a meditation on the Irish situation in relation to world politics. The first version was finished at Coole in September 1923, in the atmosphere of political instability resulting from the Irish Civil War. Yeats told Lady Gregory of "his long belief that the reign of democracy is over for the present, and in reaction there will be violent government from above, as now in Russia, and is beginning here. It is the thought of this force coming into the world that he is expressing in his Leda poem."[16] The swan-god, it seems, originated as a "rough beast," an unlikely amalgam of Lenin and President Cosgrave, subduing the anarchic masses personified by Leda; but Yeats insisted that, "as I wrote, bird and lady took such possession of the scene that all politics went out of it, and my friend tells me that his 'conservative readers would misunderstand the poem.'"[17] All politics did not evaporate in the alchemy of the creative process, however: class politics were overshadowed though not entirely effaced by the politics of sexuality.

The poem, first titled "Annunciation,"[18] was too hot for AE's [George William Russell] Irish Statesman to handle. When a group of young intellectuals decided to start a radical monthly paper, Yeats gave them "Leda and the Swan" for the first number. The other contributions included a short story by Lennox Robinson, "The Madonna of Slieve Dun,"[19] about a peasant girl who, raped by a tramp while unconscious, believes that she is pregnant with the Messiah, but dies while giving birth to a girl. To-morrow thus offered its readership not one but two rapes. Yeats's "violent annunciation from above"[20] was paired with a parody annunciation from below: both the brutish tramp and the bestial swan-god can be read as blasphemous stand-ins for the Holy Spirit. Like "Leda," Robinson's story had been refused by another periodical "because it was indecent and dealt with rape."[21]

The topic, however indirectly treated, was taboo. "The Madonna of Slieve Dun" is not explicit: the rape, unlike Leda's, takes place in the white space between paragraphs. In positing a naturalistic explanation for the girl's pregnancy, however, the story suggests that there may also be one for the Virgin Mary's. The Madonna of Slieve Dun could be read as casting doubt upon the Virgin Birth.[22] So the printers reasoned, for, operating their own extralegal censorship, they refused to produce the paper. When a year later the Christian Brothers took the law into their own hands in publicly burning "The Cherry Tree Carol" because it depicts St. Joseph's suspicion that the pregnant Virgin has cuckolded him, they were displaying a similar sensitivity to the depiction of Mary as a sexual and reproductive being. Mary's body was systematically erased by Irish Catholic devotion to the Virgin: the Christian Brothers would have been scandalized by those medieval Madonnas who offer a bare breast to the nursing Christ child.[23]

The printers provided Yeats with an opportunity to engage the forces of Catholic public opinion head on. "I am in high spirits this morning, seeing my way to a most admirable row," he wrote. [24] After his supposedly heretical play "The Countess Cathleen" Yeats had been regularly abused by Catholic newspapers, but during the twenties, with his accession to national prominence as senator and Nobel Prize recipient, the attacks increased in number and venom.[25] Sean O'Casey frequently brought copies of The Irish Rosary, The Leader, and The Catholic Bulletin to the attention of Lady Gregory,[26] so Yeats knew that his name had become a byword for paganism, anti-Catholicism, opposition to Gaelic culture, and snobbery. He was part of what The Catholic Bulletin called "The New Ascendancy."

Although the Dublin printers objected to Lennox Robinson's story and not to Yeats's poem, Yeats had clearly chosen "Leda" as the most provocative work he could offer the editors of To-morrow. The poem that we encounter in this highly political context differs radically from the "Leda and the Swan" that was published in the exclusive (and expensive) Cuala Press edition of The Cat and the Moon and Certain Poems;[27] and in the avant-garde American Dial;[28] or later as epigraph to the historical section of A Vision, "Dove or Swan?"[29] It also differs from the poem that appears in the canonical Collected Works.[30] The context provided by the other material in the paper, the hostile Catholic audience, and the desire to create public scandal unite to produce a text that rhetorically intervenes in the field of cultural politics via the representation of a female body and the enactment of a male desire for power.

Inevitably Yeats's antipurity crusade encompassed the work of James Joyce. At the Tailteann Games in August 1924 Yeats chose to endorse Ulysses in a prestigious cultural forum: "Mr. James Joyce's book, though as obscene as Rabelais, and, therefore, forbidden by law in England and the United States, is more indubitably a work of genius than any prose written by an Irishman since the death of Synge."[31] His defense of a banned book provoked an attack from a nonecclesiastical Protestant source: Professor Wilbraham Trench of Trinity College, who wrote to the *Statesman*:

> J. Joyce rakes hell, and the sewers, for dirt to throw at the fair face of life, and for poison to make beauty shrivel and die . . . and Dr. Yeats undertakes that no citizen of Dublin shall fail to know his name. In season and out of season he has proclaimed him a genius. . . . But there have been geniuses who wallowed in the mire before, though whether any quite equally foul-minded, who shall say?[32]

The diction of this letter set the terms for the debate that followed: sewers, dirt, mire, and foulness were the linguistic counters taken up by *The Catholic Bulletin*, and used interchangeably of the authors of *Ulysses* and of "Leda and the Swan." By rhetorical contamination, Joyce's interest in defecation was associated with Yeats's interest in rape. Yeats and his friends were subsequently and repeatedly abused as "the Sewage School"[33] and "the Cloacal Combine."[34] *The Catholic Bulletin*, developing the cloacal metaphor with prurient relish, reprinted Trench's letter and announced that in *To-morrow* "the Dublin aesthetes . . . have provided themselves with a new literary cesspool."[35] In the November issue of the *Bulletin*, though Lennox Robinson is granted "pride of place" in the "unsavory netherworld," the bitterest invective is reserved for "Leda and the Swan,"

> which exhibits Senator Pollexfen Yeats in open rivalry with the "bestial genius" which Senator Yeats has so recently championed. For bestial is the precise and fitting word for this outburst of "poetry" . . . Professor W. F. Trench is answered. We may even say that J. Joyce will be envious when he reads the effort of Yeats, and will call for a more effective rake. "Hell and the sewers" are not in it. It is when resort is had to the pagan world for inspiration in the "poetry" of the obscene, that the mere moderns can be outclassed in bestiality.[36]

Yeats had claimed in the Senate, "Ireland has been put into our hands that we may shape it."[37] From *The Catholic Bulletin*'s point of view, to grant Yeats that shaping power would be to continue the English occupation of Ireland by cultural rather than political means. Anglo-Ireland was construed as a sexual fifth column, the aristocratic serpent in the bourgeois Gaelic paradise. Sexuality and its representation in print, therefore, became a site of class as well as religious struggle. After the publication of *To-morrow*, "the filthy Swan Song of Senator W. B. Yeats," the "Stinking Sonnet," or the "putrid 'Swan Poem,'"[38] as it was variously and monotonously termed, was used as a continual reminder of the danger to a Gaelic Catholic nation represented by the Cloacal Combine, denizens of the literary cesspool of Anglo-Ireland.

Yeats, who frequently compared Joyce to Rabelais, was himself designated as "Rabelaisian" by The Catholic Bulletin.[39] Bakhtin's reading of Rabelais, which emphasizes the power of the low, the dirty, and the grotesque to unsettle the Law, may explain some of the impact of To-morrow. Stallybrass and White discard Bakhtin's occasionally simplistic opposition between the grotesque and the classical (or canonical) for his more complex appreciation of the way in which "the grotesque is formed through a process of hybridization or inmixing of binary opposites, particularly of high and low."[40] "Hybridization" is a possible paradigm for "Leda and the Swan," which posits no simple opposition between the carnal and the spiritual. Despite the physicality of the rape, Yeats's swan is also a god, omniscient as well as brutally powerful. This confounding of categories is mirrored in the form: Leda's "loosening thighs" and the swan's orgasmic "shudder in the loins" insert the transgressive Bakhtinian lower-body strata into the classical structure of the Petrarchan sonnet,[41] where they have seldom been found before. The fact that Yeats rarely used the sonnet[42] makes his deployment of it here the more striking: he thematizes the mixture between a hegemonic "high" form and a deliberately "low," or sexually explicit, treatment of his subject matter.

Yeats found the concept of the hybrid strategically useful as a corrective to the unitary, totalizing vision of the "one Gaelic tradition." In the interests of an Anglo-Ireland popularly represented as "silly, sordid and segregated,"[43] he claimed that the real Irish tradition was mongrel rather than purebred. In 1925, introducing a translation of "The Midnight Court" by the eighteenth-century Gaelic poet Brian Merriman, he praised what to the Gaelic advocates of purity must have been a considerable embarrassment: a bawdy comic masterpiece in the Irish language. With an irony available only to those who had been following the "Leda" controversy, he wished "that a Gaelic scholar had been found, or failing that some man of known sobriety of manner and of mind—Professor Trench of Trinity College, let us say—to introduce to the Irish reading public this vital, extravagant, immoral, preposterous poem."[44] "The Midnight Court" is a parody inversion of normal legal practice, a Bakhtinian world-turned-upside-down in which the women are on top. The sheriff who calls the poet to the court is a gigantic woman; the judge is the Queen of the Munster fairies, Eevell; judgment is given in favor of the women plaintiffs, who protest the Irish practice of marrying for money rather than sex, attack clerical celibacy, and want to punish men for failing to satisfy their carnal appetites. Desire is sanctioned rather than restrained by the Law. Yeats notes that Merriman, writing in penal times, had seen Ireland's dismal political and economic state reflected in her loss of sexual energy: "your lads and lasses have left off breeding."[45] He pretends to be scandalized by Merriman's crudity: "Certainly it is not possible to read his verses without being shocked and horrified as city onlookers were perhaps shocked and horrified at the free speech and buffoonery of some traditional country festival."[46] In identifying Merriman's poem with Bakhtinian carnival buffoonery, Yeats claims the grotesque for Gaelic literature. He also hybridizes "The Midnight Court" by crossing it with Anglo-Ireland, arguing that Merriman borrowed the structure of his poem from Swift's *Cadenus and Vanessa*.[47] The great Gaelic language poem is not only "immoral," it is a literary half-breed. The vigor of bastardy is a major theme in the poem itself, and Yeats quotes a passage that could be read as a protest against "legitimate" legal identity:

> For why call a Priest in to bind and to bless
> Before candid nature can give one caress? . . .
> Since Mary the Mother of God did conceive
> Without calling the clergy or begging their leave . . .
> For love is a lustier sire than law. [48]

Merriman's cheerful deployment of Mary's extramarital impregnation, at issue in both the To-morrow and "Cherry Tree Carol" controversies, delighted Yeats, who never lost an opportunity of turning the Virgin against her clerical advocates.

"Leda and the Swan" can thus be read as an aristocratic liberal intervention in the cultural debate about post-Treaty Irish identity, an insistence that in bringing to birth a new, independent Ireland, "love is a lustier sire than law." Was Ireland to become, as Yeats wished, "a modern, tolerant, liberal nation,"[49] free to deploy the resources of classical mythology and to admire naked Greek statuary; or was it to surrender to the obscurantism of the clergy, soon to be reified in the legislation of the new state? Sexuality, bodies, and their representations occupy center stage in this ideological struggle. The Swan, originating in Yeats's mind as an image of the violent imposition of the law, ironically comes to symbolize all those desires the censors found threatening: in the context of the poem's reception its brutal energy represents the forces of sexual liberation. Despite Foucault's warnings against construing erotic self-expression as politically emancipatory, the subsequent cultural and social history of Ireland makes it hard to dismiss this reading, especially as the clerical regulation of sexuality weighed most heavily upon women.[50]

The moral and political debate about "filth" and its exclusion from the national self-image, however, was conducted almost entirely between men. At issue was not the right of women to control and represent their own sexuality, but the male writer's freedom to use rape as a subject in a legitimate journal. Yeats's demand that the body be recognized as "the whole handiwork of God"[51] is admirable, but no one at the time seriously questioned whether this liberalism justified his graphic depiction of the body of a woman attacked and violently raped by an animal. Yeats himself, however, was aware of the potential female response: when he was asked for a copy of the poem, he replied, "there is no typist here I would ask to copy it— one a few days ago wept because put to type a speech in favour of divorce I was to deliver in the Senate."[52]

Would Yeats's woman reader have objected because of the poem's obscenity, or because of its sexism? Might she have seen in the relation of the famous male poet to a subordinate female stenographer a version of the power relations between the Swan and Leda? Women had had the vote for six years, but political representation did not guarantee access to economic or cultural power: Yeats's putative female reader is still a typist, a copier of other people's texts. The poem she would have read in 1924, however, is different from the poem women readers encounter today: not simply because Yeats revised his words, but because the feminist movement has created radically new conditions of reception for a poem about rape. Contemporary feminists challenge the credentials of a liberalism that privileges male subjectivity and freedom of speech at the price of female objectification. As Catherine MacKinnon argues, "Understanding free speech as an abstract system is a liberal position. Understanding how speech also exists within a substantive system of power relations is a feminist position."[53] The Irish historicist reading therefore needs to be articulated with a radical feminist approach that takes account of other histories: women's history, the history of pornography, the history of the sonnet form, the textual history of the poem.

Contemporary feminist reactions to "Leda" must also negotiate the strategic problem of appearing to echo the original religious outrage. Objections to sexism are not the same as objections to sex, but they may sound alike. In a recent interview the Irish lesbian feminist Mary Dorcey sums up the problem posed by depictions of rape or violence against women in the Irish cultural context:

> When pornography is discussed by feminists . . . we run into trouble immediately with liberals and others who are determined to protect the small area of secular liberalism that has been won in Ireland. It is very difficult to make a case that is anti-pornographic but does not seem pro-censorship by the Catholic church and its various right-wing militias.[54]

As Susanne Kappeler has argued, the right-wing and religious guardians of morality "do not object to the degradation of women in pornography, but to the presence of a particular kind of 'sex.'"[55] They are also likely to be the opponents of contraception, abortion, and divorce, the last two of which are still legally prohibited in Ireland. For this reason the feminist antipornography position has to be articulated with the greatest precision.

"Pornography" may seem an extreme term to apply to "Leda and the Swan," which is protected from such judgments by its canonical status as "high" art. Artistic merit is, of course, one of the grounds on which a work can be defined in law as not pornographic.[56] But as Kappeler argues, "What women find objectionable in pornography, they have learnt to accept in products of 'high' art and literature."[57] Stripped of its canonical privilege and examined in terms of its content alone, "Leda and the Swan" certainly qualifies as pornography, which is, according to MacKinnon:

> the graphic sexually explicit subordination of women through pictures or words that also includes women dehumanized as sexual objects, things, or commodities; enjoying pain or humiliation or rape; being tied up, cut up, mutilated, bruised, or physically hurt; in postures of sexual submission or servility or display; reduced to body parts, penetrated by objects or animals, or presented in scenarios of degradation, injury, torture.[58]

Subordination, dehumanization, pain, rape, being reduced to body parts and penetrated by an animal: Leda has it all. Yeats's subject, moreover, is one that has been employed for centuries on the pornographic fringe of the fine arts. Representations of Jove's amours (accompanied by Aretine's licentious verses) were fashionable in Elizabethan bedchambers;[59] while Dijkstra catalogues the enduring popularity of Leda in titillating turn-of-the-century painting.[60] Bestiality has always been an established subgenre of pornography: offering a visual image of female degradation, it abrogates a woman's claim to be considered human.[61] When we encounter "Leda and the Swan" in its frame as modernist masterpiece, dirty postcards featuring women and donkeys do not suggest themselves as valid analogies, and we are likely to forget its extracanonical pornographic pedigree.

Kappeler, however, claims that what she calls "the pornography of representation" inevitably controls the focus of any poem written by a man depicting the body (let alone the bodily violation) of a woman. The male author/subject invites the male reader to enjoy a visual spectacle in which the woman becomes an object for his scrutiny and pleasure. Although in theory the representer may be female and the represented male, this possibility has not been historically realized: "The history of representation is the history of the male gender representing itself to itself—the power of naming is men's. . . . Culture, as we know it, is patriarchy's self-image."[62] Kappeler, who is indebted to John Berger and Laura Mulvey, goes further than Berger in assuming that the structure of all male representation of women is pornographic: she sees no justification for female pleasure in viewing or reading the works of men except the (dubious) delights of masochism.[63] If we agree, it is pointless to approach "Leda and the Swan" or, indeed, most Western art and literature. Berger, who draws a distinction between the objectification of most female nudes and the exceptional portrait of Hélène Fourment by Rubens, allows for the occasional rupture of the straitjacket of representation.[64] His less exclusivist theory allows us to read "Leda and the Swan" in search of Leda's almost obliterated subjectivity.

"Leda and the Swan" is a representation of a representation.[65] Lady Gregory notes that "W. B. Y. finished his poem on Leda—showed me the reproduction of the carving on which it is founded,"[66] confirming the hypothesis of Charles Madge that the immediate visual source for "Leda" was a Hellenistic bas-relief reproduced in Elie Faure's *History of Art* (1921), which Yeats owned (see Figure 1).[67] The carving corresponds to the configuration of bird and lady in Yeats's sonnet, and Faure's overheated commentary isolates precisely the features of the bas-relief that attracted Yeats's attention:

> look at the "Leda" as she stands to receive the great swan with the beating wings, letting the beak seize her neck, the foot tighten on her thigh— the trembling woman subjected to the fatal force which reveals to her the whole of life, even while penetrating her with voluptuousness and pain.[68]

The Sadean collocation of fatal force, voluptuousness, and pain identifies Faure as a Decadent, convinced not only that Leda did "put on his knowledge with his power," but that she did so willingly: she "receives" the God, "letting" his beak seize her neck. Faure interprets Leda's rape as consensual intercourse.

The sestet of Yeats's poem remained the same in all printings, but the octave as it appeared in *To-morrow* was closer than later versions to its visual source:

> A rush, a sudden wheel, and hovering still
> The bird descends, and her frail thighs are pressed
> By the webbed toes, and that all-powerful bill
> Has laid her helpless face upon his breast.
> How can those terrified vague fingers push
> The feathered glory from her loosening thighs!
> All the stretched body's laid on the white rush
> And feels the strange heart beating where it lies.[69]

As in the carving, the bird is "hovering" in the air, and Leda's head is pressed against his breast. The image is grotesque. The anatomical improbability of rape by a swan, which has an extremely small penis, is surmounted by transferring phallic prominence to "that all-powerful bill."[70] The awkward disposition of the swan's "webbed toes" is more apparent in the carving than in the sonnet, but the disparity in height between a standing woman and an attacking bird evokes an absurdly athletic image of an airborne rapist, beating his wings furiously just to stay in place.

Yeats addresses these problems, which are simultaneously problems of poetics and of power, in the final version of his first quatrain.[71] He decreases the clumsiness of the God, increases his violence, and frames that violence as seductive:

> A sudden blow: the great wings beating still
> Above the staggering girl, her thighs caressed
> By the dark webs, her nape caught in his bill,
> He holds her helpless breast upon his breast.[72]

The vagueness of "rush" and "wheel" and the discursiveness of "the bird descends" are condensed into the immediacy of "a sudden blow" that comes from nowhere. The absurdity of the hovering rapist is transformed into the violent image of "great" wings "beating." The bird no longer hovers and descends at the same time: he is poised in the superior position, "above" his victim. Leda, previously no more than a pair of "frail thighs" and a "helpless face," is finally characterized as "the staggering girl." "Staggering" conveys precisely the body's lurch under the weight from above: the violence has a specific target and physical effect. The use of the patronizing word "girl" for a mythological heroine suggests Yeats's later poetic coaching of Swami Purohit, who was delighted to discover that "he can call a goddess, 'this handsome girl' or even 'a pretty girl' instead of 'a maiden of surpassing loveliness.' "[73] "Girl" has a shockingly intimate effect, its colloquiality eliding the gap between the mythological past and the present. It increases the erotic charge for the male reader, who can transfer the action to "girls" of his own acquaintance. The improvement in poetics intensifies the sexual and kinetic power of the verse. The notion that the "higher" the art the less pornographic it is requires reconsideration.

The poetically effective replacement of "her frail thighs are pressed / By the webbed toes" with "her thighs caressed / By the dark webs" also strengthens the connection between male violence and male eroticism. The action in the first version is a straightforward exercise of force, corroborating those who claim that rape is "about" violence and not "about" sex at all. MacKinnon insists, however, that for men violence and sexuality are often indistinguishable.[74] "Caressed" develops this terrifying ambiguity. The blow followed by the caress becomes a sinister form of seduction, as the swan's poetically ridiculous "webbed toes" are transformed into the metaphorically threatening "dark webs." Leda is entangled in sexual webs constructed by the deceptive promise of gentleness. Her face is not merely "laid" on the swan's breast, her "nape" (another increase in physical and verbal precision at the expense of Leda's human individuality) is "caught" in his bill. The imbalance of face/breast is replaced by a constrained equivalence: "he holds her helpless breast upon his breast." Leda is "held," but in a position that suggests lovemaking: the bird's expression of desire mimics the gestures of tenderness until physical satiation reveals his utter indifference to his victim.

Yeats's insistence on the power differential between rapist and victim is more forcibly rendered in language of the second version. The descriptive, sequential, paratactic syntax—"and hovering still," "and her frail thighs are pressed," "and that all-powerful bill"—is replaced by a series of appositional clauses whose connectives have been suppressed in the interests of terseness. We are hurried on in search of the main verb, which appears dramatically late, at the beginning of the fourth line, emphasized by heavy alliteration: "He holds her helpless." Yeats thought "Leda" was a poem in which "it is not clear whether the speaker is man or woman."[75] Can we imagine it as voiced from the subject position of the "helpless" victim of male power?

The major obstacle to such a reading occurs in the second quatrain, in which the ambiguous relationship between male force and female consent, the heart of all legal discussion of rape, is linguistically played out. For what Susan Estrich calls "real rape," sexual intercourse by force, against the will and without the consent of the victim, is required (see following essay). "Leda and the Swan" begins as real rape, but Yeats's language hints at the possibility of consent in *medias res*. In many previous versions of the myth, Leda is clearly so willing as to be hardly a victim at all. Spenser represents her as complicit with the Swan:

> Whiles the proud Bird ruffing his fethers wyde,
> And brushing his faire brest, did her inuade;
> She slept, yet twixt her eyelids closely spyde,
> How towards her he rusht, and smiled at his pryde.[76]

This is not rape but male pornographic pretense. Leda likes swans: she allows Jove to act out the violation scenario while secretly pursuing her own gratification. The scene embodies a number of classic male assumptions about female sexuality: women love a bit of force; or when a woman says no she means yes; or women like to degrade themselves with animals. In *The Player Queen* (1919) Yeats had taken a Spenserian view of his inherited material. Decima chooses deliberately between actors dressed as beasts:

> Shall I fancy beast or fowl?
> Queen Pasiphae chose a bull,
> While a passion for a swan
> Made Queen Leda stretch and yawn.[77]

In "The Adoration of the Magi," which originally contained no reference to Leda,[78] and which Yeats revised at the time of the To-morrow controversy, the message given to the old men will "so transform the world that another Leda would open her knees to the swan, another Achilles beleaguer Troy."[79] "Open her knees to the swan" is a decidedly voluntaristic way of putting it.

Yeats's later lyric, "Lullaby," also implies that the woman enjoyed the experience. Violence is elided as a mother wishes for her child

> Such a sleep and sound as fell
> Upon Eurotas' grassy bank
> When the holy bird, that there
> Accomplished his predestined will,
> From the limbs of Leda sank
> But not from her protecting care.[80]

The male rapist's "indifferent beak" contrasts with the "protecting care" offered by the woman to the sleeping bird at the end of "Lullaby." Yet as Olivia Shakespear perspicaciously observed: "Your lullaby, though very beautiful, is extremely unsuitable for the young! Leda seems to have a peculiar charm for you—personally I'm so terrified of swans, that the idea horrifies me—a feminine point of view."[81] Her half-humorous objection demonstrates how from "a feminine point of view" Yeats's obsession with this mythological rape may be cause for terror unmitigated by pleasure.

In comparison with Spenser or with Yeats's other versions of the story, however, "Leda and the Swan" initially presents the rape as rape: the forcible violation of an unsuspecting victim. After the brutal attack Yeats moves into the interrogative mode to test the possibility of female resistance: arguing the case for the prosecution, he suggests that it was no wonder she did not struggle more purposefully, or make her unwillingness more clear:

> How can those terrified vague fingers push
> The feathered glory from her loosening thighs?
> And how can body, laid in that white rush,
> But feel the strange heart beating where it lies?[82]

In seeking to adopt the victim's point of view, Yeats takes a tentative step toward granting her a subject position of her own. Although the divine rapist's state of mind is never explored, the narrating voice tries to gain access to Leda's consciousness via two unanswered questions. The epithet "vague" suggests that Leda is too numb with shock to fight back: unlike Spenser's peeping and smiling Leda, she is "terrified." Fear and disorientation render effective resistance impossible: Yeats's first rhetorical question implies that she could not have prevented the rape, and therefore was not legally responsible for her own predicament.

The questions, however, also contain certain assumptions in which male author and male reader are directly complicit. Those "vague" fingers and "loosening" thighs suggest that, although she is hurt and stunned, Leda's body, if not her will, responds to the rapist as physically erotic. Is it Leda's consciousness or the narrator's that approvingly tropes her aggressor as "the feathered glory"? Kappeler argues that the idea that the woman's body will involuntarily desire the rapist panders to the male view of women as "naturally" lustful creatures: "The unwillingness of the woman-victim is thus the cultural state of woman, coded by the patriarchal economy of the exchange of women, its laws and religions. The willingness of the woman-object is the natural state to which she has been returned through the offices of men."[83] Pursuing Merriman's idea that "love is a lustier sire than law," Yeats uses his description of rape to flout Irish patriarchal laws against the verbal expression of sexuality. In its repetition of male cultural assumptions about women's bodies, however, his poem paradoxically contributes to the imprisonment of the female rape victim in a legal trap: if she brings a case against her abuser, the idea that women "naturally" desire their own violation will be used to discredit her testimony. Leda's "loosening thighs" imply a moment of consenting, mutual erotic pleasure, and the omission of the possessive pronoun before "body" suggests that both bodies "feel" the beating of the other's "strange" heart. The "heart" is culturally coded to suggest emotion: in Yeats's early poem "The Heart of the Woman" the line "My heart upon his warm heart lies"[84] expresses the complete surrender of the female speaker. This rhetoric of feeling suggests to the male reader that if he behaves like the swan, women will find him emotionally as well as physically irresistible.

The question of Leda's putative sexual and emotional arousal engages with the legal attitude to the complainant in a rape trial: if a woman appears as a sexual being in her dress, deportment, or actions; if it can be proved that she has had and enjoyed sex with other men, we have prima facie evidence of her consent: she must have enjoyed the rape too, and no crime has been committed. The definition of sexual actions is formidably wide, and apparently includes hitchhiking: in 1982 Judge Bertram Richards fined a rapist instead of imprisoning him, "on the grounds that the woman whom he had raped was guilty of 'a great deal of contributory negligence' in accepting a lift home with him, despite the fact that there was no other form of transport home available."[85]

Roland Barthes suggests that the victim of Sadean violence can choose her relationship to what is being done to her: "The scream is the victim's mark; she makes herself a victim because she chooses to scream; if, under the same vexation she were to ejaculate, she would cease to be a victim, would be transformed into a libertine."[86] Do Leda's loosening thighs make her "a libertine"? I cannot be certain that women never find real rape erotic, although I imagine they rarely do. I have been told about a woman who did find her body responding to her attacker in just such an involuntary manner as Leda's: her recovery from the trauma of the rape itself was much impeded by the additional burden of guilt and shame she experienced as a result of her physical arousal. I reject, however, Barthes's notion of choice.[87] The rape happened to Leda; she was subjected to the desire of the swan. If centuries of cultural conditioning have defined women as passive and masochistic, constructing female desire as the desire to be acted upon rather than to act, then the existence of female rape fantasies is not surprising. But the gap between fantasy (which a woman can control and which involves no actual pain) and the real thing (in which she is powerless and often suffers physical harm) makes male representations of rape as pleasurable for women extremely dangerous. Not only do they invite imitation on the grounds that a rapist is giving a woman what she really wants, but, as MacKinnon argues, "pornography institutionalizes the sexuality of male supremacy, which fuses the erotization of dominance and submission with the social construction of male and female."[88] Men represent submission as both erotic and feminine: women internalize male representations of their desire and their identity as women.

In Portnoy's Complaint that clever pornographer Philip Roth uses "Leda and the Swan" in a way that exemplifies MacKinnon's contention about the social construction of gender. Portnoy picks up a woman he describes as "the star of all those pornographic films that I had been producing in my head." The Monkey (appropriately bestialized by her nickname) is ill educated, but she has a compensatory talent for fellatio; one of her finest blow jobs (an image of total female submission) moves Portnoy to a recitation of "Leda and the Swan." Although The Monkey doesn't understand poems, Portnoy insists:

> "You'll understand this one. It's about fucking. A swan fucks a beautiful girl."
> She looked up, batting her false eyelashes. "Oh, goody."
> "But it's a serious poem."
> "Well," she said, licking my prick, "it's a serious offense."[89]

When Portnoy recites "the dirty poem," The Monkey is humiliated by her ignorance of high culture, but plays submissive student to Portnoy's professor: "Okay, what's Agamemnon?"[90] Once he has explained all the classical allusions, she makes him recite the poem again, and this time she gets the point:

> "Feel. It made my pussy all wet."
> "Sweetheart! You understood the poem!" . . .

"Hey, I did! I understood a poem!"

"And with your cunt, no less."[91]

Roth plays knowingly with his readers' assumption that a poem by Yeats, something one studies in college, is high art, and therefore cannot be pornography. He gets a double thrill out of exposing it as a "dirty poem" while confirming its canonical status and using it to "educate" an ignorant woman. Not until she has learned about Agamemnon, Zeus, Clytemnestra, Helen, Paris, and Troy can The Monkey have the proper response to a poem about rape: "It made my pussy all wet." Score one for Western Civilization.

Not surprisingly a female novelist, Pamela Hansford Johnson, takes a diametrically opposed view of Yeats's poem and its relation to pornography. In The Unspeakable Skipton[92] a group of pretentious expatriates watch a private pornographic charade in which a Belgian prostitute and a flabby young man impersonate Leda and the Swan. Their pathetic and disgusting costume-drama copulation is accompanied in the mind of the novel's anti-hero, Daniel, by a recitation of Yeats's poem. The effect is grotesque, and the irony is at the expense of both Daniel and Yeats: "high art" cannot redeem the squalor of low life, and the representation of rape for the benefit of voyeurs is pornographic even when it is framed by the canonical form of the sonnet.[93]

Paul Fussell's analysis of the structure of the sonnet form, one of the constants of Western Civilization since the early Renaissance, reveals how permeated by the male point of view are even the supposedly abstract shapes of canonical genres. "The [octave] builds up the pressure, the [sestet] releases it; and the turn is the dramatic and climactic center of the poem. . . . We may even suggest that one of the emotional archetypes of the Petrarchan sonnet structure is the pattern of sexual pressure and release."[94] Fussell's analogy is based on the mechanics of male sexual response, with its single climactic moment. His orgasmic poetics are certainly appropriate to "Leda and the Swan." "A shudder in the loins" is both linguistically graphic and physically climactic. Yeats's placement of this brutally naturalistic "low" diction at the "turn" between the octave and sestet, the place of maximum formal effect, demonstrates both his fidelity to the male shape of the genre and, paradoxically, the way in which his attitude to the traditionally sublimated sexuality of the Petrarchan sonnet has changed.

Like all modifications of a generic form, the poem depends for its full effect on our knowledge of the convention that is being inverted. Originally the sonnet was the vehicle of idealized woman-worship,[95] in which the Lady disdained the helpless male lover, who was suspended in perennially unfulfilled desire; in Yeats's poem the woman is "helpless" before the "brute blood" of her male ravisher. Having overpaid his courtly dues in his youth,

Yeats swung with corresponding intensity toward the opposite extreme: rape can be construed as the dark underside of Romance. In troubadour poetry the knight who restrains his desire for his idealized lady is positively encouraged to take advantage of peasant girls.[96] Yeats also alters the static poetics of the praise-sonnet, which represents the female beloved as a series of unlinked body parts suspended in the timeless present of her lover's vain desire.[97] Leda too is physically characterized through the canonical technique of the anatomical blazon, which represents her as thighs, nape, breast, fingers; but the achievement of the swan's orgasm, the "shudder in the loins" (that could, since the possessive is suppressed, also indicate a simultaneous shudder in Leda's loins) breaks the Petrarchan pattern of eternal frustration. If the momentous engendering of a new historical cycle is represented as no more than a mechanical spasm, it nonetheless releases the poet from the limbo of high diction and no action.

Sharon Cameron argues that one of the distinguishing features of the canonical lyric is its attempt to "freeze time."[98] In "Leda and the Swan," however, Yeats attempts to incorporate time into the process of the poem. Although the traditional province of the sonnet is private experience,[99] in three lines typographically broken away from the sestet Yeats ruptures the shape of his poem and opens the present moment to its future consequences. Rape produces history, as

> A shudder in the loins engenders there
> The broken wall, the burning roof and tower
> And Agamemnon dead.[100]

Yeats imagined Helen and Pollux issuing from one of the eggs of Leda, Clytemnestra and Castor from the other.[101] Graphic physical imagery of Leda's sexual violation ("the broken wall, the burning roof and tower") leads directly to murder, as though Clytemnestra's killing of Agamemnon were coterminous with the rape. Clytemnestra, although not named in the sonnet, inhabits it as the subtextual threat of female retaliation against male brutality: she killed her husband because he sacrificed their daughter Iphigenia. Asking if Leda could foresee what was "engendered" by the rape, the narrating voice wonders if her daughter Clytemnestra's revenge would have consoled her:

> ... Being so caught up,
> So mastered by the brute blood of the air,
> Did she put on his knowledge with his power
> Before the indifferent beak could let her drop? [102]

The phrase "caught up" suggests both the swan's physical manipulation of Leda and her intense participation in the event. In asking whether she "put on" his divine "knowledge" as he had carnal "knowledge" of her, Yeats evokes a moment of Epiphany similar to the one posited by Faure, in which the "fatal force" of the swan "reveals to her the whole of life." The verb "put on" is ambiguous, and might suggest that she was not only "over/powered" but "em/powered" by the knowledge of her engendering role in future events. The contemporary poet Mona Van Duyn, however, refuses to construe rape as Epiphany: to Yeats's "did she?" she responds with an emphatic negative:

> Not even for a moment. He knew, for one thing, what he was.
> When he saw the swan in her eyes he could let her drop.
> In the first look of love men find their great disguise,
> and collecting these rare pictures of himself was his life.[103]

Leda confirms the subjectivity of the male through her objectification. The "love" evoked in her by his violence turns her into a mirror for his vanity, a means by which he can represent himself to himself.

But Yeats finally resists the temptation, implicit in the way he constructs the question, to assume that being raped by a god must be a glamorous experience worth any amount of incidental inconvenience. Despite the ambiguity of the rhetorical question in the penultimate line, the last line, although syntactically interrogative, has the force of a declarative. Yeats places at the conclusion of his poem, and thus formally emphasizes, the fact that Leda has been victimized by an indifferent brute. The god, combining overwhelming force with seductive hints of tenderness, has betrayed Leda into a human response to a creature both less and more than human, who can never engage with her. When his "indifferent beak" lets her drop we understand, as Yeats does, that Leda has been both physically and emotionally used, objectified, and discarded.

When the Virgin Mary said, "Be it done unto me according to Thy Will," she too became a vessel of the Divine (Male) Purpose. As we have seen, the question of Mary's instrumental sexual relation to the Godhead was part of the controversy over the original publication of "Leda and the Swan," and in the first edition of The Tower Yeats affirmed the relation between Leda and Mary by juxtaposing his sonnet with the poem "Wisdom." "Wisdom" contrasts the clerical, elaborately hieratical image of Mary and Jesus with the naturalistic reality of the child's conception and infancy. Giving a "chryselephantine" throne and "damask" robes to God's mother, the Byzantine church erased the embarrassment of their deity's working-class origins. Through highly formalized artistic representations, they

> Amended what was told awry
> By some peasant gospeller;

Swept the sawdust from the floor
Of that working-carpenter.[104]

But for Yeats, if Leda's rape was an Annunciation, Mary's Annunciation was a rape: a physical fact he wanted to rescue from bourgeois clerical obfuscation. In "The Mother of God"[105] the Annunciation is a "terror" borne, like Leda's, by "wings beating about the room"; the co-option of a "common woman" by indifferent forces that care nothing for her individuality.[106] The rhetoric of religious representation deliberately erases Mary's bodily experience. In "Wisdom"[107] her rape is sanitized by abstract formulae, which have been chosen by the priests because they sound good and obscure the horror of the real events:

King Abundance got Him on
Innocence; and Wisdom He
That cognomen sounded best
Considering what wild infancy
Drove horror from His Mother's breast.[108]

The "horror" dispelled by the child's normal, wild infancy is the horror of his conception: "the three-fold terror of love."[109] The personifications Abundance, Innocence, and Wisdom disguise the trio of rapist, victim, and bastard child. "Wisdom," like "Leda and the Swan," demonstrates Yeats's identification with the human against the divine, with the peasant gospeller and the common woman against the priesthood. Defending the folk vision of the pregnant Virgin in "The Cherry Tree Carol," he declared, "the Mother of God is no Catholic possession; she is a part of our imagination."[110]

Yeats's personal empathy with two female rape victims who were closely associated in his mythological imagination does not, however, dispel the doubts and questions of a feminist reader. Following the gendered distribution of power and the established structures of patriarchy, both "Leda and the Swan" and "Wisdom" figure humanity as female, Godhead as male. Does Yeats essentialize the subordination and victimage of women, and therefore perpetuate it even as he sympathizes poetically with Leda and Mary? In bringing their physical reality to the attention of a priesthood and a culture that systematically ignored and denigrated the female body, does he expose and so pornographically abuse them? Is Leda thus represented Leda raped twice?

"Leda and the Swan" demonstrates what happens when a writer cares more about using sexuality as a strategy for tilting at establishment authority than with the implications of that strategy for women, who are both the subjects of and subject to the power of his imagination. Yet it also exposes vividly the brutality of the male or divine exercise of force. We cannot make a tidy separation between a positive historicist hermeneutic and a negative feminist one. Analysing Jonathan Swift's combination of misogyny with an early critique of imperialism, Laura Brown argues that we should bring "positive and negative hermeneutics together" to expose what she sees as "the necessary intimacy of structures of liberation and oppression in eighteenth-century culture." [111] Although the cases of Swift and Yeats are not precisely analogous, to read "Leda and the Swan" along contrasting axes of Irish history and women's history reveals a similar intimacy between liberation and oppression. In a Catholic culture the revision of Virgin into rape victim challenges the repressive ideology of female purity but risks reinscribing the woman into the equally repressive category "loose" (as in "loosening thighs"). To challenge the gathering impetus toward censorship Yeats flirts with pornography. A Foucauldian feminist might emphasize the negative outcome of Yeats's attempt to stick a needle into the national being through verbal sexual transgression; but a consideration of the effects of censorship in Ireland upon the dissemination of information about contraception suggests that the virtues of resistance should never be underestimated. Liberation in complicity with oppression is surely better than oppression *tout court*?

Notes

An earlier version of this essay appeared in *Gender and History in Yeats's Love Poetry* (1993); reprinted by permission.

1. Nancy Scheper-Hughes, *Saints, Scholars, and Schizophrenics* 152 (1979).

2. Adrian Frazier, *Behind the Scenes: Yeats, Horniman and the Struggle for the Abbey Theatre* 81 (1990).

3. Cheryl Herr, "The Erotics of Irishness," 17.1 *Critical Inquiry* 1 (1990).

4. Scheper-Hughes, *supra* note 1, at 119.

5. David Cairns & Shaun Richards, *Writing Ireland: Colonialism, Nationalism and Culture* 60–63 (1988).

6. Roy Foster, *Modern Ireland, 1600–1972*, at 534–35 (1988).

7. Mary Douglas, *Purity and Danger* 124 (1966).

8. 2 W. B. Yeats, *Uncollected Prose* 438 (J.P. Frayne ed., 1970).

9. *Irish Catholic Register* 559 (1925).

10. 14.10 *Catholic Bulletin* 877 (1924).

11. Joseph J. Lee, *Ireland 1912–1985: Politics and Society* 157–58 (1989).

12. J. H. Whyte, *Church and State in Modern Ireland 1923–1970*, at 59 (1971).

13. W. B. Yeats, *Senate Speeches* 52 (Donald Pearse ed., 1961); *see* Catherine MacKinnon, *Feminism Unmodified: Discourses on Life and Law* 184–86 (1987) (discussing the appeal of art to our imitative faculties in the context of pornography).

14. Douglas, *supra* note 7, at 53.

15. 1.1 *To-morrow* (1924).

16. 1 Isabella A. Gregory, *Lady Gregory's Journals* 477 (Daniel Murphy ed., 1978).

17. W. B. Yeats, *Variorum Poems* 828 (Peter Allt & Russell Alspach eds., 1957).

18. Giorgio Melchiori, *The Whole Mystery of Art* 77 (1979).

19. Lennox Robinson, "The Madonna of Slieve Dun," 1.1 *To-morrow* (1924).

20. Yeats, *supra* note 17, at 828.

21. Gregory, *supra* note 16, at 477.

22. Id. at 584, 592.

23. Margaret Miles, "The Virgin's One Bare Breast: Female Nudity and Religious Meaning in Tuscan Early Renaissance Culture," in *The Female Body in Western Culture* 193–208 (Susan Suleiman ed., 1985).

24. W. B. Yeats, *Letters* 705 (Allan Wade ed., 1954).

25. Donald T. Torchiana, *W. B. Yeats and Georgian Ireland* 142–44 (1966); Peter Costello, *The Heart Grown Brutal* 249–53 (1977).

26. Gregory, *supra* note 16, at 609, 614, 624.

27. W. B. Yeats, *The Cat and the Moon and Certain Poems* (1924).

28. *American Dial*, June 1924.

29. W. B. Yeats, *A Vision* (1962).

30. W. B. Yeats, *Poems* 214 (Richard Finneran ed., 1983).

31. *Irish Statesman*, Aug. 23, 1924, at 753.

32. *Irish Statesman*, Aug. 30, 1924, at 790.

33. 15.1 *Catholic Bulletin* 1 (1925).

34. 14.12 *Catholic Bulletin* 1020 (1924).

35. 14.10 *Catholic Bulletin* 837 (1924).

36. 14.11 *Catholic Bulletin* 930 (1924).

37. Yeats, *supra* note 13, at 168.

38. 15.1 *Catholic Bulletin* 4, 5 (1925); 14.11 *Catholic Bulletin* 934 (1924).

39. 14.12 *Catholic Bulletin* 1027 (1924).

40. Peter Stallybrass & Allon White, *The Politics and Poetics of Transgression* 44 (1986).

41. Yeats does not use the closed rhyme *abba/abba* in the octave, preferring the greater freedom of the open rhyme *abab/cdcd*, but his sestet displays an impeccably traditional *cde/cde*.

42. Patrick Cruttwell, *The English Sonnet* 51 (1966).

43. 15.2 *Catholic Bulletin* 102–03 (1925).

44. W. B. Yeats, *Explorations* 281 (1962).

45. Id. at 284.

46. Id. at 283–84.

47. Id. at 281–82.

48. Id. at 285.

49. Yeats, *supra* note 13, at 160.

50. Marjorie Howes, "The Winding Stair," Lecture delivered at the Yeats International Summer School, Sligo (1990).

51. Yeats, *supra* note 8, at 438.

52. Yeats, *supra* note 24, at 709.

53. MacKinnon, *supra* note 13, at 140–41.

54. Mary Dorcey, "The Spaces Between the Words: Mary Dorcey Talks to Nuala Archer," 8.3 *Women's Rev. of Books* 23 (1990).

55. Susanne Kappeler, *The Pornography of Representation* 102 (1982).

56. *See id.* at 53–57 (discussing the privileging of the aesthetic category).

57. *Id.* at 103.

58. MacKinnon, *supra* note 13, at 176.

59. Melchiori, *supra* note 18, at 280–81.

60. Bram Dijkstra, *Idols of Perversity* 314–18 (1986).

61. Susan Griffin, Pornography and Silence 24–29 (1981).

62. Kappeler, *supra* note 55, at 52–53.

63. *See* Lynda Boose, "The Family in Shakespeare Studies," 40.4 *Renaissance Quarterly* 725 (1987) (discussing the opposition between feminism and pleasure).

64. John Berger, *Ways of Seeing* 60–61 (1972).

65. *See* Melchiori, *supra* note 18, at 151–63; Ian Fletcher, "'Leda and the Swan' as Iconic Poem," 1 *Yeats Annual* 82 (1982).

66. Gregory, *supra* note 16, at 476.

67. Charles Madge, "Leda and the Swan," *Times Literary Supplement*, July 20, 1962, at 532.

68. 1 Elie Faure, *History of Art* 197 (1921). The carving is reproduced on page 168.

69. To-morrow, *supra* note 15, at 2.

70. Fletcher, *supra* note 65, at 106.

71. *See* Thomas Parkinson, *W. B. Yeats: The Later Poetry* 136–42 (1971) (supplying a study of the poem's evolution that includes some comment on the To-morrow version).

72. Yeats, *supra* note 30, at 214.

73. W. B. Yeats, *Letters to Dorothy Wellseley* 44 (1964).

74. MacKinnon, *supra* note 13, at 85–92.

75. W. B. Yeats, *Ah! Sweet Dancer: Margot Ruddock: A Correspondence* 30 (Roger McHugh ed., 1970).

76. *See* Melchiori, *supra* note 18, at 112.

77. W. B. Yeats, Collected Plays 416 (1952).

78. W. B. Yeats, *The Secret Rose, Stories by W.B. Yeats: A Variorum Edition* 166 (Philip L. Marcus et al. eds., 1981).

79. W. B. Yeats, Mythologies 310 (1959).

80. Yeats, *supra* note 30, at 265.

81. John Harwood ed., "Olivia Shakespear: Letters to W. B. Yeats," 6 *Yeats Annual* 59–107 (1988).

82. Yeats, *supra* note 30, at 214.

83. Kappeler, *supra* note 55, at 158.

84. Yeats, *supra* note 30, at 61.

85. Melissa Ben et al., *The Rape Controversy* 18 (1986).

86. Kappeler, *supra* note 55, at 90.

87. In this I am in agreement with Kappeler. *Id.* at 91.

88. MacKinnon, *supra* note 13, at 148.

89. Philip Roth, *Portnoy's Complaint* 191 (1967).

90. *Id.* at 193.

91. *Id.* at 194.

92. Pamela H. Johnson, *The Unspeakable Skipton* (1959).

93. *Id.* at 58–66.

94. Paul Fussell, *Poetic Meter and Poetic Form* 116 (1979).

95. John Fuller, *The Sonnet* 6–7 (1972).

96. Joan M. Ferrante, "Male Fantasy and Female Reality in Courtly Literature," 11/12.1 *Women's Studies* 69 (1984).

97. Nancy J. Vickers, "Diana Described: Scattered Women and Scattered Rhyme," in *Writing and Sexual Difference* 96–97 (Elizabeth Abel ed., 1982).

98. Sharon Cameron, *Lyric Time* 20–23 (1979).

99. Even Milton uses the sonnet more for autobiography than for purely political or public verses. *See* Fuller, *supra* note 95, at 7.

100. Yeats, *supra* note 30, at 214.

101. Yeats, *supra* note 29, at 51.

102. Yeats, *supra* note 30, at 215.

103. Mona Van Duyn, *To See, to Take* 98 (1970); Gloria C. Klines, *The Last Courtly Lover: Yeats and the Idea of Woman* 38 (1983) (noting also Van Duyn's poem).

104. Yeats, *supra* note 30, at 219.

105. *Id.* at 249.

106. *Id.*

107. *Id.* at 219.

108. *Id.*

109. *Id.* at 249.

110. Yeats, *supra* note 8, at 464.

111. Laura Brown, "Reading Race and Gender: Jonathan Swift," 23.4 *Eighteenth Century Studies* 425, 426 (1990).

SEX

AT WORK

Susan B. Estrich

▼

1. Introduction: The Modern Law of Rape

During the 1970s and 1980s, rape law reform occupied a prominent place on the agendas of feminist organizations across the country. It was said by many, and with good reason, that the history of rape law was a history of both sexism and racism; that too often the victim was victimized a second time by a legal system that focused more on determining her fault than the man's; that far from protecting women, rape prosecutions served to stigmatize all but a few as liars and whores, as vindictive and spiteful, as villains rather than victims. All of these criticisms were voiced loudly; all were largely true. And, unfortunately, they still are.[1]

This is not to say that feminist law reformers lacked the ability or skill to change the laws. In fact, the laws *were* changed, in virtually every state. So why wasn't the problem solved?

Part of the answer is that in practice the law had long drawn distinctions between different kinds of rape. These distinctions survived, and in some cases obscured, attempts at law reform. When a woman was raped by a stranger, or better yet, by two strangers jumping from the bushes and brandishing weapons, courts waved aside the substantive requirement of resistance. The procedural requirements of a prompt complaint and of other evidence to corroborate the woman's testimony, though often formally applicable, were quickly found to be met, or excused outright. Even the relevance of a woman's sexual past was considered dubious at best. These are the cases that the system has long considered to be "real rapes," and "real rape" has always been considered a serious crime.

Of course, prosecuting even a "real rape" charge may still be a painful experience for a woman despite these relaxed requirements. Law reform could ease that pain by at least formally shielding a woman from questions about her sexual past with other men. Yet however painful the legal process was for the woman, the chances of a prosecutor prosecuting her case, a jury convicting her assailant, an appellate court upholding the conviction, and a man serving a long sentence were and are very substantial.

That has not been the case when the man is a friend, neighbor, or coworker; or when the force consists of words and hands instead of guns and knives. Technically, such cases meet the definition of rape: sexual intercourse, by force or threat of force, against the will and without the consent of the victim.[2] In practice, however, few of these cases follow the legal route of "real rape" cases. Reform or no reform, most such cases are never reported by their victims, most that are reported do not lead to prosecution and conviction, and those that do result in successful prosecutions are disproportionately likely to result in either reversal on appeal or suspension of sentence.[3]

With the benefit of hindsight, it is certainly possible to see the flaws in the reform statutes. The focus on force as a substitute for consent looks shortsighted at best. The obsessive attention to names of crimes and kinds of sexual acts, rather than traditional issues of mens rea, seems out of place. It would be far better to criminalize negligent sexual intercourse than to debate what kinds of acts constitute criminal sexual conduct in the fourth degree. At best, such delineations only provide plea bargaining material. Perhaps most fundamentally, the reformers often failed to insist on explicit statutory language to provide that a nonstranger who forces sex by words or fists commits the crime of rape, leaving some of the new statutes as susceptible to antivictim interpretations of forced sex as the old ones.

Even so, the new statutes could easily have served as vehicles for meaningful reform. Though these statutes did not always mandate reform in language that hindsight would applaud, they surely did not preclude it. And in many cases, the results under the best-written statutes have been no different than those under their less artfully drafted predecessors. Good statutes, like mediocre and old-fashioned ones, have all served as mechanisms for prosecutors to downgrade or dismiss the complaints of women raped by friends, neighbors, and employers (not to mention current or former lovers); for juries to disbelieve these complaints; for appellate courts to reverse convictions based on them. In practice, the revised statutes have not always protected women from being judged blameworthy. The inquiry has too often remained focused on the appropriateness of the male-female relationship and the woman's role in provoking, accepting, endorsing, and affirming the rightness of her rape.[4]

In the last analysis, reform failed not because feminists are not good at writing statutes, but because if there is one area of social behavior where sexism is entrenched in law—one realm where traditional male prerogatives are most protected, male power most jealously preserved, and female power most jealously limited—it is in the area of sex itself, even forced sex. Guns and gangs may be recognized as criminal, but to go beyond that is to enter a man's protected preserve, in life and in law. In life, this male domain is protected by the wielding of real power—economic, physical, psychological, and emotional. In law, it is protected by doctrines of consent, corroboration, fresh complaint, and provocation. It is protected by manipulating these doctrines to embrace female stereotypes that real women cannot meet. It is protected by a definition of reasonableness that pits this woman against that ideal, that pits one woman against the rest. It is protected by punishing women who are weak for their weakness, and women who are exceptional for their strength. It is protected, in short, by the operation of sexism in law.

There is simply no other explanation for the unique rules governing rape prosecutions.[5] Rape is the only crime whose victims are almost exclusively female. And it is the only crime that is defined more by the actions, reactions, motives, and inadequacies of the victim than by those of the defendant. As a result, the victim finds herself bound by a set of rules that she—and the voice of women—are excluded from shaping, a set of rules few women can hope to meet. In practice, this means that our legal system imposes obligations on the mostly female victims of rape that are imposed on no other victim of any other crime. We do not require people to resist a mugger, even if the mugger was once a friend. We do not insist on witnesses to robbery. We rarely question the virtue of the robbed store clerk or even the defrauded company owner. We do not downgrade larceny if the victim wore an expensive suit or walked on a dangerous street, or even if he contributed to panhandlers in the past. Yet we require rape victims to prove their virtue, and we impose obligations of actual resistance, corroboration, and fresh complaint on them.

These very same doctrines, unique in the criminal law, are becoming familiar tools in sexual harassment cases. The rules and prejudices have been borrowed almost wholesale from traditional rape law. The focus on the conduct of the woman—her reactions or lack of them, her resistance or lack of it—reappears with only the most minor changes. The evaluative stance is distressingly familiar: One judges the woman's injury from a perspective that ignores women's views; or one compares her view to that of some ideal reasonable woman, or that of women afraid to speak out against harassment for fear of losing their jobs; and thus one applies a standard that the victim cannot and does not meet. The old demons, such as corroboration and fresh complaint, are invoked as if decades of criticism of the criminal law had never taken place. All this is attached to a cause of action that carries no prison sentence, nor even the possibility of compensatory damages, let alone punitive ones, and where relief is limited to an often toothless remedy in equity.

While the crime of rape is centuries old, the federal cause of action for sexual harassment is an invention of our times. The prohibiting statute was not passed until the 1960s; its application to "sexual harassment"—a term that was not even coined until the 1970s—was not recognized in trial courts until the late 1970s, and was affirmed by the United States Supreme Court only in the 1980s. The very existence of such a cause of action is a triumph for feminist scholars and practitioners, as well as for victims of sexual harassment. But the glass is most assuredly half empty.

Given their recent vintage, sexual harassment suits presented unique opportunities to shape the cause of action with a heightened awareness of the traditional sexist doctrines that the feminist efforts to reform rape laws highlighted. The fact that many federal courts jettison such opportunities daily, that the worst of rape litigation stands more as an example followed than one rejected, is the most persuasive and painful evidence of the durability of sexism in the law's judgment of the sexual relations of men and women.[6] This article seeks to present and evaluate just that evidence, in the hope that in the harshness of light such evidence will appear, as it should, untenable.

2. Finding a Cause of Action:
The Application of Title VII to Sexual Harassment
The Title VII Cause of Action

Title VII of the Civil Rights Act of 1964 prohibits discrimination in employment on the basis of race, religion, national origin, or sex.[7] The inclusion of the category of sex was something of an accident, at best. It was added as an amendment one day before House passage of the Civil Rights Act; its proponents included a number of congressmen opposed to the Act, who hoped that the inclusion of "sex" would highlight the absurdity of the effort as a whole, and contribute to its defeat.[8] The strategy obviously failed, but it explains why there was no legislative history to guide the courts and the Equal Employment Opportunity Commission (EEOC), the statutorily created enforcement agency, in deciding what discrimination based on sex means.

Early decisions struggled with issues that to most people now seem easy. Is it sex discrimination to refuse to hire mothers of small children, while continuing to hire women who are not mothers and all men (including fathers of small children)? The courts ultimately answered yes: Discriminating on the basis of sex plus some other factor, such as parenthood, nonetheless establishes actionable sex distinctions.[9] This was not so for a policy that discriminated against pregnant persons; after the Supreme Court concluded that pregnancy discrimination was not sex discrimination at all, it took an act of Congress to strike down such policies.[10]

Even so, Title VII emerged as a powerful tool in many respects. First, it afforded a federal cause of action, to be tried before a federal judge, thus avoiding the strictures of state tort law and the possible prejudices of state court juries. Second, its procedural rules were, at least until recently, structured to ease the plaintiff's burden of establishing a prima facie case, by having the plaintiff show, through the use of quantitative data or testimony about particular events, the discriminatory effects of policies, rather than by having the plaintiff meet the far more elusive constitutional requirement of proving invidious intent.[11] Therefore, it was not very surprising that as feminist scholars and popular magazines[12] focused attention on the problems of sexual coercion and harassment in the workplace, Title VII's prohibitions on sex discrimination would be viewed as a possible and desirable avenue for litigation.

In a landmark theoretical work published in 1979, Professor Catharine MacKinnon argued that sexual harassment, which she defined as "the unwanted imposition of sexual requirements in the context of a relationship of unequal power," should be considered sex discrimination, actionable under Title VII.[13] The following year the EEOC agreed, and issued guidelines finding harassment on the basis of sex to be a violation of Title VII, and labeling as sexual harassment "[u]nwelcome sexual advances, requests for sexual favors, and other verbal or physical conduct of a sexual nature," when such behavior occurred in any of three circumstances:

> (1) [where] submission to such conduct is made either explicitly or implicitly a term or condition of an individual's employment, (2) [where] submission to or rejection of such conduct by an individual is used as the basis for employment decisions affecting such individual, or (3) [where] such conduct has the purpose or effect of unreasonably interfering with an individual's work performance or creating an intimidating, hostile, or offensive working environment.[14]

The various definitions are obviously fraught with uncertainties: Whose point of view is determinative? What counts as an implicit threat? When does interference become unreasonable? What happens if one loses a job promotion to a woman who is having a "voluntary" affair with the boss? What happens if supervisors impose no requirements, but coworkers create an environment that some but not all women find intolerable? At least in the EEOC's eyes, these were questions for the courts to resolve on a case-by-case basis. First, however, the courts had to accept the existence of the cause of action.

The Early Decisions—and the Usual Arguments

The early cases focused on a rather standard set of arguments.[15] One argument frequently heard was "Congress never intended such a cause of action." Certainly this was true, but then Congress barely intended that sex discrimination be prohibited in employment at all. Some argued that state tort law already provided a remedy. But the outlook in tort was—and still is—uncertain. In theory, relief might be available in tort for intentional infliction of emotional distress but in practice the traditional rule was (and remains) that soliciting sexual favors is not extreme and outrageous conduct, because "there is no harm in asking."[16] Assault and battery required more than words, while wrongful discharge suits were wholly dependent on the various developments in employment-at-will laws.[17]

Not all of the arguments, however, were as predictable, or so far beside the point. At least two of the major arguments put forth by employers in the 1970s, and accepted by a number of courts, presaged some of the basic theoretical tensions inherent in the Title VII sexual harassment action. Both arguments were ultimately resolved to allow suits to go forward, but in a larger sense, the failure to address these issues at their core continues to plague the cause of action that the suits ostensibly support.

The first argument was, in its narrow form, based on the slippery slope to bisexuality. Even if one takes the view that homosexual advances (e.g., by a man to a man) would also be sex discrimination (because if he weren't a man . . .), the possibility of a bisexual supervisor making advances to both sexes illustrates the folly of considering either homosexual or heterosexual overtures to be sex discrimination. As one court put it:

> It would be ludicrous to hold that the sort of activity involved here [sexual advances by a male supervisor to a female worker] was contemplated by the Act because to do so would mean that if the conduct complained of was directed equally to males there would be no basis for suit.[18]

The narrow answer to this argument is that if a woman is being sexually harassed, or denied higher wages, because she is a woman, then she is suffering from gender discrimination. When conditions are imposed on a person that would not be imposed but for her being a woman, that is sex discrimination regardless of the nature of the offensive conditions. If the boss harasses everyone, or denies everyone higher wages, he may well be a philanderer, a terrible person, and a cheapskate to boot, but he would not be engaging in sex discrimination. This is the conventional response. Eventually, this view came to be accepted, sometimes reluctantly to be sure, by all district courts. Today, it seems so obvious that commentators barely pause to consider it.

Unfortunately, this conventional answer ignores the "sexual" aspect of sexual harassment and the unique meaning of such harassment in a male-female context. We fit such cases into the Title VII rubric by pretending that they are no different than wage cases or other working condition cases. We treat the issue of sexuality, and the special nature of sexual coercion, as entirely beside the point: The sole issue becomes whether the coercion, whatever form it takes, would have been imposed on a man. But this issue is not analogous to issues in other Title VII cases. A man might pat another man on the back (if he is, as one court described it, a "physical person" [19]) but in our society, the meaning of this behavior inevitably differs if the person being patted is a woman. What makes sexual harassment more offensive, more debilitating, and more dehumanizing to its victims than other forms of discrimination is precisely the fact that it is sexual. Not only are men exercising power over women, but they are operating in a realm that is still judged according to a gender double standard, itself a reflection of the extent to which sexuality is used to penalize women. In my view, these cases are such a disaster in doctrinal terms precisely because, as with rape, they involve sex and sexuality. And yet however clear all that might be, the argument for treating these cases as violations of Title VII begins from the premise that the sexuality that lies at their core is legally invisible: they are simply cases of differential treatment based on gender.

Later courts have split on where and how "sexuality" fits into sexual harassment. Some courts consider sexuality beside the point and have consequently adopted a definition of harassment that requires no proof that it was "sexual" in nature. They have managed to expand the offense by ignoring what is generally at its core, even in cases they find questionable.[20] This approach carries with it the danger that, by ignoring the "sexual" element that is almost always present and which aggravates the injury, violations that are indeed substantial may look rather trivial. Other courts have insisted that harassment must be "sexual" in nature to fit within Title VII, and then have limited the scope of the action by adopting what seems a uniquely male perspective on issues such as men touching women at work.[21] Obviously, the latter view is less than ideal, not because these courts acknowledge the sexual element, but because they define it so one-sidedly. The middle ground is yet to be found.

The second argument, heard even more often in the early cases, rests on the alleged pervasiveness of what attorneys for one employer termed "sexual consideration" in the workplace.[22] To find Title VII liability in such cases, another court reasoned, would mean "a potential federal lawsuit every time any employee made amorous or sexually oriented advances toward another. The only sure way an employer could avoid such charges would be to have employees who were asexual."[23] Or as a third court stated:

> It is conceivable, under plaintiff's theory, that flirtations of the smallest order would give rise to liability. The attraction of males to females and females to males is a natural sex phenomenon and it is probable that this attraction plays at least a subtle part in most personnel decisions. Such being the case, it would seem wise for the Courts to refrain from delving into these matters . . . .[24]

There is no question that sexual consideration, flirtations, and advances *are* as pervasive in the workplace as these opinions suggest, although their victims surely find them more offensive and threatening than did these particular courts. In 1976, *Redbook* magazine (hardly a mouthpiece of the feminist left) asked its readers whether they had been subject to unwanted sexual "attention" at work from male bosses or colleagues; 9 out of 10 women who responded said yes, and 75 percent called the advances embarrassing, demeaning, or intimidating.[25] In a more scientific study by the federal government four years later, 42 percent of the women respondents reported being subjected to some form of "sexual harassment," at an estimated cost to the federal government of $189 million from 1978 to 1980.[26] The harassment figures were roughly the same when the government resurveyed in 1987, but the costs over a two-year period rose to $267 million.[27] Smaller surveys during this period, sometimes phrased in terms of harassment or unwelcome advances, consistently found that anywhere from 36 to 53 percent of the women questioned identified themselves as victims.[28]

But the facts of many of the early cases provided an all too easy route to evade the reality of pervasive sexual harassment. None of these early cases involved what anyone would consider minor episodes of harassment. All of them involved, as early test cases often do, rather egregious incidents in which, at least for motion purposes, courts accepted as true complaints that women were being coerced into sexual intercourse with their bosses as a condition of keeping their jobs or receiving a promotion.[29] It is often said that hard cases make bad law. Sometimes easy cases are worse still. The obvious answer in easy cases like these—the one that appellate courts and commentators seized upon most when reversing or criticizing denials of liability by lower courts—was to use the egregious facts of the particular case to paint a picture of sexual harassment as an extreme and rare event.

In real life, sexual harassment is a pervasive and common problem, but the cause of action was premised on its being unusual and rare. Perhaps there was no other way to win the early battles. But the choice ensured that the war would be a long one.

In hindsight, it seems that the early district courts were, as the law reviews often like to put it, wrong—but for the right reasons. They were right in recognizing that the fact that such cases involved sex made them inherently different from, and not simply another form of, the usual Title VII wage-and-hours or hiring-and-firing cases. And they were right to recognize that sexual harassment (although they certainly would not have called it that) was pervasive in the workplace. To prohibit it in all cases, rather than in only the most egregious, presented a fundamental challenge to the way business is conducted in America. These early district courts were, in my view, very wrong in citing these facts as reasons not to act, rather than as imperatives demanding strong action. But by treating sex as irrelevant and harassment as a rare event, the courts that reversed the district courts sowed the seeds of what so drastically limits the efficacy of the current cause of action for sexual harassment.

In 1986, the Supreme Court finally resolved the question of the *existence* of a Title VII cause of action for sexual harassment, even though by that point most courts seemed willing to accept such an action in some form. However, the Supreme Court's decision in *Meritor Savings Bank v. Vinson*[30] can hardly be construed as an unqualified victory.

Mechelle Vinson began work at the Meritor Savings Bank as a teller-trainee. Her boss, who had also hired her, was Sidney Taylor, a vice president of the bank and manager of one of its branch offices. With Taylor as her supervisor for the next four years, Vinson was promoted to teller, head teller, and finally assistant branch manager; according to the Court, it was "undisputed that her advancement there was based on merit alone."[31] In September 1978, she notified Taylor that she intended to take sick leave for an indefinite time; on November 1 of that year, the bank fired her for over-using her leave.[32] Vinson sued, alleging that during her employment she had "constantly been subjected to sexual harassment" by Taylor.[33] According to Vinson's trial testimony, shortly after her probationary period as a teller-trainee, Taylor invited her out to dinner—and to have sex with him at a motel. At first she refused, but, afraid of losing her job, she eventually agreed. Over the next three years, Taylor repeatedly demanded sexual relations with Vinson. She testified that she had intercourse with him forty or fifty times. He fondled her in front of other employees, followed her into the women's restroom, exposed himself to her, and forcibly raped her on several occasions.[34]

Taylor denied everything, claiming that Vinson fabricated the allegations due to a business-related dispute. The bank also denied everything, and denied knowledge or approval of any sexual harassment.[35]

The district court found it unnecessary to resolve the conflicting testimony, concluding that no sex discrimination existed in any event. "If [Vinson] and Taylor did engage in an intimate or sexual relationship during the time of [her] employment with [the bank], that relationship was a voluntary one . . . having nothing to do with her continued employment at [the bank] or her advancement or promotions at that institution."[36] Furthermore, the trial judge concluded that given the bank's policy against sexual harassment and Vinson's failure to lodge an internal complaint, the bank would not be liable even if sexual harassment did take place.[37]

The trial court's insistence on proof of a "nexus" between alleged sexual harassment and job-related decisions imposed strict limits on the sexual harassment cause of action. Under this view, which a number of courts shared at the time, unless the woman could prove that her sexual relationship affected job-related decisions by her employer, no claim for employment discrimination would stand. Sometimes the theory's application strained common sense: could it be, as one court suggested, that a department chairman with whom the plaintiff refused to have sex would have no voice at all in denying her tenure?[38] More often, as modern cases demonstrate, the theory leads to a great deal of testimony about the woman's tardiness, or other minor infractions, which is paraded with great energy as the reason for her firing.[39] But the most curious cases of all are those like *Vinson*, where a woman's competence is used *against* her: The circuit court found it "undisputed" that Mechelle Vinson was promoted not because she was sleeping with her boss (and being fondled by him in public, and even occasionally raped by him in private), but because of her merit.[40] After all, in whose interest would it be to admit otherwise? "Yes, your honor, I slept my way to the top. . . ." Hardly. The reality, of course, as even some of the worst early district courts almost recognized, is that sex may enter into a decision that could and should have been made strictly on the merits. Competent people are not always promoted, and tardy ones not always fired.

Not all courts at the time of *Vinson* viewed establishing a nexus between sex and job-related decisions as the only means to prove sex discrimination. The Court of Appeals for the District of Columbia reversed the trial judge and held that a Title VII violation might rest on either of two types of sexual harassment claims: harassment that conditions concrete employment benefits on granting sexual favors (often called the quid pro quo type, the functional expression of the nexus theory), and harassment that creates a hostile or offensive work environment without affecting economic benefits.[41] The court concluded that Vinson's grievance was of the hostile environment type, that the district court had not considered this claim, and that a remand was necessary as a result.[42] It also suggested that the lower court's finding of "voluntariness" might have been based on "the voluminous testimony regarding Vinson's dress and personal fantasies," testimony that the appellate court believed "had no place in this litigation."[43] Finally, the court held that the bank, like employers in all Title VII cases, would be absolutely liable for the discriminatory acts of its supervisor, regardless of whether the employer knew of the misconduct.[44]

The bank appealed, making *Vinson* the first, and to date the only, sexual harassment case to reach the Supreme Court. The Court's holding marks the conclusion of the first part of our story, the birth of a federal cause of action, and the introduction to the second, the dominance of sexism in defining that cause of action.

Then Justice and now Chief Justice Rehnquist delivered the opinion of the Court. The Court rejected the bank's claim that only sexual harassment that related to a "tangible loss" of "an economic character," as opposed to "purely psychological aspects of the workplace environment," could give rise to Title VII liability.[45] Pointing to the EEOC guidelines, precedent in racial harassment cases, and recent appellate court decisions, the Court held that "hostile environment" harassment, like quid pro quo harassment, may violate Title VII.[46]

To this holding, however, the Court attached three very significant reservations. First, "not all workplace conduct that may be described as 'harassment' affects a 'term, condition, or privilege' of employment within the meaning of Title VII."[47] For instance, the Court quoted a Fifth Circuit racial discrimination case to suggest that the " 'mere utterance of an ethnic or racial epithet which engenders offensive feelings in an employee' would not affect the conditions of employment to a sufficiently significant degree to violate Title VII."[48] To be actionable, sexual harassment "must be sufficiently severe or pervasive 'to alter the conditions of [the victim's] employment and create an abusive working environment.' "[49]

Second, while "voluntariness" in the sense of consent is not a defense to a claim of sexual harassment, "[t]he gravamen of any sexual harassment claim is that the alleged sexual advances were 'unwelcome.' . . . The correct inquiry is whether respondent by her conduct indicated that the alleged sexual advances were unwelcome, not whether her actual participation in sexual intercourse was voluntary."[50] And contrary to the Court of Appeals, the Court held that "it does not follow that a complainant's sexually provocative speech or dress is irrelevant as a matter of law in determining whether he or she found particular sexual advances unwelcome. *To the contrary, such evidence is obviously relevant.*"[51]

Third, while finding that the question of the employer's liability had "a rather abstract quality about it given the state of the record," the Court none-theless held that the appellate court "erred in concluding that employers are always automatically liable for sexual harassment by their supervisors." [52] The usual rule in Title VII cases is strict liability, and four Justices, concurring in the judgment, argued that the same rule should apply to sexual harass-ment claims, too. [53] The majority disagreed. Those in the majority implicitly suggested that in hostile environment cases no employer, or at least none with a policy against harassment, should be found liable in the absence of actual or constructive knowledge. [54]

Thus, having established a Title VII cause of action, the Court immedi-ately imposed restrictions on it. Whether by design or not, these restrictions not only make litigation more difficult for particular claimants like Mechelle Vinson, but also reinforce some of the most demeaning sexual stereotypes of women. Such restrictions operate to preserve male access to "traditional" workplace sex.

In the following sections of this article, I examine the reservations ar-ticulated in *Vinson* and the limits that the Supreme Court and lower courts have placed on sexual harassment suits. Section 3 addresses the "unwel-comeness" requirement, which the *Vinson* Court termed the "gravamen" of the action. Section 4 discusses the nexus requirement as applied in quid pro quo cases, while Section 5 addresses the requirement of pervasiveness in hostile environment cases. Section 6 examines the issues of credibility and proof that confront women complainants in both hostile environment and quid pro quo cases. Finally, Section 7 focuses on the limits of employer liability and on the paucity of remedies even where the elements of sexual harassment can be proven.

3. The Gravamen of the Action: Unwelcomeness

"Unwelcomeness" has served as a ve-hicle to import some of the most pernicious doctrines of rape law into Title VII cases. Given the additional prerequisites for establishing sexual harass-ment in any event, the unwelcomeness requirement is unnecessary even as a means to protect what some would consider legitimate, consensual sex in the workplace.

The district court's holding that Mechelle Vinson engaged in voluntary sexual intercourse with Sidney Taylor ignores the coercive nature of their employer-employee relationship, including her potential need for her job and her likely dependence on Taylor for it, as well as any implicit threat of retaliation should she reject his advances. There were, apparently, no guns or knives involved; under the strictest definitions of the criminal law, this coercion was not rape. But that does not make it simply sex.

Perhaps the Supreme Court, when it decided *Vinson*, implicitly recognized this in concluding that the district court was, if not answering wrongly, at least asking the wrong question. The Court held that the district court had erred in focusing on the "voluntariness" of Ms. Vinson's participation in the claimed sexual episodes. Rather than completely abandon the inquiry into consent, however, the Court held that "[t]he correct inquiry is whether respondent by her conduct indicated that the alleged sexual advances were unwelcome," terming unwelcomeness the "gravamen of any sexual harassment claim." [55]

The shift in inquiry from the voluntariness of the sexual act to the welcomeness of the sexual advances can be counted as a victory for women, at least in legal terms, for it provided a basis for concluding that the district court had erred. But the victory is limited at best: Unwelcomeness has emerged as the doctrinal stepchild of the rape standards of consent and resistance, and shares virtually all of their problems.

The consent standard in rape law shifts the focus of the inquiry from the conduct of the man to that of the woman. She, rather than he, goes on trial, and if her conduct is the focus of the trial, then a range of evidence relating to her—how she lives, how she dresses, how she acts—becomes, arguably, relevant to the inquiry. That she is the victim of a violent crime may be lost in the scrutiny of her lifestyle.

To be sure, one can imagine a consent standard that empowers women, at least if their accounts were believed. Such a standard might allay the burden inherent in the shift of focus from the man's conduct to the woman's. If nonconsent were defined as a "no" and if a woman's saying no made sex criminal, then a focus on nonconsent might actually give some women power to define for themselves the permissible range of "force" in sex. But that is not how the law understands nonconsent.

Nonconsent in rape has been defined not by what a woman says, but by what she does. The focus has been her conduct, not her words. While the requirement of "utmost resistance" has been formally abandoned in every jurisdiction, men who do not use guns and knives have been privileged to ignore women's words, to use at least the force of their own bodies, and to call their violation of women sex nonetheless.

With this background, the Supreme Court's conclusion that the "gravamen" of a sexual harassment case is unwelcomeness seems all too painfully familiar. On its face, the standard presents at least three serious problems. First, as in rape cases, the focus is on the victim, not on the man: she may be less powerful, and economically dependent, but she still is expected to express unwelcomeness. Unless she does, no burden is placed on him to refrain from abusing his position of power. A doctor may be required, by tort law, to secure affirmative and informed assent *before* he lays his hands on a woman; but a boss may freely touch any woman subordinate, until and unless she expresses, through her conduct, her nonassent. The justification for imposing the notice requirement on the woman, according to one leading commentator, is "[a]s the saying goes, 'even dirty old men need love.' "[56] Perhaps this is so, but why the law should protect this quest—at the expense of the emotional and bodily integrity of the female employee—is not so obvious. At the very least, we might demand that such men look for "love" outside of work, or at least ask for it first.

The second problem with the unwelcomeness standard, as defined by the Supreme Court, is that "conduct" is the yardstick by which we measure assent. The plain implication is that a polite "no" may not suffice. Though it is bad enough to presume consent in the absence of words, it is worse still to presume it notwithstanding a woman's words.

Third, and most pernicious of all, since the focus of inquiry is on the plaintiff, and since the unwelcomeness test must be met by her conduct, should we be surprised if the trial focuses on what the plaintiff wears, how she talks, even who else she sleeps with? Whatever unwelcomeness means, the Court in *Vinson* squarely held that a "complainant's sexually provocative speech or dress" is "obviously relevant" in determining whether she found the particular sexual advances unwelcome.[57]

What is "sexually provocative" dress? Does the Court mean that women who wear short skirts intend to invite sexual advances? That tight sweaters may justly be pled as provocation for otherwise offensive conduct? That men are legally entitled to treat women whose clothes fit snugly with less respect than women whose clothes fit loosely? By accepting the notion of "sexually provocative" clothing, the Court effectively denies women the right to dress as they wish. Women who wear short skirts, take pride in their own bodies, dress for themselves, go out directly from work, wear hand-me-down clothes, have gained weight lately, or even are trying to be attractive to their husbands and boyfriends are all, under the Court's view, presumed to welcome advances by *any* man on the job.

The consequences of this approach are devastating for women. Women are invisible as anything other than potential sexual objects of men—invisible to the Court and, ultimately by its rules, invisible to themselves. And in making the determination of the harassment of women dependent upon the extent of "sexually provocative" behavior by women, the Court adopts a rule that holds women responsible for their own torment. Thus, the victim of harassment, like the rape victim, suffers not only the direct injury of sexual abuse, but also the indignity of the Court's presumption that she is to blame.

Indeed, in determining whether advances are welcome, some courts have gone further still, borrowing from rape law the all too familiar "no means yes, or at least maybe" rule: "Although Plaintiff rejected [her boss's sexual overtures], her initial rejections were neither unpleasant nor unambiguous, and gave [her boss] no reason to believe that his moves were unwelcome."[58] Therefore, unwelcomeness may be judged not according to what the woman meant, but by the implication that the man felt entitled to draw. The ambiguity plainly existed only in his perception, not hers. The courts, however, privilege his interpretation.

A related technique, also familiar from rape cases, penalizes the woman who does not act like a man, and enforces a double standard of proof. In *Kresko v. Rulli*, for example, a student intern working in county government filed suit complaining that her supervisor had continuously sexually harassed her.[59] The court found that his advances were not unwelcome, noting that she had frequent lunches with her boss, wrote him "at least one personal, affectionate note," and engaged in "mutual kissing and petting."[60] Most important to the court was that she did not complain about her treatment, except to another intern, even though she was the sort of young woman who was active in school politics, and had no qualms about filing a complaint against a dentist who was treating her family unfairly. "The logical conclusion is that [she] did not complain because either the advances were welcome, or at least she had ambivalent feelings."[61]

Logical to the court, perhaps, but empirical studies have consistently found that women do not talk about sexual harassment even to friends.[62] Silence is not necessarily proof of welcomeness; it may well signal the shame, humiliation, fear, and dependence of a victim. It is precisely this humiliation and fear that makes simply untenable the analogy between complaints about a dentist treating you unjustly and complaints about your boss forcing you to have sex with him.

Even more troubling is the court's finding that the woman must have been "ambivalent." One rarely hears women testifying that their feelings about a sexual advance by their supervisor are ambivalent. Indeed, the studies suggest that men, more than women, seem ambivalent about sexual advances; men are far more likely than women to be flattered by sexual attention in the workplace, and to assume that women will be flattered as well.[63]

In practice, both traditional and nontraditional women may find that their own actions are used against them in the unwelcomeness analysis. A woman who behaves in the most stereotypical ways—complimenting men, straightening their ties, "mov[ing] her body in a provocative manner,"[64] let alone eating dinner with the boss on a business trip, or remaining friendly even after rejecting his advances—may find that the sexual advances she rejects are, as a matter of law, not unwelcome.[65] Similarly, women who act too much like men—who use "crude and vulgar language," or choose to eat with the men in the employee lunchroom—cannot be heard to complain of a worksite that is "permeated by an extensive amount of lewd and vulgar conversation and conduct."[66] Their "unfeminine" behavior apparently deprives them of protection, whatever the statutory mandate. Like women in rape cases who have sexual pasts, their conduct makes them fair game.

In short, the unwelcomeness requirement performs the doctrinal dirty work of the consent standard in rape law. At a minimum, it shifts the focus from the man to the woman. In too many cases, her conduct is evaluated in terms that see women only as the sexual objects of men. The standard of judgment is painfully male: Women who act like most women—who act "friendly," or dress stylishly, or keep silent—discredit themselves, but no more than do women who act too much like men—who use lewd language, or eat lunch with the boys. The apparent difficulty that many judges have finding the deserving victim raises the question whether, at least in some courts, the very point of the inquiry might be in effect to protect a broad category of sexual relations in the workplace, so long as these relations appear, at least to the men judging them, typical and acceptable.

Certainly, that is the rule in rape cases. The consent standard—and the corresponding inquiries into what a woman did or said, how she "led the man on," or how she failed adequately to signal her nonconsent—have, at least until recently, made successful prosecution of acquaintance rape all but impossible. Where the relationship is "appropriate," at least to the court's eyes, judges tend to see sex, not rape. Similarly, in Title VII cases they see sex, not sexual harassment. In both types of cases, they are often wrong. That a certain relationship might be appropriate does not necessarily mean that the man's behavior has been.

The strongest justification for the welcomeness doctrine is that the rule ensures that consensual workplace sex does not provide the basis for a civil action. The more radical response to this argument is that there is no such thing as truly "welcome" sex between a male boss and a female employee who needs her job. And if there is, then the women who welcome it will not be bringing lawsuits in any event. Certainly from my experience teaching this subject, it seems much easier for men putting themselves in the shoes of the powerful to assume that their advances are welcome than it is for women putting themselves in the shoes of the powerless to think that even a "yes" is a real or free choice.

One need not adopt the more radical approach, however, to reject the welcomeness inquiry as unnecessary. The fact is that in both the quid pro quo and the hostile environment cases, additional requirements exist for proving that sex is harassment, making the unwelcomeness inquiry superfluous, and leaving no justification for the burden it imposes.

Consider, first, the case of quid pro quo harassment. In such a case, the woman is required to establish a direct connection between her acceptance or rejection of sexual advances and a job benefit or loss. The prototype fact pattern is simple: If you sleep with me, you'll be promoted; if you don't, you'll be fired. The question of whether such a bargain is "welcomed" by the woman should startle even those who reject the more radical approach to workplace sex. Even if you believe that I might freely consent to sex with my supervisor in some other circumstances, can free will exist in the face of coercion? With a gun to my head, would you even ask about philanthropy?

Nothing in Title VII requires one to afford protection to such an employer. When a boss threatens (or if you believe in welcomeness, "offers") to fire you if you don't sleep with him, or promote you if you do, we are not dealing simply with workplace sex, welcome or not. Sex in this context determines the conditions of employment. Title VII leaves the employer free to hire or fire for any reason he chooses other than sex; here, it is plainly sex—both the gender of the offeree, which renders her subject to such a bargain, and the very terms of the bargain—that functions as the basis for the employment decision. And this is so regardless of welcomeness.

Indeed, at least some courts have recognized as much, albeit in suits brought by third parties. The Court of Appeals for the District of Columbia, in *King v. Palmer*, upheld a sex discrimination claim where a promotion that the plaintiff sought went instead to another woman with whom their boss was having a sexual relationship.[67] The issue on appeal was whether the plaintiff was required to produce evidence that the sexual relationship had actually been "consummated."[68] The court found her evidence of "sexual conduct" sufficient to support her claim that sex was a substantial factor in the other woman's promotion.[69] The unwelcomeness of the sex was simply not an issue.[70]

Now, one can certainly argue that third-party suits such as these raise privacy issues that direct suits do not. Should people be free to initiate lawsuits, complete with comprehensive discovery and the like, as a way to ferret out sexual relationships of third parties? One can argue that Title VII was intended to be enforced by the direct victims of sex discrimination, not by those once removed. But, I would submit, it is very difficult to argue that the underlying bargain—sex for a job or promotion—is worthy of protection, or does not constitute sex-based discrimination, when viewed one step away. This is not because such a valuable offer must be made available to everyone, regardless of gender; it is, rather, because whatever other preferences and penalties may be traded in the workplace for jobs or promotions, sex should not be one of them. The irony is that this may be easier to see from the perspective of the third party than from the perspective of the immediate victim.

Thus, eliminating unwelcomeness as an element in quid pro quo cases would not, for better or worse, bar sex that many men and some women might consider welcome or consensual. Rather, doing so would prohibit only conditioning job benefits upon sex. The man who chooses to make the workplace his sexplace would in theory remain free to do so. He would simply be barred from using extortion—threats of harm and promises of benefit—to win his welcome.

Unwelcomeness is no more necessary in hostile environment cases, although for different reasons. The irony of the hostile environment case is that the subjective welcomeness inquiry, gravamen or not, is fundamentally at odds with all the other elements of the cause of action. A hostile environment, the courts have consistently held, must be based on objective criteria, evaluated from an "objective" viewpoint.[71] The fact that a particular woman found the environment totally debilitating is beside the point; the question is what other persons, often mythic, would think. Thus the welcomeness inquiry is either utterly gratuitous or gratuitously punitive. It is gratuitous when the environment is not proven objectively to be hostile, because an unwelcome environment that is not objectively hostile does not give rise to liability in any event. It is gratuitously punitive if the environment is found objectively hostile, for in that case the employer can nonetheless escape the burden of addressing the issue, by portraying this particular woman as so base as to be unworthy of respect or decency, and by arguing that she thus welcomed, through her conduct, an environment that a "reasonable" woman would have perceived as hostile. In either case, welcomeness serves as a means to keep the focus on the woman rather than the supervisor; on what she, rather than he, has done wrong; and on whether she deserves to be treated with human decency, rather than whether he violated the standards of decency and humanity.

Under the old rule in rape cases, a woman's sexual history might be relevant regardless of the circumstances of the assault. In most cases, the effect was not to improve the truth-seeking process of the courts, but to discourage women from filing complaints in the first instance. "Welcomeness"—defined in sexual harassment doctrine to include the woman's dress, language, habits, and even sex life—may play a similar role.

It should be obvious that the system already contains serious disincentives to women filing sexual harassment complaints. Start with embarrassment, loss of privacy, and sometimes shame. If the woman remains employed, she faces the prospect that her harasser and others will make her life impossible. If she has quit or been fired (and it seems no coincidence that women who are no longer employed bring most of the complaints), the danger is that she will be branded a troublemaker, and find it difficult to find another job. Empirical studies suggest that possibly actionable harassment is widespread, even endemic, but the number of lawsuits, not surprisingly, does not bear out this possibility. Anything that adds another disincentive, as the Supreme Court's unwelcomeness requirement surely does, ought to be supported by a strong justification. In my view, the unwelcomeness inquiry certainly is not.

4. Proving the Quid Pro Quo

The division between quid pro quo harassment and hostile environment harassment rests on the assumption that only in the former, and not the latter, does harassment directly determine economic benefits and losses. In practice, this is rarely so; the distinction between these two forms of harassment takes the form of a continuum rather than a divide.[72] When a woman is told to have sex or be fired (the classic quid pro quo), economic benefits are undoubtedly affected. But is the case so different when a boss propositions a female employee daily, or when in order to do her job, a woman must endure a range of physical and emotional abuse? There may be no manifest threat, at least in legal terms, to fire or not promote her. In practical terms, however, the impact on the woman will often be virtually identical: The victim will submit, quit, or end up being fired or held back for "cause," such as working too slowly, making too many mistakes, or taking too many sick days.[73]

The distinction is, however, significant in legal terms. The plaintiff in a quid pro quo case is not required, as a hostile environment claimant is, to prove that the harassment is pervasive and objectively intolerable. In practice, less harassment is necessary to satisfy the threshold requirement of a quid pro quo case.

There is, not surprisingly, a catch: While the quid pro quo plaintiff need not establish that harassment was pervasive, she faces two obstacles so substantial as to spell failure for many claimants. First, she must establish the existence of an actual threat. Second, she must prove that her reaction to the threat, rather than some other factor, resulted in her firing or demotion. In practice, these obstacles produce a working definition of quid pro quo harassment that may be so narrow as to make all but the most perfect plaintiffs unable to establish the requisite nexus, and all but the most perfectly stupid defendants able to rebut successfully a prima facie case.

Establishing the requisite threat is no easy matter. Only on rare occasions will a boss admit that he threatened a female employee with termination if she refused to sleep with him. Indeed, in all the cases I have reviewed, I cannot recall one instance where an employer admitted to threatening a female employee. As in many rape cases, there are rarely witnesses, leaving the factfinder to weigh one person's word against another's. Moreover, no words need ever be spoken to make such a threat effective.

In *Spencer v. General Electric Co.*,[74] for instance, the plaintiff testified that on a number of occasions, her boss asked her to have sex with him and to see him at her home. He also asked a coworker whether the plaintiff was any good in bed. She "understood" that her employment would suffer if she refused him, although no explicit threats or promises were made. At trial, she presented evidence of two promotions received by a coworker with whom the same man was having an affair. This evidence was not enough, according to the court, to prove that job benefits were contingent upon her submission to her supervisor's sexual advances.[75] The court emphasized that the employer took no adverse action against her; of course, the court ignored the fact that she was never promoted. More importantly, the court noted that the plaintiff introduced no testimony that her promoted coworker was unqualified, leaving the court satisfied that the other woman's promotions and salary increases were based on merit, not sexual favors.[76]

One cannot know simply from reading a court opinion whether Ms. Spencer's progress was retarded by the rejection of her boss's advances. Still, the court's opinion raises troubling questions in at least two respects. First, it fails to acknowledge what is obvious to most employees: bosses need not flaunt their power in order to exercise it. A "request" from a superior carries with it a different message than one from an equal. If the early district courts were right that "sexual consideration," as it was termed, pervades workplace decision-making, then on what basis can one presume that rejection of a request for sexual access will be considered irrelevant in future decisions that the boss makes about the one who rejected him? The better rule, it seems, would place on the man an affirmative burden of production, if not also of persuasion, to make clear that no threat was intended in his request. But at present no court imposes such a rule.

The second troubling aspect of *Spencer* is its invitation to women to discredit one another. It is not enough to prove that a coworker is having an affair with her boss; a plaintiff must also prove both that she herself is qualified, and that the coworker is not. Such a rule not only pits women against each other, but also misplaces the appropriate burdens. It may be true that the other woman *was* qualified, but it is also true that not all qualified people are promoted. If her affair played *any* part in her promotion (and is there anyone who believes that it is humanly possible that it would not?), then sex has indeed become a condition of employment, prohibited under Title VII.

In any event, most quid pro quo cases focus not so much on whether a threat was made, but on the related question of whether the woman's response to her boss's proposition or threat motivated the decision to deprive her of an economic benefit. If the nexus between proposition and economic deprivation is established, her claim that there was at least an implicit threat will usually be accepted.[77] Not surprisingly, establishing that nexus is even more difficult than establishing the threat.

Obviously, the easiest way to establish the basis for a personnel decision is from personnel files or statements. Not so long ago, for example, a woman brought suit on Fifth Amendment due process grounds against a member of Congress who actually wrote her a letter explaining that she did not get a particular job because she was a woman. He claimed that the actual reason was because she was unqualified; he just told her it was her gender so as not to hurt her feelings.[78] Since that time most, but not all, congressmen have become smarter.[79] But even at their most naive, most employers would not write letters to women, or place notes in personnel files, explaining that Mrs. S. did not receive a promotion because she refused sexual intercourse with her boss. These are things one seldom writes down, or even tells to close friends.

The absence of perfectly stupid employers necessitates the perfect employee. An employer can always find good reasons to fire people, as labor organizers have long understood. In case after case, one reads of women who were tardy for work, women (like Mechelle Vinson) who were out sick too often, women whose typing or phone skills are found, after some time on the job, to be less than par.[80] In theory, if one could show that other equally sick, tardy, or incompetent workers are not fired, one might convince a court that the stated reason is a pretext. In practice, finding other identically situated women may prove difficult if not impossible. Generally, only in cases where harassment was truly endemic to the workplace—and other women came forward to attest to it—have plaintiffs succeeded in establishing that the stated reason for their firing was only a pretext.[81]

At a more fundamental level, the quest for perfection begs the real question. For a fired employee, the real question is not whether she is perfect, but whether her sexual rejection of her boss played a role in his concluding that she is not. Or, to frame the inquiry in a more telling way, *would she still have been fired if she had said yes?* One sees many cases of women who said no and were fired, and very few of women who said yes and lost their jobs. Frequently there is evidence, as there was in *Spencer* and *Kresko*, that the same man had "welcome" relationships with other women in the workplace, and that these women remained nonlitigious and employed.[82] If a woman understands that she can keep her job by saying yes, she should be protected from firing if she says no. If an employer allows sex to have currency in his workplace, then Title VII at a bare minimum should require that those who say no be treated no worse than those who say yes. But that is not the way the courts ask the question, or answer it.

In *Dockter v. Rudolf Wolff Futures, Inc.*,[83] for example, the plaintiff was "an attractive female in her mid-twenties," who had "a ninth grade education, with a concomitant [sic] level of diction and oral presentation, and a somewhat querulous or testy personality."[84] She was working nights as a bartender; he was a customer trying to impress her. They engaged in some mutual flirting, and he hired her as his administrative assistant. "For the first few weeks, James, as he occasionally did with other female employees at the office, made sexual overtures to—in the vernacular of the modern generation, 'came on to'—her."[85] Ms. Dockter rejected these efforts, and reprimanded her boss for fondling her breast. James accepted his defeat, and not long after, the company fired Ms. Dockter.[86]

Ms. Dockter found herself in something of a Catch-22. The court found that she had failed to establish quid pro quo harassment because she was not perfect: The court credited the employer's explanation that she had been fired for incompetence. Of course, one could ask whether she might have kept her job by putting up with a more extreme version of the same conduct that helped her get it. One could ask how the women who responded positively to James's fondling and overtures fared. One could ask those questions and, in doing so, put employers who engage in "consensual" office sex at risk when they fire women who refuse to go along. The *Dockter* court chose not to ask those questions. The question it *did* ask—whether there was a good explanation for her firing—was answered solely by reference to her word-processing abilities and her demeanor around coworkers.[87] As for her hostile environment claim, James's conduct was not sufficiently offensive and unwelcome to satisfy the requirements of a hostile environment cause of action.[88]

The fact pattern is a common one. In *Christoforou v. Ryder Truck Rental, Inc.*,[89] a supervisor fondled the plaintiff's rear end and breasts, propositioned the plaintiff, and tried to force a kiss at a Christmas party.[90] The court readily found evidence of "sexual tension" at the workplace.[91] Although sufficient to make out a prima facie case of quid pro quo harassment, this evidence, in the court's eyes, was fully rebutted by proof that she was fired not for rejecting sexual advances but because she was tardy and her boss had a difficult temper.[92] The hostile environment claim likewise failed because the advances, though sufficient to establish her half of the quid pro quo claim, were considered too sporadic and innocuous to support a finding of a hostile environment.[93]

It is possible that the women in these cases were in fact highly unqualified, and would have been discharged even if they had had sex with their bosses. The mere fact that the plaintiffs lost is not a basis for condemning judicial decisions. What is troubling is the theory behind these opinions, namely the judges' simplistic presumption that an employer can evaluate a woman's "qualifications" wholly apart from the sexual interactions that occurred, and that a court can and should do similarly. And what is so disappointing about these opinions in practice is that their embrace of this artificial meritocracy leaves all but the most ideal women without protection from sexual blackmail at work. Real women—women who are sometimes tardy, sometimes slow, and rarely perfect—are vulnerable women. This aspect of the quid pro quo doctrine bears an uncanny resemblance to the law's traditional willingness to protect only the Madonna in a rape case, and to brand her more common sister the whore, even though no woman remains a Madonna once she has been raped (which is the cruelest irony, or perhaps the point).

Neither law nor policy commands such a result in sexual harassment cases. If the goal is to protect all women from sexual blackmail, and there is no basis to argue that it should be anything less, then the governing doctrines should be structured to serve that goal, and not to protect sexual access to everyone who might later be termed "unqualified." This means that we should find a prima facie case of sexual harassment whenever a woman can establish that she was subjected to an adverse employment action— whether she was fired, demoted, or not promoted—and that she rejected sexual advances of her superior. The law should impose on the employer the burden of showing not simply that she was "unqualified," but that the adverse action would have been taken even if she had said yes to sex.

Such a rule would be a significant advance for women in two respects. First, it would relieve them of the obligation of proving the elusive nexus between their responses to their bosses' propositions and the deprivation of an economic benefit. Instead it would place the burden of proving the absence of a nexus on the employer. Second, it would require the blackmailer or his employer to bear the responsibility for his blackmail: if an employer chooses to make sex a positive consideration in employment decisions, then all women should be entitled to the benefit, *regardless of whether they say yes or no.*

To be sure, an employer under this rule would be less free to fire than if he had never resorted to sexual extortion in the first place. So be it. No one forced him to engage in blackmail. Surely the law does not need to *encourage* sex in the workplace, let alone do so by affirmatively protecting sexual blackmail. It hardly seems too much to expect that as between the powerful blackmailer and his less powerful victim, he, rather than she, should bear the burden of the blackmail. Perhaps most important, once sexual blackmail has been introduced, it is foolish and even punitive for courts to close their eyes and pretend that employment decisions can somehow be made and judged without regard to it.

Of course, no legal rule will stop all blackmail in the workplace. There will always be women who cannot afford the risk of unemployment, cannot bear the expense of litigation, and cannot stomach the pains of disclosure and discovery. But the legal rule should say to all women, even if it cannot make good its assurance in every case, that they are protected from sexual blackmail. Women are entitled to know that saying no will leave them no worse off than if they had said yes. Hopefully, such a rule will make at least a few more women feel a little more free to choose for themselves.

5. Establishing a Hostile Environment

The great victory of Vinson,[94] if it can be called that, was the Supreme Court's willingness to recognize the second and less widely accepted form of sexual harassment: the hostile environment.[95] But the acceptance was hardly unconditional. Hostile environment claimants, before and since Vinson, have faced substantial difficulties establishing that their worksites violate Title VII.[96]

At least two obstacles regularly complicate hostile environment lawsuits, in addition to the unwelcomeness gravamen. First, the woman must prove that the offensive conduct was "based upon sex."[97] Second, she must show that the harassment was "sufficiently pervasive so as to alter the conditions of employment and create an abusive working environment."[98]

The "Based on Sex" Requirement

Technically, the requirement that the harassment be based on sex is a burden shared by quid pro quo and hostile environment claimants alike. In practice, though, courts readily agree that propositions to have sex, the most common "quid," are gender-based. Notwithstanding the early courts' concerns about the hypothetical bisexual supervisor,[99] most judges will simply assume that a similar proposition would not be forthcoming to a member of the same sex. However, some courts have held that worksite conditions— foul language, obscene cartoons, and physical gestures short of sex or the demand for it—are not always based on sex.[100]

In theory, one could argue that the "based on sex" requirement is an absolute mandate of Title VII. After all, the Act bars only discrimination in the conditions of employment based on sex.[101] But Title VII in no way mandates the practical obstacle that the "based on sex" requirement has come to represent in many courts.

While the test is often stated, in legal terms, as whether the harassment is "equally offensive" to both sexes, it is often applied in practice as a question of whether the action is itself sexual.[102] Presumably, nonsexual acts are directed at both men and women, and are equally offensive to both. Sexual acts, by contrast, are directed at women and are offensive only to them. Such a test might work for women if "sexual" acts were broadly defined, and viewed from a woman's perspective. The problem is that courts tend to define "sexual" very narrowly, based on a man's view of a man's acts.

In *Wendorf v. Metropolitan Life Insurance Co.*,[103] for example, the court found that the boss "was a 'physical person' and felt a need to touch people in order to communicate."[104] The court had no doubt that his behavior was "impolite and possibly annoying;"[105] nor did the court question that he might have been "unpleasant to the plaintiff" on a number of occasions.[106] But the court concluded that his acts did not constitute sexual harassment, since "this behavior . . . was directed at both male and female workers and was clearly not sexual in nature."[107]

What is striking about *Wendorf* is the court's rather facile assumption that a physical touch is the same behavior when done by a man to a man as when done by a man to a woman. Perhaps that is true among some groups of family and friends, but it is hardly typical of the American workplace, let alone the workplace where the man is a boss and the woman his employee. There was no showing, nor did the court require one, that Metropolitan Life was a uniquely familial work environment. The fact that men were touched as well may not be irrelevant to a sexual harassment claim, but it surely should not be dispositive.

One problem, plainly, is perspective: even if the man who touched (the boss) and the man who reviewed his behavior (the judge) view such touching as nonsexual, it does not follow that it would be viewed that way either by the woman touched (Ms. Wendorf) or by most women. So the dispositive question here may be simply this: *whose perspective should govern?* And if that is the right question, the male perspective is not necessarily the right answer.

When criminal penalties are imposed, and mens rea required, one expects to hear the argument that the law should require a blameworthy choice by the man. Thus, it is said, his perspective, narrowly construed, should define the offense. Even that argument, however, is not necessarily irrefutable: If negligence is sufficient to give rise to criminal liability, as it is in some areas of the law,[108] then the question should be not what the man thought was reasonable, but what we as a society decide is reasonable. And there is nothing inherently reasonable about a perspective that maximizes both sexual access of men and sexual injury to women.

If there are strong reasons for adopting a reasonableness standard in the criminal law, and I believe there are,[109] these grounds are even more persuasive in the civil context, where the very purpose of the law is to protect women, and where the deprivation of liberty and the stigma inherent in criminal punishment are absent. Why, after all, should the courts protect a man's right to maul women? This is the only "right" to be lost if courts presume what most women would indeed assume: that being touched by a man is different than being touched by a woman, and that as a rule, men should keep their hands off.

Consider, for a moment, what would have happened if Ms. Wendorf had touched her boss back. I have little doubt: the issue would no longer be whether his touching of her was sexual, but whether by her actions she had demonstrated that it was welcome. In *Downes v. FAA*,[110] for example, a male supervisor argued that his record should be cleared of any charge of sexual harassment. Among the behavior at issue was his touching of a female employee's hair on at least two occasions, an act he described as "a gesture of friendliness."[111] In ruling for him on the grounds that there was no pattern of harassment, the court emphasized that "context" was critical to the hair touching; context included whether she had called him or been personal toward him in the past.[112] If she had, the court assumed, the behavior might be sexual but also welcome; if not, perhaps not sexual at all.

Touching hair and body are not the only examples. One woman learned of, and then found, offensive cartoons labeled with her name in the men's room. These were not based on sex, the court ruled, since there were also men's names on the cartoons.[113] Another woman felt harassed by the language common to her workplace, which included "frequent references . . . to female and male genitalia and to sexual activity." The language, the court found, bespoke no intent to discriminate based on sex, but might merely have relieved the pressure in the workplace.[114]

The judicial opinions do not detail the exact content of the cartoons or the speech in these cases. But I would be very surprised if they did not reflect the most traditional and most sexist attitudes, portraying women as sex objects, who are invisible in every other respect. I would be amazed if they did not embrace a philosophy of male-female sexual relations that judged women anatomically and celebrated sexual triumph over them. Were I applying the "based on sex" test, I would have no trouble condemning these messages. Even by the judiciary's own definitions, the reality remains that such images are not, at least not yet, "equally offensive to men and women."[115] But the test is not being applied by me, nor by many others who share my perspective, and this is, of course, the point.

The second obstacle women complainants face is the requirement that they prove that the harassment is sufficiently severe or pervasive. As the Supreme Court held in *Vinson*, it is not enough that the employee herself is offended.[116] It is not enough, for example, that the source of offense is an intentionally insulting, gender-based comment. For sexual harassment to be actionable, the woman must establish that it was sufficient "to alter the conditions of [the victim's] employment and create an abusive working environment."[117] Or, as one leading appellate court decision put it, the harassment must be "sufficiently severe and persistent to affect seriously the psychological well being of employees, [which] is a question to be determined with regard to the totality of the circumstances."[118]

Certainly the pervasiveness of the harassment should be relevant to the question of what relief is appropriate: for example, was the harassment sufficiently severe as to result in a constructive discharge of the plaintiff? But it does not inevitably follow that there is no harm in harassing, so long as it is sporadic.

One justification for the pervasiveness requirement seems, plainly, that every workplace insult should not be treated, quite literally, as a federal case. But in defining what counts as trivial or "de minimis," many courts have wrongly looked to social interaction outside the workplace as the standard, ignoring not only the "captive audience" nature of the employment context but also the fact that "society" hardly reflects a normative standard that women have had an equal role in shaping. Precisely this rationale was adopted in *Rabidue v. Osceola Refining Co.*[119] to dismiss complaints of vulgar language and offensive posters. The court characterized the impact on the environment of admittedly sexually oriented poster displays as "de minimis . . . when considered in the context of a society that condones and publicly features and commercially exploits open displays of written and pictorial erotica at the newsstands, on prime-time television, at the cinema, and in other public places."[120] In short, the subordination and exploitation of women outside of work rendered acceptable similar treatment inside. Equally troubling about *Rabidue* is just how nontrivial and pervasive the harassment in that workplace apparently was. According to the dissenting judge, pictures of nude and scantily clad women abounded, including one, which hung on a wall for eight years, of a woman with a golf ball on her breasts and a man with his golf club, standing over her and yelling "fore."[121] The language was equally offensive: one coworker, never disciplined despite repeated complaints, routinely referred to women as "whores," "cunts," and "pussy."[122] But the Sixth Circuit found all this de minimis.[123] A second and related justification for the pervasiveness requirement may be the recognition by federal courts that what even *they* would consider nontrivial harassment is itself pervasive in the workplace. *Rabidue* sounded this theme as well:

> [I]t cannot seriously be disputed that in some work environments, humor and language are rough hewn and vulgar. Sexual jokes, sexual conversations and girlie magazines may abound. Title VII was not meant to—or can— change this . . . Title VII is the federal court mainstay in the struggle for equal employment opportunity for the female workers of America. But it is quite different to claim that Title VII was designed to bring about a magical transformation in the social mores of American workers.[124]

The early federal courts recognized the highly sexualized atmosphere of many workplaces, and cited it as a reason not to afford protection under Title VII. More recent decisions that have reached the opposite result, including *Vinson*, have done so by stressing the limited application of the Title VII action to only the most extreme cases of sexual harassment.[125]

But the fact that a hazard is widespread should be a reason to ban it, not to tolerate it. The greater the number of women who are exposed to sexual harassment, the more of a reason strict standards are needed. If harassment is viewed as a wrong, then its very commonness is an argument to "get tough." Consider the analogy to drug use. Few would accept the argument that its prevalence means that employers should be more tolerant of it. There is no analogous view in the narcotics situation of "there's no harm in trying—as long as it's sporadic or casual." On the contrary, spot checks of everyone, suspected or not, have become the rule of the day. Vigilance. Zero tolerance. No leniency. These are the catchwords of the day. Yet harassment can destroy a woman's health and well-being more quickly than marijuana use. Our insistence on thinking about sexual harassment differently reveals the depth of our acceptance of sexual harassment as appropriate workplace behavior.

Even in this context, however, the standards applied by some courts in enforcing the "pervasiveness" requirement remain extreme. Formally, the pervasiveness test is wholly objective: The harassment must be "so significant a factor that the average female employee finds that her overall work experience is substantially and adversely affected by the conduct."[126] Who is this average female? Sometimes, she is constructed out of whole cloth by the court. For example, the average female, according to a Michigan judge, would not consider herself harassed if a flashlight were shined up her skirt, but would merely dismiss it as "childish."[127] In other cases, she is not even a woman, but a "reasonable person" of no explicit gender.[128] This construct is at best meaningless, given that men and women do not view harassment in the same way; at worst, it implies that the reasonable person is male. More often, she is fashioned out of the court's view of the *other* women in the workplace: other women who, according to one court, "simply ignored" pictures of naked women on doors and sexual objects in the work area;[129] or other women who find their bosses sitting on their laps, talking about his tongue and penis, to be merely "horseplay" that is "funny and inoffensive."[130]

Women who fail to meet this objective standard—women who find flirtation by their boss debilitating, or who are adversely affected by the "romantic ambience" of the boss's conduct—are vulnerable to being judged "hypersensitive to conduct by men."[131] But while women who complain too much are "hypersensitive," women who do not complain at all may fare no better. Those who suffer in silence often find that their silence is used against them, either because of the courts' assumption that had they complained the harassment would have stopped,[132] or, more often, because of the presumption that the harassment couldn't have been so bad—and therefore not so pervasive or debilitating—if the woman didn't even complain.[133]

Superwomen—women who not only do not complain, but also continue to get their jobs done, at least for a time, and even excel at them—often fare least well of all. Where a woman was able to work regular shifts for ten days after an alleged instance of forced intercourse, the court found the harassment did not impact significantly upon the conditions of employment.[134] Similarly, where a woman continued to perform her job—notwithstanding her supervisor's propositions, winks, and suggestions of a rubdown, along with the ribbing of coworkers—her continued performance in itself suggested that the harassment failed to meet the "psychologically debilitating" test.[135] Nor was harassment considered significant for a woman who not only continued in her job, but was even praised for her work, after being patted on the rear end and the breast and rebuffing her inebriated boss on a business trip.[136]

These cases illustrate at least two problems that go beyond their particular facts. First, for at least some of the courts, the objective standard of pervasiveness is defined by an idealized woman who simply may not exist. Such a woman is tough, not "hypersensitive"; she is aggressive, not passive. Such a woman complains in a way that effectively stops the harassment. Such a woman does not suffer in silence or confide only in other women. In short, the "reasonable woman" is very much a man.

By requiring women to behave like men, Title VII courts are following a pattern well established in rape cases. In defining the "force" that makes sex rape, a number of courts have adopted the rules of schoolboy fights, demanding that the man actually use his fists, and condemning the woman who, like a playground "sissy," cries rather than fights back.[137]

Moreover, even those courts that base their standard on the reactions of real women—of the particular plaintiff, or of others in the workplace—

end up with a definition of pervasiveness that is often no broader than that of courts that cling to the idealized model. Few of these courts recognize that the extent to which women react to insults, propositions, and physical abuse may have far less to do with the severity of the harassment than with the need of women to keep their jobs. Contrary to the Sixth Circuit's holding in *Rabidue*, the decision to enter an offensive workplace is rarely a truly "voluntary" one. That court's suggestion that the legal standard should be defined by the "reasonable expectation of the plaintiff upon voluntarily entering that [admittedly crude and offensive] environment" [138] is either disingenuous or, at best, a reflection of the distance between appellate judges and the reality of working women. In truth, the "strongest" women may simply be the most needy, and the reality is that most working women are needy women.

Because courts fail to recognize this, or perhaps choose not to, many courts in hostile environment cases end up doing silently what the Sixth Circuit in *Rabidue* did explicitly: translating the tolerance of powerless women for offensive conditions into a normative standard of acceptable workplace conduct. Thus, what the powerless must tolerate because of their need becomes what the law defines as acceptable conduct.

And yet, the very point of Title VII—indeed, the only point—should be to ensure that precisely this kind of "tolerance" by the powerless *not* define the prerogatives of the powerful. That women would be "willing" to work with hazardous chemicals, or for subminimum pay, or for fifty hours without overtime, is hardly a justification for those unlawful working conditions. Because the market does not protect women against these conditions, the law does. So, too, for discrimination—at least in theory. But the pervasiveness requirement, particularly as it has been most strictly interpreted, signals our (or at least judges') unwillingness to clearly state that sexual insults have no place on the worksite. Sexual harassment, unlike sweatshop conditions, remains an acceptable aspect of the American workplace.

It is one thing to believe that an isolated trivial comment should not give rise to a federal lawsuit; it is quite another to limit the hostile environment test so as to shield all but the most extremely offensive workplaces from even the possibility of liability. To be sure, the wrong should determine the remedy. But by holding that short of pervasiveness there is no wrong at *all*, courts have stripped the Title VII action of its teeth. And what is worse is that they have done so by taking women's neediness and turning it against them, making women responsible under the law for the insults and abuse hurled at them.

6. Questions of Credibility

While doctrinal elements like unwelcomeness, nexus, and pervasiveness decide many sexual harassment cases, my reading of the case law suggests that credibility questions probably decide nearly as many. By credibility, I mean, quite simply, whether the judge believes the woman's account of victimization or the man's exhortations of innocence.

One problem with addressing questions of credibility is that their resolution ultimately depends on being there. If you weren't at the trial, if you didn't hear the evidence and see the witnesses yourself, or even read the transcript in its entirety, you are certainly in no position to second-guess the court's judgment. At least that is the approach of most appellate courts, and it works quite effectively to protect credibility judgments from reversal.

But my point is not so much whether case X or case Y was rightly decided, as whether there emerges, from the courts' discussions of fact-finding, patterns of judgment that raise legitimate questions as to the enterprise as a whole. Based on my review, serious questions are raised in at least three respects. First, some courts, though perhaps only a minority, have structured the relevancy rules in sexual harassment cases to frame the credibility question as a one-way ratchet against women. Second, and even more troubling, virtually every decision on credibility seems to assume the relevance of factors such as the presence of corroboration and the freshness of the woman's complaint, treating these factors as neutral indicia of credibility rather than as cards categorically stacked against women. Finally, in making judgments about women's motivations, a number of courts have embraced stereotypes of women that punish real women for both their strengths and their weaknesses, and leave unchallenged the most traditional "scorned woman" explanations for why women complain of harassment.

The 1988 decision in *Kresko v. Rulli*,[139] discussed earlier,[140] serves as the worst example of the one-way ratchet. In *Kresko*, a Minnesota court upheld the trial court's simultaneous *exclusion* of evidence of the boss's sexual relations with other workers and *inclusion* of evidence of the plaintiff's subsequent relations with other men. As to the former, the court emphasized that "most of the other women did not consider the incidents sexual harassment," and that since he admitted that most of the incidents occurred, but claimed they were consensual, they were not necessary to show motive or opportunity.[141] As for the woman's sex life, the court held the evidence relevant and probative because she "affirmatively placed this aspect of her life at issue."[142]

Kresko is easy to attack. In criminal cases, there may be a justification for applying different rules of proof to victim and defendant, for such cases are contests not between plaintiff and defendant, but between the state and the individual, and the deck is supposed to be stacked on the individual's side. But that justification disappears in a civil suit. Moreover, if sex life is relevant at all, surely sex at the office is more relevant than sex outside of it. The *Kresko* court's plain bias against women turns that commonsense observation on its head, finding *his* work-related sexual activity less relevant than *her* outside dating. Ultimately, though, what makes *Kresko* and other cases like it so vulnerable to attack is the unjustifiable lack of symmetry that lies at their core: the application of harsher evidentiary rules to her than to him.[143] But the more important question is whether the system *should* be symmetrical.

Plainly, whether a man has had sexual relations with other female employees seems relevant, regardless of whether they "consented" at the time. Such a pattern might well define the "understandings" at work on the job site. Indeed, in a number of cases, it is the third or fourth woman who brings the suit, and often she succeeds only because of the testimony of her heretofore uncomplaining predecessors.[144] And it is not always obvious, at least in *his* case, that the line should be drawn at work. If he has harassed women outside of work, that seems relevant; if he is a "Don Juan" on the outside claiming to be a choirboy at the office, even that may seem relevant. But are these same patterns equally relevant to the woman complainant: does it matter if she has had relationships with other men at work, or with other men outside of work, or if she has complained before or since, as Ms. Kresko apparently did, of date rape outside the office?[145]

Symmetry is neat, applying the same rules of relevancy to both men and women, to both aggressor and victim; with symmetry, the ratchet runs both ways. Unfortunately, we do not live in a neat world. A rule treating evidence of a woman's other sexual relationships the same as such evidence about the man may seem egalitarian; the impact of such evidence may not be. Men with active sex lives are normal, desirable, successful. Women are loose, easy, unworthy. Men are "Don Juans." Women are whores. True, we respond to the story differently if we are told that she was a virgin. But that extra ounce of probative value in the unusual case (since most women complainants are not virgins) will come at great cost for the more common woman. The fear of having one's sex life paraded before a court, and the fear that what is average for women will, when exposed, look exceptional (because for women, the gap between the male-defined ideal and the usually male-imposed average is so great) lead not only to shame in the courtroom but acquiescence in the workplace. If this form of evidentiary symmetry is enforced, it may substantially enhance the asymmetry of power and powerlessness inside the workplace.[146]

So if there is to be symmetry—and I have yet to read an opinion embracing a one-way ratchet *favoring* women—it must be of a more limited kind.

Lines must be drawn to limit the admissibility of evidence in order to protect women, even if those legal parameters also protect men. We must draw evidentiary lines at the workplace that render purely personal life irrelevant. We must draw lines between sex and aggression that make evidence of the latter admissible, even if the line between the two is an artificial one. I want to know if the man has been prosecuted or sued for rape elsewhere, or arrested for domestic assault, and I want to know even if the cost of knowing is also asking whether the woman has ever complained of rape.

At least most judges, most of the time, recognize the need to be at least somewhat careful when dealing with evidence of other sexual activity. They may still fail to admit or exclude the proper amount of evidence, but generally they are paying attention. This is not so when dealing with factors such as corroboration and the freshness of the complaint. For most judges, it seems, these look like neutral criteria, beyond reproach as a basis for judging. Few even hesitate before embracing them in making credibility decisions. They should.[147]

In rape law, similar rules were established, both formally and informally, to guide the fact-finding process, rules that emphasized such things as the presence of corroboration, the availability of eyewitness accounts, and the freshness of the woman's complaint.[148] The rules served, quite intentionally, to make rape cases more difficult to prove than other crimes. The reason, originally quite explicit and only later shrouded in legalese, was the fear that women, particularly scorned women and nonvirgins, would use rape complaints vindictively against men. In short, the rules were intended, and served, to stack the deck against women.[149]

With law reform in the 1960s and 1970s, American jurisdictions formally abandoned these special proof rules. Although empirical evidence suggests that corroboration and the freshness of the complaint may continue to have some practical impact on the handling of cases, formally, at least, they are dirty words.[150] That is in part because of a growing recognition, again at least formally, that there is no need to stack the deck against women. It should also be because the proof rules were never a particularly accurate guide to the realities of how rapes happen and how victims respond.

After all, what would count as corroboration? Witnesses, perhaps? Or bruises and other signs of resistance? The reality is that rapists rarely perform before witnesses. The reality is that bruises may be the expected scars of schoolboy fights, but that threatened women rarely behave like schoolboys. Many of them do not "fight back," at least not with their fists, and to require them to do so could jeopardize their survival. Even medical corroboration may be unwittingly destroyed, given the natural instinct of women who have been violated to wash, to douche, to clean themselves. And as for requiring a fresh complaint, the notion that a truly victimized woman's first response to her rape would be to complain publicly, or even privately, belies the sense of shame and embarrassment that many rape victims feel, itself a rather understandable response to how the law has regarded and treated rape victims. Thus while the presence of witnesses, bruises, sperm, and a fresh complaint obviously may be relevant evidence, they are likely to be the exception rather than the rule, and their absence should not signal that the woman should not be believed.

And if this is true in rape cases, it should surely be true in sexual harassment suits. After all, the standard of proof for rape is the law's highest, permitting no reasonable doubt of the defendant's guilt; the standard for sexual harassment, a preponderance of the evidence, is the law's lowest. Rape is punishable as a crime, and those convicted of it face both the stigma of the felon and lengthy incarceration; sexual harassment suits, when successful, rarely result even in significant monetary judgments.

It is therefore somewhat surprising, and even more disquieting, to read again and again in sexual harassment suits not only that the woman loses, but that her credibility suffers because no witnesses were present, or because she did not complain swiftly or publicly enough.[151] Ironically, the forms of harassment most likely to occur in public, and thus be corroborated, are also those that courts are most likely to dismiss as trivial jokes and gestures rather than treat as harassment. But one should rarely expect nontrivial harassment, at least as judicially defined, to take place in public in front of witnesses, or to be memorialized in personnel files. More serious forms of harassment—explicit sexual overtures, threats of firing or promises of promotion, and actual acts of sexual intercourse—are less likely to be accompanied by corroboration, and consequently, the woman is less likely to be believed.

Similarly, to read the judges' opinions, one would expect that the first response of a harassed woman is to complain, both officially and privately. But in fact, one sees few cases of women who do this. Indeed, the opinions that most emphatically announce this standard of conduct almost always involve women who did not complain.[152] The surveys, noted earlier, bear out the pattern: one survey found that while over half of the women questioned reported having experienced sexual harassment, only 22.5 percent reported having ever even talked about the general subject matter—let alone the particular instance—with a coworker.[153]

Yet the corroboration rule lives on in sexual harassment cases as if it were a neutral criterion, as if absence of corroboration were as probative as its presence. In reality, corroboration should be treated as a one-way ratchet. It should be persuasive when present—for no one would argue that witnesses should be ignored, bruises discounted, or cries for help dismissed— and irrelevant when not. The fact that the corroboration rule continues to be embraced unembarrassedly in sexual harassment cases, long after it has at least been formally rejected in rape cases, raises the question of whether it serves, here as there, its more traditional and deservingly vilified purpose: not as a neutral guide to truth, but as a mechanism reflecting the disfavored status of sexual complaints and complainants.[154]

Finally, women who are considered by courts or coworkers to be "outspoken" or "assertive" are expected to be outspoken or assertive about the sexual wrongs of their bosses. The fact that such assertiveness might bring embarrassment, or even dismissal, is routinely ignored, as is the fact that women in these cases are always relatively powerless. As one court put it: "Choosing what version to believe is not merely a question of witness credibility, but also a question of what version logically makes better sense." [155] The court maintained that "an outspoken employee whose rights had been violated [would not] have remained silent. . . ." [156] The particular woman, the court noted in passing, had recently undergone a bilateral mastectomy, and had requested and been granted a transfer because of all the talk and gossip about her surgery.[157] Nowhere does the court note the irony of expecting, indeed of demanding, assertiveness from a cancer patient who has recently lost both her breasts.

The question, as the court put it, of "what version logically makes better sense" largely depends on who does the asking. I have no doubt that many of these judges honestly believe that women would complain if they were subject to sexual advances, or at least to unwelcome ones. I also have no doubt that in many cases, these judges are simply wrong. Yet because these erroneous views have become guides to credibility and truth, they have also become not simply rules of proof but elements of the offense: absent such complaint, there is no wrong. But that is only half the story. One cannot read a random sample of sexual harassment opinions without recognizing the sense in which these are not cases of people judging other people. They are cases of men judging women—judging women on the topic of sex. And on that topic, women, because they are women, bear an enormous burden of proof.

7. Limits on Liability

It should be clear, I hope, that making out a case of sexual harassment under federal law is not easy. It is not enough to show that one has been harassed at work. A quid pro quo must be shown, the existence of a pervasively hostile environment must be established, or arguments that employers had cause to fire or not promote the plaintiff must be defeated. And to meet these burdens, one must first be believed—no easy task when the rules of credibility are stacked against women.

Unfortunately, even if the elements of the action are proven and the judge is persuaded, the question of relief remains. Given the magnitude of the obstacles to proving a claim of sexual harassment, one might think that the relief available was substantial. Regrettably, in many cases the relief available to a successful claimant ranges from not much to nothing at all.

First of all, there is the question of whether the employer is even liable for the violation. In any other type of Title VII action, that is not a question at all. Where a supervisor discriminates in wages, hours, or working conditions, the employer must remedy that discrimination, whether or not the employer knew about it, should have known about it, or approved it.[158] Having hired supervisors, and entrusted them with authority, the employer is held to violate federal law whenever they do.

Although strict liability for employers is applied automatically in quid pro quo cases, a number of federal courts have refused to apply it to hostile environment claims. That refusal won the support of the Supreme Court, in dicta at least, in *Vinson*.[159]

The rationale for this "differing treatment" was explained in greatest detail by the Court of Appeals for the Eleventh Circuit in *Henson v. Dundee*.[160] According to the *Henson* court:

> The environment in which an employee works can be rendered offensive in an equal degree by the acts of supervisors, coworkers, or even strangers to the workplace. The capacity of any person to create a hostile or offensive environment is not necessarily enhanced or diminished by any degree of authority which the employer confers upon that individual. When a supervisor gratuitously insults an employee, he generally does so for his reasons and by his own means. He thus acts outside the actual or apparent scope of the authority he possesses as a supervisor. His conduct cannot automatically be imputed to the employer any more so than can the conduct of an ordinary employee.
>
> The typical case of quid pro quo sexual harassment is fundamentally different. In such a case, the supervisor relies upon his apparent or actual authority to extort sexual consideration from an employee. Therein lies the quid pro quo. . . . Because the supervisor is acting within at least the apparent scope of the authority entrusted to him by the employer when he makes employment decisions, his conduct can fairly be imputed to the source of his authority.[161]

The *Henson* court's reasoning cannot withstand analysis. First, by equating harassment by a workplace supervisor with the insults of a stranger, the court closes its eyes to a fact that the woman worker cannot avoid: Her supervisor, unlike a stranger, is not only there every day, responsible for the workplace, but also has power over her. His power to supervise—to hire and fire, and to set work schedules and pay rates—does not disappear, except perhaps in the eyes of the *Henson* court, when he chooses to harass through insults and offensive gestures rather than directly with threats of firing or promises of promotion. To pretend, as the *Henson* court does, that "the capacity of any person to create a hostile or offensive environment is not necessarily enhanced or diminished by any degree of authority which the employer confers upon that individual" is to leave the powerless, who know they lack power, utterly without protection against the powerful, who know they have it.[162]

Second, the *Henson* court errs in seeking to draw a neat line between insults and threats. According to the court, when a supervisor insults an employee, he "does so for his own reasons";[163] when he threatens to fire her, he is acting on behalf of the employer. But extortionate firings do not serve the employer's interests any more than gratuitous insults, or at least one hopes they do not. In both cases, the supervisor is abusing the power that has been entrusted to him. In both cases, he is acting for his own reasons and not the employer's. In both cases, his threats carry weight and his insults must be tolerated precisely because he is the supervisor, this is a workplace, and most women need their jobs. To be sure, the supervisor may have been specifically delegated the power to hire and fire, but he is also delegated the power to define the acceptable working conditions of the workplace. Nor can it be the case, empirically at least, that it is harsher to hold the employer responsible for a hostile environment than to do so for quid pro quo harassment, on the grounds that the employer is less likely to be aware of the former. On the contrary, threats and promises tied to sex are far more likely to take place in private, whereas the hostility of the environment is often all too obvious and patent. Moreover, the additional requirement in hostile environment claims that the harassment be sufficiently widespread and serious to qualify as "pervasive" suggests that any employer who wanted to know what was going on, or wanted to assume responsibility for the workplace, could and would do so. Thus, a number of courts have adopted something of a middle-ground position, holding employers liable for "failing to remedy or prevent a hostile or offensive work environment of which management-level employees knew, or in the exercise of reasonable care should have known."[164] If anything, it is much harder to learn about who is sleeping with whom, and why.

Finally, the differential rule cannot be justified by the concern, which some courts have expressed, about expanding employer liability to include misdeeds not only by supervisors but also by coworkers. To be sure, coworkers can contribute to a hostile environment, and by definition, they may not have the authority to make threats of firing or promotion. But if ignorant employers were the concern, one might expect liability for hostile environment cases to be restricted to those situations where knowledge is clearly imputable, for instance, where a supervisor played some role in contributing to the intolerable environment. Ironically, the Henson approach, at least in theory, accomplishes just the opposite. If the supervisor participates in the creation of the hostile environment, then the employer may be spared from liability unless the woman complained to higher managers; but if coworkers or outsiders create the hostile environment, and the supervisor chooses to tolerate it, then his knowledge might well be imputed to the employer and liability found.[165] Thus, where the supervisor is himself a wrongdoer, the employer may have *more* protection than when he is simply a passive onlooker.

Ultimately, the only justification for the differential rule that can withstand even the most cursory analysis is that courts simply perceive this form of harassment as less serious than quid pro quo harassment. They were slower to recognize hostile environments in the first instance, and are now more reluctant to impose liability for them. No courts say this outright, but their decisions seem unjustifiable on any other basis.

What is particularly troubling about this differential rule is how limited the relief available for hostile environment claims is in any event, unless they fully resemble quid pro quo complaints. Under Title VII, only equitable relief is available; compensatory and punitive damages are not.[166] There is no relief for pain and suffering, nor are there damages for humiliation. A court of equity can order the harassment stopped, but cannot order compensation for those who suffered under it. The usual remedy in Title VII cases is reinstatement and back pay. But reinstatement and back pay are not appropriate remedies unless the plaintiff lost her job as a result of the illegal action.[167] Thus in hostile environment cases, relief generally turns not only on a showing that the hostile environment was pervasive, but also on a showing that it resulted in the constructive discharge of the plaintiff.

To establish constructive discharge, an employee must demonstrate not only that she resigned because of the harassment, but also that working conditions were so intolerable that any reasonable person in her position would have been compelled to resign.[168] That standard invites a familiar host of problems: Who is the reasonable person? Is that person male or female, needy or independent, real or idealized?[169] But whatever its other faults, and they are many, the standard on its face collapses a doctrinal distinction between quid pro quo and hostile environment cases that is critical to the stated reasoning of Henson. For it is only when hostile environment harassment crosses the line and directly determines conditions of employment—

only when the hostile environment is, to an objective eye, the direct equivalent of a firing—that liability exists. Thus there is no need for the *Henson* rule, even if one accepted its unstated premise that hostile environment cases are generically less serious than quid pro quo cases, for the former would rarely result in meaningful relief in any event. The most that plaintiffs who have not been discharged can usually hope for is that the defendants receive a slap on the hand.

Quid pro quo claimants, or successful constructive discharge claimants, do not fare much better. Although reinstatement may be available, women who have been driven from a job, or fired from it, are understandably reluctant to go back to work for the man who harassed and fired them. As for back pay, the less you earn, the less it is, and the easier courts seem to think it is to mitigate your damages by finding an "equivalent" job. Thus, it is not unusual even in cases of firing to see small or even token awards, reflecting both the duty to mitigate and the below-average wages paid to working women in the first place.[170]

All of this is equally true in other Title VII cases, with one important exception. The most significant wage discrimination cases brought under Title VII are class actions; the relief represents not back pay to one woman, but to hundreds or even thousands. The important role played by Title VII class actions makes both practical and theoretical sense: practical sense because the dollars involved, and the deterrence they deliver, become meaningful only when the claims of the group are aggregated; theoretical sense because it is the shared trait of gender that determines and limits opportunity.

The individualized focus of most sexual harassment claims, by contrast, not only results in very limited relief, but is also theoretically unsatisfying. Instead of focusing on gender, the suits focus on tardiness, or typing and spelling skills. The defense attorneys need not defend their clients' attitudes or actions toward women in general, but simply destroy one particular woman. Rather than uniting women, the suits pit the one who complained against those who did not; or the one who felt forced to leave, or was fired, against those who remain. The suits become occasions to deny the importance of gender, rather than to recognize it. Class action suits may be more difficult to style in the quid pro quo context if women are threatened one by one, but intrinsically such actions should be well suited to hostile environment claims. The fact that class actions are rare in both contexts is a testament to the structure of the rules of proof and liability—rules that see even hostile environment cases in terms of individualized "welcomeness" and the individualized application of constructive discharge, rules that recognize the cause of action with one hand and deny its seriousness with the other.

8. Conclusion

The pitfalls for women in current Title VII doctrine suggest a number of doctrinal changes that the federal courts and Congress should adopt to protect women against sexual harassment at the workplace. The "welcomeness" inquiry should be eliminated in both quid pro quo and hostile environment cases, because the additional requirements of proof in both types of cases make the welcomeness inquiry doctrinally gratuitous and personally humiliating for women. In quid pro quo cases, the courts should focus on whether the boss has made sexual overtures and followed them with an adverse employment decision, not whether the woman meets an abstract idealized standard. Stated doctrinally, judges should ask not whether the woman could have been fired anyway, but whether she would have been fired had she said yes. And on that question, the burden of proof should be on the man. In hostile environment cases, the degree of pervasiveness should be a measure of relief, rather than a requirement to establish a violation. I would argue that subjective hostility should at least make out a prima facie hostile environment case, but if an objective standard is to be applied at all, then it should be defined by reference to a normative standard of a nonhostile workplace, not to a standard of what powerless and economically dependent women are "willing" to tolerate. Credibility rules should be reformulated to eliminate the double standard and sharply limit, if not entirely eliminate, the persuasive value of the absence of corroboration or a fresh complaint. Liability rules should be restructured, within the limits of Title VII, to make the constructive discharge standard more realistic, and meaningful recovery more possible. Class actions should be encouraged, not discouraged. At least some courts may be ready to meet the challenge. As this article was going to press, the Court of Appeals for the Ninth Circuit held in *Ellison v. Brady* that the appropriate perspective for judging a hostile environment claim is that of the "reasonable woman" and recognized that a woman's perspective may differ substantially from a man's.[171]

But the broader prospects for making any of these changes are uncertain at best. At its inception, Title VII's grounding in the federal equity jurisdiction seemed an ideal alternative to conservative and unsympathetic state judges and juries. Today, while some exceptions remain, the increasing conservativism of the federal judiciary raises the question of whether state courts and state juries might not be at least equally sympathetic, particularly in states like California, where laws provide for both compensatory and punitive damages in harassment cases.[172]

Whether in state or federal court, however, the challenge of making the law work for women, and not against them, is more than a matter of doctrinal manipulation. Underlying the system as it is currently structured and enforced rests a set of assumptions and attitudes about women and work that support both the rules and results of which I am most critical.

One of the leading theorists of sexual harassment in the workplace has argued that such behavior represents an inappropriate spillover into the workplace of the norms of conduct that exist in society generally. Under this view, socially accepted forms of male aggressiveness become unacceptable in the workplace because of the additional elements of economic power and dependence.[173]

Aggressive fondling, drunken lurches, exclusive attention to anatomy, abusive language, and the treatment of women solely as sexual objects may, empirically speaking, be considered acceptable behavior outside of the workplace, but that is in large part a reflection of the very sorts of power imbalances that we at least recognize, reluctantly, at work. What makes such conduct generally acceptable outside of work is that men say it is, and that women have no say.

It is precisely this attitude of easy acceptance, at least outside of work, that makes it so difficult to limit sexual harassment at work. The problem with the court decisions, and the attitudes they reflect, is that offensive sexuality is so routinely considered normal, abuse of power acceptable, and the dehumanizing of women in sexual relations unremarkable, that when we (or the courts, at least) see such things at work, it hardly seems a "federal case." On the contrary, both courts and commentators have expressed the view that such activity is not only common but desirable. As Judge MacKinnon of the U.S. Court of Appeals pointed out, "Sexual advances may not be intrinsically offensive . . . [for they involve] social patterns that to some extent are normal and expectable."[174] Indeed, according to one commentator writing in the Harvard Law Review, "relations between the sexes may be chilled if men fear that behavior offensive to a sensitive woman may be actionable in court."[175]

The courts' answer to this concern has been the creation of the limited and inadequate legal doctrine addressed in this article. Only where they find the explicit quid pro quo, only where the employee is otherwise perfect in terms of both job performance and personal worthiness, only where the hostile environment seems hostile even to the men judging it are the courts willing to say that something aberrant is happening, and that it needs to be stopped. The Title VII action, by and large, limits its redress to the most unusual; the problem, by and large, is what is considered usual.

But this is not the only answer. As things stand now, we protect the right of a few to have "consensual" sex in the workplace (a right most women, according to the studies, do not even want), at the cost of exposing the overwhelming majority to oppression and indignity at work. Is the benefit to the few so great as to outweigh the costs to so many more? I think not. For my part, I would have no objection to rules that prohibited men and women from sexual relations in the workplace, at least with those who worked directly for them. Men and women could, of course, violate the rule; but the power to complain, once in the hands of the less powerful, might well "chill" sexual relations by evening the balance of power between the two.

I do not see this as going too far. After all, in cases of true love, one could wait a semester, or transfer to another department, or even trust the woman not to file a lawsuit. But for those who shy away from such a clear rule, the courts' sexism is not the only alternative. The doctrinal changes recommended in this article, for example, would not mean an end to all sexual relations at work. They would, however, enhance the scrutiny of employment decisions that men make about women with whom they have been sexually involved, and about women who have rejected them sexually. These changes would also require employers to take responsibility for their workplaces, to ensure that they are no more dangerous to a woman's psyche than to her body. Though not a major revolution perhaps, and not as clear-cut as I would ideally like, these changes would nonetheless be steps in the right direction.

As with rape, the reality is that many men will not change unless and until forced to change. After all, few give up power, or its perquisites, without a fight. But there are some signs that the fight has begun. Women who for years routinely accepted harassment as part of the environment—indeed, by men's definition, as a prize of it—are beginning to say no, to speak out, to force employers and institutions to recognize and address the question of what counts as harassment.

Take, for instance, the case of Congressman Jim Bates (D-CA), whose idea of "just joking around" apparently included requests for daily hugs from female staffers, during which he patted their buttocks; discussions of whether an aide would sleep with him if she were stranded on a desert island; and wrapping his legs around the leg of another staffer, in full view of his office staff, and swaying back and forth, grinning.[176] Representative Bates is surely not the first member of Congress to engage in such "joking around." But his staffers complained to the House Ethics Committee, which found the allegations sufficiently serious to investigate and to require an apology. This is at least a beginning.

It is a beginning because the women had the courage to speak up, and because the men on the Ethics Committee knew that however acceptable such behavior was in the past, in 1990 it could not be officially approved. This case was not a "federal" one perhaps, but it was not acceptable either. For all the grousing, my guess is that congressional homes are a little more pleasant to work in today because of the complaint against Congressman Bates. And that is certainly a step in the right direction.

Notes

Originally published in 43 *Stanford Law Review* 813 (1991). © 1991 by the Board of Trustees of the Leland Stanford Junior University; reprinted by permission.

1. My conclusions on rape law, as well as specific examples of statutes and cases, are based on my research in Susan Estrich, "Rape," 95 *Yale L.J.* 1087 (1986) and Susan Estrich, *Real Rape* (1987).

2. The essential elements of rape—sexual intercourse or contact, force, and non-consent—have remained largely unchanged. *Compare, e.g.,* Act effective May 2, 1895, ch. 370, § 2, 1895 Wis. Laws 753, 753 with Mich. Stat. Ann. § § 28.788(2)–(4) (Callaghan 1990). *See generally* Leigh Bienen, "Rape III—National Developments in Rape Reform Legislation," 6 *Women's Rts. L. Rep.* 170 (1980).

3. Estrich, *Real Rape, supra* note 1, at 15–26.

4. A major study of the Michigan reform statute, for example, concluded that "the law has very little impact on the system's approach to sexual assault cases." Jeanne Marsh et al., *Rape and the Limits of Law Reform* 65 (1982). *See generally* Wallace D. Loh, "The Impact of Common Law and Reform Rape Statutes on Prosecution: An Empirical Study," 55 *Wash. L. Rev.* 542, 552–54 (1980) (discussing features of the Michigan reform statute); Kenneth Polk, "Rape Reform and Criminal Justice Processing," 31 *Crime & Delinquency* 191 (1985) (empirical study of effects of rape reform laws).

5. Indeed, the distrust of women is an explicit justification for these rules. Three centuries ago the English Lord Chief Justice Matthew Hale warned that rape is a charge "easily to be made and hard to be proved, and harder to be defended by the party accused, tho' never so innocent." 1 Matthew Hale, *The History of the Pleas of the Crown* 635 (1736). Hale's observation that women could and would easily fabricate rape charges was the basis of a cautionary instruction often given to juries in rape cases. Professor Wigmore, for his part, thought it was the "unchaste . . . mentality" of rape complainants that led them to lie and justified special rules of proof on that basis. 3A John H. Wigmore, *Evidence in Trials at Common Law* § 924a, at 736 (J. Chadbourn rev. ed., 1970). Freud has also been invoked to support the claim that women unconsciously want to be raped: "[A] woman's need for sexual satisfaction may lead to the unconscious desire for forceful penetration, the coercion serving neatly to avoid the guilt feelings which might arise after willing participation." Note, "Forcible and Statutory Rape: An Exploration of the Operation and Objectives of the Consent Standard," 62 *Yale L.J.* 55, 67 & nn. 85 & 87 (1952).

6. In researching this article, I have read hundreds of trial and appellate court decisions in sexual harassment cases, as well as most of the available empirical studies of sexual harassment. My purpose, however, is not to write a hornbook chapter of a practitioner's guide to the current state of the law. It is, instead, to reveal the attitudes

and understandings underlying legal doctrine in this area. If anything, I have focused on what could be considered the most extreme opinions because of the light they shed on the enduring sexism in the law.

7. 42 U.S.C. § 2000e (1988). Title VII prohibits an "employer," defined as "a person engaged in an industry affecting commerce who has fifteen or more employees . . . and any agent of such a person," id. § 2000e(b), from discriminating in "compensation, terms, conditions, or privileges of employment, because of [an] individual's race, color, religion, sex, or national origin." Id. § 2000e-2(a).

8. See 110 Cong. Rec. 2577–84 (1964) (remarks of Reps. Smith, Tuten, Andrews, and Rivers). See generally Francis J. Vaas, "Title VII: Legislative History," 7 B.C. Indus. & Com. L. Rev. 431, 441–42 (1966).

9. See Phillips v. Martin Marietta Corp., 400 U.S. 542 (1971). Other "sex plus" distinctions include sex plus marriage. See, e.g., Sprogis v. United Air Lines, 444 F.2d 1194 (7th Cir. 1971) (company policy requiring stewardesses but not male cabin attendants to remain unmarried constitutes sex discrimination).

10. See General Elec. Co. v. Gilbert, 429 U.S. 125 (1976) (disability benefits plan denying coverage to pregnancy-related disabilities does not violate Title VII); Pregnancy Discrimination Act of 1978, 42 U.S.C. § 2000e(k) (1988).

11. See McDonnell Douglas Corp. v. Green, 411 U.S. 792, 802–06 (1972) (discussing allocation of burdens of proof in racial discrimination cases); Griggs v. Duke Power Co., 401 U.S. 424 (1971) (use of preemployment test having discriminatory impact violates Title VII despite absence of discriminatory intent). President Bush recently vetoed the Civil Rights Act of 1990, which would have codified the Griggs test and reinforced its holding in the face of recent Supreme Court attempts to increase the plaintiff's evidentiary burden. See, e.g., Wards Cove Packing v. Antonio, 490 U.S. 642 (1989) (after plaintiff establishes prima facie case of employment discrimination under Title VII, burden of producing evidence of business justification falls to employer, but burden of persuasion remains with plaintiff).

12. See, e.g., Paula Bernstein, "Sexual Harassment on the Job," Harper's Bazaar, Aug. 1976, at 12; Judith Coburn & Mary Cunningham, "So Successful, She Had to Fail," Mademoiselle, Jan. 1981, at 24; Claire Safran, "What Men Do to Women on the Job: A Shocking Look at Sexual Harassment," Redbook, Nov. 1976, at 149; Nancy J. White, "Sex in the Office—It's Mostly Bad Business," Ladies Home J., Oct. 1982, at 104.

13. Catharine A. MacKinnon, Sexual Harassment of Working Women 1 (1979).

14. 29 C.F.R. § 1604.11(a) (1990).

15. See, e.g., Corne v. Bausch & Lomb, Inc., 390 F. Supp. 161, 163 (D. Ariz. 1975), vacated without opinion, 562 F.2d 55 (9th Cir. 1977); Barnes v. Train, 13 Fair Empl. Prac. Cas. (BNA) 123, 124 (D.D.C. 1974), rev'd sub nom. Barnes v. Costle, 561 F.2d 983 (D.C. Cir. 1977).

16. Calvert Magruder, "Mental and Emotional Disturbance in the Law of Torts," 49 Harv. L. Rev. 1033, 1055 (1936); see, e.g., Andrews v. City of Philadelphia, 895 F.2d 1469, 1486–87 (3d Cir. 1990) (sexual harassment allegations not sufficiently outrageous and intolerable under Pennsylvania law); Paroline v. Unisys Corp., 879 F.2d 100, 112 (4th

Cir. 1989) (same under Virginia law); Studstill v. Borg Warner Leasing, 806 F.2d 1005, 1008 (11th Cir. 1986) (same under Florida law).

17. See generally Terry M. Dworkin et al., "Theories of Recovery for Sexual Harassment Going Beyond Title VII," 25 San Diego L. Rev. 125 (1988) (structure of sexual harassment claims inhibits possibility of recovery in tort). While tort claims may afford monetary damages, they generally require proof of intent by the wrongdoer and knowledge by the employer. Joan Vermeulen, "Preparing Sexual Harassment Litigation Under Title VII," 7 Women's Rts. L. Rep. 331, 337 (1982). Moreover, contributory fault notions of tort law explicitly open the door to all evidence of the plaintiff's so-called "fault." See id. at 340–43. See generally Guess v. Bethlehem Steel Corp., 913 F.2d 463 (7th Cir. 1990) (employer not strictly liable for sexual harassment of plaintiff by co-worker; negligence standard applies); Weiss v. International Bd. of Elec. Workers, 729 F. Supp. 144 (D.D.C. 1990) (complaints of sexual harassment dismissed on procedural grounds).

18. Corne, 390 F. Supp. at 163. Indeed, the conventional wisdom seems to be that while homosexual harassment is covered by Title VII, see, e.g., Wright v. Methodist Youth Serv., Inc., 511 F. Supp. 307 (N.D. Ill. 1981), bisexual harassment is not covered, see Bundy v. Jackson, 641 F.2d 934, 942 n.7 (D.C. Cir. 1981); see also Vinson v. Taylor, 760 F.2d 1330, 1333 n.7 (D.C. Cir. 1985) (Bork, J., dissenting from denial of rehearing) (questioning whether Congress in fact intended to prohibit any form of sexual harassment, given that statute does not cover bisexual harassment), aff'd on other grounds sub nom. Meritor Sav. Bank v. Vinson, 477 U.S. 57 (1986); Katherine S. Anderson, "Employer Liability Under Title VII for Sexual Harassment After Meritor Savings Bank v. Vinson," 87 Colum. L. Rev. 1258, 1259 n.13 (1987).

19. See Wendorf v. Metropolitan Life Ins. Co., 47 Empl. Prac. Dec. (CCH) par. 38,316, at 53,795 (E.D. N.Y. 1988).

20. See, e.g., Hicks v. Gates Rubber Co., 833 F.2d 1406 (10th Cir. 1987) (reversing district court judgment for employer and holding that harassment need not be sexual to constitute hostile environment; physical or verbal abuse because of gender may be sufficient); McKinney v. Dole, 765 F.2d 1129 (D.C. Cir. 1985) (reversing district court grant of summary judgment for employer and holding that physically aggressive acts by a male supervisor against a female employee, even if not explicitly sexual, can constitute sexual harassment in violation of Title VII if it would not occur but for the sex of the employee).

21. See, e.g., Wendorf, 47 Empl. Prac. Dec. (CCH) par. 38,316 at 53,795; Turley v. Union Carbide Corp, 618 F. Supp 1438, 1441–42 (S.D. Va. 1985) (brought under state law, but relying on Title VII cases).

22. Williams v. Saxbe, 413 F. Supp. 654, 657 (D.D.C. 1976), rev'd sub nom. Williams v. Bell, 587 F.2d 1240 (D.C. Cir. 1978) (on procedural grounds), on remand, Williams v. Civiletti, 487 F. Supp. 1387 (D.D.C. 1980). The Williams case was the first to recognize a cause of action for sexual harassment under Title VII. Williams, 413 F. Supp. at 657–58. The defendant in Williams—the United States Department of Justice—argued that the "primary variable" in the case was not gender, but "willingness vel non to furnish

sexual consideration. . . . Plaintiff was allegedly denied employment enhancement not because she was a woman, but rather because she decided not to furnish the sexual consideration claimed to have been demanded." Id. at 657. The judge, while finding the argument "appealing," ultimately rejected it. Id.

23. Corne v. Bausch & Lomb, Inc., 390 F. Supp. 161, 163–64 (D. Ariz. 1975), vacated without opinion, 562 F.2d 55 (9th Cir. 1977).

24. Miller v. Bank of America, 418 F. Supp. 233, 236 (N.D. Cal. 1976), rev'd, 600 F.2d 211 (9th Cir. 1979); see also Tomkins v. Public Serv. Elec. & Gas Co., 422 F. Supp. 553, 557 (D.N.J. 1976) (permitting such actions would create the need for "4,000 federal trial judges instead of some 400"), rev'd, 568 F.2d 1044 (3d Cir. 1977).

Ten years later, the EEOC adopted virtually the same position as the Miller district court in arguing that the plaintiff in Meritor Savings Bank v. Vinson had failed to state an actionable claim. See Brief for the United States and the Equal Employment Opportunity Commission as Amici Curiae at 13, Meritor Sav. Bank v. Vinson, 477 U.S. 57 (1986) (No. 84-1979) ("Sexual attraction is a fact of life, and it may often play a role in the day-to-day social exchange between employees in the workplace.").

25. Safran, supra note 12, at 217. The Redbook survey found: "[N]early 9 out of 10 women report that they have experienced one or more forms of unwanted attentions on the job. This can be visual (leering and ogling) or verbal (sexual remarks and teasing). It can escalate to pinching, grabbing and touching, to subtle hints and pressures, to overt requests for dates and sexual favors—with the implied threat that it will go against the woman if she refuses." Id.

26. United States Merit Systems Protection Board, Sexual Harassment in the Federal Workplace: Is It a Problem? 2–3 (1981).

27. United States Merit Systems Protection Board, Sexual Harassment in the Federal Government: An Update 39 (1988).

28. See Barbara A. Gutek, Sex and the Workplace 46 (1985) (53.1 percent of women surveyed identified themselves as victims of sexual harassment); Terri C. Fain & Douglas L. Anderson, "Sexual Harassment: Organizational Context and Diffuse Status," 17 Sex Roles 291, 298–304 (1987) (breakdown of data by type of harassment and other factors); Donald E. Maypole, "Sexual Harassment at Work: Review of Research and Theory," 2 Affilia 24, 30 (1987) (36% of women surveyed identified themselves as victims of sexual harassment); Working Women's Institute, "The Impact of Sexual Harassment on the Job: A Profile of the Experiences of 92 Women," Research Series Report No. 3 (1979).

29. See, e.g., Williams v. Civiletti, 487 F. Supp. 1387 (D.D.C. 1980) (supervisor kept changing his story; plaintiff consistently alleged that she was fired because she failed to accede to his demands); Miller v. Bank of America, 418 F. Supp. 233, 234 (N.D. Cal. 1976) (allegation by black female employee that her male supervisor promised her a better job if she would be sexually cooperative and caused her dismissal when she refused).

30. 477 U.S. 57 (1986). Mechelle Vinson, the plaintiff, is an African-American woman. Whether and to what extent racism plays a role in sexual harassment, and in

the legal system's treatment of such cases, is an important question that is beyond the scope of this article.

31. Id. at 60.

32. Id.

33. Id.

34. Id. Vinson also testified that Taylor "touched and fondled" other female employees, id. at 60, but the district court did not permit her "to present evidence of a pattern and practice relating to sexual advances to other female employees in her case in chief, but advised her that she might well be able to present such evidence in rebuttal to the defendants' cases." Id. at 61 (quoting Vinson v. Taylor, 23 Fair Empl. Prac. Cas. (BNA) 37, 38 n.1 (D.D.C. 1980)).

35. Vinson, 477 U.S. at 61.

36. Vinson, 23 Fair Empl. Prac. Cas. (BNA) at 42.

37. Id. Vinson testified that because she feared Taylor, she did not report his harassment to his supervisors and did not use the bank's complaint procedure. Vinson, 477 U.S. at 61.

38. Fisher v. Flynn, 598 F.2d 663, 665 (1st Cir. 1979).

39. See, e.g., Dockter v. Rudolf Wolff Futures, Inc., 684 F. Supp. 532, 534–35 (N.D. Ill 1988), aff'd, 913 F.2d 456 (7th Cir. 1990); Christoforou v. Ryder Truck Rental, Inc., 668 F. Supp. 294, 296–97 (S.D.N.Y. 1987); see also text accompanying notes 80–93 infra.

40. Vinson v. Taylor, 753 F.2d 141, 143 (D.C. Cir. 1985), aff'd on other grounds sub nom. Meritor Sav. Bank v. Vinson, 477 U.S. 57 (1986).

41. Vinson, 753 F.2d at 145 n.30.

42. Id. at 145.

43. Id. at 146 n.36. In the view of the court of appeals, if the evidence showed that "Taylor made Vinson's toleration of sexual harassment a condition of her employment," her voluntariness "had no materiality whatsoever." Id. at 146.

44. Id. at 150–51.

45. Brief for Petitioner at 30–31, 34–36, Meritor Sav. Bank v. Vinson, 477 U.S. 57 (1986) (No. 84-1979); see Meritor Sav. Bank v. Vinson, 477 U.S. 57, 64 (1986).

46. Vinson, 477 U.S. at 65–66.

47. Id. at 67.

48. Id. (quoting Rogers v. EEOC, 454 F.2d 234, 238 (5th Cir. 1971), cert. denied, 406 U.S. 957 (1972)).

49. Id. (quoting Henson v. Dundee, 682 F.2d 897, 904 (11th Cir. 1982)).

50. Id. at 68 (citing 29 C.F.R. § 1604.11(a) (1985)).

51. Id. at 69 (emphasis added).

52. Id. at 72.

53. Id. at 74–78 (Marshall, J., concurring in the judgment).

54. See id. at 72–73 (While "declin[ing] the parties' invitation to issue a definitive rule on employer liability . . . we do agree with the EEOC that Congress wanted courts to look to agency principles for guidance in this area. While such common-law prin-

ciples may not be transferable in all their particulars to Title VII, Congress' decision to define 'employer' to include any 'agent' of an employer, 47 U.S.C. § 2000e(b), surely evinces an intent to place some limits on the acts of employers for which employers under Title VII are to be held responsible.").

55. Meritor Sav. Bank v. Vinson, 477 U.S. 57, 68 (1986).

56. 1 Arthur Larson & Lex K. Larson, *Employment Discrimination: Sex* § 41.63(c), at 8-160 to 8-161 (1990). For a bit of comic relief on this issue, Professors Larson and Larson quote the argument of defense counsel in Jones v. Wesco Invs., Inc., 846 F.2d 1154 (8th Cir. 1988) that "[i]f civil liability is implanted on an employer for its employees [sic] natural interaction between the genders, either the collapse of our commercial system or the end of the human race can be foreseen. No employer could safely employ both males and females and the number of marriages with children will be substantially decreased . . . In [asking a female employee out on a date] the man should not have to gamble civil liability on her 'yes' response. See 1 Larson & Larson, *supra* § 41.63(c), at 8-161 n.56. I have yet to see a case in which a man was found liable for politely asking a woman out on a date; I have never even seen an unsuccessful case where that was the complaint. Indeed, in Jones, the supervisor had made persistent sexual advances to a married female employee, who had repeatedly and clearly indicated her unwelcomeness. *See id.*

57. *Vinson*, 477 U.S. at 69.

58. Docter v. Rudolf Wolff Futures, Inc., 684 F. Supp. 532, 533 (N.D. Ill. 1988), aff'd, 913 F.2d 456 (7th Cir. 1990).

59. 432 N.W.2d 764, 766–67 (Minn. Ct. App. 1988) (suit filed under federal and state law).

60. Id. at 768.

61. Id.; *see also* Grubka v. Department of Treasury, 858 F.2d 1570 (Fed. Cir. 1988) (overturning as not supported by substantial evidence the demotion of a supervisor for sexual harassment, where the employee involved had flirted with the supervisor and where the supervisor had at most stolen a kiss); Bouchet v. National Urban League, 33 Fair Empl. Prac. Cas. (BNA) 536 (D.D.C. 1982), aff'd, 730 F.2d 799 (D.C. Cir. 1984) (judgment for employer where plaintiff was aware that she had been hired in part because of her employer's personal attraction to her).

62. See. e.g., Gutek, *supra* note 28, at 46, 54 (while 53.1% of the women in the sample reported having directly experienced sexual harassment, only 22.5% reported even having talked about the general subject matter to a coworker). Plainly, more empirical work needs to be done in this area, but here, as in rape research, problems of definition coupled with personal and socially imposed embarrassment may complicate efforts to discover the truth of women's experiences.

63. Gutek found that the single biggest discrepancy between men and women in their attitudes toward workplaces came on the question whether the respondent would feel "flattered" if asked to have sex: 67.2% of the men, as compared to 16.8% of the women, responded that they would be flattered, while 15% of the men, and 62.8% of the women, reported that they would be insulted. Id. at 96.

64. Richman v. Bureau of Affirmative Action, 536 F. Supp. 1149, 1164 (M.D. Pa. 1982).

65. *See id.* at 1164, 1177; *see also* Sardigal v. St. Louis Nat'l Stockyards Co., 42 Fair Empl. Prac. Cas. (BNA) 497, 501 (S.D. Ill. 1986) (in finding for the employer, court emphasized that the plaintiff voluntarily associated with her alleged harasser, went for a drive with him, and even allowed him in her home).

66. Gan v. Kepro Circuit Sys., 28 Fair Empl. Prac. Cas. (BNA) 639, 640–41 (E.D. Mo. 1982); *see also* Loftin-Boggs v. City of Meridian, 633 F. Supp. 1323, 1327 (S.D. Miss. 1986) (where plaintiff herself used coarse language and participated in workplace banter and joking, court concluded that "[a]ny harassment plaintiff received . . . was prompted by her own actions, including her tasteless joking" and that the environment could not oppress her, since she contributed to it), *aff'd*, 824 F.2d 971 (5th Cir. 1987), *cert. denied.* 484 U.S. 1063 (1988).

67. 778 F.2d 878 (D.C. Cir. 1985). The EEOC guidelines similarly provide that:

> Where employment opportunities or benefits are granted because of an individual's submission to the employer's sexual advances or requests for sexual favors, the employer may be held liable for unlawful sex discrimination against other persons who were qualified for but denied that employment opportunity or benefit.

29 C.R.R. § 1604.11(g) (1990); *see also* Kersul v. Skulls Angels, Inc., 130 Misc.2d 345, 347–48, 495 N.Y.S.2d 886 (Sup. Ct. 1985) (in case brought under New York State Human Rights Laws court relied on EEOC guidelines and *King v. Palmer* to hold that plaintiff could state a cause of action based on allegations that she had been denied benefits given to a coworker who was sexually involved with the employer). *Contra* DeCintio v. Westchester County Medical Ctr., 807 F.2d 304 (2d Cir. 1986) (holding that male plaintiffs were not victims of sex discrimination because their employer preferred his female lover in defining and filling a job opening), *cert. denied,* 484 U.S. 825 (1987); Miller v. Alcoa, 45 Fair Empl. Prac. Cas. (BNA) 1775, 1778–79 (W.D. Pa. 1988) (holding that "preferential treatment on the basis of a consensual romantic relationship between a supervisor and an employee is not gender-based discrimination," but implying that a third-party suit may lie if the relationship is nonconsensual).

68. *King,* 778 F.2d at 882.

69. *Id.*

70. The question whether third parties should, in the first instance, be permitted to bring such suits was apparently not raised by either of the parties on appeal. *See id.* at 883 (Bork, J., concurring in the denial of rehearing en banc).

71. *See* notes 126–138 *infra* and accompanying text.

72. One of the few cases to recognize this was Jeppson v. Wunnicke, 611 F. Supp. 78 (D. Alaska 1985), a pre-*Vinson* decision which recognized that tangible job benefits cannot be meaningfully distinguished from intangible ones and refused to enforce different rules regarding employer knowledge of sex discrimination in a hostile environment versus quid pro quo cases. Four judges also rejected the notion of different employer liability rules for each form of harassment.

73. Empirical research also casts doubt on the sharp distinction drawn by the

courts. Surveys indicate that a highly sexualized environment—one in which sexual joking is common and flirtatious behavior is encouraged—is also one where specific sexual overtures are more likely to occur. *See* Gutek, *supra* note 28, at 124.

74. 697 F. Supp. 204 (E.D. Va. 1988).

75. Id. at 217.

76. Id. at 208.

77. *See* Vermeulen, *supra* note 17, at 340–42 & n.81.

78. *See* Davis v. Passman, 442 U.S. 228, 230 n.3 (1979); *see also* Price Waterhouse v. Hopkins, 490 U.S. 228 (1989) (discriminatory notes in personnel file). Only a few such cases need to reach the Supreme Court before all but the most unsophisticated employers get smart and avoid such practices.

79. *See* note 176 *infra* and accompanying text.

80. *See, e.g.*, Valdez v. Church's Fried Chicken, Inc., 683 F. Supp. 596 (W.D. Tex. 1988) (absenteeism); Bouchet v. National Urban League, 33 Fair Empl. Prac. Cas. (BNA) 536 (D.D.C. 1982) (unsatisfactory overall work performance), *aff'd*, 730 F.2d 799 (D.C. Cir. 1984) Ramsey v. Olin Corp., 39 Fair Empl. Prac. Cas. (BNA) 959 (S.D.N.Y. 1984) (high error rate); Sand v. Johnson Co., 33 Fair Empl. Prac. Cas. (BNA) 716 (E.D. Mich. 1982) (tardiness).

81. *See, e.g.*, Horn v. Duke Homes, 755 F.2d 599, 602 (7th Cir. 1985) (three other women employees came forward to testify that the same supervisor had repeatedly harassed them); Priest v. Rotary, 634 F. Supp. 571, 574–76 (N.D. Cal. 1986) (plaintiff managed, with the help of other women employees, to establish a pattern of sexual harassment by restaurant owner).

82. *See* Spencer v. General Elec. Co., 697 F. Supp. 204, 213–15 (E.D. Va. 1988); Kresko v. Rulli, 432 N.W.2d 764, 768–69 (Minn. Ct. App. 1988); *see also Horn*, 755 F.2d at 602–3; *Priest*, 634 F. Supp. at 581–82.

83. 684 F. Supp. 532 (N.D. Ill. 1988), *aff'd*, 913 F.2d 456 (7th Cir. 1990).

84. Id. at 531.

85. Id.

86. See id.

87. Id. at 534, 535. Indeed, some courts go further still, implicitly blaming the "unqualified" woman for being in a job that, in the court's view, she did not deserve and received only because of her sexuality. There is certainly a flavor of this in the *Dockter* opinion. There is more than a flavor in Bouchet v. National Urban League, 33 Fair Empl. Prac. Cas. (BNA) 536 (D.D.C. 1982), *aff'd*, 730 F.2d 799 (D.C. Cir. 1984), where the court in holding that no quid pro quo had been demanded, emphasized that the "unqualified" plaintiff had been hired because her supervisor allowed his attraction to her to "overcome his better judgment" and that she, though knowing this full well, "*did nothing to discourage* [him]." Id. at 540 (emphasis added).

88. *Dockter*, 684 F. Supp. at 535.

89. 668 F. Supp. 294 (S.D.N.Y. 1987).

90. Id. at 296–300.

91. Id. at 300.

92. See also King v. Board of Regents, 898 F.2d 533, 540 (7th Cir. 1990) (plaintiff established that her dean sexually harassed her, but failed to establish that the harassment was the reason her contract was not renewed; court emphasized that evidence of "tenure-quality work" was absent).

93. Christoforou, 668 F. Supp. at 301.

94. Meritor Sav. Bank v. Vinson, 477 U.S. 57 (1986).

95. See note 46 supra and accompanying text. The first appellate court to recognize a hostile environment claim for sexual harassment was the U.S. Court of Appeals for the District of Columbia Circuit, in Bundy v. Jackson, 641 F.2d 934 (1981). While relying as well on other Title VII categories, where liability was based on a discriminatory environment regardless of whether specific and tangible job benefits were involved, the court, rather than emphasizing the differences between quid pro quo and hostile environment cases, focused instead on the connections between them as well as their complementary nature. Without this expansion in liability, the court recognized, any employer could lawfully and freely harass an employee "by carefully stopping short of firing the employee or taking any other tangible actions against her in response to her resistance." Id. at 945.

96. See, e.g., Drinkwater v. Union Carbide Corp., 904 F.2d 853 (3d Cir. 1990); Halpert v. Wertheim & Co., 27 Fair Empl. Prac. Cas. (BNA) 21 (S.D.N.Y. 1980).

97. Henson v. City of Dundee, 682 F.2d 897, 903 (11th Cir. 1982).

98. Id. at 904.

99. See note 18 supra and accompanying text.

100. See text accompanying notes 103–114 infra.

101. See note 7 supra and accompanying text.

102. Not every court has held, at least formally, that sexual harassment must be sexual in order to be considered based on sex. See McKinney v. Dole, 765 F.2d 1129, 1138 (D.C. Cir. 1985) ("We have never held that sexual harassment . . . that occurs because of the sex of the employee must, to be illegal under Title VII, take the form of sexual advances or of other incidents with clearly sexual overtones."); Hicks v. Gates Rubber Co., 833 F.2d 1406, 1415 (10th Cir. 1987) (agreeing with the McKinney court that harassment that is not sexual in nature may constitute illegal sex discrimination if the conduct would not have happened but for the employee's sex); Andrews v. City of Philadelphia, 895 F.2d 1469, 1485 (3d Cir. 1990) (sexually discriminatory conduct need not be sexual); see also Ellison v. Brady, No. 89-15248, 1991 U.S. App. LEXIS 875 (9th Cir. Jan. 23, 1991) (finding it unnecessary to decide whether conduct must be sexual). But even these courts have insisted that the plaintiff prove that men are treated differently.

103. 47 Empl. Prac. Dec. (CCH) par. 38,316 at 53,788 (E.D.N.Y. 1988).

104. Id. at 53,795.

105. Id.

106. Id. at 53,794.

107. Id. at 53,795; see also Turley v. Union Carbide Corp., 618 F. Supp. 1438, 1441–42

(S.D. W. Va. 1985) (to be actionable, harassment must not only be directed at a member of the female sex, but must be "harassment which plays upon the stereotypical role of the female as a sexual object").

108. *See Model Penal Code* § 2.02 comment 4 (1980) (justifying negligence liability); *see also* H.L.A. Hart, *Punishment and Responsibility* 152–57 (1968); Glanville Williams, *Criminal Law: The General Part* § 43 (2d ed. 1961).

109. *See* Estrich, "Rape," *supra* note 1, at 1182–83.

110. 775 F.2d 288 (Fed. Cir. 1985).

111. Id. at 295; *see also* Walter v. KFGO Radio, 518 F. Supp. 1309 (D.N.D. 1981) (supervisor claimed that patting female employee on the bottom was to show support and encouragement; no harassment found).

112. *Downes* 775 F.2d at 295.

113. Bennett v. Corroon & Black Corp., 517 So. 2d 1245 (La. Ct. App. 1987), *writ denied*, 520 So. 2d 425 (La. 1988). Notably, there were no cartoons labeled with men's names in the place where men were denied access: the women's room.

114. Halpert v. Wertheim & Co., 27 Fair Empl. Prac. Cas. (BNA) 21, 23–24 (S.D.N.Y. 1980).

115. Rabidue v. Osceola Ref. Co., 805 F.2d 611, 620 (6th Cir. 1986).

116. Meritor Sav. Bank v. Vinson, 477 U.S. 57, 67 (1986).

117. Id. (quoting Henson v. City of Dundee, 682 F.2d 897, 904 (11th Cir. 1982)). Applying this standard, courts have been reluctant to recognize sexual harassment in the absence of at least the old "quid" of the quid pro quo cases—repeated sexual demands. Mere "sexual derision," as Professor Kathryn Abrams terms it, has generally been held insufficient to create a hostile environment, and even sporadic sexual demands have often proven insufficient. Kathryn Abrams, "Gender Discrimination and the Transformation of Workplace Norms," 42 *Vand. L. Rev.* 1183, 1199–1200 (1989); *see, e.g.*, Jones v. Flagship Int'l, 793 F.2d 714 (5th Cir. 1986) (three requests for sexual contact, plus office party decorations of bare-chested mermaids, insufficient for establishing sexual harassment claim); Rabidue v. Osceola Ref. Co., 805 F.2d 611 (6th Cir. 1986) (offensive posters and vulgar language insufficient), *cert. denied*, 481 U.S. 1041 (1987); Highlander v. KFC Nat'l Management Co., 805 F.2d 644 (6th Cir. 1986) (fondling and verbal proposition insufficient); Dockter v. Rudolf Wolff Futures, Inc., 684 F. Supp. 532, 535 (N.D. Ill. 1988) (breast fondling not sufficient to constitute hostile environment, and other advances found "essentially inoffensive"), *aff'd*, 913 F.2d 456 (7th Cir. 1990); Strickland v. Sears, Roebuck & Co., 46 Fair Empl. Prac. Cas. (BNA) 1024 (E.D. Va. 1987) (inappropriate joking and touching insufficient); Harris v. Bolger, 599 F. Supp. 1414 (C.D. Cal. 1984) (allegations of suggestive gestures on four or five occasions insufficient to support claim of sexual or racial harassment). *See generally* 1 Larson & Larson, *supra* note 56, § 41.64(d)(ii), at 8-183 to 8-186; Abrams, *supra*, at 1199–1200; Note, "Sexual Harassment Claims of Abusive Work Environment Under Title VII," 97 *Harv. L. Rev.* 1449 (1984).

119. 805 F.2d at 620–22.

120. *Id.* at 622.

121. *Id.* at 623–24 (Keith, J., concurring in part and dissenting in part).

122. *Id.* at 624 (Keith, J., concurring in part and dissenting in part).

123. *Id.* at 622. The Court of Appeals for the Seventh Circuit adopted a similar approach in Scott v. Sears, Roebuck & Co., 798 F.2d 210 (1986), where the plaintiff was repeatedly propositioned by her supervisors, where her requests for assistance were met with sexual innuendos, and where coworkers slapped her rear and openly commented on how she must behave during sex. In the Court's view, such activities did not sufficiently poison the work environment. *Id.* at 211–14. *But see* Andrews v. City of Philadelphia, 895 F.2d 1469, 1485 (3d Cir. 1990) (finding hostile environment); Davis v. Monsanto Chem. Co., 858 F.2d 345, 350 (6th Cir. 1988) (criticizing *Rabidue*): Yates v. Avco Corp., 819 F.2d 630, 637 (6th Cir. 1987) (adopting victim's perspective).

124. *Rabidue*, 805 F.2d at 620–21 (quoting Rabidue v. Osceola Ref. Co., 584 F. Supp. 419, 430 (E.D. Mich. 1984)).

125. *See* Meritor Sav. Bank v. Vinson. 477 U.S. 57, 67 (1986); Henson v. City of Dundee, 682 F.2d 897, 904 (11th Cir. 1982).

126. Rabidue v. Osceola Ref. Co., 584 F. Supp. 419, 433 (E.D. Mich. 1984), *aff'd*, 805 F.2d 611 (6th Cir. 1986).

127. Vermett v. Hough, 627 F. Supp. 587, 607 (W.D. Mich. 1986).

128. *See, e.g., Rabidue*, 805 F.2d at 620.

129. Kelsey-Andrews v. City of Philadelphia, No. 88-4101, 1988 WL 137284, at *2 (E.D. Pa. Dec. 19, 1988).

130. Spencer v. General Elec. Co., 697 F. Supp. 204, 214 (E.D. Va. 1988).

131. Sand v. Johnson Co., 33 Fair Empl. Prac. Cas. (BNA) 716, 720, 727 (E.D. Mich. 1982).

132. *Kelsey-Andrews* No. 88-4101, at *2.

133. *See, e.g.,* Walter v. KFGO Radio, 518 F. Supp. 1309, 1314–15 (D.N.D. 1981); *see also Sand,* 33 Fair Empl. Prac. Cas. (BNA) at 726–27 (causal nexus between sexual harassment and plaintiff's termination from employment not established because plaintiff did not make her first complaint until a few weeks after she was fired).

134. Staton v. Maries County, 868 F.2d 996, 998 (8th Cir. 1989).

135. Scott v. Sears, Roebuck & Co., 798 F.2d 210, 214 (7th Cir. 1986).

136. *Walter,* 518 F. Supp. at 1315–16.

137. *See, e.g.,* Slate v. Alston, 312 S.E.2d 470 (N.C. 1984); State v. Lester, 321 S.E.2d 166 (N.C. 1984); Commonwealth v. Biggs, 467 A.2d 31 (Pa. 1983). *See generally* Estrich, *Real Rape, supra* note 1, at 60–63.

138. Rabidue v. Osceola Ref. Co., 805 F.2d 611, 620 (6th Cir. 1986).

139. 432 N.W.2d 764 (Minn. Ct. App. 1988). But *Kresko* is hardly unique. The lower court in *Vinson,* for example, excluded evidence regarding Taylor's other alleged sexual activity at work. *See* Vinson v. Taylor, 23 Fair Empl. Prac. Cas. (BNA) 37, 38–39 & n.1 (D.D.C. 1980).

140. *See* text accompanying notes 59–61 *supra.*

141. *Kresko*, 432 N.W.2d at 768–69.

142. *Id.* at 770.

143. It is almost as easy to attack those courts that rely on the absence of harassment complaints from other female workers, while refusing to allow plaintiffs' attorneys to question female coworkers on precisely this topic. Surely if a "fact" is to be dispositive, it must be considered relevant. *See, e.g.,* the discussion of the lower court decision in Henson v. City of Dundee, 682 F.2d 897, 899 (11th Cir. 1982), where the trial judge held against the plaintiff, relying on the fact that her boss had never sexually propositioned her female coworker. In fact, however, the judge would not allow plaintiff's attorney to question the other woman on this, upholding the relevancy objection. A new trial was eventually granted.

144. *See, e.g.,* Horn v. Duke Homes, 755 F.2d 599 (7th Cir. 1985) (two former female employees testified that they had been harassed, and another that she had had a "voluntary" affair with the same man).

145. In Priest v. Rotary, 98 FR D 755, 756 n.1, 32 Fair Empl. Prac. Cas. (BNA) 1064, 1065 n.1 (N.D. Cal. 1983), *later proceeding,* 634 F. Supp. 571 (N.D. Cal. 1986), a California district court refused to grant a motion to compel a plaintiff to answer questions such as: "Would you tell me the name of each person that you have had sexual relations with in the last ten years?"

146. Similar problems in rape prosecutions have led to the widespread enactment of rape shield statutes, which limit consideration of the victim's sexual activities with men other than the defendant. Even so, most such statutes afford discretion to the trial court to balance probative value and prejudicial effect, and appellate courts have in some cases insisted, notwithstanding statutory language to the contrary, that such discretion be exercised in favor of admission. *See, e.g.,* State v. Colbath, 130 N.H. 316, 324, 540 A.2d 1212, 1216 (1988) (Souter, J.) ("evidence of public displays of general interest in sexual activity can be taken to indicate a contemporaneous receptiveness to sexual advances"). *See generally* Kathleen Winters, Note, "United States v. Shaw: What Constitutes an 'Injury' under the Federal Rape-Shield Statute?" 43 *U. Miami L. Rev.* 947 (1989); Andrew Z. Soshnick, Note, "The Rape Shield Paradox: Complainant Protection Amidst Oscillating Trends of State Judicial Interpretation," 78 J. Crim. L. & Criminology 644 (1987).

147. *See* notes 151–57 *infra* and accompanying text.

148. While most jurisdictions have formally abandoned such rules, the Model Penal Code retains a corroboration provision and a fresh complaint rule in its proposals. *See Model Penal Code* § 213.6(4)–(5); Estrich, "Rape," *supra* note 1, at 1087.

149. *See, e.g.,* 3A Wigmore, *supra* note 5 § 924a, at 736; "Forcible and Statutory Rape: An Exploration of the Operation and Objectives of the Consent Standard," *supra* note 5, at 61, 67–68 (there is an "unusual inducement to malicious or psychopathic accusation inherent in the sexual nature of the crime").

150. *See* Estrich, *Real Rape, supra* note 1, at 88–91.

151. *See, e.g.,* Carter v. Sedgwick County, 705 F. Supp. 1474, 1477–78 (D. Kan. 1988); Spencer v. General Elec. Co., 697 F. Supp. 204 (E.D. Va. 1988); Christoforou v. Ryder

> claimant will pause long before enduring the humiliation of making public the indignities which she has suffered in private, as well as the anticipated claims that she has "consented," and the attempts to trivialize her concerns, when she is precluded from recovering damages for her perpetrators' behavior. It is, however, the responsibility of Congress, rather than this Court, to recognize and repair this deficiency in the statute.

Mitchell, 629 F. Supp. at 643.

168. See, e.g., Steele v. Offshore Bldg., 867 F.2d 1311, 1317–18 (11th Cir. 1989); Coley v. Consolidated Rail Corp., 561 F. Supp. 645, 651 (E.D. Mich. 1982); Robson v. Eva's Super Market, 538 F. Supp. 857, 862 (N.D. Ohio 1982); Brown v. City of Guthrie, 22 Fair Empl. Prac. Cas. (BNA) 1627, 1633–34 (W.D. Okla. 1980). Some courts go further still, requiring proof that the employer actually intended the discharge. See, e.g., Dornhecker v. Malibu Grand Prix Corp., 828 F.2d 307, 310 (5th Cir. 1987) (to establish constructive discharge, plaintiff must prove that the "employer *deliberately* makes an employee's working conditions so intolerable that the employee is *forced* into an involuntary resignation") (quoting Wilkins v. University of Houston, 654 F.2d 388, 390 (5th Cir. 1991)); Ross v. Double Diamond, 672 F. Supp. 261, 277–78 (N.D. Tex. 1987).

169. "[E]ven under the less stringent standard, the requirement that the working conditions be 'intolerable' makes constructive discharge tough to prove." 1 Larson & Larson, *supra* note 56, § 41.64(c), at 8-179.

170. See, e.g., Coley, 561 F. Supp. at 651–52 (back pay limited to $5200 in light of failure to mitigate; fear of middle-aged men no excuse). The lawyers, not surprisingly, often fare better than the plaintiffs; even nominal damages are enough to support an award of attorneys' fees. The real deterrent, if there is one, and the real explanation for the *Henson* result may be lawyers' fees, even though the judgment is framed in terms of the woman's lack of rights, not the lawyers' need for payment.

171. No. 89-15248, 1991 U.S. App. LEXIS 875, *18–21 (Jan. 23, 1991); see also Nancy S. Ehrenreich, "Pluralist Myths and Powerless Men: The Ideology of Reasonableness in Sexual Harassment Law," 99 *Yale L.J.* 1177, 1207–08 (1990).

172. See Commodore Home Sys., Inc. v. Superior Court, 649 P.2d 912 (Cal. 1983).

173. See Gutek, *supra* note 28. Gutek argues that this is because sex roles are more basic cognitive categories than work roles; many women adopt sex roles at work because they "feel more comfortable" with these roles, while many men, uncomfortable with women in the workplace, revert to familiar sex roles. Noticeably missing from Gutek's analysis is any emphasis on the general power imbalances between men and women which, I would argue, are reflected in traditional sex roles—inside or outside of work. Similarly, the suggestion that women adopt these roles at work out of comfort ignores the possibility that the only one comforted is the man, not the woman, and that women do what those in power expect, indeed demand, of them. Gutek's own empirical reports suggest that men, far more than women, welcome the sexualization of the workplace. Id. at 96.

174. Barnes v. Costle, 561 F.2d 983, 1001 (D.C. Cir. 1977) (MacKinnon, J., concurring).

175. "Sexual Harassment Claims of Abusive Work Environment Under Title VII," *supra* note 118, at 1458.

176. See "Sex Probes to Target 3 Lawmakers," *L.A. Times*, Aug. 5, 1989, at 2, col. 1.

REVISING

ANCIENT TALES

III

The essays in this section indicate just how deeply entrenched is the idea that women who can read and write, and thus might tell tales, are a persistent danger to the status quo. "Revising Ancient Tales" places in historical context the oft-repeated claim that women's capacity to represent themselves has always been severely limited by the manner in which they tell stories about themselves, the conditions under which they can tell those stories, and the spaces to which their storytelling has been confined. This section also demonstrates that individual solutions to structural and systemic biases sometimes merely soften protest rather than lead to transformations of a social or political kind, even though one woman's story has the potential to force the recognition of a need for that transformation, as did Anita Hill's.

The words women use, the stories to which they appeal, the characters they construct cannot escape the tradition of biased interpretations governing what judges, juries, readers—or senate subcommittees—can hear. What is more, the hierarchies and stereotypes that inhere in traditions of representation shape even women's understanding of their own identities and behaviors. Despite the fact that these essays chart a history of misrepresentation, from medieval heretic trials and eighteenth-century law to nineteenth-century fiction and twentieth-century courtrooms, they also insist that women's power to talk back is enhanced by our self-conscious and strategic revisions of the stories that have been used against us.

Rita Copeland's essay, "Why Women Can't Read: Medieval Hermeneutics, Statutory Law, and the Lollard Heresy Trials," deals with two dimensions of misogynist hermeneutics in the Middle Ages: the clerical construction of women as bad readers who shouldn't be allowed to mix with books, and a symbolic identification of literalism, vernacular texts, and the laity with the female body. Both these dimensions, clerical misogyny and the symbolic association of literal reading and vernacular texts with feminine carnality, represent implicit "laws" of reading that preserve an official "masculinist" control of reading and interpretation; these "laws" also secure the professional prerogative of the clergy over interpretation and teaching of sacred Scripture. But this implicit and symbolic "law" of reading was codified in statutory law, in the legal code that defined the grounds for criminal prosecution of the Lollard heresy in fifteenth-century England. In official attempts to suppress the Lollard heresy among the laity, possession and use of the vernacular Bible was classified as evidence of heretical activity. Of course this law was directed at both men and women readers. But the Lollard hermeneutic proclaims the very principles that are associated with "bad" feminine reading: it promotes literalism, vernacular texts, and lay reading. The real object of official prosecution was the Lollard hermeneutic, which is symbolically a feminine hermeneutic, regardless of the gender of the reader.

As we see from the records of heresy investigations and trials, women readers, or women who participated in a textual community, were readily perceived as the embodiments, the living exemplars, of this feminine hermeneutic. Because literacy among lay women was fairly unusual, lay women who could read or who possessed books came under particular suspicion of heretical activity. This essay focuses on the trial record of one woman, Margery Baxter, who was tried for heresy in Norwich in 1428–29. The unusually detailed court records concerning Margery Baxter allow us to pinpoint the intersection of hermeneutical law and the realization of that law in the historical prosecution of a particular woman.

In "Voices of Record: Women as Witnesses and Defendants in the Old Bailey Sessions Papers," Margaret Anne Doody culls women's voices from one of the few historical sources in which women might be seen actively revising social and self-representation. Reviewing cases of theft, infanticide, and assault heard at London's Old Bailey during the 1740s, Doody gives us evidence of how women defended themselves and speculates on the reasons women may have been heard as they were, or silenced. "Voices of Record" provides us with pieces, however fragmentary, of the long history of women's public speech, a valuable perspective for us as we cope with new examples of women's traumatic experience as witnesses. This evidence resists any easy generalizations about women's access to public speech. Defendants might be allowed to wax long, all the while condemning themselves with their own words. Or, they may effectively turn their accusers' stories against them. Of equal importance to these examples of women's voices is the analysis Doody gives us of the media through which their witness is given and preserved. The courtroom drama "scripts" its characters—defendants and witnesses—and allows for "intermittent improvisation" at best. Furthermore, the Sessions Papers, journalistic accounts of trials published for sale in a period without formal trial records, but at a time when theatrical drama and the novel were burgeoning, are examples of how popular culture both constructs and affects the representation of women and contributes to the creation of an elite tradition of literary representation. As Rita Copeland's essay demonstrates, legal (and theological) discourse shared many of the conventions and practices of literary discourse, and women therefore spoke in the apparently discrete space of courtrooms not only as witnesses in the legal sense, but also as witnesses to the construction of their self-representation in the elite and popular culture of which the law courts were a part.

It is this double-edged witnessing by women that is explored in Susan Sage Heinzelman's essay, "Guilty in Law, Implausible in Fiction: Jurisprudential and Literary Narratives in the Case of Mary Blandy, Parricide, 1752."

Taking the occasion of the trial of Mary Blandy in 1752 for the poisoning of her father as a particularly sensational model of the manner in which both high and low culture employ stereotypes of women readers and writers as suspect, Heinzelman positions Mary Blandy's story within the larger cultural narrative of the rise of the novel. The essay situates Mary Blandy's case at the intersection of several forms of storytelling and delineates the manner in which shifts in the value of certain kinds of representations of reality, although potentially liberating for women, may, in fact, end up controlling their voices even more significantly than before. In the late seventeenth and early eighteenth centuries, women writers discovered that economic and social affect might be within their grasp as the novel began to encroach upon previously privileged forms of representation. Dismissed by early reviewers as work for women, the production of the early novel—sentimental fiction—was dominated by women writers, and its reception was dominated by women readers. What opportunities did this novel way of speaking about one's individual and social self offer to women? How did such opportunities conflict with and threaten to undermine the representations associated with more authoritative narratives—like those of the law, or theology, or history?

Heinzelman's essay juxtaposes three accounts of the events leading up to the hanging of Mary Blandy for the murder of her father: the quasi-legal account as recorded in the State Trials; the "history" of God's intervention in human affairs, as recorded by Henry Fielding in his *Examples of the Interposition of Providence in the Detection and Punishment of Murder* (1752); and the autobiographical account written by Mary Blandy in her Oxford gaol cell, *Miss Blandy's Own Account of the Affair Between Her and Mr. Cranstoun* (1752). It is the latter account that Heinzelman suggests partakes of those novelistic conventions that simultaneously promise some resistance to the dominant language of the law and inscribe the weaknesses and evils of women even more insistently in the culture. Even as women turned, then, to literary conventions to assist in their self-representation and to compensate for their misrepresentation in other authoritative discourses, they found themselves engaged in contending with the same damaging stereotypes of women as witnesses, writers, and readers.

Women also turned directly to literary representation to campaign against their exclusion from legal representation, an exclusion that became more determined and rigid after the late eighteenth century. Christine L. Krueger, in "Witnessing Women: Trial Testimony in Novels by Tonna, Gaskell, and Eliot," examines the critiques of gender bias in legal and literary practice made by three politically influential nineteenth-century British writers. Whereas Doody and Heinzelman give us evidence of the discursive structures that shaped what women could say in courts of law and in their own defense in autobiographical narratives, Krueger shows that by the mid-nineteenth century women were using the novel's self-conscious narrative strategies to attack the power structures that underlay ostensibly neutral jurisprudential theories, courtroom practices, and literary judgments. The novel afforded these writers a forum in which transgressive—"illegal"—female stories could be represented and, unlike in the male-dominated courtroom, be authorized—that is, shown as credible and realistic. Additionally, for novelists who justified their work as contributing to social reform, the law symbolized not only the legal barriers to women's equality, but the panoply of misogynistic critical standards ranged against them. From *ad feminam* attacks on their chastity to misreadings that appropriate female protest for reform agendas serving exclusively male interests, female novelists suffered for their attempts to revise ancient tales in many of the ways we associate with women witnessing against men in courts of law. As a consequence, they were acutely aware of the need for women to author social reality, if not in law, then in literature.

Anne B. Goldstein's essay, "Representing the Lesbian in Law and Literature," confronts directly this need for women to employ the various literary and legal representations of reality in their efforts to retell ancient stories about women's sexuality. Goldstein brings the insights of generations of female novelists representing women's characters to bear on the challenges of litigation for lesbian clients. Terming litigation a "storytelling contest," she surveys the range of stories told by and about lesbians in fiction of the last century in order to assist lawyers who need to tell compelling stories about lesbian clients they represent. Lawyers, Goldstein argues, must imagine any client's character, and given the unfavorable stereotypes that prevail in the culture, imagining and representing lesbian clients in a positive manner poses a particular challenge. Lesbian novels are useful to lawyers, not because they necessarily present realistic portrayals of lesbians' lives, but because their aim is generally that of litigators: to explain and justify the characters they represent to a potentially hostile audience. Goldstein identifies five general strategies evident in fiction about lesbians—including *The Well of Loneliness, The Price of Salt, The Color Purple,* and *Patience and Sarah*—and applies these strategies to two cases. The first is the well-known case of Sharon Kowalski and Karen Thompson, in which Thompson "successfully recast the meaning of 'lesbian lover' " so that she might be made Kowalski's legal guardian when Kowalski was severely injured in an auto accident. The second, a case Goldstein litigated, involves a woman who was threatened with dismissal from her job for "being a lesbian." Both cases illustrate the necessity of confronting stereotypes about lesbian identity and the value of fictional representations in enabling lesbians to tell their own stories about their identities.

What these essays all attest to is the potential for transforming the social and political realities that attend on women's daily life and that such transformations are both the impetus for and the result of legal and literary representations. It is to the power of representation, then, that women must pay attention if they are first to reimagine, and then retell, those ancient tales that have thus far so severely constrained them.

WHY WOMEN CAN'T READ

Medieval Hermeneutics, Statutory Law, and the Lollard Heresy Trials

Rita Copeland

▽

It is a clerical commonplace of the Middle Ages that women and books don't mix. This particular strain of misogynistic tradition constitutes a hermeneutical "law," a code that governs theories of reading in academic and theological circles from the early church fathers to the late medieval universities and preaching orders. But this "law" of reading, the doctrine of the text that proclaims women to be innately bad readers, also has real legal ramifications. It is an operative assumption of one late medieval legal code, the set of statutes that defined the grounds for criminal prosecution of heresy in fifteenth-century England. In official attempts to suppress the Lollard heresy among the laity, possession and use of the vernacular Bible was classified as evidence of heretical activity. Such legally sponsored suspicion could be directed especially at the textual activity of lay women. In this essay I want to trace the way in which a literary discourse of misogyny is actualized in historical legal practice. I am concerned here with the legal ramifications of how women use literature.[1]

There are two broad issues to be considered here: the implicit laws that establish hermeneutical propriety by defining the proper "gender" of reading, and the explicit heresy laws that forbade or regulated the circulation of vernacular texts, laws that were also used to identify women as a potentially subversive readership. We will thus see how a gendering of hermeneutics is overlaid upon the social and legal ordering of sexual difference.[2] The laws of hermeneutics are the more difficult to trace because they are implicit, a formation of attitudes and theoretical postures rather than formalized legal rulings. But it is also a more powerful and culturally comprehensive discourse than any given set of actual regulations, which are circumstantially and historically contingent. It is this uncodified code excluding women from the fraternity of textual exegesis that I will consider first, and afterward show how its central precepts are realized in the legal thought and practice associated with the historical moment of Lollardy, the English pre-Reformation heresy that evolved from the political and eucharistic teachings of the fourteenth-century Oxford theologian John Wyclif.

Textual Exegesis and the Feminine

Ancient traditions of misogamy (hatred of marriage) joined with misogynistic currents to produce the topos that a wife is a worldly distraction from the rigors of philosophy and the company of books.[3] The formulation that was most popular with medieval satirists was contained in the *Liber aureolus de nuptiis* (*The Golden Book on Marriage*), attributed to the Greek philosopher Theophrastus (third century B.C.), which survived only in excerpted form in St. Jerome's defense of virginity, *Adversus Jovinianum*. Theophrastus, and through him Jerome, sets the terms for the opposition between wives and books:

> A wise man therefore must not take a wife. For in the first place his study of philosophy will be hindered, and it is impossible for anyone to attend to his books and his wife. Matrons want many things: costly dresses, jewels, great outlay, maidservants, all kinds of furniture, litters and gilded coaches. . . . There may be in some neighboring city the wisest of teachers; but if we have a wife we can neither leave her behind, nor take the burden with us. To support a poor wife is hard: to put up with a rich one is torture. . . . Men marry, indeed, so as to get a manager for the house, solace weariness, to banish solitude; but a faithful slave is a far better manager, more submissive to the master, more observant of his ways than a wife who thinks she proves herself mistress if she acts in opposition to her husband, that is, if she does what pleases her, not what she is commanded. . . . A wise man can never be alone. He has with him the good men of all time, and turns his mind freely whenever he chooses. What is inaccessible to him in person he can embrace in thought. And if men are scarce, he converses with God. He is never less alone than when alone.[4]

The asceticism and spirituality of the scholar's retreat cannot sustain the jangling intrusions of worldliness. To preserve its authenticity it must preserve its remove, even where that remove is merely fictive, as the scholar's leisure is necessarily a corollary of his relative wealth, which frees him from labor. Here the submissive slave is preferred to a wife, for the (male) slave, as property, can function as an extension of the master's identity to maintain the illusion of solitude even in the midst of worldly affairs. But a wife, whose status is also that of property, is an intrusive other whose sexual presence (her reproductive function) belies the fiction of retreat from worldly interests.[5]

The representation of the wife as a forceful incursion of material demands into the otherwise chaste, sexually homogeneous world of the scholar is related to a more pervasive theme in ancient thought, the association of femininity with base and willful corporeality, and of masculinity with reason and spirit. This topos received its most famous scientific legitimation in Aristotelian physiology and politics.[6] In the Theophrastus fragment the common dualism of spirit/body, male/female is extended to support the more particular opposition between ascetic masculine bookishness and garrulous female domesticity. The imperative of the Theophrastus passage, or at least the use to which it was put in Jerome's quotation of it, was to promote an ascetic misogamy.[7] Later medieval authorities took the Theophrastus fragment in a somewhat different spirit to produce a particularly clerical form of satire on marriage.[8] In his autobiographical *Historia calamitatum (The Story of Misfortunes)* Peter Abelard places the Theophrastan theme of marriage versus study in the mouth of Heloise. Heloise, although pregnant, rejects Abelard's proposal of marriage, appealing first to Pauline spirituality ("Has your marriage been dissolved? Do not seek a wife . . . those who marry will have pain and grief in this bodily life," 1 Corinthians 7), then to Jerome's defense of virginity, and finally to a philosophical misogamy that bespeaks the interests of a professional academic class: [9]

> What harmony can there be between pupils and nursemaids, desks and cradles, books or tablets and distaffs, pen or stylus and spindles? Who can concentrate on thoughts of Scripture or philosophy and be able to endure babies crying, nurses soothing them with lullabies, and all the noisy coming and going of men and women about the house? Will he put up with the constant muddle and squalor which small children bring into the home? . . . the great philosophers of the past have despised the world, not renouncing it so much as escaping from it, and have denied themselves every pleasure so as to find peace in the arms of philosophy alone.[10]

Abelard also used the Theophrastan opposition between philosophy and marriage in another treatise, the *Theologia christiana*, in a vein that was to gain popularity in twelfth-century clerical satire on marriage, that Philosophy herself is a wife, sufficient to all the needs of the scholar.[11] That Abelard would voice these misogynistic arguments against marriage through the persona of Heloise is a fine irony, as Wilson and Makowski point out.[12] Heloise was herself a scholar of great accomplishment, and while the misogamous arguments were historically applied to both sexes, the misogynistic cast of her discourse, playing out the ancient opposition between women and books, is really continuous with the rhetorical interests of Abelard's narrative, which recounts the devastating consequences for his reputation and career of his liaison with Heloise.

The antifeminism of Theophrastan polemic engages traditional social mechanisms to underwrite the exclusiveness of intellectual privilege: it makes the exclusion of women from the domain of philosophy a natural and inevitable concomitant of women's disenfranchisement from economic and institutional bases of power in marriage. But there is a larger theoretical framework within which this system of exclusion—the opposition between women and books—justifies itself. As noted, the formal, scientific foundation of this logic of exclusion is the identification of woman with body and of man with spirit or intellect. The hermeneutical correlative of this metaphysic of gender also provides a powerful justification for male intellectual privilege. Women are not simply boisterous and demanding intruders on the scholar's spiritual retreat: by their very nature, their willful carnality, women are bad readers. Good reading is reading like a man, reading always according to the spiritual sense.

From Neoplatonist criticism to Christian exegesis, spiritual reading is the privileged mode of interpretation. Augustine comments on Paul's famous dictum, "the letter kills but the spirit gives life" (2 Corinthians 3:6):

> that is, when that which is said figuratively is taken as through it were literal, it is understood carnally. Nor can anything more appropriately be called the death of the soul than that condition in which the thing which distinguishes us from beasts, which is the understanding, is subjected to the flesh in pursuit of the letter.[13]

The literal level of the text is identified with carnality, with the flesh that must give way to the spirit. Augustine's influential hermeneutics articulates the relationship between reading spiritually and spiritual faith: to be able to read a text or any other sign not just for itself (carnally) but for its significance in love of God (charitably) is to be able to comprehend and act upon the basic tenets of Christianity, its doctrines of love and salvation. The dualism of body and soul is fundamental to this model of reading. As we have seen, this metaphysic is figured and understood through gender oppositions, and the hierarchy of gender is similarly encoded in Christian hermeneutics. To read spiritually, that is, to read through faith and the doctrine of charity, is to read as a man. St. Ambrose represents the progression from carnality to spiritual faith in terms of a "progress" from womanhood to manhood:

> She who does not believe is a woman and should be designated by the name of her bodily sex, whereas she who believes progresses to complete manhood, to the measure of the adulthood of Christ.[14]

Good reading is tantamount to good faith, and to read as a woman is to read with a gross carnality, resistant to the spiritual sense. Individual women can of course learn how to read spiritually and become believers, as Ambrose indicates; but in so doing they leave their carnal feminine natures behind, assuming a chaste, "masculine" spirituality.[15] Thus on the terms of this metaphysical law, women are hermeneutically handicapped; or we might say that reading is gendered, such that good, productive, spiritual reading that leads to faith is identified with a masculine essence, and perverse reading, which is literal and self-interested, is associated with a feminine principle of carnality.[16]

Yet as Carolyn Dinshaw has recently shown, the hermeneutical association of women with carnality has yet another dimension.[17] What she calls "the exegetical assimilation of literality and carnality to femininity" is also to be understood in terms of the gendered identity of the text itself.[18] The very text, especially the literal level of the text, is represented as a feminine object. Just as Paul associated the letter of the text with death and the fleshly body, so the carnality of the text, in turn, can be—and often is—identified with a woman, with the female body.[19] Dinshaw cites Jerome's comparison of the beautiful pagan text with the beautiful captive woman of Deuteronomy 21:10–13 as a richly suggestive example.[20] The heathen captive may be transformed into a good Hebrew wife if she is ritually cleansed: her hair shorn, her nails pared, her old clothing taken away, she will mourn for her parents in her captor-husband's house and then be his wife. Jerome uses this passage to speak of his desire for the classical pagan text, which he will purify by "translating" it—carrying it over, like a captive—into an application to Christian wisdom:

> Is it surprising that I, too, admiring the fairness of her form and the grace of her eloquence, desire to make that secular wisdom, which is my captive and handmaid, a matron of the true Israel? Or that shaving off and cutting away all in her that is dead whether this be idolatry, pleasure, error, or lust, I take her to myself clean and pure and beget by her servants for the Lord of Sabaoth?[21]

Here Jerome enunciates what were to become the basic hermeneutical principles that guided medieval Christian reception of the texts of pagan antiquity, especially mythology and poetic fiction or fable. The text must be stripped of its literal layer, must be read allegorically for the philosophical or spiritual truths that lie concealed within it.

Figured in this way the text is a passive, albeit seductive or attractive, object that benefits from the ministrations of an active reader. The *locus classicus* for the identification of text with woman is Macrobius' *Commentary on the Dream of Scipio* (ca. 400 A.D.), which justifies the reading of poetic fiction (*fabula*) on the grounds that Philosophy (which is personified as a woman) must be modestly veiled from the eyes of the uninitiated, and thus wraps her truths in the covering of fiction or poetic allegory.[22] The immodest exposure of Philosophy is compared with prostitution in a famous analogy:

> Numenius, a philosopher with a curiosity for occult things, had revealed to him in a dream the outrage he had committed against the gods by proclaiming his interpretation of the Eleusinian mysteries. The Eleusinian goddesses themselves, dressed in the garments of courtesans, appeared to him standing before an open brothel, and when in his astonishment he asked the reason for this shocking conduct, they angrily replied that he had driven them from their sanctuary of modesty and had prostituted them to every passer-by.[23]

Not only is the text a feminized object, a female body reserved only for the gaze of initiates, but reading is figured as a kind of sexual mastery, an act of bodily control (stripping, penetrating, even sometimes cleansing) which is represented along the lines of a male prerogative.

The exclusion of women from reading, the law that women and books don't mix, is encoded hermeneutically. According to one version of the code, reading is a masculine performance enacted on a feminine text; another dimension of this is that good reading is spiritual, and thus necessarily masculine, while the literal text is carnal in nature and thus associated with female bodiliness. In addition, reading as a woman is reading carnally; for a woman to read spiritually is for her to read in an "immasculated" way, to "progress" to the spirituality of manhood.[24] Women are carnal readers and woman as text is a carnal or literal text. The metaphysics of this combination are striking. The carnality of a female reader would never be able to penetrate and purge the carnality of a literal text. That is, a woman cannot read beyond the literal level because she *is* the literal level. Moreover, if reading is a fundamentally masculine sexual act performed on a female body, a woman cannot (should not) perform that sexualized act on a female body. For a woman to read as a woman is metaphysically on the order of a sexual taboo, a female carnal act performed on a feminized textual body.[25]

How is this hermeneutical law encoded institutionally? How is gender reflected in the social organization of reading? Paul's injunctions about the public silence of women, "Let women keep silence in churches" (1 Corinthians 14:34–35) and "Let women learn in silence . . . I suffer not a woman to teach" (1 Timothy 2:11–12), which bank on and augment a tradition of philosophical misogyny, also authorized the prohibition of women from the office of preaching, the work most directly tied to the institution of reading. But canonical prohibitions against women preaching or serving the office of priest are enforced in much broader terms through regulation of the practice of reading itself.

From the central Middle Ages onward, reading as an academic practice is synonymous with Latin culture, or Latinity. As early as the fourth century A.D. in Rome, the language of the Latin classics was becoming an antiquated academic language to be reclaimed and preserved by a cadre of professional grammarians. By the seventh century, the language of Jerome's Latin Vulgate translation of the Scriptures was no longer readily accessible even to speakers of Romance, or Latin-derived, vernaculars. Latin, the language of classical and Christian learning and of the Bible, became throughout Europe an academic language, the linguistic identity of a professional class. The ranks of this professional intelligentsia were almost exclusively male. Latinity, synonymous with literacy, is thus also identical with masculinity.

Throughout the Middle Ages, Latinity is associated with a professional class of clerks: Latin is international, masculine, learned rather than native, and as Walter Ong points out, literate rather than oral.[26] It transcends the boundaries of geography and historical temporality. The vernacular (standing for many languages) is identified, by contrast, with the general laity: its character is regional, its speakers are men and women, it is the lingua materna, the native mother tongue, and until the later Middle Ages, it is associated with orality and nonliteracy. The institutional significance of gender as a defining category of language use is reinforced at a symbolic level. If Latinity is associated with a masculine preserve of clerical education (what Ong calls a male "puberty rite"[27]), ecclesiastical community, and priestly office, vernacularity is figured in feminine terms. The users of the vernacular languages are, of course, men and women of all classes. But such strong divisions of gender, economic and legal status, and political and demographic positioning are nevertheless internal distinctions within the laity as a whole. Along symbolic lines, clergy defines itself in distinction from laity, as the spiritual estate that must rule the secular estates. As Hugh of St. Victor (1096–1141) puts it:

> There are two lives, the one earthly, the other heavenly; the one corporeal, the other spiritual; one by which the body lives from the soul, the other by which the soul lives from God. . . . On this account powers were established in both peoples distributed according to both lives. Indeed, among the laics, to whose zeal and providence those things which are necessary for the earthly life belong, is earthly power. But among the clerics to whose office look those things which are the goods of the spiritual life, is divine

power. Thus the one power is said to be secular, the other is called spiritual. . . . Now the more worthy the spiritual life is than the earthly and the spirit than the body, so much does the spiritual power precede the earthly or the secular in honor and in dignity.[28]

Hugh distinguishes between the temporal and the spiritual orders along the same lines that Pauline exegesis distinguishes between the spiritual and literal levels, or indeed along the same lines that traditional metaphysics distinguishes between the spirituality of men and the carnality of women. In a symbolic sense (and to some extent in a very real sense) the laity is a feminized entity. Its defining characteristics, when taken as a whole in counterdistinction to clergy, are reducible to the same terms that define women in relation to men: it is carnal and it is subordinate to a higher principle of rule. The laity in relation to clergy occupies the same structural position in discourse as women in relation to men.

The vernacular, the *lingua vulgaris* or common tongue, is also conceived and represented in feminine terms. In simplest terms it is the *lingua materna*, the language learned through the mother in infancy. In the context of clerical Latinity, it is the language first learned in the domestic female interiors of the household, before the boy is removed from his natural family and instated in a monastery or other school setting which provides a substitute family and family hierarchy within the structure of the ecclesiastical organization. In other ways as well vernacularity is identified with the world of women: it is local, domestic (the word "vernacular" comes from the Latin *vernaculus*, meaning domestic servant), and because cut off from the world of official learning, it is also ignorant and powerless. It is precisely to rectify this marginalization that Dante defends his use of the vernacular for philosophical poetry and learned commentary, explaining his love for his native tongue on the grounds that the language was his own "efficient cause":

> This vernacular of mine joined together my parents, since they spoke to each other in it. . . . For this reason it is clear that my vernacular had a part in my generation, and so was one of the causes of my coming into being.[29]

Moreover, his vernacular poetics will provide not only all men but also women and children ("to the extent that nature permits") access to intellectual affairs.[30] Thus even for the greatest vernacular poet of the Middle Ages, the *lingua vulgaris* is linked with the feminine realm of courtship and with the limited horizon of female intellect.

Laity and vernacularity are like Paul's docile wife, subject to her husband's private instruction (1 Corinthians 14:35). The intervention of vernacularity in an official public sphere of learning is deemed subversive, just as a wife's intervention would be. This theoretical model of the place of the vernacular [31] is quite irrelevant to the realities of cultural practice, where by the twelfth century (in France) the vernacular achieves a strong and permanent foothold in literary and even learned production. But the very reason for the irrelevance is telling: even where the vernacular identifies itself with cultural empowerment through strong appropriation of traditions of learning—as, for example, in the works of twelfth-century poets such as Chrétien de Troyes and Marie de France—such encroachments have little or no impact on academic consciousness, not, that is, until the vernacular claims as its rightful domain the Bible itself and the work of biblical hermeneutics. We will return to this point later.

Women of course read a great deal in the Middle Ages. But women as learned, Latinate scholars were rare, rare enough to be noteworthy, both in their own times, as in the near-mythical status of figures like Heloise or Hildegard of Bingen, and in ours, where these women and others like them continue to receive attention in specialized studies of medieval learning and literature.[32] On the other hand, as recent scholarship has shown, there is considerable evidence of women as book owners in the Middle Ages. Susan Groag Bell has looked to wills and other material records to find evidence of women book owners from as early as the ninth century, with the numbers of owners and books owned rising dramatically in the fourteenth and fifteenth centuries with the increased production and circulation of vernacular devotional books.[33] We also know that in many cases girls received reasonably sound educations at convent schools, and that at some convents nuns were involved in the copying of manuscripts.[34]

But the social fact of women as readers of learned texts does little to undermine the antifeminist essentialism of hermeneutical tradition. The difference between social practice and hermeneutical law is important. Social practice changes; hermeneutical law, carrying a legacy of official and ancient sanction, is conservative and resistant to change. And indeed because of its immutability, because it reproduces itself over and over again in a powerful discourse of learned culture, it is hermeneutical law, rather than social practice, that shapes attitudes. Recent feminist scholarship on women's learning in the Middle Ages has been concerned to discover facts from a relative paucity of evidence, and to retrieve such evidence from the obfuscating myth of women's intellectual inferiority. My purpose, in contrast, is to account for the prevailing power of this myth and to consider how it is used in complicity with dominant professional and economic interests to suppress potentially subversive social practice. The moment that the ideology of misogyny, expressed so persuasively in a comprehensive hermeneutical discourse, comes up against social practice and is seriously challenged by it, it asserts its claims by asking to have itself codified in social practice, in law.

The sphere of literacy with which women readers are historically associated is the vernacular, and especially with secular vernacular genres such as lyric poetry and romance. The emergence of vernacular devotional genres such as meditative poetry and prose, and didactic and mystical works, has also been associated with the tastes and demands of a newly literate class of pious lay women. But as noted, the vernacular represents a realm of literary production outside the parameters of official clerical, hermeneutical interests, and not important enough to be hermeneutically regulated in the same ways as Latin. After the Fourth Lateran Council of 1215, which made annual confession compulsory, the vernacular becomes an important instrument for doctrinal instruction of the laity, and thus an institutional means of larger social regulation. In this situation, the vernacular as a whole is regulated by official Latinity: it is not itself the site of operation of complex hermeneutical systems. As separate discursive orders, one dominant and one subordinate, Latin and vernacular serve as categories to differentiate other associated discursive orders: clergy and laity, masculine and feminine, the Bible and secular writings, the spiritual sense and the literal sense, closed and open interpretive systems, learned and "lewd."

Official Hermeneutics and Vernacular Scriptures

Where rigid and fiercely guarded hermeneutical codes, the "laws" of textual criticism, have their most severe and restrictive force is in the reading and interpretation of the Bible. The institutional mystification of the Bible and its exegetical encrusting is the most contested textual ground of the Middle Ages. As Margaret Deanesly notes, the attitude of the medieval church toward vernacular translations of the Bible was divided between tolerant indifference and anxious protectiveness of official privilege:

> If [the] translation [was] made for some king or exalted personage, or by some solitary student, and remained a hallowed but practically unused volume in a royal or monastic library, no objection was taken to the translation as such: but if the translation was used to popularise a knowledge of the biblical text among lay people, prohibition immediately followed.[35]

Vernacular translation of the Bible was an important consideration in a number of European heretical movements that preceded Wyclif and the Lollards in England. The Waldensian movement, which began in southern France in the late twelfth century, and the Cathars, a heretical sect of Lombardy, both gave much impetus to the production and dissemination of vernacular Scripture, often with expository glosses, which would enable lay learning and even preaching.[36] These early heretical movements forced official orthodoxy to formalize its position on vernacular Bible translation and lay reading as potential threats to the professional hegemony of the priestly class. Among these heterodox movements, lay reading of the Bible was almost always promoted along with lay preaching. The activity of lay preaching, together with reformist zeal and various doctrinal heresies (e.g., rejection of the doctrine of transubstantiation, or revivals of the old heresy of Donatism, which denied the validity of sacraments administered by a sinful priest), posed a serious threat to the authority of the ecclesiastical hierarchy, which availed itself of all feasible means to combat the spread of these movements and to suppress them whenever they sprang up.

It is interesting, although not surprising, that so much official repression was directed, not only against doctrinal heterodoxies, but against the dissemination of vernacular Scriptures. Insofar as these heresies were premised on increased lay independence from the interpretive and sacramental ministrations of established clergy, they were also premised on increased lay access to Scripture.[37] There was a great practical strategy in combating the heresy by attacking its basic machinery along with its belief systems. It was a more comprehensive plan to forbid vernacular Scriptures in general than to argue against each doctrinal error produced by unregulated lay reading and interpretation of the Bible. Moreover, the possession of vernacular translations of the Bible provided solid material evidence of heretical activity or associations. In the late twelfth century, the ecclesiastical establishment under Innocent III developed a sophisticated line of theoretical response to the heretical advocacy of vernacular translations, theory that could be used in conjunction with official edicts and condemnations and which provided the grounds for inquisitorial practices of burning vernacular books. Although Pope Innocent himself never actually prohibited the use of vernacular Scriptures, his pastoral letter of 1199 discussing this problem and prohibiting lay preaching was incorporated into canon law and was interpreted by inquisitors and theologians as a legal basis for suppressing such books among the laity.[38]

The terms by which the official establishment, prior to the advent of Wyclif and the Lollards, represents lay reading of vernacular Scriptures are illuminating for their discursive relationship with the tradition of hermeneutical misogyny. The recurring theme of these criticisms is that unguided lay reading of vernacular Scriptures can only unlock the literal sense, and that lay teachers, "arguing falsely from the letter," perpetuate certain doctrinal errors when they instruct their lay fellows.[39] One of the earliest accounts of the Waldensians is given by an Englishman, Walter Map, who witnessed their appeal to the Pope at the Third Lateran Council of 1179:

We saw the Waldensians at the council celebrated at Rome under Pope Alexander III. They were simple and illiterate men, named after their leader, Waldo, who was a citizen of Lyons on the Rhone: and they presented to the lord pope a book written in the French tongue, in which were contained a text and gloss on the psalter, and on very many other books of both testaments. These besought with great urgency that authority to preach should be confirmed to them, for they thought themselves expert, when they were scarcely learned at all. . . . For in every small point of the sacred page, so many meanings fly on the wings of virtue, such stores of wealth are accumulated, that only he can fully exhaust them whom God has inspired. Shall not therefore the Word given to the unlearned be as *pearls before swine*, when we know them to be fitted neither to receive it nor to give out what they have received? Away with this idea, and let it be rooted out.[40]

In the mid-fourteenth century an Italian Dominican, Passavanti, makes an argument against vernacular translation which is less derisory than Map's, but more explicit in its identification of the vernacular with enchainment to the literal sense:

In certain books of scriptures and of the doctors which are translated into the vulgar tongue, one may read, but with great caution: because many of them are found false and corrupt, either through the fault of the scribes, who do not generally fully understand them, or through the fault of the translators, who do not understand the deep passages of the scriptures, or the subtle and obscure sayings of the saints, and do not explain them according to the interior and spiritual understanding, but only the rind of the letter, according to grammar, when they turn them into the vulgar tongue. And because they have not the spiritual understanding, and because our vulgar tongue is lacking in the right words, they expound it often coarsely and rudely, and often not truly. In short, it is too perilous: for they may fall so easily into error.[41]

The message is clear: the laity, untutored in Latin and ignorant of the finer points of theology and of exegetical procedure, should not meddle with Scripture in the vulgar tongue. But it is the symbolic status and discursive affiliations of the vernacular that we must consider more closely. In Map and more explicitly in Passavanti, the vulgar tongue is identified with hopeless and unrelenting literalism. In the large context of the hermeneutical tradition that we have considered here, literalism is identified with feminine textuality. Reading literally, according to the letter alone, is metaphysically equivalent to feminine carnality. It is also significant that the vernacular is represented, notably in Passavanti, as the linguistic locus of such literalist entrapment. Here we must also recall that in medieval sociolinguistic consciousness, the vernacular is associated with the realm of women, with the localism, domesticity, and orality of feminine linguistic use.

Thus the official theoretical responses to lay use of vernacular Scriptures can be seen to participate in a large discursive order in which the two key terms of condemnation, literalism and the vernacular, are metaphysically identified with femininity. Moreover, as we see in Map and Passavanti, vernacular and literal are also mutually equivalent. That equivalence is reinforced by their individual association with femininity, which becomes the common and definitive element in the system. By association, the laity as a whole is feminized and indeed infantilized by the repressive measures taken against its claims to theological and sacramental self-determination. Laity and woman, we recall, occupy the same structural position in discourse. Thus we see that literalism, vernacularity, and laity are all, in metaphysical as well as social-discursive terms, reducible to a common identification with woman. In terms of their discursive order, the laws enacted and theories promulgated against the laity using vernacular Scriptures are no less than laws against feminine textuality, against female reading.

The Lollard Heresy: Hermeneutical Law and Positive Law

The various injunctions against vernacular Scriptures, designed to root out heresy, can thus be seen as an extension of the symbolic order of hermeneutical misogyny: hermeneutical "laws" against feminine reading are translated into actual legal measures against the seditious influence of the vernacular, which in metaphysical terms is identical with femininity. The English heresy of Lollardy provides a particularly urgent case of this passage of the metaphysical into the real, for a number of reasons. First, the laws enacted in England against vernacular translations of Scripture were very specific and were enforced with considerable severity. Second, women were conspicuously singled out for their role in this vernacular textual culture, and we have a good many records of their activities, from the orthodox point of view in chronicles and anti-Lollard tracts, and indirectly from their own point of view, in trial transcripts. Third, Lollardy claimed, as one of its own doctrinal hallmarks, a distinct preference for the literal sense of Scripture, thus providing, on its own terms, an affirmation, indeed a positive recovery, of a feminine hermeneutic.[42] It also thereby made itself a prime target for the most severe official repressions, which could call forth the combined force of theological orthodoxy and institutionalized misogyny to combat the spread of the Lollard heresy.

Broadly speaking, the Wycliffite or Lollard movement falls into two phases: the period up to the condemnation of Wyclif and his doctrines by the Blackfriars' Council of 1382 (a council of clerics, theologians, and lawyers convened in London by the Archbishop of Canterbury to examine Wyclif's doctrines for heretical content), and the long period of Lollard prosecutions after the Oxford condemnation, lasting well into the sixteenth century. The Blackfriars' Council of 1382 is the dividing line between the two phases of the movement.[43] Lollardy began in the academic environment of Oxford and from there was disseminated to popular audiences by the academicians who comprised Wyclif's Oxford circle. (The word "Lollard," from a Dutch word meaning "to mumble," was a term of opprobrium applied to Wyclif's followers.) But after 1382, the movement lost its academic foothold. Wyclif died of natural causes in 1384, and over the next two decades Oxford was purged of its Wycliffites, the most important leaders of the movement recanting under prosecution. The promulgation and interpretation of Wycliffite doctrine was for the next century left almost entirely to the popular constituents of the heresy. With the suppression of the heresy at Oxford the movement became decentralized, and endured in regional pockets throughout villages, towns, and cities, where it had its strongest following among the artisan classes. Thus in this second and much longer phase of the movement the Lollard schools were no longer regulated by links with an "authoritative" academic apparatus; instead the transmission of points of dogma was carried on at a rank-and-file level, through the efforts of regional evangelists (some of whom had had academic ties with Oxford), or in the structural environment of local cells or "covens" where individuals might secretly instruct friends, family, and servants, and where a contraband English book (a Wycliffite translation of the gospels or an anthology of tracts) would provide the focal point for a heretical gathering.[44]

Lollard doctrine is neither canonical nor systematic. It persisted under many different conditions in a great variety of environments, and was not formally codified within the ranks of the movement. Indeed the terms of Lollard doctrine may be said to have been stabilized most by the orthodox prosecutors and inquisitors who from 1382 onward periodically drew up lists of points to be condemned (the Blackfriars' Council found ten of Wyclif's propositions heretical and fourteen erroneous) and throughout the fifteenth century devised examination questions for suspected heretics and formula abjurations for those found guilty.[45] But there are certain points of continuity between the thought of the Wyclif circle at Oxford and the many provincial Lollard sects that survived into the early sixteenth century.

The basic tenets of Lollard belief, the points of doctrinal heresy on which they were prosecuted, can be summarized briefly. The two most consistent points, deriving directly from Wyclif's thought, concern his arguments against the eucharistic miracle of transubstantiation and in favor of the temporal disendowment of the clergy. Wyclif, and his later Lollard followers, argued against the orthodox position that the bread and wine change their substance, when consecrated on the altar, into the veritable body and blood of Christ.[46] For Wyclif's lay followers this was a strong rallying point, for it provided the focus for a popular reformist anticlericalism. As a (purportedly) Lollard text of 1395 puts it, "the feynid miracle of the sacrament of bred inducith alle men but a fewe to ydolatrie," a position that calls into question not only the validity of sacramental symbolism, but also the special authority invested in priests through their sacramental role.[47] Lollard reformism extended to rejection of other sacraments, especially confession and the priestly power of absolution, and to various forms of ritual show, notably pilgrimages, images, and foundations of chantry priests, all of which involve the exchange of money for a supposed spiritual good. Similarly the power of the clergy was questioned along several lines. What proved to be Wyclif's most dangerous opinions concerned his call (not without some orthodox precedent) for disendowment of the clergy in temporal goods, and strict delineation between the domains of clergy and of secular rulers.[48] This attack on clerical dominion was linked in Lollard thought with other forms of anticlericalism, notably a rejection of "private religion" (monasticism and other practices that removed the religious from public involvement), and rejection of both papal and priestly authority to pronounce absolution, to excommunicate, and even to mediate the word of God. The guiding foundations of Lollard thought are two assumptions articulated throughout their polemics: Holy Scripture as the only real ground of truth, which promotes literal interpretation of the Bible, and the "priesthood of all believers," a priesthood of which virtue, faith, and contrition are the requirements.[49]

These two founding assumptions bring us to the exigencies of lay readership. If the Bible is the single source of doctrinal authority, and if all Christians are priestly interpreters of its truths, then of course the laity must have access to the Bible in the vernacular. But it was precisely such universal access that would encourage the notion of a "priesthood of all believers," which, along with the many subsidiary doctrinal heresies, posed an incalculable threat to secular as well as clerical authority.[50] Thus lay reading of the Bible had to be suppressed, not because it was an inherently heretical activity, but because it made heresy and oppositional attitudes possible.

What forms did the suppression of lay reading of the Bible take? By 1400, two Wycliffite translations of the Bible were in circulation, the first a very literal version (often associated with Nicholas Hereford, who recanted in 1391), and the second a much more idiomatic rendering (attributed, although without conclusive evidence, to John Purvey, who recanted in 1401). In the wake of the condemnation of Wyclif in 1382, and in the context of continuing investigations of Lollardy at Oxford and elsewhere, first under Archbishop

Courtenay and then under Archbishop Arundel, the ecclesiastical establishment began to formulate and propagate its opinions and determinations on vernacular Bible translation.[51] The general tenor of these opinions is reflected, somewhat crudely, in the late fourteenth-century chronicler Henry Knighton's account of Wyclif:

> John Wyclif translated into the English tongue the gospel, which Christ conferred upon clerics and doctors of the church so that by them it might be sweetly ministered to the laity and more feeble persons according to the exigencies of the time, the needs of persons, and the hunger of their minds.[52] . . . Whence because of him, that which belonged to the very literate and highly intelligent clergy has been made the more vulgarly accessible to the laity, and *even to women who know how to read* [emphasis mine]. Thus the pearl of gospel is scattered and trampled underfoot by swine, and what was once beloved by clerk and layman is now turned into something of a joke between them. The jewel of clergy has become the sport of laymen, and what was once a celestial endowment for clergy and doctors of the church will ever be a commonplace to laymen.[53]

More to the point, the statute *De heretico comburendo* (1401) which instituted the death penalty for heretics (thereby bringing England into line with Continental practice), emphasized, as Margaret Aston notes, Lollard literacy as a feature of their sedition. In the words of the statute, "they make unlawful conventicles and confederacies, they hold and exercise schools, they make and write books, they do wickedly instruct and inform people." [54]

Such views are elaborated with scholastic subtlety by clerics who engaged the Wycliffite position on translation in setting forth official arguments against it. In 1401, Friar William Butler, a regent master of the Franciscans at Oxford, presented a very detailed determination against the lawfulness of any translation of the Bible.[55] Butler's opinion develops two assumptions: the difficulty of Scripture and the divinely ordained inferiority of the populace to the priestly estate, whose natural role it is to regulate the dissemination of doctrine and the interpretation of Scripture. The reasoning appeals to certain time-honored pragmatic concerns: any translation is prone to error, even the standard Latin Vulgate translation. But under controlled conditions, these errors can be remedied:

> The church ordained for there to be universities in which the Scriptures are taught and books are copied which, if they contain errors, can easily be corrected. Such revision cannot easily be accomplished when the books are widely circulated among the populace.[56]

Here the focus is not on the inadequacy of certain classes of readers, but rather on the mechanical perils of translating and copying. It is dangerous to allow the free circulation of incorrect texts, as the incidence of error would multiply and lead unwitting readers to serious misconceptions. Better then for the texts to be contained and reviewed in a controlled environment such as the university, which is equipped to rectify errors.

From this pragmatic rationale, however, Butler proceeds to certain metaphysical arguments, including the identification of the Christian community with the mystical body of Christ. All of the faithful are members of Christ's body, and are thus like parts of the body: hands, feet, throat, back, belly, hands, fingers, legs, toes, and eyes. All bodily members have their distinct functions. The job of reading is performed by the eyes, not by the feet and toes. The "vulgar populace" is metaphorically the equivalent of the feet, and by the logic of this metaphor, the populace has no business doing the work of the eyes. Butler then changes metaphorical direction slightly to develop his last argument: that priests are like the stomach which draws in the food of Scripture and digests it, thereby nourishing the rest of the body. Only the priests can properly digest Scripture because they can read the spiritual sense. To give Scripture directly to the people is to deny them nourishment, for on their own all that they can take in is the useless rind of the literal sense.[57]

Butler's determination exemplifies the metaphysical "laws" that could be invoked to justify the suppression of vernacular Scriptures and lay reading. In its identification of the vulgar populace with intractable literalism it builds on the precedent of earlier antiheretical rhetoric, and like those precedents implements the orthodoxies of literary theoretical tradition, which reserves good reading for the spiritually elect.

The legal implementation of this theoretical orthodoxy came in 1407, when Thomas Arundel, Archbishop of Canterbury, drafted a set of thirteen anti-Lollard statutes known as the Constitutiones, which were formally issued in 1409. The Constitutiones forbade unauthorized preaching in English, and any preaching sympathetic to Lollard doctrine, tightened the supervision of preachers, forbade the promulgation of heterodoxies in the grammar schools and public disputation of doctrinal matters outside of the schools and universities, and ordered monthly investigations of Oxford scholars and colleges to eradicate any latent pockets of sympathy in what was once the Wycliffite stronghold. For our purposes here the most important statutes concern the circulation of Lollard books. Article 6 forbade the reading of any texts by Wyclif or his associates or followers unless the text was examined and approved by authorities to be appointed by the universities of Oxford or Cambridge. Article 7 prohibited any new English translations of the Bible and forbade any reading or ownership of the Wycliffite translation of the Bible, in whole or in part, upon pain of excommunication, unless the translation was approved by the authorities.[58]

As Anne Hudson has argued, the impact of this last statute was to suppress the use of English for any theological matters that had hitherto been expressed in Latin, and even more, to make "the expression of ideas gained from Latin books and expressed in English . . . *ipso facto* evidence of heresy."[59] The enforcement of this statute led to some rigorous positions, as in the ordinance issued in 1426–27 by John Whethamstede, abbot of St. Albans, proclaiming that the cause of heresy is "the possession and reading of books in our vulgar tongue." [60] It also led to some curious extremes, such as the case in the late fifteenth century when the possession of a copy of the The Canterbury Tales was produced as evidence of heresy in the prosecution of a Lollard suspect.[61] More generally, Arundel's statutes gave great momentum to the investigation and prosecution of Lollards by articulating precise terms for uncovering evidence of heresy. The significance of the Constitutiones was to specify the vernacular as a site of illegal activity. Thus investigations of Lollard suspects routinely mention the possession of English books and typically required a search of the suspect's house to turn up evidence of book ownership.[62] In Lollard trials, the scripted abjurations often include the promise to forfeit any books written by or for the suspect and to inform the authorities of any other illicit book production that may be known to the suspect.[63]

As Claire Cross has shown, the activity of women Lollards in most communities centered on books, whether it was by passing on Lollard doctrine and knowledge of the gospel to family and friends, or by organizing book distribution.[64] This is certainly the way that the establishment defined their activity: denunciations of Lollard women by churchmen and other establishment figures often include remarks about women's improper and arrogant bookishness. Reginald Pecock, writing in the mid-fifteenth century, comments on the inveterate literalism of Lollard women readers:

> . . . thilk wommen whiche maken hem silf so wise bi the Bible, that thei non deede wollen allowe to be vertuose and to be doon in mannis vertuose conversacioun, save what thei kunnen fynde expressli in the Bible, and ben ful coppid of speche anentis clerkis, and avaunten and profren hem silf whanne thei ben in her iolite and in her owne housis forto argue and dispute ayens clerkis . . . [65]

This makes the standard construction of women as bad readers. The notion of false and intractable literalism is reinforced by linkage with the traditional antifeminist opposition between wife and clerk. Here the gospel-reading wives proudly and willfully hold forth on their interpretations of Scripture, disputing the more subtle readings of clerks, and speaking scornfully of clergy. It would seem that the most direct and serviceable line of attack on Lollard women is to seize on their textual activity as a monstrous sign of the social and sexual aberrations that the Lollard heresy has brought about. The Carmelite Thomas Netter, for example, writing in the early 1420s, sees the prominence of women in the roles of readers and preachers of gospel as evidence of the spread of the heresy: "in the city of London the most foolish of women set up on stools, publicly read and taught the scriptures in a congregation of men."[66]

Thus we see how hermeneutical tradition informs social practice. The official denunciation of Lollard women, leading to their legal prosecution, is generated out of the same discourse that comprises hermeneutical "law." In the inquiry records and trials of Lollard women, it is their activity as readers that surfaces with remarkable frequency, and as heretics what they really give evidence of is reading. But it is important to note that their reading is profiled only through their legal prosecution. As in hermeneutical "law," so in historical legal practice, feminine reading is notable only as a sign of error. Women's textual activity cannot be registered as a positive norm.[67] Much as earthquakes and other natural disasters were used in medieval chronicles and narratives as signs and omens of great upheaval in human affairs (indeed, the Blackfriars' Council of 1382 was referred to as the Earthquake Council because a tremor broke up the proceedings), so in anti-Lollard literature women's reading becomes a sign of the transgressive violence that heresy has wrought against political and hermeneutical order. Women's reading is the consummate symbol of the threat of vernacular, lay reading of the Bible.

Women's reading becomes evidence of heresy. The illiterate mystic Margery Kempe, whose eccentric and emotional expressions of piety often brought her hostile public attention, virtually had to prove herself a non-reader when her knowledge of gospel made the authorities in York suspect her as a Lollard.[68] Along similar lines, the Norwich Lollard Margery Baxter had a confrontation with a Carmelite friar in which she expounded the gospels to him in English. Her familiarity with Scripture apparently raised his suspicions, for he accused her of heresy.[69] Reading is so much linked with heresy that women were known to conceal their ability to read when under investigation by authorities. In the examinations of a group of Coventry Lollards in 1511, one suspect, Juliana Young, initially denied that she could read, and admitted to literacy only when confronted with the testimony of another suspect, Robert Silkby.[70] Another Lollard from Coventry, Joan Smith, who abjured in 1511, was investigated again in 1520, and although initially acquitted, was rearrested and condemned to death as a relapsed heretic when the bishop's officials discovered English books in her possession.[71] Cross also suggests that in a number of Lollard communities the need to conceal evidence of reading accounts largely for the learning and transmission of the Lollard Bible by memory, an activity dominated by women.[72]

The suppression of Lollard books was not necessarily or exclusively directed against women: women and men were equally subject to prosecution for ownership, reading, and circulation of prohibited books.[73] The real enemy, the object of official repression, is the Lollard hermeneutic itself. This is a feminine hermeneutic: it is open and popular, vernacular, and literal. All participants in this hermeneutic, women and men, are discursively feminized, in sociolinguistic as well as in metaphysical terms. But I wish to focus, in the remainder of this essay, on the particular conditions of women's textuality and consider how the feminization of hermeneutics under Lollardy creates a context for the representation of women as subversive readers.

Women as Subversive Readers

The records of investigations and trials, from which we get most of our information about the activities of Lollards, provide us with a useful perspective on official views of Lollard women. The authorities recorded what they considered to be important facts about suspects. It is no doubt for this reason that we have so many details about Lollard women's textual activities. Thus at least in terms of the information preserved in official records, women's reading is a construction of legal interests.

What kinds of activities are recorded and thus constructed as subversive? Most importantly, women were instrumental in setting up autonomous and self-reproducing textual communities in the family, the household, and in towns, readerly networks that displaced the authoritative interpretive apparatus of clerical preaching. The sense of autonomy was keenly felt in Lollard communities. One woman of the Chilterns is recorded as claiming that "she was as well learned as was the parish priest, in all things, except only in saying mass."[74] The Norwich community, which was prosecuted in 1428, had been converted by William White, a Kentish missonary who considered himself a disciple of Wyclif.[75] Margery Baxter carried White's books from Yarmouth to her home village of Martham near Norwich, an action that is recorded (along with her concealment of him in her house) because it indicates the degree of her direct involvement with White's evangelical mission. As the trial transcripts put it, she "secretly carried the books of William White from the village of Yarmouth to the village of Martham and hid them." [76] Margery also encouraged Joan Cliffland (who later testified against Margery) and Joan's servant to come to her rooms at night to hear Margery's husband William read the "law of Christ," a practice of secret readings which was apparently customary in this household, as in many others.[77]

Margery's husband William testified about the literacy and book ownership of many of his fellow Lollards in the Norwich community, including the daughter of Thomas and Hawise Moon, who could read English, and Alice, the servant of William White, to whom White had bequeathed a copy of the New Testament.[78]

The proceedings of 1511 against the Coventry heretics reveal considerable activity among women who formed connections with communities as far away as London. Joan Washingby had learned her heresy from Alice Rowley, and on moving from Coventry to Northampton and then London (possibly from one Lollard household to another) may have brought a Lollard book from Agnes Johnson in Coventry to Joan Blackbyre in London.[79] Also among the Coventry Lollards, "little mother Agnes" taught Rose Fournour, who had served in the house of another Lollard, Robert Hachet. Thomasina Viller's mother took her to hear readings from a Lollard book in the house of Roger Landesdale. Years later Thomasina brought her husband to Landesdale's house for instruction. Roger Landesdale in turn had received a number of his books from Joan Smith, who had been converted to heresy by her first husband, Richard Landesdale. Joan had later passed her husband's books on to his relative Roger. This Joan Smith is probably the same Joan Smith (or "widow Smith") tried and burned as a relapsed heretic in 1520 when it was discovered that she still possessed English books. The dominant figure of the Coventry women, Alice Rowley, was attracted to Lollardy on account of its writings, although she herself was apparently illiterate. She owned numerous books and loaned them, including a copy of Paul's Epistles, to Roger Landesdale, and the same book or another copy to Thomas Bowen. She confessed to destroying many of her books in the wake of the heresy proceedings. [80] A sense of the talismanic value that attached to books in the secretive world of Lollard textual communities is evident in her remark that she believed God would protect her "because of our good steadfast faith, and good books."[81] Similar patterns of women forming covert and tenacious book networks are observable in other Lollard communities, such as the Chilterns and London, where heresy trials were conducted in the early sixteenth century.[82]

In metaphysical terms, the danger of such communities of women readers and teachers sharing books and interpretations among themselves is that they dramatize and augment the possibility of an exclusively female textual "eros." The patriarchal metaphysic defines good reading in heterosexual terms, as a sexual mastery (stripping or penetration) performed by a masculinized reader upon a feminized text. The reader, whether man or woman, is enjoined to read spiritually, that is, to read in a way that is male-identified. But the Lollard community of women readers presents an oppositional model: women reading in an insistently literal way (which is the standard of the popular Lollard hermeneutic), and thus performing feminized read-ings upon the always feminine object of the text. This symbolic order of opposition is further reinforced by the social reality of a self-determining and largely self-sufficient community of women who circulate books and readings among themselves and their families, ingeniously circumventing official controls as well as the prohibitive expense of acquiring books.[83]

The court records suggest the anxiety of the legal authorities about the transgression of a symbolic order of reading. The records offer considerable documentation about the hermeneutical activity of women. They note, for example, the ways in which women exercise hermeneutical agency. One instance, which I mentioned above, is the triumphant displacement of cleri-cal authority expressed by the woman who claimed to be as learned as the parish priest in all things except saying mass. Here, in addition to the obvious professional judgment leveled against the clerical competitor, we may detect some irony in her willingness to concede his superiority in the techniques of the mass, for the mass is of small value in the antisacramen-talism of Lollard belief. In other words, the priest has superior mastery of nothing that matters in the heretic's hierarchy of values, and the individual worshipper is entitled to her own professional opinion about matters of Scriptural interpretation. A similar instance of the exercise of interpretive control is recorded in the trials of London Lollards in 1511–12. Joan Baker is reported to have advanced a number of heretical opinions, among them that the crucifix is a false god, the Pope has no power to bind and loose, and that "she cold here a better sermond at home in hur howse than any doctor or prist colde make at Poulis crosse or any other place."[84] To insist that she could hear a better sermon in the domestic conventicles of her fellow heretics than anything the official clergy could offer is at once to appropriate the prerogative of hermeneutical control and to claim a measure of public recognition for her critical judgments which would be denied to her in the orthodox church community. As Claire Cross notes, the late medieval English church offered fewer avenues of religious expression for women than for men, and if the laity in general had little voice in doctrinal matters, lay women had even less, given their position in the hierarchic systems of economic class and gender. Thus it is not difficult to see the attractiveness for women of heretical sects that invited them to participate as learned and competent members, recognizing and rewarding their textual knowledge by calling on them for recitations of Scripture or by fostering their expression of oppositional hermeneutics.[85]

In the view of the orthodox church, a pronouncement such as Joan Baker's is abhorrent and thereby noteworthy not only because it indicates the degree of interpretive autonomy that developed under the Lollard heresy, but also because it fulfills traditional expectations of feminine hermeneutics: wayward, intemperate, and false. In this way the Lollard hermeneutic is identical with what is negatively constructed as a feminine hermeneutic. The official anxiety about this doubly seditious hermeneutic is reflected in the representation of women's textual activity. In the detailed transcript of the trial and abjuration of Margery Baxter at Norwich in 1428–29 we have an extraordinary record of the interdependence of official and oppositional textual ideologies.

The Case of Margery Baxter

The deposition against Margery Baxter by the episcopal court's witness, Joan Cliffland, shows how Baxter embraces and elaborates the very literalism for which feminine and Lollard hermeneutics are officially denounced. All that we know of Margery Baxter is said not by her, but against her. We do not hear her voice, but her voice several times removed: what the court scribe recorded, in Latin, of Joan Cliffland's testimony, in English, of Baxter's own words.

Margery Baxter is the woman who carried the books of the Lollard evangelist and mentor William White from Yarmouth to her village of Martham. She and her husband William gave refuge to White. She also witnessed White's execution at which, according to the deposition, she observed that when he tried to preach to the crowd and incite the people to

> rise up and kill all the traitors who stood against him and his teaching, which was the law of Christ . . . a devil, a disciple of the bishop Caiaphus [a Lollard epithet for the bishop of Norwich], struck the said William White on his lips and covered with his hand the mouth of the said sacred doctor so that in no way might he propound the will of God.[86]

The scene of the bishop's man striking and covering the mouth of the evangelist has its own literal, iconic force in Baxter's narrative (or in the witness's narrative). According to the testimony, she speaks of White as "a great saint in heaven and a most saintly doctor, sent and ordained by God," to whom she prayed every day that he might "intercede for her before God in heaven."[87] This may seem inconsistent with her espousal of standard Lollard doctrine rejecting worship of the saints and of images as false idolatry designed to extract money from simple people. But her cultivation of White as a saint is actually continuous with her rejection of images and of the official canon of saints. Her devotional enterprise is based on a literalist hermeneutic of direct witnessing, without symbolic mediation: she knew White, could count herself among his acolytes, and indeed could assume an apostolic role in carrying forward the mission of the martyred evangelist. The church-sponsored practice of image worship is for her an empty, supervenient symbolism; her relationship to White, by contrast, is direct and experienced, summed up in her witnessing of the evangelist's mouth, the fleshly, living vehicle of his message, being closed by the bishop's official. Her work as an apostle is to open his mouth again, to be in her turn a martyr (the word means "witness"), by carrying and storing his books and by teaching his message.

Baxter's interpretation of Wyclif's eucharistic doctrine, the centerpiece of Lollard thought, also exemplifies how her literalist hermeneutics cuts through symbolism and abstraction. Wyclif had rejected orthodox arguments on transubstantiation, claiming that it was impossible for the consecrated host to become in *substance* the veritable body of Christ. On good logical grounds he argued that a substance cannot be altered to become another substance: thus if the bread becomes the body of Christ it still necessarily retains the substance of bread. Baxter's interpretation elides Wyclif's logical niceties, proposing instead a most fundamental, literalist objection to the symbolism of the host. According to the deposition, she asserted to Joan Cliffland that

> if the sacrament were God and the true body of Christ, there would be infinite number of gods, because every day a thousand priests and more make a thousand such gods and afterwards eat a thousand such gods and then disgustingly excrete what they have eaten through their backsides in stinking privies, where you can find enough of such gods if you want to look for them.[88]

On the face of it, this is a seditious view, because it denies the central, church-sponsored mystery of the Eucharist, and because it willfully wrests the job of interpretive explanation away from clergy. The "absurdity" of the explanation only proves the danger of letting the business of interpretation fall to unsupervised and eccentric individuals. But more profoundly, the seditious threat of Baxter's explanation lies in the very astuteness of its logic. If indeed one accepts as true that the host becomes the very body of Christ, then one must wonder what becomes of that "body" when the priest consumes and digests it. If the church asks the faithful to believe literally and unconditionally in the transubstantiation of the host, then at what point in the miraculous process is that literalist vision to stop? What Wyclif had argued is that the host is symbolically, but not literally, the body of Christ. If that view is heretical, then, as Baxter asks, what are the consequences of the literalism of belief that the church sanctions?

According to the deposition, Baxter asserted that "she ought not to be burned, even if convicted of Lollardy, because . . . she had and has a charter of salvation in her womb [in utero suo]."[89] This may remind us of Alice Rowley's belief in the talismanic power of "good books" which, she believed, would save her Lollard community. In terms of its effect in the official deposition against Baxter, it doubtless served as another example of the egregious extremes of Lollard textual culture, an ignorant woman invoking the salvific power of a mysterious and unspecified text lodged within the secret places of her womb, a text that cannot be officially authenticated or even traced. But it is also a provocative image of the power of literalism. It may be distantly reminiscent of Apocalypse imagery, in which John is enjoined by the angel to "take the book and eat it up. . . . and it was in my mouth, sweet as honey; and when I had eaten it my belly was bitter" (Revelations 10:9–10), which is similarly an image of making the salvific text a literal object to be consumed and stored within the body.[90] But the closest affinity of Baxter's "charter of salvation in her womb" is with the imagery of the Virgin Mary, that is, with the Annunciation and the moment of Christ's Incarnation.

Baxter's image of the salvific charter in her womb suggests a conflation of the conception of Christ in the Virgin's womb and Christ as the Incarnation of the Word, thus the Word made flesh in the Virgin's womb. The central mystery of Christian doctrine involves a consummate literalism, the Word that was God becoming incarnate, the spirit becoming flesh, in the body of a mortal woman. Late medieval iconography of the Annunciation reinforces the literal impact of the association between the Virgin and the Word. Many fourteenth- and fifteenth-century devotional images show the Virgin reading at the moment of the Annunciation. As Susan Groag Bell notes, this detail has no Scriptural foundation: the image of the Virgin as reader at the Annunciation (or at confinement, or after childbirth, or even on the flight to Egypt) was supplied by artists who, Bell suggests, were responding to a contemporary phenomenon, the increasingly visible and important participation of women in the culture of devotional literature, as patrons, readers, and book owners: "the developing association of the Virgin with books in fact coincides with the rise in numbers of women book owners during the fourteenth and fifteenth centuries."[91] In such images, the book itself is a symbol of the Word, that is Christ, who becomes incarnate in the Virgin's womb.

Thus late medieval devotional iconography makes the literal connection between women's textual power and the Virgin who carried the Word incarnate in her womb. I would argue that this is the very connection that Margery Baxter makes between her textual activity and the central mystery of the faith, the Incarnation of the Word. She has seized that fundamental literalization of Christian theology, making the spirit carnal, out of the control of official mystification and has made it her own drama, continuous with her role as the apostle of William White. She carried White's books to safety and hid them away in a secret place out of reach of the authorities;

similarly she carries the text of her own safekeeping in her womb, a place of utterly private sanctity beyond the powers of official examination or authentication. Like the private chamber in which her husband read her the "lex Christi," and like the secret reading covens of the Lollards in general, the hiding of the text of salvation in her womb represents the exercise of private and thus autonomous interpretive power. Within the secret confines of her womb Baxter exercises her interpretive prerogative of literalism by literalizing her doctrinal independence from orthodox supervision: like the Virgin, with whom she achieves a literal identification, she holds within her the transformation of spirit into letter, of salvation into her own personalized charter.

Baxter takes the incarnational mystery of Christian doctrine so thoroughly into her own hands as to authorize her own salvation. This is precisely the kind of resistant autonomy that official orthodoxy most fears and that it takes severe measures to suppress. Yet Baxter's highly individual response is not wholly radical in its origins. Her personal literalization of the mystery of salvation can be seen as simply a more pronounced expression of the very kind of affective response to Christ that the orthodox establishment (especially the Franciscans) encouraged in popular worship. The mystic Margery Kempe often found herself at odds with standards of public behavior as well as of religious propriety for her intense devotional identification with such affective images as the Nativity or the Passion (her typical response was to sob uncontrollably at any suggestion of these scenes); but while her extreme responses to such devotional imperatives may have made her a public nuisance and a worry to clerical authorities, they did not qualify her to be judged a heretic.[92] Margery Baxter differs from Margery Kempe only in degree, not in kind: whereas Kempe did not (or could not) take her direct and private investment in religious mystery to the point of liberating herself from clerical regulation, Baxter did.[93] For the church-sponsored devotional images that Margery Kempe so embraced and which Margery Baxter, as a Lollard, despised, Baxter substituted her own apocalyptic eschatology, her own martyrology (her devotion to White and his books as relics), and her own apostolic mission. But the literalism that marks her hermeneutic as heretical is in essence the same literalism that the late medieval church encouraged in the form of affective devotion to images of Christ's life.

Baxter is an ideal candidate for official prosecution, not only because she was a professed Lollard, but because the deposition allows her to be constructed as a veritable prototype, an admonitory example, of what Dinshaw calls "the exegetical assimilation of literality and carnality to femininity."[94] For Baxter, the literal sense and the female body are as one: her literal text of salvation is lodged within the private space of her womb. The letter of the text and her body are domains over which she can aspire to exert absolute, self-determining control. Indeed, her Lollard hermeneutics are so identified with her body that she articulates the accusation of heresy in terms of rape. She was certainly aware of her vulnerability to exposure for her heresy. Even as she tried to convert Joan Cliffland, she sensed that Cliffland would betray her to the authorities. In Cliffland's deposition, Baxter is quoted as saying to her: "Joan, it seems from the look on your face that you intend and propose to reveal the council I have given you to the bishop." When Cliffland denies any intention of reporting her to the bishop, Baxter threatens that if Cliffland does report her, she will do to her what she did to a certain Carmelite friar of Yarmouth, "the most learned friar in the whole country." This leads to an account of Baxter's confrontation with the friar, which I mentioned in brief earlier. When Baxter denounces his mendicant habits, the friar invites her to "teach him something." She responds by expounding the gospels to him in English. This raises his suspicions, and he accuses her of heresy. Hearing that the friar has accused her, Baxter in turn accuses the friar of trying to seduce her, saying that when she would not consent, the friar accused her of heresy. She adds that her husband wants to kill the friar. The nervous friar falls silent and departs in disgrace.

This episode provides two views of the relationship between law, gender, and reading. On one view, this is a power play over the prerogatives of gender, class, and professionalism: the male cleric accuses a lay woman of heresy because she usurps his professional prerogative of expounding the Bible; and the woman accuses the cleric of sexual indecency, using her social-sexual identity as a wife as an effective weapon to neutralize his credibility as a clerical accuser. Moreover, if he will invoke misogynistic convention to accuse her of heresy on the evidence of her scriptural knowledge, she will invoke popular antifraternal convention to accuse the friar of sexual license, one of the more common complaints leveled at mendicants.[95] But on the other view, her accusation of sexual affrontery, even though technically false (as far as the deposition suggests), is at another level true. His exposure of her heresy is the same as a sexual attack, so deeply identified is her salvific knowledge with her bodily integrity. The accusation of heresy represents a kind of intimate bodily violation, an assault upon her sexual-textual self, imaged as the charter of salvation contained in her womb.

The unusually detailed court records concerning Margery Baxter allow us to pinpoint the intersection of hermeneutical law and the realization of that law in the historical prosecution of a particular woman. This essay has dealt with two dimensions of misogynist hermeneutics, the construction of women as bad readers and the metaphysical identification of a certain kind of reading—reading that is literal, vernacular, and lay—with femininity. The latter is often personified by specific women such as Margery Baxter (or her fictional prototype, Chaucer's incurably literal Wife of Bath). But the laws of reading, hermeneutical as well as statutory, are not directed so much against women reading as against a kind of reading associated with "feminine" attributes of literalism, carnality, ignorance, and waywardness. It is thus the gender of reading, rather than the sexual identity of the readers, that is at stake in hermeneutical law and its encoding in historical statutory law. As I have also suggested, the "femininity" of the Lollard hermeneutic is the real object of orthodox prohibition and prosecution, not the femininity of the readers. But as we find, however, in the records of heresy investigations and trials, and especially in the case of Margery Baxter, women readers, or women who participated in a textual community, were readily seen as the embodiments, the living exemplars, of this feminine hermeneutics. If the Lollard hermeneutic is a reclaiming of the literal sense and of the power of individual hermeneutical agency, then Lollard women, acting upon this textual entitlement, mirrored back to the legal establishment the law's own gendered construction of subversive reading.

Notes

1. At the outset I wish to acknowledge my debt to Ralph Hanna, who read and commented on this essay, and whose own work on Lollard textuality has informed my approach to this material. I want to mention in particular an article that he showed me before its publication, "The Difficulty of Ricardian Prose Translation: The Case of the Lollards," 51 *Modern Language Quarterly* 319 (1990), which concerns Lollard women readers, and the manuscript of a book in preparation, which contains material on Lollard hermeneutics.

2. For a reconsideration of the distinction between gender and the historicity of sexual difference, *see* Joan Wallach Scott, *Gender and the Politics of History* 1–11 (1988).

3. On the relationship between misogamy and misogyny, *see* Katherina M. Wilson and Elizabeth M. Makowski, *Wykked Wyves and the Woes of Marriage: Misogamous Literature from Juvenal to Chaucer* 1–11 (1990).

4. *The Principal Works of St. Jerome* (orig. publ. 1893), *Select Library of Nicene and Post-Nicene Fathers* 2d. ser. 6, 383–84 (W. H. Fremantle trans., 1954); *Adversus Jovinianum,* in *Patrologia latina,* 23:313–15 (J. P. Migne ed.) (hereinafter PL).

5. *See* G. E. M. de Ste. Croix, *The Class Struggle in the Ancient Greek World from the Archaic Age to the Arab Conquests* 98–111, 114–47, 418–25 (1981).

6. *See,* among many loci, Aristotle, *Generation of Animals* 738b 25 and *Politics* 1254b 6–15. *See also* the study by Prudence Allen, R.S.M., *The Concept of Woman: The Aristotelian Revolution 750 B.C. to A.D. 1250* (1985).

7. Wilson and Makowski, *supra* note 3, at 44–60.

8. On the institutional structure of philosophical misogyny, *see* Wilson and Makowski, id. at 108.

9. On the new professional identity of the academic, *see* Jacques Le Goff, "How Did the Medieval University Conceive of Itself?" in Jacques Le Goff, *Time, Work, and Culture in the Middle Ages* 122–34 (Arthur Goldhammer trans., 1980).

10. *The Letters of Abelard and Heloise* 71–72 (Betty Radice trans., 1974); *Historia calamitatum* 76–77 (J. Monfrin ed., 1978).

11. Wilson and Makowski, *supra* note 3, at 74–75, and more generally on this vein of satire, id. at 74–108. *See also* Robert A. Pratt, "Jankyn's Book of Wikked Wyves: Medieval Antimatrimonial Propaganda in the Universities," 3 *Annuale Mediaevale* 5–27 (1962).

12. Wilson and Makowski, *supra* note 3, at 77.

13. Augustine, *On Christian Doctrine* 3.5.9 (D. W. Robertson trans., 1958); *De doctrina christiana*, in *Corpus scriptorum ecclesiasticorum latinorum* 80 (William M. Green ed., 1963) (hereinafter CSEL).

14. Ambrose, *Expositio evangeliis secundum Lucam*, PL 15:1844; translation cited from Vern L. Bullough, "Medieval Medical and Scientific Views of Women," 4 *Viator* 499 (1973). This passage is cited and discussed in Carolyn Dinshaw, *Chaucer's Sexual Poetics* 204–5 (1989). The following account of literalism and its identification with femininity has been greatly informed by Dinshaw's important study.

15. Cf. Jerome: "As long as woman is for birth and children, she is different from man as body is from soul. But if she wishes to serve Christ more than the world, then she will cease to be a woman and will be called man." *Commentum in Epistolam ad Ephesios* 3.5, PL 26:533; translation cited from Wilson and Makowski, *supra* note 3, at 57. Cf. discussion by Dinshaw, *supra* note 14, at 205.

16. For a useful account of the philosophical and feminist issue of essence and essentialism, see Diana Fuss, *Essentially Speaking: Feminism, Nature, and Difference* 1–6 (1989). See further the critique of gender itself as a category of historical, philosophical, and feminist analysis in Judith Butler, *Gender Trouble* (1990).

17. Dinshaw, *supra* note 14, at 3–27, 113–31.

18. Id. at 200 n.46.

19. Cf. R. Howard Bloch, "Medieval Misogyny," 20 *Representations* 1–24 (1987); Patricia Parker, "Literary Fat Ladies and the Generation of the Text," in Patricia Parker, *Literary Fat Ladies: Rhetoric, Gender, Property* 8–35 (1987).

20. Dinshaw, *supra* note 14, at 23.

21. Epistle 70, CSEL 54, 1.702 (I. Hilberg ed., 1910); *The Principal Works of St. Jerome*, *supra* note 4, at 149. It is not surprising that Jerome also speaks of the activity of textual translation in terms of taking meaning captive; see Epistle 57, in CSEL 54 *supra*, at 1:512.

22. *See* Dinshaw, *supra* note 14, at 21–25, for an acute distinction between the Macrobian model of reading, where the truth hidden beneath modest veils is the naked body of a woman, and the Pauline model, where the female body is the carnal or literal level of the text, which one passes through and discards to arrive at its spiritual essence.

23. *Macrobius: Commentary on the Dream of Scipio* 86–87 (William Harris Stahl trans., 1952); *Commentarii in Somnium Scipionis* 7–8 (J. Willis ed., 1963).

24. On the term "immasculation" and its implications for reading in the Middle

Ages, *see* Susan Schibanoff, "Taking the Gold Out of Egypt: The Art of Reading as a Woman," in *Gender and Reading: Essays on Readers, Texts, and Contexts* 83–106, esp. 85, 103 n.8 (Elizabeth A. Flynn & Patrocinio P. Schweickart eds., 1986). Schibanoff borrows the term from Judith Fetterley, *The Resisting Reader: A Feminist Approach to American Fiction* xx (1978).

25. Here we may refer again to Jerome's statement (quoted above) comparing the pagan text to the captive heathen woman. It is worth noting that Jerome speaks of "begetting" by the purified text "servants for the Lord of Sabaoth." If reading is a masculine possession of a feminine text, it is also designated as a procreative activity, whereby the reader "sires" a new interpretive product upon the carnal letter of the text. We may suggest, therefore, that on the terms of this metaphysic, reading as a woman, feminine possession of the feminized textual body, is seen to violate the order of heterosexual procreation.

26. Walter Ong, *Orality and Literacy: The Technologizing of the Word* 112–15 (1982).

27. Walter Ong, "Latin Language Study as a Renaissance Puberty Rite," 56 *Studies in Philology* 103–24 (1959).

28. Hugh of St. Victor, *On the Sacraments of the Christian Faith* 256 (Roy J. DeFerrari trans., 1951); *De sacramentis christianae fidei*, PL 176:417–18.

29. Dante, *Convivio* 1.13.4, in *Literary Criticism of Dante Alighieri* 65 (Robert S. Haller trans., 1973); *Il Convivio* (G. Busnelli and G. Vandelli eds., 1934–37).

30. Dante, *De vulgari eloquentia* 1.1, in *Literary Criticism of Dante Alighieri*, *supra* note 29, at 3; Dante, *De vulgari eloquentia* (Aristide Marigo ed., 1938). Cf. *Convivio* 1.9 and *Epistle to Can Grande* 10: "And if we consider the manner of speaking [of the *Commedia*], it is unstudied and low, since its speech is the vernacular, in which even women communicate," in *Literary Criticism of Dante Alighieri*, *supra* note 29, at 101.

31. If it can even be called a model, since the vernacular is so virtually invisible to the insulated world of monastic and clerical Latinity that there is scarcely any theoretical consciousness of it. See Serge Lusignan, *Parler vulgairement: les intellectuels et la langue française aux XIIIe et XIVe siècles* (1986).

32. For two recent examples, *see* Joan M. Ferrante, "The Education of Women in the Middle Ages in Theory, Fact, and Fantasy," in *Beyond Their Sex: Learned Women of the European Past* 9–42 (Patricia H. Labalme ed., 1980); Peter Dronke, *Women Writers of the Middle Ages: A Critical Study of Texts from Perpetua (d. 203) to Marguerite Porete (d. 1310)* (1984).

33. Susan Groag Bell, "Medieval Women Book Owners: Arbiters of Lay Piety and Ambassadors of Culture," in *Sisters and Workers in the Middle Ages* 135–61 (Judith M. Bennett et al. eds., 1989) (orig. publ. in 7 *Signs* 742–68 (1982)).

34. *See* Bernhard Bischoff, "Die kölner Nonnenhandschriften in das Skriptorium von Chelles," (orig. publ. 1957) *reprinted in* 1 *Mittelalterliche Studien* 16–34 (1966); Suzanne Fonay Wemple, *Women in Frankish Society: Marriage and the Cloister 500–900*, at 175–88 (1981); Eileen Power, *Medieval Women* 76–88 (M. M. Postan ed., 1975).

35. Margaret Deanesly, *The Lollard Bible and Other Medieval Biblical Versions* 18 (1920).

36. Deanesly, id. at 25–44.

37. See M. D. Lambert, *Medieval Heresy: Popular Movements from Bogomil to Hus* 77–78, 230–32 (1977).

38. Deanesly, *supra* note 35, at 30–35.

39. Deanesly, *id.* at 29.

40. *De nugis curialium,* quoted in translation in *id.* at 26–27.

41. J. Passavanti, *Trattato della scienza,* quoted in translation in *id.* at 46.

42. For discussions of literal interpretation as a hallmark of Lollard thought, see K. B. McFarlane, *John Wycliffe and the Beginnings of English Nonconformity* 90–91 (1952); Anne Hudson, *The Premature Reformation: Wycliffite Texts and Lollard History* 271–72 (1988); Peggy Knapp, *Chaucer and the Social Contest* 71–76 (1990). Among Wyclif's own writings the main source for his theory of literal reading is *De veritate sacrae Scripturae* (Rudolf Buddensieg ed., 1905–07).

43. Hudson, *supra* note 42, at 62.

44. See John A. F. Thomson, *The Later Lollards, 1414–1520,* at 1–5 (1965); cf. Margaret Aston's comments on the "vulgarization" and "simplification" of doctrine in regional cells: "William White's Lollard Followers," in Margaret Aston, *Lollards and Reformers: Images and Literacy in Late Medieval Religion* 71–99, esp. 91–93, 99 (1984) (hereinafter *Lollards and Reformers*).

45. See, e.g., Anne Hudson, "The Examination of Lollards," in Anne Hudson, *Lollards and Their Books* 125–40 (1985).

46. For background on Wyclif's *De eucharistia,* see McFarlane, *supra* note 42, at 93–97; for further discussion, *see* M. J. Wilks, "The Early Oxford Wyclif: Papalist or Nominalist?" 5 *Studies in Church History* 69–98 (1969).

47. "Twelve Conclusions of the Lollards," in *Selections from English Wycliffite Writings* 25 (Anne Hudson ed., 1978). Orthography has been modernized.

48. The principle of "disendowment of the clergy" called for ecclesiastical institutions to give up their lands and other forms of secular wealth. *See* McFarlane, *supra* note 42, at 58–88; Janet Coleman, *English Literature in History, 1350–1400: Medieval Readers and Writers* 209–18 (1981); Michael Wilks, "Predestination, Property, and Power: Wyclif's Theory of Dominion and Grace," 2 *Studies in Church History* 220–36 (1965).

49. *See* Anne Hudson, Introduction to *Selections from English Wycliffite Writings, supra* note 47, at 4–5.

50. *See* Margaret Aston, "Lollardy and Sedition," in *Lollards and Reformers, supra* note 44, at 15. *See also* the perceptive discussion of lay literacy and Lollard textuality by Janet Coleman, "The Social and Political Significance of Lollardy," in Coleman, *English Literature in History, 1350–1400, supra* note 48, at 209–31.

51. Aston, "Lollardy and Sedition," in *Lollards and Reformers, supra* note 44, at 1–47.

52. Despite long traditions associating Wyclif with the translation of Scripture, there is no evidence that Wyclif himself was responsible for this or any other vernacular production. *See* Margaret Aston, "Wyclif and the Vernacular," in *From Ockham to Wyclif* (Studies in Church History Subsidia 5) 281–330 (Anne Hudson & Michael Wilks eds., 1987).

53. Henry Knighton, Chronicon 2:151–52 (J. R. Lumby ed., London, Rolls Series 1895).

54. Quoted from Aston, "Lollardy and Literacy," in *Lollards and Reformers, supra* note 44, at 198.

55. On Butler, *see* Deanesly, *supra* note 35, at 289–90; for the text of Butler's determination, *see* id. at 401–08.

56. Id. at 401.

57. Id. at 415–18.

58. Text in *Concilia Magnae Britanniae et Hiberniae A.D.* 446–1717, at 3:314–19 (D. Wilkins ed., London, 1737); translation in *The Acts and Monuments of John Foxe*, 3:242–48 (Josiah Pratt ed., London, 1870).

59. Anne Hudson, "Lollardy: The English Heresy?" in *Lollards and Their Books, supra* note 45, at 149.

60. Cited in id.

61. *See* Thomson, *supra* note 44, at 243, and Hudson, "Lollardy: The English Heresy?" *supra* note 59, at 142.

62. *See* Anne Hudson, "Some Aspects of Lollard Book Production," in *Lollards and Their Books, supra* note 45, at 182.

63. Id.; for an example of this formula in abjurations, see the text in Hudson, "The Examination of Lollards," in *Lollards and Their Books, supra* note 45, at 136.

64. Claire Cross, " 'Great Reasoners in Scripture': The Activity of Women Lollards 1380–1530," in *Medieval Women* 378 (*Studies in Church History Subsidia* 1) (Derek Baker ed., 1978).

65. [. . . those women who make themselves so wise by the Bible that they will hold no deed to be virtuous and to be done in man's virtuous conversation except what they can find expressly in the Bible, and are most scornful in their speech against clerks, and boast and press themselves forward—when they are making merry in their own houses—to argue and dispute against clerks . . .]. Reginald Pecock, "Repressor of Overmuch Blaming of the Clergy," in *Chronicles and Memorials of Great Britain and Ireland*, 1:123 (C. Babington ed., London, 1860). On this passage from Pecock, *see* Margaret Aston, "Lollard Women Priests?" 31 *Journal of Ecclesiastical History* 443 (1980).

66. Cited in Aston, *supra* note 65, at 457.

67. Deanesly discusses some instances of women who were encouraged or at least permitted to read Scripture, but only under strict ecclesiastical supervision. Such cases offer models of good women who submit to orthodox regulation. *See* Deansley, *supra* note 35, at 336–40. For an acute discussion of the representation of "good women" as opposed to (Lollard) "bad women" readers, *see* Hanna, *supra* note 1.

68. *The Book of Margery Kempe*, in *Early English Text Society*, ch. 52 (orig. ser. 212) (Sanford B. Meech & Hope Emily Allen eds., 1940). On this see Alcuin Blamires, "The Wife of Bath and Lollardy," 58 *Medium Aevum* 230–31 (1989).

69. *Heresy Trials in the Diocese of Norwich*, 1428–31, at 48 (Norman P. Tanner ed., Camden Fourth Series 20, 1977) (hereinafter *Norwich Heresy Trials*). Margery Baxter herself may not have been literate, but the suspicious sign of heresy, just as in the case of

the orthodox Margery Kempe, was a fluent command of the text of Scripture. On Margery Baxter's knowledge of Scripture, see Hanna, *supra* note 1.

70. Cited in Cross, *supra* note 64, at 367.

71. Cited in id., and Thomson, *supra* note 44, at 116.

72. Cross, *supra* note 64, at 371.

73. See Thomson, *supra* note 44, at 112, 222–36. More generally, see Margaret Aston, "Lollardy and Literacy," in *Lollards and Reformers*, *supra* note 44, at 193–217.

74. Cited in Cross, *supra* note 64, at 371.

75. On White's background and influence, see Aston, "William White's Lollard Followers," in *Lollards and Reformers*, *supra* note 64, at 71–99.

76. *Norwich Heresy Trials*, *supra* note 69, at 41.

77. Id. at 47–48; *The Acts of and Monuments of John Foxe*, *supra* note 58, at 3:595.

78. *The Acts and Monuments of John Foxe*, *supra* note 58, at 3:597.

79. Thomson, *supra* note 44, at 114; Cross, *supra* note 64, at 366.

80. Cross, *supra* note 64, at 366–67; Thomson, *supra* note 44, at 108–15, 243.

81. Cited in Cross, *supra* note 64, at 367. On the talismanic power of books for Lollards, see Margaret Aston, "Devotional Literacy," in *Lollards and Reformers*, *supra* note 44, at 108–09.

82. See Cross, *supra* note 64, at 369–72, 375–78.

83. This kind of oppositional discourse is of a different but related order to the model of women's subversive speech described by Deborah S. Ellis, "The Merchant's Wife's Tale: Language, Sex, and Commerce in Margery Kempe and in Chaucer," 2 *Exemplaria* 595–626 (1990).

84. Cited in Cross, *supra* note 64, at 376, and Hudson, *supra* note 42, at 199–200.

85. Cross, *supra* note 64, at 378.

86. *Norwich Heresy Trials*, *supra* note 69, at 47. Substantial portions of the deposition against Margery Baxter are also translated in *The Acts and Monuments of John Foxe*, *supra* note 58, at 3:594–96.

87. *Norwich Heresy Trials*, *supra* note 69, at 47.

88. Id. at 45. In my translation I have followed the rather clinical terms of the Latin text, which expresses what the priests do with the host after consuming it in the following, rather colorless way: "et commestos emittunt per posteriora in sepibus turpiter fetentibus." This points up how mediated our access to Margery Baxter's voice really is, and how much the voice of the law defines the speaker by distancing us from her. The scribe has recorded in Latin what the witness reported of Baxter's pronouncement in English. Doubtless Baxter would have expressed her no-nonsense view of the fortunes of a thousand eucharistic wafers in the bowels of a thousand priests in more direct and sturdy language.

89. Id. at 49. I am grateful to Ralph Hanna for bringing this curious statement to my attention.

90. See, e.g., Jesse M. Gellrich, *The Idea of the Book in the Middle Ages: Language Theory, Mythology, and Fiction* 21 (1985).

speaker's relation to other persons, to goods, to work, to money. When we investigate the records of the courtroom's tight drama, we should see them not as seamless records but as prisms, artificial works emitting flashes of light from different surfaces. The flashes, I still insist, do give us some vision of lived experience, and we owe some respect to the subjectivity of the speakers. That may seem all the more difficult, not only because our own contemporary theories have boiled away "subjectivity" and left us with only the bones, the skeletal outline, of a "subject position," but because in this case the records are courtroom records, and not the work of the woman in question, be she defendant, accuser, or witness. No real-life Pamela, pen in hand, writes to us here. Instead, the records are shaped by the recorders, the journalists who write down, rewrite, and reinterpret what they have heard.

I am drawing on a body of printed material known as the *Old Bailey Sessions Papers*, taking some accounts of trials in the early 1740s—the decade, incidentally, of the freshly invigorated English novel, the decade of *Pamela* and *Tom Jones* and *Clarissa* and *Roderick Random*.[1] The County of Middlesex and the city of London (that is, most of greater London) tried felons in "sessions" at the court of the Old Bailey every month or six weeks during legal terms. The *Sessions Papers* are accounts of trials for offenses categorized as "common felonies"—for which the penalties ranged from whipping, the pillory, and branding, to transportation or hanging. Despite the gravity of such trials for the defendants, no court records were kept. The *Old Bailey Sessions Papers* (OBSP) were the work of journalists.[2] These *Sessions Papers* began as mere broadsides (the earliest surviving date from 1674) and developed into full pamphlets, becoming more and more detailed as the eighteenth century progressed. Early in the century, the testimony of witnesses and the defenses of prisoners were given (most of the time) in short summary. By the 1730s, the OBSP settled into their amplified format, which continued to extend into even more detailed renditions, looking on the printed page very like the printed texts of plays. The courtroom drama is obviously felt by the journalists who render it, and by the readers who peruse the accounts, even as the courtroom itself bears (as it always does bear) a marked relation to contemporary theater.

These *Sessions Papers*, as John Langbein notes, were written by journalists for lay readers, but there are no superior sources.[3] The OBSP are not a popular substitute for a grave official record. The court of law had no idea of generating its own records of mere felony cases until the journalists entered the scene with what was at first regarded as an uncomfortable, even unconstitutional, intrusion upon the workings of the Crown. Journalists were controlled, subject to licensing in the seventeenth century, and by the mid-eighteenth century the civic authorities succeeded in appointing a shorthand expert and journalists of their own choice as reporters for the

Sessions Papers.[4] If civil authorities, magistrates, and judges were somewhat suspicious at first, their fears were justified. They did learn how to turn the Sessions Papers to their own use in some ways (including as reference material), but the very writing itself, while apparently reinforcing the court's power, at the same time to some extent demystifies it.[5] In taking over authorial control, however anonymously, the journalists take a certain "authority" (the authority of authorship) upon themselves, and judges and jurymen (as well as prisoners) inevitably become characters, if anonymous characters, in the drama or narrative. It was doubtless to guard against such a contingency that the authorities impressed upon the reporters the desirability of not characterizing members of the court in particular during the reporting of a trial. We are not to know what judge (or juror) framed a question; all are subsumed under the phrase "the Court." Yet, the more insistent and cluttering the detail offered by a journalistic account, the less "pure" the magisterial role becomes—and, as we shall see, the journalists offered an avalanche of gritty detail.

The journalists' accounts, however, made the desirability of complete records evident, and by the end of the century the court began to make records of its own. If we want to criticize the journalists for implicit biases, sensationalism, writing for effect, we must first admit that they performed an important service in asserting the public's right to know and in ensuring that Justice would have to keep track of itself.

The OBSP are all we have in this period as a record of felony trials— they are the closest thing to a transcript. We have no "tape recordings" of eighteenth-century speakers, and these transcripts are not true transcripts, and certainly not recordings. Yet they are, tantalizingly, the closest thing we have to recording of the eighteenth-century common people (largely invisible in history and even in drama and the novel). The printed record was offered to the public for entertainment as well as for information and warning. The journalists are obviously aware of the duty of pleasing the public. At the same time, the records in their own way adopt a scientific manner, a manner of objectivity. The Sessions Papers are much less emotional than their rival or complement, the Ordinary's Accounts. As the Sessions Papers grew in volume and importance, the chaplain (or Ordinary) of Newgate Prison had also discovered that he could make a good thing of writing accounts of the lives and last behaviors of the prisoners who were to be executed, especially for dramatic or highly interesting crimes (coining, highway robbery, murder). The climax was the story of execution day itself. The Ordinary's Account was one of the primary modes of biographical writing of the period.[6]

The Ordinary of Newgate (always an identifiable individual) could of course bring his skills to bear in shaping a story, and could vary the tone (comic, pathetic, satiric, sententious) in order to give different forms of entertainment and instruction to the reader. It was the Ordinary's perceived duty to editorialize, to moralize.[7] The *Ordinary's Accounts* thus bear the marks of authorship. The *Old Bailey Sessions Papers* must be considered to be authored also, but in a different manner. They are not narrative but drily descriptive where they do not become—as they frequently do—dramatically mimetic. Some cases are written out at great length, with statements of witnesses given quite fully, and even some questions from judge (or jury) and/or "Council." We do not know what principles of artistic selection prompted a writer to devote much more space to one case than another, especially in cases of dull crimes, such as petty theft. We may assume that not only the social standing of the plaintiff (the "Prosecutor") and accused (the "Prisoner") played a part, but that even factors we cannot begin to evaluate, such as the personal appearance of the accused, led to judgments about which case to give at length and which to give in one sentence. The decisive factor is not the weight of the verdict. Death or transportation is nearly as frequently awarded to the convicts whose cases come to us in one brief statement as to those whose cases are given at great length. Part of the "fun" of reading the OBSP must have been (as it is now) trying to second-guess the jury and judge—first as to "Verdict" (which is given at the end of the case as it occurs)—and then as to "Sentence." For Sentence, one must flip to the back of the pamphlet, which lists the prisoners described in that section under categories of penalties awarded: e.g., "Received Sentence of Death, 13" (followed by list of names, each with case number); "Transportation for 14 Years, 1"; Transported for 7 Years, 31"; "Burnt in the Hand, 5"; "Whipt, 5." That is the list as it appears at the end of *The Proceedings of the King's Commissions of the Peace, Over and Terminer, and Gaol Delivery for the City of London; and also the Gaol Delivery for the County of Middlesex . . .* Number II (for sessions of January 13–16 of 1744). The authenticity is vouched for on the back page, under the list of those condemned, and also of those condemned in former sessions who have had their sentences commuted or carried out. This information is included, it is stated, "In Order to render these Trials yet more acceptable to the Gentlemen who preserve Sets of them." That is, it is assumed that there are readers who regularly buy and keep these papers, and like to follow cases through to the very end. And it is presumed that such readers for whom the OBSP must be tailored are "Gentlemen." The *Sessions Papers* meet their requirements in being fully informative and accurate.

The *Sessions Papers* announce their credibility by their standard device of naming persons and locations. The accounts do not emanate from the universe, or from Justice at large; a specific individual, who can be found at a certain place, is the authentic recorder:

Trials at Law, &c. are carefully taken in Short-Hand by N. Fromanteel, at the

Two Black Boys within White-Chapel Bars (I, Pt. 2 (January), 40; cf. III (February), 84).[8] The OBSP are authenticated—they are responsible. The shorthand writer is named, and can be found—these papers are legitimate writings, records meant to bear historical inspection, and they indicate a concept of accuracy by which to judge them. The name of the shop or tavern may seem to us regrettably pertinent. "The Two Black Boys" reminds us of the curse of slavery and of the slave-labor that sustains the wealth of the nation that could produce Sessions Papers and "Gentlemen" to read them. "The Two Black Boys" may be taken as persons silenced in these and all such proceedings—and yet not uninterested in them. There are many who are silenced in these papers, too—the accused whose cases get recorded and put away without their being overheard on paper.

What first struck me about the OBSP was not the silence, but the babble of voices. And I am still struck by that crowd of voices. With every reservation announced and allowed for, with the contaminated nature of this medium considered, yet it is a medium. This is one of our few slender, defective lines to the past, and not to the official past—the eighteenth century of the green lawns and great houses, of Parliament and Laws—nor even of Covent Garden or of Richardson's and Fielding's novels. This is an eighteenth-century world so much in action that it can (in some measure) forget to idealize and defend itself. Thus within the confines of its Sessions Papers—which in a semiofficial manner do proclaim "British Justice" (a commodity much advertised through the centuries but always in short supply)—within those confines of a certain grey and half-louche respectability, there is represented a world of the poor and of the minorities (women, blacks, and Jews) that we cannot otherwise glimpse.

The subject is vast, and the material offers a mine of information of all kinds. Here I am merely going to deal with a few cases of the 1740s, cases in which women are strongly involved. In other essays I have dealt with the murderesses, whose cases evoked usually excited public response.[9] Those were women who were invited to speak out, and whose speeches were recorded at some length. Some, like Mrs. Brownrigg, who murdered her apprentice, could say but little for themselves, while others, such as Mary Blandy (notorious for poisoning her father), and even the poor thief Sarah Malcolm (accused of murdering her employer's household), take up the pen in their own defense, as well as speaking with all the eloquence they could muster at their own trials. Most of these women had something to say, and the public wanted to hear them speak. Defending her life in a public court was, I have pointed out elsewhere, one of the few occasions in the eighteenth century in which a woman was urged to take command of the public forum—or at least to have a voice in it.

But the women in lesser cases were obviously defending their own lives too, very often, though not robed in the glamor that hung about the murderess. I am going to present some of these women—and some of the many female witnesses who spoke in court—as well as musing upon the silenced woman, women not given a transcribed voice. It is certainly worth noting that the journalist's report does not really tell us with certainty whether someone present said anything or not. John Langbein in his invaluable research into the notes made in the 1750s by Sir Dudley Ryder, Chief Justice of King's bench, during criminal trials, finds the OBSP in general are corroborated, but notes that some testimony has occasionally been deleted.

> Ryder's notes often preserve significant aspects of the trial evidence that the OBSP editors deleted from their narratives. For example, there are a couple of cases in which the OBSP state, "[t]he prisoner had nothing to say in his defense," which might mean that the accused simply kept silent. Ryder shows us that the accused did speak up, but that what he had to say was not consequential. . . . In another case we learn from Ryder that the OBSP deleted most of the accused's defense from a case seemingly fully reported.[10]

Such deletion is not, however, a consistent practice, except when the OBSP gives only a short summary of a case, which Langbein calls a "squib report." Silencing can occur at two levels—within the courtroom and within the written record. Often the written record reflects the tendency of the court, the inclination to find someone's testimony worth hearing, or worthless and thus inaudible. There were undoubtedly cases in which the judges did not want an accused person they were trying to help to say too much, as well as cases in which they were anxious to convict. My interest is in the way the women are silenced within the one evidentiary account we have and that the public was meant to read, the written record of the *Sessions Papers*. My approach is certainly not scientific; it is anecdotal. What I am presently doing might be described as "cruising" among the cases of 1744.

Silencing the accused is, it should be noted, not always the symptom of legal violence or oppression, at least not in a simple way—it doesn't always *necessarily* coincide with a "guilty" verdict. For instance, we may read a "squib report" like this:

> MARY BROWN was indicted for stealing two pairs of men's leather pumps, value 2s.6d., the goods of *Evan Williams*, March 10. Acquitted. (IV (April), 103)

More seriously, there is the case of child-murder.

> MARTHA SHACKLETON, otherwise HILL . . . was indicted for the Murder of her Female Bastard Child, by casting and throwing it into a Privy belonging to the Dwelling-House of *William Porter*. . . . (I (January), 16)

William Porter, her employer, gives a very circumstantial account in January of a conversation with Martha Shackleton on the previous 18th of September. In his speech the accused Martha is extensively *ventriloquized*; not speaking here herself, she hears another speak her alleged words:

> I thought she was not well, and asked her what was the Matter with her, she said she was extremely Ill with the Gravel and Stone; I desired her to send for Mr. *Warner*, a Surgeon . . . but in talking with her, I thought I observed that she was fallen away, and suspected she had been with Child. . . . I talked to her of having the necessary House opened, to search if any Child was there, which she insisted upon in order to clear her Character. . . . On the 9th of November, I received a Letter from Mrs. *Porter* from Lincoln, where the Prisoner came from, in which she acquainted me, that she was two Months gone with Child before she came from thence; I told her of the Letter, and asked her concerning it; she then owned she had miscarried and that she was five Months gone with Child when she miscarried; I sent for a Carpenter, and had the Vault opened, and there was a Child found. (16)

Porter had called in Warner the Surgeon, who was present to give testimony in court. Having viewed the body when it was discovered, the Surgeon could not decide whether "there had been any Violence done" or even be certain what sex the infant was ("to the best of my Judgment . . . a Female Child")—but added, damagingly, "I said it was so large, that I believed it might be about nine Months . . ." (16).

All of this, you will note, involves conversation *about* Martha—including Mrs. Porter's epistolary conversation about her—and conversation with her is internally reported. Martha Shackleton does not appear to speak during her own trial (according to this account) until one line near the end.

> *Q to the Prisoner.* Are you married?
> *Prisoner.* Yes—My Husband is at Sea, his name is Hill.
> Acquitted. The Jury found that the Child was still-born. (17)

Poor Martha "speaks" (at least on the page) only one line—having had other lines attributed to her. But that one line is efficacious. Her assertion of her marriage evidently gives the Jury the excuse it wants to acquit her, and she is not required to produce a husband or evidence of marriage.

In another case, a woman had married only too much, apparently. "ELIZABETH FIRES, otherwise ELIZABETH, the Wife of ANTHONY TERRY, otherwise ELIZABETH, the Wife of BENJAMIN BRADSHAW" was indicted on the grounds that after having married Anthony Terry in the 12th year of George the Ist, she did in the 9th year of George II "feloniously marry and take to her Husband *Benjamin Bradshaw*, the aforesaid *Anthony Terry* being then

Living, against the Form of the Statute in that Case made and provided" (I, Pt. 2 (January), 24). The woman thus charged with polyandry must have been present in court, but the only person questioned is Benjamin Bradshaw. He undergoes a brisk catechism:

> Benjamin Bradshaw—I am married to that Woman, I was married eight Years ago at St. John Wapping.
> Q. Who married you?
> Bradshaw. I cannot tell the Name of the Parson.
> Q. Did he appear to be a Clergyman?
> Bradshaw. Yes.
> Q. Was the ceremony of the Church of England read over?
> Bradshaw. Yes.
> Q. Were you married with a Ring?
> Bradshaw. Yes.
> Q. Did you cohabit together as Man and Wife?
> Bradshaw. Yes—about eight Years.
> Q. When did you part?
> Bradshaw. Never; we have always lived together.
> Q. Have you had any children?
> Bradshaw. Yes.
> Q. Have you any proof of her Marriage with her first Husband?
> Bradshaw. No.
> Q. Are you willing to keep her, and have her still?
> Bradshaw. Yes, and please you my Lord.
> Acquitted. (24–25)

One would think Benjamin Bradshaw was on trial, but he is not the person indicted. How did this case come to be presented? What Enoch Arden story—or some prosaic story of jealous neighbors—lies behind it? We cannot tell. Neither can we tell whether Elizabeth Fires/Terry/Bradshaw was as willing to sustain this marriage as Benjamin was, or whether in fact she and her husband needed this case to be brought to put an end to queries about their union's legitimacy. What is evident is that the Court—that is, the judges—were not at all anxious to intervene in a viable marriage or to go searching after former arrangements made by dwellers in Wapping. This viable marriage was peaceful and ensured that wife and children would not be thrown upon the parish. We cannot of course tell whether they questioned Elizabeth or not. The impression we gather from this account is that the judge did not want to ask her questions, for fear of what he might hear, and that the safest mode of procedure was to tackle the innocent Benjamin. If there is contempt for Elizabeth in the procedure, it is not to be found simply in the suppression of her voice from the evidence we are offered.

Silence or silencing might well mean safety—but it might not. The absence of a woman's voice from the record is certainly no guarantee that she escaped from penalty—even the Death Penalty.

> ANN LEWIS, was indicted for stealing a silk damask counterpane, value 30 s;
> a holland shirt, 2 s; and a silk handkerchief, 12 d, the goods of A—— B——.
> Jan. 1. Guilty. (III (February), 83)

And when we turn to the back of this pamphlet (84), we find the name of Ann Lewis among those condemned to death. The silk counterpane did the damage—it was valuable. People were executed for stealing goods over a certain value (40 shillings, or 5 shillings worth from a shop).[11] Prosecutions were, however, very often brought for the lowest and most humble objects—a tub, a pair of old boots, a pound of chocolate, two candlesticks, and a length of cloth. We see here a society that does produce consumer goods, and an array of objects, but in which the goods are in short supply and expected to endure. Small households could be seriously threatened by the loss of a tub, a cooking pot, a shirt. And in the realm of necessity, in the day-to-day struggle, women of course participate very fully. That is why they are Prosecutors as often as Prisoners, and references to them in various capacities as nurses, washerwomen, landladies, pawnbrokers, etc. turn up with great regularity.

Sometimes a felony case involves a more glamorous theft. Consider the case of William Pitt's gold watch and diamond.

> ELIZABETH MILLER, otherwise BAREFOOT, of St. Martin's in the Fields, was
> indicted for stealing a Gold Watch, with a large Diamond on the Pendant,
> the Property of William Pitt, Esq; in the Shop of Isaac Duhammel, Nov. 15, 1741.
> (I (January), 10)

The watch, left to be mended, was stolen out of the shop. Abraham Jacobs deposed that the watch had been offered to him in "Rag-Fair": "the Prisoner said to me, are you a Jew? I said, yes; she said, she had got a Gold Watch to dispose of, and she wanted me to help her to a Chap for it." He called in his father, who suspected a theft, saw the advertisement for the watch, went to Duhammel and ensured the prisoner's arrest. She was on this occasion discharged, Duhammel not turning up at the court in time. One John Berry deposed that he had seen

> "a Gold Watch with two Diamonds, which the Prisoner showed me; says
> she, I have got a Chance, and if you help me to a Chap for it, I will satisfy
> you. . . . I told her there were twenty Guineas Reward offered for it, and
> advised her to carry it to Mr. Duhammel; she said, she would not, for she
> could make thirty Guineas for it. There was one Harris who kept her Com-

pany, but is gone off, said to her, *You will come to be hanged for this Practice. Oh!* says she, *I am not afraid of that by Jesus God,* as that is their *Irish* way of talking. I told Mr. *Duhammel* I could inform him where the Watch was, but she had so many Thieves about her, that if we went into *Rag-Fair* to take her, we would be knocked on the Head." (11)

Elizabeth Miller is richly quoted throughout the case as to past utterances, but she is reported as saying very little for herself in court. What she does say comes immediately after John Berry's evidence:

The Prisoner being called upon to make her Defence, said, that *Berry* was a Thief-taker, and desired he might go out of Court while her Witnesses were examined. (11)

Berry immediately responds to this request for his absence:

Berry. She wants me to go out, because I should not discover who the Persons are, that come in her Behalf; for they are all like herself. (11)

Elizabeth Miller says nothing more in this account, and the Constable takes up the tale, giving details of her arrest:

she came quietly along with us; we stripped her naked, all but her Shift, and searched every Part of her, and made her extend her Legs, for fear she should have concealed it; we went to her House, and searched that narrowly; we cut the very Beds open, but could not find it. (11)

Elizabeth Miller is searched very narrowly, but her words are not weighed or searched—at least they cannot be by the reader, who is not given them. The details of the search of her body have a certain salacious interest, perhaps.

The court reporter (or reporters) may seem often to display a cautious salacious interest. Among the minor felonies, most cases involving prostitutes receive slightly more (sometimes much more) attention than cases of common stealing, even if the value of the goods lost or claimed lost is the same.

MARGARET NEWTON, of *St. Martins in the Fields*, was indicted for stealing half a Guinea, and one shilling, the money of *George Jennings*, privately from his person, *Feb. 18. George Jennings.* Last *Saturday*, about 10 o'clock at night, as I was going home to my master's (Mr. *Haddock*, who keeps bagnio) the Prisoner picked my pocket of half a Guinea in the *Strand*, between *Hungerford* and *St. Martin's Lane*. (III (February), 70)

This Prosecutor was shrewdly questioned by the Court, in a number of short queries, as to precisely how the money was abstracted, how much it was and in what denomination of coin. He said he had "14 s in gold, and the rest in silver" after changing "a guinea at the *Ship*" (70).

Q. How much had you spent?

Jennings. I believe nine pence, for three pots of beer.

Q. Nine pence was a pretty deal, was not you disguised in liquor?

Jennings. Very little, if anything. (70)

In response to further questions, he said he could not open Margaret Newton's hand to retrieve the money; he called "the watch" or watchmen, the early and inefficient form of police:

I had her to the watch-house, kept her there all night, and the next morning had her before a Justice, and then she owned she took a halfpenny out of my pocket, and no more. (70)

At this point Margaret Newton herself surprisingly enters the catechistical lists:

Prisoner. Did not you offer me three pence at the water side, if I would oblige you?

Jennings. No, I did not.

Prisoner. You said so at the watch-house. . . . Did not you pull me and haul me about, and wanted to have to do with me?

Jennings. By virtue of my oath, I did not.

Prisoner. You said you had been spending of money, or you would have given me more.

Jennings. By virtue of my oath, it is false.

Q. Upon what pretence did she come up to you? Did she speak to you?

Jennings. Yes, she came to pick me up.

Q. Did you pick her up, or did she pick you up?

Jennings. She picked me up; when she came up to me, she took hold of me with one arm, and with the other picked my pocket . . . she was not searched, for when I proposed searching of her, she said, if she had three or four half guineas about her, what was that to any body. (70–71)

The Prisoner, having joined in the interrogation and cross-examined her Prosecutor, now gives her own statement:

I was coming from my mistress's where I had been at work, by St. Martin's Lane; he asked me to drink, I said, No, I will not; then he said, he would give me three pence if I would go with him under the gate-way; I said, I did not value his three pence; he said he had been spending money, or else he would have given me more; and because I would not go with him, he d——d me and called me bitch, and charged the watch with me in a minute. Acquitted. (71)

Here the Prisoner has successfully employed her wits and language in making her accuser visibly appear as a drunken lecher and not as an innocent victim; she had, however, the sympathy of the Court, as that was the line indicated by the Court's questions. Margaret Newton seems fully responsive to her situation in the law court. Less fortunate women—less fortunate in the outcome—are unsuccessful in an attempt to elicit the court's sympathies. In April 1744 Elizabeth Milward brought a criminal suit against Richard Carberry for assault and theft supposedly committed on January 26, 1744—although the prosecutor herself is vague about the date:

> Eliza[Beth] Milward. About 8 or 9, or it may be 10 weeks ago, I cannot tell which, as I was coming over Flemish church yard, near Tower-hill . . . with a butter tub . . . Dick Carberry knocked me down; then he tore my apron off my sides, and took my pocket with five or six shillings in it—I knew him . . . He had a room in the next house to my mother's, that came over her shop— . . . After I got up I said, Pray Mr. Carberry don't meddle with me. And he beat me, and said, you B——h, I will knock your brains out. (IV (April), 99)

The Prisoner (Carberry) turns Milward's story around by giving another sort of background to the incident:

> Prisoner. The night before this happened, another midshipman and I went into the bawdy-house which is kept by her or her mother, and we drank pretty freely. She took a laced hat and a guinea from this gentleman, and three shillings and six-pence from me. Said I, my girl, you have got a guinea from this gentleman, and a laced hat. She said she knew nothing of it. They had stripped us so, that we had not money to pay our reckoning. And then they and their bullies fell upon us so, that we had like to have been murdered. There were a matter of sixteen whores of them together. So the next day, about three o'clock I met this girl, and said, You B——h, you are one of the whores that robbed me last night. And so she charges me with robbing her. (99)

Catharine Milward, the mother, in a separate indictment, claimed that Carberry "came bodily into the house" "in a great passion" and broke furniture and windows, and threw goods into the street, starting a riot so that there gathered "a mob of 100 people about the door" (100). He took a box of valuables and gave it to his wife and landlady, who took away the Milwards' goods and money (to a value of over 14 guineas).

In this case, as in so many, witnesses and neighbors were important. The same female neighbors testified in both these cases, and were universally for Richard Carberry against the Milwards. One of these neighbors, Sarah Cooper, asserted that Catharine "kept a vile house"; she had seen Carberry throw Elizabeth down, but said the girl made at the time no complaint of robbery. Another witness, Elizabeth Studly, added, "As to his robbing her, I believe he robbed her of nothing, for I believe she had not a farthing in the world—I never heard any harm of *Elizabeth Milward*—the mother has the character of keeping a disorderly house" (100). In the case of Catharine Milward's complaint of housebreaking, Sarah Cooper exclaimed, "I don't believe the Prisoner took the value of this bit of paper away, for all the neighbourhood believes they were not robbed of a pin" (101). The neighbor women repeatedly asserted that the Milwards would accuse anybody; Carberry's landlady, Sarah Mills (who is closely involved in the case), says "I believe they don't care whose life they swear away" (101), and Elizabeth Studly agrees that the Milwards would swear falsely: "I believe they would not stick at it in order to obtain their ends" (101). Carberry was acquitted on both counts. In such a case we can see the power of female witnesses in registering neighborhood values (or appearing to stand for them).

Women are of great importance in the OBSP as *witnesses*. As witnesses, they appear in two important categories—as Prosecutor, and thus as chief witness for the Prosecution, and as character witness. Women are chiefly Prosecutors for thefts from shop or home, and they are most likely to appear against a female employee in the shop or home. Maidservants stealing clothing and sheets and pawning or selling them seems to have been a source of household distress (as in Fielding's *Amelia*).[12] We should not, however, see these Prosecutors in a purely domestic context. Many are shop-owners or are engaged in paid work of some kind; a number are washerwomen or clear-starchers who must have goods of some value temporarily in their dwelling, which is also the place of business.

One of the many all-female cases involves a female publican, Mary Ann Conliff, who formerly kept "a publick house in the little piazzas in *Covent Garden*," and a female [bartender], Jane Morris, who, the publican claimed, stole clothes and linen from her. Jane Morris evidently persuaded the jury that her version was credible: "The washerwoman has all the linnen [sic] entirely. She (Conliff) owes her four pound fourteen shillings and odd pence" (IV (April), 101). Jane Morris was acquitted. The commonplace of our time that the eighteenth century saw a diminution of women's work may have to be revised or at least interestingly modified as we look at the realities of eighteenth-century city life.[13] The *Old Bailey Sessions Papers* offer a window (if a dim and dirty window) on the realities of that life, and could serve as a mine of sociological information—including valuable information as to standards of living and the actual processes of eighteenth-century consumerism. Here is one decidedly domestic case:

> MARY CAWDELL, was indicted for stealing a pink coloured silk damask gown, value 50 s. a blue silk gown, value 10 s. a flowered cotton gown, value 10 s. a white silk damask gown, value 20 s. a red and white sattin [sic] gown, value 10 s. some linen, a child's scarlet cloth cloak, a velvet cap, and

a parcel of children's wearing apparel, &. the property of *Charles Corbet*, in his dwelling house, *Dec.* 12th. (I, Pt. 2 (January), 53)

Mr. Corbet is the official employer of the former maidservant, the official owner of all the gowns, and the Prosecutor (and it is he who must pay out the five guineas reward to the pawnbroker). But Mrs. Corbet is the chief prosecution witness, and thus chief speaker:

> Mrs. *Corbet*. My gowns were locked up in my drawers, and the children's clothes lay in a closet in the room where the Prisoner lay. I missed them on *Sunday* the 11th of *Dec.* I went up for something for Mr. *Corbet*, and found that all these things were gone—I cannot say when I saw the gowns last, for I do not dress myself much in winter time—I saw one of them about three weeks before. (53)

There is something plangent about the statement "I do not dress myself much in winter time"—a sort of Barbara Pym resonance. One is led to ponder the frugal way of life of Mrs. Corbet, who has clothes too good to wear, kept locked away in drawers—the property, after all, of her husband. Mary Cawdel may have been tempted, one speculates, because the lovely dresses went unused. The Corbets were evidently persons of some income, in order to be able to buy the "pink coloured silk damask" and to have a dress made up of it, a fifty-shilling gown. The status of this middle-class gown is perhaps something like that of a "consumer durable," for clothes, as we see in these accounts, are too valuable to middle-class and poor to be readily allowed to be perishable. The pawnbroker, however, could turn unwieldly solid goods into liquid money. In another case, a (male) witness claims in defense of the Prisoner, Margaret Saunders, that her landlady, Hannah Harding, lent her the sheets she has allegedly stolen. The landlady, he claims, lent Margaret Saunders the sheets to pawn, and is now supporting the prosecution only because Mrs. Harding had not dared to tell her husband of this transaction, for fear of his beating her (I, Pt. 2 (January), 60). The Prisoner was acquitted. The claim of the defense was very credible; we may speculate that covert access to the pawnshop was often sought by women who had no property in their own gowns and sheets, but might find means of making away with these stealthily and converting them into cash.

The pawnshop seems to have loomed fairly large in the lives of many women. In another all-female case, Mary Fisk was accused of stealing a sheet (value 18 d.) and a brass saucepan and other goods from Sarah Verney, her landlady:

> She said, she had given them to her sister (who is a good honest woman) to pawn them. I found some at Mr. *Granger's*, and the saucepan at another

place. I catched her in bed with my servant on *Monday* last, which frightened me very much.

Q. I hope it was a maid servant?

Verney: No; it was a man servant. (I, Pt. 2 (January), 57)

The sister-in-law, Sarah Daniel, said she had pawned the things, but claimed that when she found out from Mrs. Verney that the things were stolen "I went and fetched the sheet and throwed it into Mrs. *Verney's* House." Sarah Daniel denies pawning the sheet to help her brother, and disassociates herself from Mary Fisk. "I would scorn to say a false thing." The Prisoner insists that the sheet and plate were pawned by Mrs. Daniel for her brother's use: "They were pawned for the use of my husband when he broke his arm, before he went to sea." This is Mary Fisk's only defense (according to the record) and it seems designed rather to make Sarah Daniel share the guilt than to get herself off. The verdict of "Guilty" follows close upon Fisk's speech—but Mary Fisk gets in the last word in the case: "I return the old bawd thanks for her favour"—perhaps a fling at the landlady as prosecutor, but more likely a jeer at Sarah Daniel who would not tell a lie to help her out (57).

Of course, women do not appear as prosecutors, or as witnesses for the prosecution, all the time. They may be invited to participate very fully as witnesses for the defense. A witness for the defense might supply an alibi or might appear as a character witness in order to describe the good conduct of the Prisoner hitherto, asserting directly or by implication that the alleged misconduct is unlikely or even impossible. There was at least a theoretical difference in types of witnesses. Character witnesses for the prosecution (showing that the accused had a bad reputation) could be invoked only if the Prisoner summoned character witnesses in his/her own behalf. Some women were reluctant to appear as defense witnesses. A man who claimed that he was in fact listening to some ballad-singers when the theft in question took place wanted the singers as witnesses but they did not show up: "The ballad-singers were called, but did not come to the character of the Prisoner" (III (February), 69). We see in this instance that there is often in fact no clear distinction made between a *substantial* witness who offers an alibi and a *character* witness. In the case of William Pitt's gold watch and diamond, the witnesses become very hesitant—probably because of John Berry's emphatic indication that all the witnesses the accused brings in on her own behalf are thieves, like herself. One of the witnesses, Elizabeth Carlow, the old-clothes dealer, is visibly under suspicion herself, and has reason to be cautious in speaking of Elizabeth Miller:

I have known the Prisoner ever since she was a Child . . . she is a Child's Coat-Maker; I never heard of any Dishonesty by her in my Life— . . . I buy and sell Clothes—I have bought Things of her, and never was challenged for any Thing that I bought of her. (I (January), 11)

Another female witness speaks more warmly in favor of the prisoner:

> Ann Brown. I have known her for seven years; I never knew any Thing but what was just and fair of her—She is a Stay-maker, and buys and sells that sort of Goods. (11)

Ann Austin is more cautious in testifying to the character of the prisoner:

> Ann Austin. I have known her five years; I know her to be a Dealer in the Fair, I know nothing of her Character.
> Q. Pray don't you know her to be a Woman of a very bad Character?
> Austin. I don't dive into that; I have enough to do at Home; I only say what I know. (11)

Note that Ann Austin's caution does not lead her into agreeing with the tendency of the Court. She will not swerve off into the negative direction when speaking of Elizabeth Miller, even though the Court points that direction out to her in a very leading manner. Who, we may ask, is "Q"? The Q (which stands for "Query") presumably masks a judge (the most probable identity), but queries may also be put by a prosecuting attorney (rare but more common as time goes on) or even a member of the Jury. Most commonly, a long dash before a remark made by Prosecutor, Witness, or Prisoner indicates that the following remark is an answer to a question without any other indication of a query. The effect of the record is to have Prisoner and Witnesses interrogated by an impersonal and unidentified power, the power of the Court to ask questions.

We may also note that the concept of "Character" (such as is at work in a phrase like "character reference") would seem to demand the presence of women. Women represent the unofficial domestic history; they stand for the local memory of a person, running back even to childhood. What a man or woman's character is can be known only to the women who have observed him or her from childhood, the women who are themselves the guardians of the neighborhood mores. Women as character witnesses sustain a kind of choric value in the drama of the courtroom; they represent the nurses of the community and of its morals.

The women who served as witnesses did not of course see their function as choric, nor were they necessarily reluctantly dragooned into appearing on behalf of another. Often the women witnesses actively intervene for the benefit of a person accused of a crime (including other women accused). Indeed, one might suppose that women play a key role in women's cases, as witnesses for good or ill, because they are often the only people present to and attentive to certain kinds of crime—not only the domestic sort, but the crimes of the streets involving prostitutes. Women are not only moral witnesses to each other, but are expected to be in some sort useful guardians of morals. There are also the women on the wild side who, as participants of the life of the streets, can change our view of what went on. Consider the case of Susannah Hughes, indicted "for stealing a Silk Purse, value 1 d. and two Ducats, value 19 s., the property of Charles Harrison, privately from his Person, Dec. 2" (I, Pt. 2 (January), 38).

> Charles Harrison. I met Susannah Hughes and another Woman in the Strand, and asked them to drink a Glass of something; they took me to the Lebeck's Head, and we had an eighteen Penny Tiff of Punch; the Prisoner clapped her Hand upon my Breeches (I supposed she wanted Money more than any Thing) and told me I had nothing; she clapped herself down upon my Knee, and exposed her Legs and Thighs very much; I found her Hand Going into her Bosum, and I took hold of it with my Purse in it.—I am Positive of it— . . . I belong to my Lord Herbert, I have been thirty four Years in the Service—I was in such Company* before that Evening; I will not deny it, but I did not pull any Gold out there.

> *The Prosecutor was asked how he came to go into such Company, and whether he was sober; he said, I was between both; I know what I did; Sed nemo sine crimine vivit. (38–39)

The question of the court thus entered here as an interesting footnote indicates a certain impatience on the part of the Court with the character of the Prosecutor himself, not infrequently to be found in the cases where men knowingly consorting with prostitutes get taken. There seems to be some unstated feeling that the man is asking for it, however low the character of the women. That feeling permits other women to use some leverage by adding confusion to the case. In this instance, two female witnesses and their evidence—not from within the public house, but from outside it.

> Esther Wood deposed that she met the Prosecutor in Fleet Street that Evening; that he had a Broomstick in his Hand, and gave her several Blows; that he was very much in Liquor, and charged her with taking his Purse. Mary Williams swore she saw and heard what the last Witness deposed. Acquitted. (39)

Esther Wood and Mary Williams must be two women of the streets, who turn the Prosecutor's behavior into repetitive frenzy. His irrationality becomes the feature of the case. The accused Susannah is meanwhile unrecognized in the written account, speaking no recorded word. One wonders whether Wood and Williams are not being very clever—they have found an effective model of discrediting the pompous middle-aged servant of Lord Herbert and his Latin quotations too. He is a nut case, a drunkard armed with the prosaic and female instrument, "a Broomstick" (like a witch or shrew), and he cannot tell one whore from another, but is always going on about his purse—perhaps obsessed by the place where his balls ought to be, where according to his own evidence Susannah told him he had "nothing." We might call this case "the Case of the Witty Witnesses"—although the witnesses' intelligence does not reflect upon their truthfulness.

It strikes me that I have given you in this essay a number of instances in which women are the guardians of commodities (tea, chocolate, sheets, old clothes, cooking pans, brocade gowns) or in which the women are commodities. But that must necessarily be the case whenever we look at such numerous cases, in any century. I also have not given you any of the cases of petty theft involving only men: the whole society seems to rest on goods that are to be traded, pawned, possessed. This is a commodity culture, a consumer culture, with too few commodities as yet. In the courts of law chiefly concerned with small property, the women must appear. They are related to property not only as domestic consumers, but as producers and processors, as traders and suppliers of service. In such a world of property, women as well as men who have a relation to property must speak—and they speak more fully as chorus than they do, on the whole, when they are at the center of the action—accused of infanticide or domestic theft. The less respectable they are as victims, prosecutors, or witnesses, the freer they seem to be to speak—or at least to have their speech recorded. We may take it that the shorthand reporter and his editor felt at liberty in printing the details of prostitutes' speeches not only as they had so little "character" to lose but as they are, so to speak, licensed entertainers. Whores' reported speech can be drawn upon for color—as in the case of Mary Clifford, called "Green-Gown Mary," who with some men committed an assault and theft upon Margaret Gyles. Mary Clifford had assaulted Mrs. Gyles's friend Mrs. Frenson earlier; when Margaret Gyles took Clifford aside from the pub to make sure of the assault, she was set upon by Clifford:

> She whistled, and said, *Now you B———h I will have my Revenge on you; I will cut your Throat from Ear to Ear;* she said she would have *my Heart's Blood,* she would present the *Blood Bowl* to me. . . . (I, Pt. 2 (January), 37)

After Mary and her gang of "Carmen" were finished with Margaret Gyles (including forcible sexual contact), there was another (reported) conversation:

> After I cried out *Stop Thief* three times, Clifford came back again with the Cloak over her Arm and the Bundle in her Hand, and knocked me down in the Mud, and said, *Take that in the room of the Blood Bowl.* (37)

The violent-speaking Mary Clifford is not recorded as saying anything during her trial. She is a silenced woman who is *represented* as a forcible speaker. The two women who testify against her, not silenced, may also report her speech. These two women are subject to questioning. They are doubted. Their story is not believed because they had not asked for assistance or identified the culprits (at the time). The explanation is that "they were in Liquor"; the gang is too large, identifications are a problem. Mary Clifford remains present purely in narration—as it were—a narration emanating from two other women. This narration presents her as a violent character with a blood-curdling turn of phrase. Such memorable language sells papers. Words substitute even for a body (of a defendant, of victim, of evidence, even at times of executed prisoner). *Take that in the room of the Blood Bowl* indeed.

Notes

1. The relationship between accounts of criminals and the developing genre of the novel has fascinated some literary historians. John Bender points out that many if not most central characters of major eighteenth-century novels are accused of crime or threatened with such accusation, and spend part of their time in a prison; he connects the imprisonment in stories with individual adjustment to social control, so that the novels embody and enact social constriction; see John Bender, *Imagining the Penitentiary: Fiction and the Architecture of Mind in Eighteenth-Century England* (1987). Like many others touching upon crime and punishment in the period, Bender has been influenced by Michel Foucault's *Surveiller et punir: Naissance de la prison* (1975), translated by Alan Sheridan as *Discipline and Punish: The Birth of the Prison* (1977). Lincoln Faller turned to his (non-Foucauldian) study of the writing of criminal lives in the eighteenth century after he had begun the study of the novelist Daniel Defoe, who wrote criminals' lives purportedly factual, as well as fictions such as *Moll Flanders* (1722) or *Colonel Jack* (1722), in which the central characters are criminals; see Lincoln B. Faller, *Turned to Account: The Forms and Functions of Criminal Biography in Late Seventeenth- and Early Eighteenth-Century England* (1987).

2. John Langbein, "The Criminal Trial before the Lawyers," 45 U. Chi. L. Rev. 263–316 (1978) (hereinafter *The Criminal Trial*). Langbein, a legal historian, is searching for the emerging presence and developing role of lawyers in criminal trials; *see also* his "Shaping the Eighteenth-Century Criminal Trial: A View from the Ryder Sources," 50 U. Chi. L. Rev. 1–136 (1983) (hereinafter *Ryder Sources*).

The relation between journalism, contemporary behavior, freedom of the press, and control of the press demands more study. Lennard Davis in *Factual Fictions: The Origins of the English Novel* (1983)—a work purporting to treat of the relation between journalism, fiction, and the laws of censorship—touches on a fascinating topic, but the book itself is practically worthless as it offers no indication of any real contact with any eighteenth-century journalism whatsoever. Someone else will eventually have to grapple with the topic, exploring actual journalism of the period.

3. See Langbein, The Criminal Trial, supra note 2, at 271: "To write legal history from the OBSP is . . . a perilous undertaking, which we would gladly avoid if superior sources availed us. However, on the present state of our knowledge about the surviving sources, it has to be said that the OBSP are probably the best accounts we shall ever have of what transpired in ordinary English criminal courts before the later eighteenth century."

4. See Langbein, Ryder Sources, supra note 2, at 12–14; the reporter Thomas Gurney, appointed in 1748, remained until 1770 when he was succeeded by his son.

5. Michael McKeon points out that criminal biography faced both ways in apparently supporting civil authority while offering us modes of swerving away from it:

> "Authority" in the criminal biography, much more thoroughly than in the picaresque narrative, is an ambiguous conflation of divine and positive law, so that the unarguable will of God is burdened with the weight of what in other contexts might well be recognized as its antithesis, its deforming secularization. It would not be surprising if readers of narratives and spectators at executions alike were distracted at least momentarily by the complacency of an identification—between God and the magistrate, divine decree and its human accommodation—which recent history had rendered extremely problematic.

Michael McKeon, The Origins of the English Novel, 1600–1740, at 98 (1987).

6. See Peter Linebaugh, "The Ordinary of Newgate and His Account," in Crime in England, 1550–1800, at 246–69 (J. S. Cockburn ed., 1977).

7. The Ordinary's Account was, however, at first a highly unofficial publication, but it increased in size, price, and respectability in the first twenty years of the eighteenth century: "From little more than a broadside, it changed over twenty years to become a small pamphlet, a change that reflected both its consolidation as a specific genre and its acceptance by City officials" (Linebaugh, id. at 247). The semiofficial status accorded the Ordinary's Account was presumably achieved largely through the frequency of overtly moralizing pronouncements, as well as in a general edifying adherence to the function of Providence. Yet, presumably in order to make the works sell, the ordinaries incorporated a variety of other tones, and even of narrative lines. So too did other authors of stories of crime, as Faller shows in Turned to Account, supra note 1.

8. All of the quotations from the Old Bailey Sessions Papers in this article are taken from the OBSP of 1744; the original publications treat dating according to the Old Style of calendar, whereby a new year begins on 21 March, so that January 1744 is to be called January 1743/4. Papers were printed in "numbers," a number sometimes appearing in two parts, as does the January (1973/4) number from which this quotation is taken. The numbering of pages was consecutive throughout the entire year, a device that encouraged the reader to purchase all the installments and thus make up the complete "book."

9. See Margaret Anne Doody, "The Law, the Page and the Body of Woman: Murder

and Murderesses in the Age of Johnson," in *The Age of Johnson* 127–60 (Paul J. Korshin ed., 1987); and Margaret Anne Doody, " 'Those Eyes Are Made So Killing': Eighteenth-Century Murderesses and the Law," 46 (1) *Princeton U. Lib. Chron.* 49–80 (1984).

10. Langbein, *Ryder Sources, supra* note 2, at 24–25. Langbein succinctly puts the case for the reliability of the OBSP: "If the OBSP report says something happened, it did; if the OBSP report does not say it happened, it still may have. Legal historical researchers can rely upon the OBSP, but not for negative inferences." *Id.* at 25.

11. *See* Roy Porter, "Power, Politics, and the Law," ch. 3 in Roy Porter, *English Society in the Eighteenth Century* 113–58 (1982). The increase in the number of crimes to which the death penalty could be applied during the eighteenth century has been usefully summarized by Leon Radzinowicz; see Leon Radzinowicz, *A History of English Criminal Law and Its Administration from 1750: Vol. I. The Movement for Reform, 1750–1833*, at 4–5, 7 (1948–68).

The administration of the death penalty in eighteenth-century England for crimes involving property has been the subject of strong controversy as well as increased investigation since the publication of Douglas Hay's "Property, Authority, and the Criminal Law" in *Albion's Fatal Tree* 17–63 (Douglas Hay, Peter Linebaugh, & E. P. Thompson eds., 1975) and E. P. Thompson's *Whigs and Hunters: The Origin of the Black Act* (1975). Thompson comments that the passage of the notorious "Black Act" of 1723 "suggests . . . some complicity between the ascendancy of the Hanoverian Whigs and the ascendancy of the gallows." Thompson, *supra* at 23. John Langbein argues against Hay's and Thompson's Marxist position in "*Albion's Fatal Flaws*," 98 *Past and Present* 96–120 (1983). Lincoln Faller is interested in the cases in which the criminal was spared, even repeatedly spared by juries and judges who ought to have sent them to the gallows if purely class interests were at stake; Faller argues that it was one thing for Parliament to make the statutes and another for judges and juries to apply them, and points to the numerous defenses of capital punishment of theft as indicating some degree of doubt rather than utter certainty (*see* Faller, *supra* note 1, at 150–67). Faller is interested in the mythmaking that made it tolerable for society to deal with criminals and punishment. The discussion has culminated (at least at present) in the publication of Peter Linebaugh's long-awaited and well-researched book, *The London Hanged* (1992). Linebaugh investigates the background and contexts of the laws and their application, while never letting us forget that it was real men and women, with their own histories and experiences, who were hanged at Tyburn.

12. In *Amelia*, Henry Fielding's novel of 1752, the hero William Booth and his wife, who are living in much reduced circumstances, are robbed of clothing by their young servant maid Betty. Booth discovers her "in a tattered Silk Gown, stepping out of a shop in Monmouth-Street," seizes her, and has her taken before a Justice of the Peace. Betty confesses: "I took no more than two Shifts of Madam's, and I pawned them for five shillings, which I gave for the Gown that's upon my Back." Booth is disgusted to find how easy it is for the pawnbroker to carry on "the Trade of receiving stolen Goods . . . with Impunity." Booth also wishes the servant punished for robbery, and the shifts are worth thirty shillings, but when he accuses her of "a felonious Breach of

Trust," the magistrate points out that "Breach of Trust is no Crime in our Law unless it be in a Servant; and then the Act of Parliament requires the Goods taken to be of the Value of forty Shillings." Booth's chagrin at finding neither the pawnbroker nor the girl will suffer evidently reflects Fielding's desire for a change in the law toward more severity; one must conclude that both Booth and the author think the little servant girl ought to be hanged. See Henry Fielding, Amelia 483–85 (Martin C. Battestin ed., Wesleyan University Press, 1983) (1752).

13. Much of our contemporary commentary on the place of women's work in the Restoration and eighteenth century ultimately rests upon Alice Clark's pioneering study of 1919, Working Life of Women in the Seventeenth Century (reprinted, Routledge and Kegan Paul, 1982). Clark pointed out how adversely women were affected economically by the change from the old female-producer-centered, rural world to the new urban and commercial world. Advancing capitalism took over productive work that was traditionally female (e.g., brewing, perfume-making), and women were brought more and more into the home, which became less and less of a workplace. Subsequent studies have emphasized the development of women of all classes into consumers rather than producers; even the wives of mechanics and petty tradesmen became expected to stay within the home, while working-class women turned into servants (or prostitutes). Whig historians such as Lawrence Stone insist on seeing a continual progress in comfort and sensibility for eighteenth-century women (see Lawrence Stone, The Family, Sex and Marriage in England 1500–1800 (1977)), but feminist scholars on the whole see an economic and social process of deprivation accompanying the domestication of women and the increasing feminization and nonproductivity of the home. See, e.g., Jane Spencer, The Rise of the Woman Novelist from Aphra Behn to Jane Austen 11–22 (1986); and Nancy Armstrong, Desire and Domestic Fiction: A Political History of the Novel 59–95 (1987). The transformation from rural producer to urban consumer could be experienced quite quickly by individuals such as Richardson's Clarissa in fiction and Hester Lynch Thrale in fact; yet the social change also happened slowly, over several generations; Jane Austen, literally a spinster, had and used a spinning wheel. Historians lamenting the loss of work involved in the change from rural to urban or urbanized life may overlook the multitude of working opportunities the urban world offers to females at the lower end of the social scale.

GUILTY IN LAW,

IMPLAUSIBLE IN FICTION

Jurisprudential and Literary Narratives in the Case of Mary Blandy, Parricide, 1752

Susan Sage Heinzelman

This essay investigates a symptomatic critical moment in mid-eighteenth-century England when cultural discourses contended one with another for the privilege of being able to speak with the greatest verisimilitude about "what really happened." With Alexander Welsh, I believe that there are "excellent reasons for consulting the history of the common law . . . [in] assessing verbal representations of reality. . . . Since the eighteenth century, at least two desiderata have stood out at trials at law: an ideal of truthfulness and an effective means of representation."[1] Those two desiderata at law can also account for the nature of the critical attention focused in the late seventeenth and early eighteenth centuries on a newly emerging form of the "verbal representation of reality"— the novel. It was precisely this anxiety over the fictionality of the novel's reality and its effectiveness in representing the truth that troubled critics, theologians, and moral philosophers. The tension between the two terms "verisimilitude" and "mimesis" was intensified when the novelist was a woman. However popular with the reading public writers like Aphra Behn, Eliza Haywood, Delariviére Manley, or Charlotte Lennox were, they always stood suspect, as women, in their capacity to authorize faithful representations of reality. The same suspicion that accompanied the texts produced by women writers also attended women witnesses in courts of law, the degree of suspicion measured precisely by the legal, moral, and epistemological value of the case.

Up to the late seventeenth and early eighteenth century, the narratives of law, theology, natural philosophy, and literature were complexly interwoven, each borrowing from the other.[2] Such interweaving produces the genre mixing that is one of the particular characteristics of early-eighteenth-century discourse: fictions that claim to tell the truth; factually based biographies and autobiographies that borrow plot and character from French romances; scientific discourses that are inseparable from theological treatises; and travel narratives that are part allegory, part scientific discourse, part theological treatise. By mid-eighteenth century, however, there had come into being a "modern" sensibility that generally considered the law to be objective, factually based, and enabled by logic and rules, but considered literature to be subjective, located in the unreal (and therefore potentially untrue) world of the imagination, and enabled by emotion and image.

Focusing on a trial for parricide held in 1752, this essay theorizes that, by the mid-eighteenth century, certain kinds of narratives—jurisprudential, theological, historical—were invested with the authority to make inquiries and render judgments about truth and lies; while other narratives—novels, biographies, autobiographies—were suspect precisely because, wittingly or not, they questioned the cause-and-effect relationships upon which, to a large extent, authoritative narratives had staked their power. What was circumstance to the novel, the biography, and the autobiography was circumstantial evidence to the law. This essay also discusses the way in which the values associated with the two categories of narrative are gendered by the uses to which those stories are put and the functions they claim to serve in cultural representation.

Mary Blandy's trial for parricide generated enormous public interest, with over thirty contemporary pamphlets produced analyzing her character and the trial. I will focus on three versions of the case: the quasi-legal account in the form of a reported trial narrative—The Trial of Mary Blandy, a compilation of public records by William Roughead; a theological-jurisprudential-literary account, in the form of a "history" authored by magistrate-novelist Henry Fielding—Examples of the Interposition of Providence in the Detection and Punishment of Murder (1752); and an autobiographical account, in the form of an apologia by Mary Blandy, written in her Oxford gaol cell immediately before her death—Miss Blandy's Own Account of the Affair Between Her and Mr. Cranstoun (1752).[3] First, however, I will briefly retell the story leading up to the trial, relying on the version published in the Notable British Trial series, edited by William Roughead.[4]

The Story of What Really Happened

On April 6th 1752, Mary Blandy was hung for murdering her father, a lawyer of Henley-upon-Thames in Oxfordshire. She was charged with poisoning him by feeding him a "love philtre" under the instructions of her lover, Mr. Cranstoun, who claimed he wished to encourage Mr. Blandy's consent to their marriage. The love philtre was actually arsenic, a fact that Mary denied knowing. Mr. Cranstoun, who was already married under Scottish law to a Roman Catholic of a Jacobite family, was apparently attracted to Mary by the rumor that her father would settle £10,000 on her at marriage. The source of the rumor was actually Mary Blandy's own father, Francis Blandy, who hoped thereby to attract the "right" sort of man for his daughter. Leading for the Crown at Blandy's trial, Mr. Bathurst, who became Lord Chancellor in 1771, excused Mr. Blandy's deception as "a pious fraud."[5]

Relying on contemporary characterizations of the Blandy family, Roughead reproduces with remarkable fidelity the gendered representations of behavior flourishing in the mid-eighteenth century. Mary Blandy's mother, for example, is described as "'an emblem of chastity and virtue; graceful in person, in mind elevated.'"[6] Mary Blandy, on the other hand, although raised by her mother in "the principles of religion and piety,"[7] shows an unusual fondness for reading, "a taste sufficiently remarkable in a girl of her day."[8] This somewhat unhealthy interest in achievements inappropriate for her gender finds its public expression in Mary's marred physical beauty: "[H]er biographers," notes Roughead, "are significantly silent regarding her physical attractions. Like many a contemporary 'toast,' she had suffered the indignity of the smallpox" (see Figure 1).[9] Offsetting Mary's physical disadvantages, however, was the prospect of a dowry of £10,000—the "pious fraud" perpetrated by her father, who alone knew that his wealth could not sustain such a sum. (In fact, when he died, he was worth less than £4,000.)

Francis Blandy hawked his daughter on the marriage market in Henley and spent a season at Bath; repeatedly Mary was wooed and repeatedly her father prevented marriage because the "catch" was insufficiently wealthy or prestigious to satisfy his social ambitions. Eventually, however, a certain captain in the army won Mr. Blandy's approval and, in 1746, Mary became engaged. Unfortunately, the captain's regiment was soon ordered abroad and, as Roughead has it, "the stern summons of duty broke in upon. . . [Mary's] temporary Eden. . . ."[10] Finally, through her father's business relationship with Lord Mark Kerr, the twenty-six-year-old Mary met Captain the Hon. William Henry Cranstoun, grandnephew of Lord Mark, who had taken a house at Henley named "The Paradise," an irony that neither the prosecuting attorney nor Roughead misses in characterizing Mary as Eve and Cranstoun as the serpent.

The thirty-two-year-old Captain Cranstoun appeared to be as physically unprepossessing as he was morally ugly (see Figure 2). Cunning and lecherous, he had fought as a First-Lieutenant of Sir Andrew Agnew's regiment of marines with the English in the 1745 rebellion and was in Henley raising

Figure 1. Miss Mary Blandy. Reprinted from William Roughead, *The Trial of Mary Blandy* (1914), facing p. 38.

volunteers to fill up the Hanoverian lines depleted by the Scottish rebels. Captain Cranstoun was the fifth of seven sons of a Scots peer, William, fifth Lord Cranstoun, and his wife, Lady Jane Kerr, eldest daughter of William, second Marquis of Lothian. Cranstoun's father had died in 1727 and his eldest son, James, had become the sixth Lord Cranstoun.

Mr. Blandy apparently encouraged Cranstoun's attentions to Mary, but it was not until the following summer, in 1747, that Cranstoun simultaneously declared himself to Mary and told her of a Scottish lady who was. he said, falsely claiming to be his wife. Accepted provisionally by Mary, Cranstoun formally asked Francis Blandy for his daughter's hand in marriage, telling him nothing of the "action of declarator of marriage" that had been raised by his wife against him in the Commissary Court at Edinburgh in October 1746.

Unfortunately for Cranstoun, his great-uncle, Lord Mark, more particular about such matters than the nephew, wrote to Francis Blandy informing him that his daughter's fiancé already had a wife and a child in Scotland.

Figure 2. Captain William Henry Cranstoun with his pompous funeral procession in Flanders. Reprinted from William Roughead, *The Trial of Mary Blandy* (1914), facing p. 190.

On May 22nd, 1744, Cranstoun had privately married Anne, daughter of David Murray, merchant of Leith, a son of the late Sir David Murray of Stanhope, Baronet. After living with his wife "in a private manner" for six months, Cranstoun returned to his regiment in London, with the marriage still unpublished for fear that, as the lady was of a Roman Catholic and Jacobite family, Cranstoun's chances for promotion might be prejudiced. On February 19th, 1745, Anne Cranstoun gave birth to a daughter. Despite having already privately acknowledged to both her family and his own that he was married to Anne Murray and that the child was indeed his daughter, Cranstoun disavowed his marriage—rather conveniently given that the Murrays had supported Prince Charlie and that Anne's brother, the current Baronet of Stanhope, had been taken prisoner at Culloden, tried at Carlisle, and was under sentence of death. (That sentence was later commuted to transportation.) Cranstoun claimed that Anne Murray had been his mistress and that, although he had promised to marry her if she would become a Presbyterian, her refusal to convert freed him from his engagement. He had, he said, pretended to be married merely to save her honor before her family.

Roughead suggests that Mary Blandy believed Cranstoun because she was desperate that she would be left an old maid and that Francis and Mrs. Blandy were blinded by the aristocratic connections of their putative son-in-law. Mr. Blandy "in the vanity of his heart ha[d] been heard to say, *he hoped still to live to be a grandfather to a lord.*"[11] Certainly Cranstoun's story, regardless of the light into which it cast him, was common enough to be believable. Many young women had been seduced and ruined by the ruse of a "secret marriage," and Cranstoun's excuses would have confirmed for the Blandys that they were dealing with a man of fashion (see Figure 3).[12]

Cranstoun remained with the Blandys until the spring of 1748, five or six months from the time he had asked for permission to marry Mary. Then he left, on regimental business, for London and Southampton. While Cranstoun was absent, Mrs. Blandy fell ill; only the arrival of Cranstoun was able to restore her to health. He remained with the Blandys for another six months, at their expense, until his regiment broke at Southampton, when he set out for London. By this time, Mr. Blandy was considerably less enthusiastic about Cranstoun's courtship of Mary; after all, he had received directly from Cranstoun's wife a copy of the Commissary Court's decree in her favor.[13] For the moment, however, Cranstoun seemed able to persuade Mr. Blandy that an appeal to the Court of Session would be successful in reversing the judgment against him.

In 1749, a few months after Cranstoun left the Blandys, Mary went with her mother to London to seek medical advice about Mrs. Blandy's health, staying in Doctor's Commons with Mrs. Blandy's brother, Sergeant Henry Stevens. With extraordinary nerve, Cranstoun proposed a secret marriage, perhaps hoping that the English courts would weigh more heavily in any determination of legitimacy than the Scottish courts. In his own account of the Blandy affair, Cranstoun claims that the marriage indeed took place at Mary's request, " 'lest he should be ungrateful to her after so material an intimacy.' "[14] Despite the medical attention she received in London, Mrs. Blandy died on September 30th, 1749, believing until the end in Cranstoun's goodness and sincerity. She begged her husband not to oppose the match after

Figure 3. Captain Cranstoun and Miss Blandy, with Mary's father. Reprinted from William Roughead, *The Trial of Mary Blandy* (1914).

her death. Mary had to borrow £40 from her godmother, Mrs. Mountenoy, so that Cranstoun could come down to Henley for the funeral. Mary forwarded Cranstoun £15 so that he could pay off the bailiffs who had kept him confined to his lodgings in London. He remained with Mary and her father for several weeks; for the first time, Cranstoun introduced Mary to the idea that Mr. Blandy's rancor against him might be softened with a love powder he could obtain from "the famous Mrs. Morgan" of Scotland.[15]

At the appearance of a dunning letter, Cranstoun, borrowing another £15 from Mary, set off to London to pay his debts. He did not return until the following August in 1750, almost a year after he had left Henley, and only then after Mr. Blandy reluctantly agreed to his visit. Without any progress in his Scottish affairs, Cranstoun was made to feel decidedly unwelcome by Mary's father. By way of proving the potency of the "love powder," some of which Cranstoun had brought with him, he apparently introduced a little into Blandy's tea and miraculously transformed his hostility into amity. Mr. Blandy appeared to suffer no ill effects.

Francis Blandy was not the only one who needed to be mollified: while at Henley, Cranstoun confessed to Mary that he had a daughter by a Miss Capel a year before he had met her. Mary forgave him and hoped he had repented his follies. It was harder for her to forgive him, a day or so afterwards, when she discovered a packet of letters among his clothes from a woman he was keeping in London, presumably supported partially by Mary Blandy's own loan to Cranstoun. Somehow Cranstoun was able to persuade Mary to forgive him again, invoking her own mother's words "not to give him up." Soon after, Cranstoun's mother became dangerously ill in Scotland and, once again relying on Mary for his solvency, Cranstoun set off to see her. It was November 1750; and it was the last time that Mary saw Cranstoun.

Determined to end the affair with Cranstoun, Francis Blandy ordered Mary to write to him telling him not to show his face until he had settled his marital difficulties. Unknown to Mr. Blandy, Cranstoun's appeal against the Commissary Court's decision had been dismissed and he was barred from marrying Mary while his wife lived. Some time in the spring of 1751, Cranstoun sent Mary a supply of Mrs. Morgan's powder, along with some Scotch pebbles, which were highly polished stones and a hot fashion item. Despite doubt about the powder and its effects upon her father's health, Mary mixed some in his tea. Apparently Mr. Blandy took some of the tea but on at least two occasions he left it untouched, unfortunately for one of the maidservants, Susan Gunnell, and an old charwoman, Ann Emmet, both of whom became violently ill after drinking Mr. Blandy's leftover tea. According to the evidence introduced at her trial, Cranstoun wrote to Mary advising her that when she wished to "clean her pebbles," she should put the powder in something of substance so that it should not " 'swim a-top of the water . . . I am afraid it will be too weak to take off their rust, or at least it will take too long a time.' "[16]

On Monday, the 5th of August, Francis Blandy ate some gruel prepared for him on Mary's instructions; on Tuesday, the 6th, he was seriously ill, in agony and vomiting, and the Henley apothecary, Mr. Norton, was summoned. That evening, he ate some more gruel and was again struck down with vomiting and intense pain. Once again, Ann Emmet finished off Mr. Blandy's uneaten food—this time, the gruel—and once again, she became seriously ill. Mary Blandy's concern over the gruel and her insistence that no fresh gruel be made alerted the maidservants. Susan Gunnell tasted the white gritty "settlement" at the bottom of the pan; immediately, the pan was locked in a closet overnight and, on Thursday, August 8th, Susan Gunnell carried the pan to Mrs. Mountenoy, who sent for the apothecary, Mr. Norton, who removed the pan for further examination.[17]

Mrs. Blandy's brother, the Rev. Mr. Stevens of Fawley, arrived on Friday the 9th and Susan Gunnell told him of her suspicions. She was advised to tell Mr. Blandy all she knew, which she did the next morning. Apparently, Mr. Blandy did not question the possibility that his daughter might be trying to murder him, wondering only where she might have obtained the poison. According to the testimony of Susan Gunnell and Betty Binfield, Mr. Blandy on several occasions that morning attempted to force a confession from Mary. In fact, Mary was seen throwing letters (and, it turned out, what was left of the powder) onto the fire. After she left the kitchen, the maids rescued from the fire a folded paper packet with the words "The powder to clean pebbles with" inscribed, apparently, in Cranstoun's handwriting. There was still some powder left, and this they gave to Mr. Norton when he visited later that day.

Mary insisted that a famous physician, Dr. Anthony Addington of Reading, be sent for, and he arrived at midnight. Confirming Mr. Norton's diagnosis that Mr. Blandy was suffering from the effects of poison, Dr. Addington warned Mary that her reputation and life would be in jeopardy if her father died. Mary's response, according to the prosecution, was to write to Cranstoun on August 11th, warning him of the danger:

Dear Willy:

> My father is so bad, that I have only time to tell you, that if you do not hear from me soon again, don't be frightened. I am better myself. Lest any accident should happen to your letters, take care what you write. My sincere compliments. I am ever yours.[18]

The letter was intercepted and shown to Mr. Norton, who read it to Mr. Blandy, who apparently remarked: " 'Poor love-sick girl! What will not a woman do for the man she loves?' " [19]

Confronted with the evidence of her complicity, Mary begged her father's forgiveness, although maintaining her innocence of any knowledge of the effects of the powder. There followed, according to the testimony of the servants, a scene of such daughterly repentance and paternal forgiveness to rival the sentimental romances of the day. Mr. Blandy died three days later, on Wednesday, August 14th. By this time, Mary had been confined to her room, guarded by Edward Herne, parish clerk of Henley.

The next morning, Mr. Herne left Mary unguarded when he went to dig a grave for Mr. Blandy. Wearing nothing but a half-sack and petticoat without a hoop, Mary ran out of the house. Her dress and manner quickly attracted an angry crowd and she was forced to take refuge in the Angel Inn. She was escorted home by Mr. Alderman Fisher, one of the jurymen summoned to the inquest. On Friday, the 16th of August, the jury found that Francis Blandy was poisoned and that Mary Blandy "did poison and murder him." The constable was issued a warrant to conduct Mary to the county jail at Oxford until her trial. That night Mr. Blandy was buried; Norton, the apothecary, Littleton, his clerk, and Harman, his footman, were the only mourners.

Apparently, Mary's alleged murder of her father posed such a threat to the stability of the social and political order that the Secretary of State, the Duke of Newcastle, solicited an opinion from Lord Chancellor Hardwicke on the question of whether the Crown would assume the cost of prosecuting Mary Blandy because her relatives (the parties that would normally prosecute) were unable to undertake the burden. The Lord Chancellor heartily endorsed the Crown's assumption of the cost of prosecution, asserting that "it would be a Reproach to the King's Justice, and I am sure would create the justest concern & Indignation in His Majesty's own mind, if such an atrocious Crime of Poisoning and Parricide should escape unpunished . . . ."[20] His letter concludes: "Forgive me for adding one thing more that it should be pointed out to Mr. Attorney [the Attorney General, Sir Dudley Ryder] to consider whether the crime of the Daughter, who, as I apprehend, lived with & was maintained by her Father, may not be Petty Treason."[21]

Petty treason, "which was an aggravated form of murder," consisted of one of the following three acts: "homicide of a master by his servant; of a husband by his wife; and of an ecclesiastical superior by his inferior."[22] It was also judged petty treason for "a son to kill his father, or master, to whom he was bound apprentice, or by whom he was maintained, or to whom he rendered any necessary service, though he received no wages."[23] It is unclear exactly under what category the Secretary of State would have Mary Blandy charged with petty treason, but clearly her dependence upon her father as a servant is dependent on her master, as a bound apprentice is dependent on his employer, is sufficient warrant for the charge. She had abused, to use Blackstone's language in his commentary on this category, "a natural, a civil or even a spiritual relation" that subsists between a superior and an inferior, and had forgotten all "obligations of duty, subjection, and allegiance."[24] A crime against the familial patriarch thus constituted a "petticoat" version of a crime against the King and his State. The " 'Noblemen and Gentlemen in the Neighborhood of Henley-upon-Thames, and the Mayor and principal

Figure 4. Miss Mary Blandy, with the scene of her execution. Reprinted from William Roughead, *The Trial of Mary Blandy* (1914), facing p. 130.

Magistrates of that Town'." thanked his grace, the Duke of Newcastle, "for King George's 'Paternal Goodness' in directing that the prisoner should be prosecuted at 'His Majesty's Expense,' stating that no endeavor would be wanting on their part to render that prosecution successful."[25]

On March 2nd, 1752, the grand jury for the county of Oxford found a true bill against Mary Blandy. Because the Oxford Town Hall, where the

Assizes were normally held, was being rebuilt, the trial was moved to the hall of the Divinity School at the University. On March 3rd, 1752, Mary Blandy appeared to answer the charges against her. The judges were the Hon. Heneage Legge and Sir Sidney Stafford Smythe, two of the Barons of His Majesty's Court of Exchequer. Including the Hon. Mr Bathurst, there were five Crown lawyers. Mary Blandy was defended by Mr. Ford and two assistants. The trial lasted thirteen hours, during which the prosecution called medical witnesses and servants in the Blandy household to testify to Mary's attendance on her father and her manner of cursing him when he was absent. The defense lawyer, who was unable under the rules of the court to offer a summation to the jury, called upon Mary to address the jury in her own defense. She complained of misrepresentations and of unfair and damning publicity before the trial had begun; moreover, she insisted that she had not known of the effect of the powder on her father.

The defense now called its own witnesses, who testified that the evidence of the servants was not to be trusted because they had a grudge against Mary. Other character witnesses asserted that they had never seen anything but filial duty from Mary to her father. Mr. Bathurst had the last word, refuting many of the defense's assertions of Mary's innocence. Judge Baron Legge gave the charge to the jury: " 'What you are to try is reduced to this single question, whether the prisoner, at the time she gave it to her father, knew that it was poison, and what effect it would have?' " [26] Without retiring, the jury consulted for five minutes and returned a verdict of guilty. She was allowed six weeks to settle her affairs before her hanging, which took place in Oxford on April 6, 1752 (see Figure 4).

Mary's lover, Cranstoun, fled to France where he stayed with a kinswoman, Mrs. Ross, and published pamphlets that rather ungallantly laid the blame for Blandy's death on Mary. It hardly mattered: by December of 1752, Cranstoun also was dead. On his deathbed, he not only converted to Roman Catholicism but also arranged for a pretentious and elaborate funeral, complete with procession.

The Trial Account

Even before Mary Blandy entered the court, her crime had been officially represented as a theological and jurisprudential narrative of filial betrayal. Mary's criminality is contextualized by political, social, and mythical narratives that specifically gender her crime and it is exactly through those narratives that she is reassigned to her properly dutiful place. In his opening statement, Henry Bathurst, Solicitor-General, suggests how the natural structures of affiliation—familial, theological, and jurisprudential—must be marshalled against the threat of Mary Blandy's undaughterly, unnatural, and finally, unnarratable behavior:

> [W]hat will be thought of one who has murdered her own father? who has designedly done the greatest of all human injuries to him from whom she received the first and greatest of all human benefits? who has wickedly taken away his life to whom she stands indebted for life? who has deliberately destroyed, in his old age, him by whose care and tenderness she was protected in her helpless infancy? who has impiously shut her ears against the loud voice of nature and of God, which bid her honor her father, and, instead of honoring him, has murdered him? [27]

The piling up of rhetorical questions amounts to an almost pathological refusal to narrate events, and joined with the increasing pitch of disbelief, constructs an accusation for which there is only one response: a confession of guilt. Emphasizing the social and political consequences of a crime whose story cannot be told, Mr. Serjeant Hayward, Crown prosecutor, directs his comments specifically to the future lawyers and political leaders of the country in the courtroom—Oxford University students:

> But you, young gentleman of this University, I particularly beg your attention, earnestly beseeching you to guard against the first approaches and temptations to vice. . . . Learn hence the dreadful consequences of disobedience to parents; and know also that the same mischief in all probability may happen to such who obstinately disregard, neglect, and despise the advice of those persons who have the charge and care of their education; of governors likewise, and of magistrates, and of all others who are put in authority over them.[28]

In this argument, the prosecutor presents parental disobedience as the prime cause of social instability, invoking both the first crime of filial disobedience—Eve against God—and also calling upon the pervasive political threat to a stable society manifest in both internal and foreign unrest.[29] The logic of this narrative of filial disobedience also parallels the logic of circumstantial evidence, which the prosecution will allude to later in the trial. Specifically, there is an inevitability in the train of circumstances that begins with the first act of disobedience and ends in crime; and it is this inevitability itself that convinces the audience of the narrative's truthfulness. The rhetoric of disobedience and punishment moves in a widening circle outward from the familiar to encompass the network of personal, social, and political bonds: from parents to teachers; to governors and magistrates; and finally, "all others" in authority. The historical and political range of the prosecution's rhetoric, the paradigmatic nature of the story of Blandy's crime, is suggested in the paraphrase of the trial offered to the readers of *Gentleman's Magazine*:

> Posterity may know and blush, that such a monster in cruelty had existed in a female form, who, without provocation, had cooly [sic] and deliberately meditated and accomplished the destruction of that life which had given her being; and that children in after ages may be warned by her example, that how secretly soever such deeds of darkness are devised and carried on, they are always open to the all-seeing eye of heaven, whose providence seldom fails to bring them to the knowledge of men.[30]

The "all-seeing eye of heaven," the final Author/Authority providentially inscribes the crime of the accused in such a way that it becomes "the knowledge of men," that is, the truth. The divine Author thus provides the human author and his all-male audience (the judge and jury) with a narrative that has intention, purpose, and most importantly, innocence. The accused, however, acts without motive, "without provocation"; for what provocation could exist that would drive a daughter to kill her father? Thus her untruth, her deceit, and her guilt are doubly condemned—as treason and as motiveless treason—and no narrative can possibly vindicate her because any story that she might tell is ipso facto uninspired and treacherous.

The prosecutor's legal narrative imitates the divine narrative in which God reveals the truth to men and such a narrative always uncovers the "hidden work of darkness."[31] The trial account is informed not only by the individual circumstances of Blandy's trial, but by the general condition of all women arraigned at the bar of, not merely human, but divine justice. Thus God's intervention in human affairs generates the true and single narrative of human history, one in which Eve embodies female deceit, just as "[d]ivine justice [generates] the normative model for human justice."[32] Such is the persuasive power of invoking God as witness for the prosecution against Mary Blandy: the prosecution avails itself of a narrative that is invested with all the authority that theological-jurisprudential rhetoric contains. Such divine and immediate Authorship is invoked again when Mr. Bathurst praised the clarity with which "Providence ha[d] interposed to bring [Mary Blandy] to . . . trial that she m[ight] suffer the consequence."[33] He was especially grateful for the interposing hand of God, which apparently had reached into a fire and snatched, unburnt, the paper containing the arsenic powder, and a potentially compromising letter from Cranstoun to Mary Blandy. Because poison is "a deed of darkness," one of the most difficult of crimes to prove by the evidence of the senses, and thus one of the most likely to elude the eye of the court, the unseen hand of God must uncover what the unseen hand of the accused has already wrought. And if God's intervention uncovers physical evidence, so much more convincing is the belief in the accused's guilt than hearsay or eyewitness accounts, which rely upon the frailty of the human memory and the inconsistency of human relationships.

God's Providential intervention in human affairs, by which the trace of arsenic is preserved, is juridically represented as circumstantial evidence; in fact, the trial of Mary Blandy is one of the first to use this term in its specifically modern legal sense.[34] Such a development is consistent with the increasing reliance upon trial by jury: a development that requires a coherent inferential theory of evidence that would replace the visible and conclusive evidence of trial by ordeal, or would outweigh the oath swearing by witnesses in trial by compurgation. Moreover, the modern conception of the jury, unlike its medieval equivalents, relies upon the juryman's ignorance of the facts of the crime. He is not there to tell what he knows about the facts of the case; instead, he is there to be persuaded of the guilt or innocence of the accused, a persuasion that must rely to an unprecedented extent upon verbal representations by witnesses of "what really happened." What cannot be seen, here and now in the courtroom, must be inferred; and to begin that process, there must be at least one irrefutable fact that generates the chain of inference linking apparently unconnected circumstances into a causal sequence. That one irrefutable fact or circumstance is the site of God's intervention; thus, it is the origin of the narrative that leads inevitably to discovery, accusation, conviction, and punishment. The relevant legal test is not the "likeliness" of an event; rather it is how well that particular event can be accommodated in a chain of events, and how inevitable that chain of cause and effect seems to be. Another way of saying this is: What counts as relevant circumstantial evidence is its capacity to be narrativized, not its capacity to imitate lived experience.

Alexander Welsh argues that this jurisprudential shift in the eighteenth century from evidence perceived as testimony to evidence as evidentiary facts corresponds to that in theology where the "testimony of singular revelations in miracle or Scripture" was gradually replaced with the inferential providential revelation of natural religion, the evidence of the senses.[35] In Mr. Serjeant Hayward's explanation of the concept of circumstantial evidence, we can find traces of this earlier sense of evidence as testimony manifest in revelation, as well as the developing modern conception of the inferential legal narrative:

> Experience has taught us that in many cases a single fact may be supported by false testimony, but where it is attended with a train of circumstances that cannot be invented (had they never happened), such a fact will always be made out to the satisfaction of a jury by the concurring assistance of circumstantial evidence. *Because circumstances that tally one with another are above*

human contrivance. And especially such as naturally arise in their order from the first contrivance of a scheme to the fatal execution of it.[36]

In the narrative of Mary Blandy's criminality, circumstantial evidence takes on the power and conviction of Providence. The jurisprudential narrative mirrors and sanctions the seemingly inevitable and thus totalizing logic of the Judeo-Christian narrative: "[C]ircumstances that tally one with another are beyond human contrivance," claims Mr. Serjeant Hayward. Or as Hayden White says of the narrative of history, " 'the events seem to tell themselves.' "[37]

This seeming inevitability and connectedness pervasive in juridical, theological, and historical narratives must be distinguished from the "*absurd and unaccountable . . . actions*"[38] that occur in seventeenth- and eighteenth-century romances or novels. Nevertheless, the novel can imitate that natural and divine ordering of events upon which eighteenth-century jurisprudence relies as its model for revealing the truth. And it is precisely this capacity to imitate authoritative, inevitable sequentiality that causes so much cultural anxiety: if fiction can be made to seem like the truth, how will the uneducated and the ill-informed know the difference between the truth and an imitation of that truth? The novel trespasses upon the moral and epistemological territory previously reserved for the law and the church; furthermore, the novel radically destabilizes conventional ideas of what constitutes logical and probable cause, as well as calling into question the way in which traditional moral philosophy, in both its legal and theological aspects, represents the relationship between man and God.

The trial account returns again and again to this question of narrativity and the manner in which the crime can be properly and truthfully narrated only within a theological-jurisprudential rhetoric and form to which, by definition, only those who can speak in court with authority (the lawyers and the judges) have access. Having established the prime cause as filial disobedience, an original cause that is sanctified by the intervention of God in the discovery of the wicked act of poisoning, the prosecution repeatedly shapes the testimony of its witnesses to reflect this originary and originating sin. The defense, likewise, reinforces this narrative of the events by bringing witnesses who dispute the reports of Mary's disobedience; thus the defense, in effect, confirms that there is no more powerful or more persuasive site than this to begin the story of a daughter's criminality.

Mary Blandy's own account of the events leading up to her father's death does not, however, follow the model proposed by the prosecution and defense; and it is, in part, precisely because she cannot displace that master narrative that she is unconvincing. Furthermore, she is already condemned as guilty even before she details her defense because she adopts a form and rhetoric that cannot speak of innocence, no matter what its content—the form of the novel. Before moving to Mary Blandy's apologia, however, I would like to look at a text that appears to position itself, generically, midway between the semiofficial legal version and the fictional histories published by the popular press, although structurally and rhetorically it aligns itself with the authority of the courts: Henry Fielding's *Examples of the Interposition of Providence in the Detection and Punishment of Murder* (1752).

Providential Intervention as Novelistic Narrative

Like the prosecutor's narrative, Fielding adopts an eschatological structure that reaches back to the first familial slaughter of Abel by Cain, and forward to the final day of judgment. Like the prosecutor's narrative, Fielding's exemplary history assumes what appears to be a natural, rather than an invented or contrived structure. Fielding achieves this effect, in part, by directly claiming authorship only for the introduction to and conclusion of the narrative, as if the intervening tales, "collected from various authors, antient and modern,"[39] had fallen into their natural and circumstantial order of their own accord. The formal structure of the text thus imitates the apparently natural and circumstantial intervention of God in human affairs. Fielding's text is simultaneously the evidence for providential intervention *and* that intervention itself. Fielding's narrative relies for its rhetorical conviction upon the very circumstantiality of evidence that it sets out to prove exists.

The stories of divine intervention, numbering thirty-three, are taken from classical and Biblical narratives, as well as popular sources. Special attention is given to stories that detail the murder of husbands by wives (usually with the assistance of a lover); wives by husbands, seduced by younger and wealthier women; revengeful mistresses against their errant lovers; and sons against fathers. In all the stories, discovery of the crime is synonymous with conclusive evidence of the guilt of the accused. In other words, divine revelation still constitutes the originating site of narrative, although the witness of human senses—the bloodstained handkerchief, the fevered confession—is brought to bear on what would otherwise be only miraculous. Theologically, we have then both the medieval reliance upon miracles, and the modern reliance upon the evidence of the human senses. Jurisprudentially, medieval conceptions of divine Providence are gradually giving way to the modern concept of circumstantial evidence.

Taken together, however, Fielding's exempla also assume the structural seriality and detail of the novel. Both within the individual tales and throughout the exemplary history as a whole, circumstances pile upon circumstances, making the implausible seem plausible; the merely accidental seem predictive; and the gestural seem concrete. Fielding's text generates that aura of authenticity and authority that the novelist seeks to create.

In the case of Mary Blandy, Fielding must go to some lengths to insist upon the veracity of what otherwise would seem unbelievable. In fact, he is required to overrule the tendency of his readers to disbelief by insisting that to be skeptical of Mary's guilt would be an "obstinate and stubborn infidelity." [40] Using specifically legal rhetoric, he transforms the fabulous and the mysterious into evidence of a providential intervention that cannot be dismissed. To support the truth of divine intervention, he argues:

> the horrors with which the minds of Murderers are particularly haunted; and the most unaccountable, indeed miraculous means, by which the most secret and cunning Murders have often been detected, do abundantly bear testimony: not to mention the many stories of apparitions on this dreadful occasion; some of which have been so well and faithfully attested, that to reject them with a hasty disbelief, seems to argue more of an obstinate and stubborn infidelity, than of a sound and sober reason. [41]

In light of the evidence that Fielding suggests ought to convince his readers of the murderer's guilt—the horrors haunting the mind and the appearance of apparitions—it might seem curious that his account of Mary Blandy's guilt should emphasize exactly the opposite: the visible, nonmysterious evidence of her parricide. It is curious, however, only if one expects a consistent and coherent jurisprudential theory of evidence and narrativity. Fielding's story of Mary Blandy perfectly illustrates the genre mixing produced by the struggle for supremacy between various forms of narrative and various theories of what constitutes evidence. Here the stuff of the fabulous (the *fabula*, the *romans*) competes with the theological and jurisprudential discourses of innocence and guilt, and of plausibility and implausibility. Wearing the hats of both the fabulist and the magistrate, Fielding weaves back and forth between sometimes contradictory cultural representations of truth.

It was, says Fielding, Blandy's "public and . . . barefac'd manner," [42] her visible hatred of her father, her unbecoming behavior and speeches, and her boldness in her guilt that convicted her. Such an account of Blandy's actions not only seems to contradict Fielding's intent in citing Blandy's case, but also contradicts the evidence presented at her trial that asserted that her deed was done in secret and alone, and therefore could not have been discovered without the intervention of God. Fielding further insists that Blandy was so bold as to draw attention to herself in her escape from Oxford gaol and thus was prevented . . . from making use of the money, and things of value in her hands, for her escape . . . And this she might easily have effected, when she walked to Henley, had she gone on in a postchaise to London, instead of returning back to her father's house, which she must know, from what had before passed, would lead to her being taken up, and tried. . . .[43]

In other words, unable to explain Blandy's actions by any "sound and sober reason,"[44] Fielding concludes that her behavior is irrational, the consequence of an original infatuation, and the very fact of her irrationality is proof of her guilt: a circular logic that perfectly reflects the potential circularity of the theory of circumstantial evidence. Because the accused is guilty, then the particular circumstance in the chain of events that retrospectively could be seen to lead to discovery, confession, and conviction becomes evidence of God's intervention in human affairs; and that God was thus required to intervene is, of course, conclusive proof of the accused's guilt.

Finding a cause for Blandy's weird behavior is essential to restoring to order the disorder that her murder has created in the familial and state body—like a gap in the text, Blandy's crime is an ellipsis of meaning; moreover, her crime disrupts the logical and necessary chain of cause and effect that operates in a "sound and sober world" to inscribe God's work. As Fielding explains:

> In the politic, as in the natural body, no disorders ever spring up without a cause; much less do any diseases become epidemical by mere accident. These must all have their causes, and such causes must be adequate to the effects which they produce.[45]

Thus the search for adequate causation, for an explanation of disease in the natural body or disorder in the political body, becomes the equivalent of identifying the moment of the narrative's origin: the point at which Providence intervenes in human affairs is synonymous with the discovery of that chain of inference that leads to an understanding of the adequacy of cause and effect. Narrative, then, in its "true" form—that is, in its historical, theological, and jurisprudential form—renders the logic and site of God's intervention in human affairs visible.

"Delicacy in Distress": Mary Blandy's Apologia

It is precisely Blandy's failure to "render the causes adequate to the effects which they produce"[46] that marks her own narrative as untrue. For *Miss Blandy's Own Account of the Affair Between Her* and Mr. Cranstoun, relying as it does upon her memory of conversations and events and her reconstruction of motive and sentiment, contends with the apparently neutral, objective, jurisprudential discourse of the law courts and the exemplary narrative of Fielding's history. These authorized versions are replaced with the contrived, self-conscious narrative of the novel. Rooted in, to use historian John Pocock's terms, the contingent world of private discourse rather than the continuous world of legal, theological, and historical discourse[47] and grounded in a detailed and domestic chronology, which she claims was "too slightly touched upon"[48] at her trial, Blandy's account falls under the suspicion that shadows all individually authored texts, particularly autobiographical ones—that truth has succumbed to self-interest, that self-representation is inherently partial and not subject to final proof.

Drawn into the textual representation of her crime, Mary Blandy took up the pen while in prison to write her own apologia, thus incriminating herself further (see Figure 5). She exposes herself as already condemned, composing a female autobiographical narrative as testament to what could only be read officially as excuse, and thus as confession. That Mary Blandy chose to defend herself outside of the courtroom had to be construed as further evidence of the depths of her deliberate treason. She had already had the opportunity to speak to the jury and the public in her trial and had clearly failed to convince them of her innocence. Properly speaking, Mary Blandy ought either to confess to parricide, and thus satisfy her readers with closure, or remain silent as a proper lady would.[49] Rather than supporting her contention that she was duped by her lover, her unladylike enthusiasm for making her actions explicable, for making sense of the evidence according to her narrative, only served to condemn her more soundly.

The apologia was published after the trial in response to considerable popular support for her case. Adopting as her model the immensely popular sentimental novels of late- seventeenth- and early- eighteenth-century women writers, Mary Blandy confirms her unwitting complicity in a self-representation that is fictional (and thus suspect) and that characterizes women either as the helpless victims of man's deceit and sexual aggression, or as taking violent revenge against those who have harmed them.[50] Despite the appeal of Blandy's story for the popular audience, an appeal reflected in the sentimental discourse of newspaper accounts of her trial that spoke of her "Delicacy in Distress,"[51] this model of women's writing only situated her more firmly against the jurisprudential and theological discourses that had condemned her. She adopted a form particularly associated with women writers who, however much read, were frequently castigated as having abandoned the proper task of their sex—the guardianship of the private, domestic space of their husbands and fathers—and who were, therefore, asserting sexual (and thus political) aggressiveness improper in ladies.[52]

Figure 5. Mary Blandy in her cell at Oxford Castle. Reprinted from William Roughead, *The Trial of Mary Blandy* (1914), facing title page.

Improper sexual behavior is precisely the sign of Mary Blandy's guilt in the prosecutor's narrative, as it was for those who were hostile to her and reported that she flirted and assumed suggestive poses during her trial. Thus for Mary Blandy an explanation is not a vindication, but rather a confession; and yet, perversely, the refusal to confess explicitly denied the official audience its satisfaction that "rebellion was forestalled, subversiveness domesticated."[53] Her protestation of innocence, relying on the conventions of sentimental novels, was read as the absence of a (true) confession, a fiction that could only comprise "an aggravation of her wickedness."[54]

Moreover, Mary's explanation of the apparently incriminating evidence against her did not merely have to counter the presumption of guilt, but had to revise what the prosecution had argued was a divinely ordered narrative: ". . . because circumstances that tally one with another are above human contrivance."[55] In attempting to substitute her own narrative, her own testimony, in place of the version offered by the prosecution, Mary Blandy not only appeared to belie the truth of legal discourse, but she also raised her voice against the voice of God: she tempted Providence. Thus Blandy's account of apparitions, distant music, and miraculous events is not like Fielding's, a witness for those of "sound and sober reason" of the invisible but powerful hand of God, but rather a sign of her "obstinate and stubborn infidelity."[56]

Mary Blandy appeals to character and event, as if, like oath swearing in trial by compurgation, the verbal representation of innocence were indeed proof of that innocence. In her detailed reconstruction of the events leading up to her father's death, she relies upon those elements of narrative that we have come to identify with the novel—what Michael McKeon summarizing Ian Watt calls "the particularization of character and background, of naming, of temporality, causation, and physical environment."[57] The daughter's text has no "theological field of action."[58] Unlike popular, and by the mid-eighteenth century, conventional, criminal autobiographies, Blandy's apologia is not both an example of sin and a model for repentance; rather Blandy's account aligns itself rhetorically and formally with the novel, and thus locates itself in that place where truth and untruth, fact and fiction, plausibility and implausibility confront each other.

Legal Facts, Feminist Fictions

The threat to jurisprudential truth lies not just in the novel's capacity to create epistemological confusion for its readers, to obscure the difference between the real and the imagined. The threat also comes from the confrontation between the value and power of the individual and the necessarily limiting and coercive power of the state. The culture's representation of selfhood and of individuality must be grounded in those discourses and stories most necessary to maintain order and stability in the state: the religious, the historical, the jurisprudential, and the economic. If, as Fielding's exemplary history suggests, the operation of divine truth-telling (and thus justice) relies on how adequately causes produce effects, then the narrative of an individual life, which like the exemplary history depends upon a causal structure for its coherent representation, must always be a potential threat to the singular and exceptional nature of the historical or jurisprudential narrative. In other words, if the fictional narrative can reproduce as if it were true the logic of cause and effect, how is the divinely inspired narrative to be distinguished from the humanly crafted one? Such a danger is especially threatening when one narrates the life of a criminal. The problem, simply put, is how to tell the story of falsehood, deceit, and moral degeneracy in such a way as to convince the reader of the "truth" of the narrative without assigning to the narrative (and its narrator) the same status as divinely sanctioned narratives of truth.

Such discursive confusion may have generated the early eighteenth century's obsession with criminal autobiographies, biographies, and news reports of trials. That obsession might not simply be, as Lincoln Faller suggests, that readers were interested in "extended narratives about 'problematic' lives."[59] It might also, and perhaps more significantly, be that crafting a narrative about those lives foregrounds issues of evidence and veracity. In other words, the interest lies not so much in the actions, characters, and motives of criminals and other marginalized individuals, but rather in the epistemological confrontation between general statements about truth and moral virtue and specific and individual representations of those assertions.

Moreover, the specific individual narrative—the stuff of fiction—is feminized in its relation to the apparently transcendent, historical or jurisprudential narrative, which both represents and constructs the patriarchy. The threat that individual narrative poses to the social text is exacerbated, therefore, when that narrative is a woman's, since female authorship only further intensifies the difference between a divine narrative and its human form.

It is not merely historical coincidence that provides the link between the codification of evidence, seen most clearly in Sir Geoffrey Gilbert's Law of Evidence (1756), and the emerging prestige of the novel. Eighteenth-century anxiety over what is true and real, on the one hand, and what is imaginary and unreal (and therefore potentially false and corruptive) on the other, coincides with the intersection of two, apparently separate, cultural narratives:

(1) The rise of women novelists, editors, critics, and printers to a position of prominence and economic visibility in the culture.[60] For example, in 1752, printer Elizabeth Nutt published the Treatise of Feme Coverts, or The Lady's Law, one of several texts published in the late seventeenth and early eighteenth century on legal issues primarily for a female readership.[61]

(2) The efforts to codify modern rules of evidence for the courts. This codification might be seen as part of the culture's attempt to establish what

authority is required to privilege one narrative over another, a response that occurs precisely when the authority to represent their experience in narrative seemed within the grasp of women writers.

This intersection of jurisprudential, historical, and fictional narratives is a fruitful site for exploring the complex codes that govern the production and reception of truth-telling and truth-claiming narratives. Seeing the protocols of historical and jurisprudential narrative as fundamentally distinct from the protocols of fictional narrative only serves to reinscribe women's writing as functioning outside the discourses of power. Indeed, one of the most important consequences of feminist legal scholarship has been a growing awareness of the transformative value of literary narrative in its relationship to legal narrative. The novel, as Carolyn Heilbrun observed, "gives women the chance to transform narrative and anecdote into jurisprudence."[62] Such a critical recognition moves literary narrative away from its oppositional and marginalized position, vis-à-vis supposedly fact-based legal narrative, and resituates both literary and legal discourse within a larger cultural system, a system constructed, in part, precisely through the mutually reinforcing relationship of law and literature. This essay is, of course, precisely the kind of text that the intersection of the narratives of feminism, law, and literature can produce: it is, itself, symptomatic of one of those moments when discourses contend for the privilege of speaking a kind of provisional truth.

Notes

Originally published in Texas Journal of Women and the Law 95 (1992); reprinted by permission. I would like to thank Jocelyn Marsh, Jane Marcus, Susan Stanford Friedman, and Zipporah Wiseman for their advice and encouragement.

1. See Alexander Welsh, "Burke and Bentham on the Narrative Potential of Circumstantial Evidence," 21.3 New Literary History 607 (1990) (establishing the association between circumstantial evidence and theory of narrative). Welsh's analysis of the historical development of the common law and its relationship to fictional representation has been extremely useful in my own work. One major point of difference between his analysis and mine, however, is that Welsh assumes that narration is a gender-free operation in its production and its reception. Obviously I do not: the effect that legal theories of evidence have on the narratibility of experience and the authenticity and credibility of that narrative is marked by gender as much outside the courts as inside.

2. See generally Douglas L. Patey, Probability and Literary Form: Philosophic Theory and Literary Practice in the Augustan Age (1984) (discussing the contributions of literary materials, medicine, law, and theology to the genesis of Augustinian probability theory);

Barbara J. Shapiro, *Probability and Certainty in Seventeenth-Century England* 3 (1983) (presenting the idea that in seventeenth-century England "a more intimate relationship between empirical, natural philosophy and religious, historical, legal, and even literary thought" developed); Brian Vickers & Nancy S. Struever, *Rhetoric and the Pursuit of Truth: Language Change in the Seventeenth and Eighteenth Centuries* (1985) (criticizing and interpreting literature, aesthetics, English philology, and rhetoric from 1500 to 1800).

3. The public outrage that surrounded Mary Blandy's arrest and trial is attributable not only to the sensitive domestic and foreign political climate of the 1750s, but also to the ancient fear that accompanies the murder of a parent by a child. Particularly when, as rarely happens, a daughter kills a father, "the event is certain to receive an almost mythic notoriety that carries with it the overtones of cultural anxiety." Lynda E. Boose, "The Father's House and the Daughter in It: The Structures of Western Culture's Daughter-Father Relationship," in *Daughters and Fathers* 19, 38–39 (Lynda E. Boose & Betty S. Flowers eds., 1989). Further, such patricides "almost inevitably [occur] inside [a] triangular structure in which the daughter is positioned between father and lover." *Id.* at 39.

4. William Roughead, *The Trial of Mary Blandy* (1914) (based on the trial account reported in the State Trials (vol. 18), documents deposited in the British Library and the Public Records Office, and letters held by private individuals). My account of Roughead is yet another unreliable version of what really happened.

5. *Id.* at 65. Henry Bathurst (1714–94) became solicitor-general in 1746 and attorney-general in 1747. On the recommendation of Lord Harwicke, the lord chancellor, Bathurst was appointed a judge of the common pleas in 1754. After the sudden death of Lord Hardwicke in 1770, Bathurst was created lord chancellor (1771), a post he held until 1778. "The 'Case of the unfortunate Martha Sophia Swordfeager' (1771), an unhappy woman entrapped into a pretended marriage, is attributed to the pen of Lord Bathurst, and the work on the 'Law relative to Trials at Nisi Prius,' which bears the name of Justice Bullar, is sometimes said to have been founded on the collections of the older lawyer." *Dictionary of National Biography* 1327–28 (1975).

6. Roughead, *supra* note 4, at 1.

7. *Id.* at 2.

8. *Id.*

9. *Id.*

10. *Id.* at 3.

11. Sylvanus Urban, "The Trial of Miss Blandy for Poisoning Her Father," *Gentleman's Magazine*, March 1752, at 108, 117.

12. *See* Lawrence Stone, *Road to Divorce* (1990): "A reasonable guess would . . . be that between 15 and 20 percent of all marriages in England in the middle of the eighteenth-century were conducted in . . . clandestine ways." *Id.* at 115. Part of the impetus for reform in the clandestine marriage system came from courts "exasperated by the unreliability of the evidence for clandestine marriages, and in the 1730s the lord chief justice and other criminal court judges at the Old Bailey began to reject Fleet registers as evidence for or against the frequent charges of bigamy in which they figured." *Id.*

at 115–16. Furthermore, the clandestine marriage plot "figures in over a third of the plots of plays from Wycherley and Vanbrugh in the late seventeenth century to Steele in the early eighteenth century. A survey of the plots of 241 comedies dating from 1660 to 1714 has shown that 91 of them involve a clandestine marriage, 70 of them false marriages or marriages performed by trickery and deception, and 26 mock or joke marriages." Id. at 118. "The Blandys might have been wiser if they had heeded the case of Creswell v. Creswell (1748), in which an heiress, Miss Warneford, discovered, after having born Mr. Creswell children, that her marriage was void because of his previous marriage to a Miss Scrope, who herself discovered an even earlier marriage to a third woman, still living." Id. at 119.

13. On March 1, 1748, the Commissary Court decreed that Cranstoun and Anne Murray were husband and wife and ordered the captain to pay his wife an annuity of £40 for her support and £10 for their daughter's. The court also ordered him to pay expenses of £100. For Cranstoun, now on half-pay, the verdict was financially disastrous. Roughead, supra note 4, at 9.

14. Id.

15. Roughead includes a contemporary advertisement for a love philtre in his account of the case. Id. at 187. Such love-drops were apparently enormously popular, despite their illegality. Apart from the obvious uses to which such love-drops could be put—woman to unloving man, man to uncompliant woman, spouse to adulterous spouse—the seller also promised success to the servant debauched by any young master "[who] after won't have her, let her give him a little of this liquor and if he don't marry her, I'll have nothing for it." Id. at 187. Apparently, local magistrates were not as zealous in prosecuting the sellers of such potions and powders as they might be, perhaps because they, like so many others less educated, more than half believed in the efficacy of such potions. In addition to their illegality in the eyes of the law, such potions were also associated with spiritual depravity: the advertisement plays upon the cultural prejudice against Roman Catholics, especially the secretive and duplicitous Jesuits: "[t]his liquor is the study of a Jesuit, one Mr. Delore." Id. at 187. See James A. Brundage, Law, Sex and Christian Society in Medieval Society 199, 503 (1987) (describing long-standing ecclesiastical opposition to such magic potions).

16. Roughead, supra note 4, at 19 (quoting from Cranstoun to Mary Blandy, July 18, 1751).

17. See Thomas R. Forbes, Surgeons at the Bailey: English Forensic Medicine to 1878, at 133 (1985) (note that "[t]he trial of Mary Blandy . . . is said to be the first, or one of the first, in which chemical tests for arsenic were accepted as evidence").

18. Roughead, supra note 4, at 71.

19. Id. at 71.

20. Roughead, supra note 4, at 143.

21. Id. at 144.

22. Leon Radzinowicz, A History of English Criminal Law and Its Administration from 1750, at 628 (1948).

23. Id. at 628 n.83.

24. Id. at 628 n.84.

25. Roughead, *supra* note 4, at 32.

26. Roughead, *supra* note 4, at 41.

27. Roughead, *supra* note 4, at 65.

28. Id. at 75–76. Alexander Welsh also points out the "didactic spirit" of Serjeant Hayward's comments in his analysis of the Mary Blandy trial in *Strong Representations: Narrative and Circumstantial Evidence in England* 46 (1991).

29. Seventeenth-century and early eighteenth-century Europe was ravaged by a series of wars and rebellions over succession and the extent and function of kingly authority. For example, the Civil War in England was followed by constant domestic and foreign unrest, leading to the Bloodless Revolution that put William of Orange on the English throne in 1688. Threats from home and abroad were only temporarily held at bay by the 1701 Act of Settlement; the War of Spanish Succession followed (1702–13); then the 1715 Jacobite Rebellion, managed and financed from France on behalf of the son of James II; war with Spain broke out again in 1720, lasting until 1729; the War of the Austrian Succession erupted in 1740, lasting until 1748; and just a few years before the Blandy trial, the 1745 Jacobite Rebellion took place, promoting the claim of James II's grandson, Bonnie Prince Charlie, to the throne of England and Scotland and ending with the Battle of Culloden in 1746. *See* William B. Willcox, *The Age of Aristocracy, 1688 to 1830* (1966).

30. Urban, *supra* note 11, at 108 (quoting counsel for the prosecution).

31. Roughead, *supra* note 4, at 74.

32. Randall McGowen, "'He Beareth Not the Sword in Vain': Religion and the Criminal Law in Eighteenth-Century England," 21.2 *Eighteenth-Century Studies* 192, 193 (1987–88).

33. Roughead, *supra* note 4, at 73.

34. Welsh, *supra* note 1, at 616. For his definition of circumstantial evidence, as distinct from direct evidence, Welsh relies, in part, on *Johnson's 1755 Dictionary*: "The adjuncts of a fact, which make it more or less criminal; or make an accusation more or less probable." Id. at 615. *See* John H. Langbein, *Torture and the Law of Proof* (1977) (discussing the history of medieval theory of proof).

35. Alexander Welsh, "The Evidence of Things Not Seen: Justice Stephen and Bishop Butler," 22 *Representations* 60, 69–70 (1988).

36. Roughead, *supra* note 4, at 74 (Welsh also quotes this particular definition in his essay on Burke and Bentham, noting how the metaphors used by Hayward "imply linear connectedness . . . and the idea of completion" (Welsh, *supra* note 1, at 616; emphasis added)).

37. Hayden White, "The Value of Narrativity in the Representation of Reality," 7 *Critial Inquiry* 5, 7 (1980), quoting Emile Benveniste, *Problems in General Linguistics* 208 (Mary Elizabeth Meek trans., 1971).

38. Michael McKeon, *The Origins of the English Novel, 1600–1740*, at 86 (1987), quoting Joseph Glanville, *Saducimus Triumphatus; Or, Full and Plain Evidence Concerning Witches and Apparitions . . .* 10 (1681).

39. Henry Fielding, *Examples of the Interposition of Providence in the Detection and Punishment of Murder* (printed for A. Millar: London) (1752).

40. Id. at 4.

41. Id.

42. Id. at 88.

43. Id.

44. Id. at 4.

45. Id. at 2.

46. Id.

47. John G. A. Pocock, *Virtue, Commerce, and History* 91–93 (1987).

48. Roughead, *supra* note 4, at 178–79.

49. Margaret Anne Doody, " 'Those Eyes Are Made So Killing': Eighteenth-Century Murderesses and the Law," *Princeton U. Lib. Chron.* 49, 53 (1984).

50. Id. at 70. This is not to say that Mary might not also have had access to novels in which female vulnerability was explored and in which the failure of the law to provide women with protection came under attack. It was the novel's capacity to engage with the apparently more powerful cultural and legal narratives that made it potentially dangerous to social stability: what cannot be acknowledged in law and theology might find expression and embodiment in the novel.

51. Id. at 72.

52. *See* Janet Todd, *The Sign of Angellica: Women, Writing and Fiction* 9 (1989): "[L]ike the man, the woman who published could no longer be entirely appropriated and made dependent. But, since women should not be independent or self-owning, this failure to be potential property was a kind of impropriety."

53. Sidonie Smith, *A Poetic of Women's Autobiography* 119 (1987).

54. Doody, *supra* note 49, at 53.

55. Roughead, *supra* note 4, at 74.

56. Fielding, *supra* note 39, at 4.

57. McKeon, *supra* note 38, at 2. *See* Ian Watt, *The Rise of the Novel* (1957).

58. Smith, *supra* note 53, at 119.

59. Lincoln B. Faller, *Turned to Account: The Forms and Functions of Criminal Biography in Late Seventeenth and Early Eighteenth-Century England* 195 (1987).

60. *See A Dictionary of British and American Women Writers, 1660–1800* (Janet Todd ed., 1988) (listing over 500 women writers).

61. I am grateful to Maureen Mulvihill for her fine research into seventeenth- and eighteenth-century instructive legal materials for women and for her willingness to share her work with me.

62. Carolyn Heilbrun, address at the *Texas Journal of Women and the Law* Conference on Feminist Practice: The Representation of Women in Law and Literature (March 1990).

WITNESSING WOMEN

Trial Testimony in Novels by Tonna, Gaskell, and Eliot

Christine L. Krueger

∇

"Stuff and nonsense!" said Alice loudly. "The idea of having the sentence first!"

"Hold your tongue!" said the Queen, turning purple.

"I won't!" said Alice.

"Off with her head!" the Queen shouted at the top of her voice. Nobody moved.

"Who cares for you?" said Alice (she had grown to her full size by this time). "You're nothing but a pack of cards!"

At this the whole pack rose up in the air, and came flying down upon her; she gave a little scream, half of fright and half of anger, and tried to beat them off, and found herself lying on the bank, with her head in the lap of her sister, who was gently brushing away some dead leaves that had fluttered down from the trees upon her face.

—Lewis Carroll, *Alice's Adventures in Wonderland* (1865)

Alice's power to challenge arbitrary authority represented by the legal system of Wonderland forms a telling contrast with the fortunes of female characters called on to give testimony before English courts of law in Victorian novels by women. Alice's contemporaries—including Charlotte Elizabeth Tonna, Elizabeth Gaskell, and George Eliot—might have found the nightmarish close of the Knave of Hearts' trial positively utopian compared with their dramatizations of a legal discourse rivaling Wonderland's judicial practices for absurdity, tyranny, and sheer cruelty. For these writers, the possibility that women's speech could be comprehended by a legal system, much less expose its misogyny, would indeed have been a dream come true. Had Alice faced the court confronted by Helen Fleetwood, Mary Barton, or Hetty Sorrell, she would suddenly have found herself on trial, whether or not she was the accused, and have been powerless to accomplish her own defense. Far from dominating the exchanges with lawyers and judge, Alice's testimony would be deemed unintelligible, condemned as "saucy," or misconstrued as an admission of guilt. In short, the authority to represent herself—in both senses of the term— would be taken away from Alice and given over to judges indifferent or hostile to her.

Trial scenes, which come at climactic points in Tonna's *Helen Fleetwood* (1841), Gaskell's *Mary Barton* (1848), and Eliot's *Adam Bede* (1859) and *Felix Holt* (1866),[1] dramatize the exclusion of women's voices from public speech through mechanisms symbolized by the law. More subtle, but effectively as powerful as the laws against seditious speech which gagged political subversives, the prejudices governing female speech, forcing it to conform to masculine ruling-class interests, are shown to have the sanction of the state. In each of these novels, a female witness experiences the trauma of being made a public spectacle and, if she is not immediately shamed into silence, she suffers the maddening frustration caused by her authorial illegality. Either she will be dismissed for transgressing the rules of evidence—that is, the court's preconception of "the facts"—or her testimony will be appropriated for a patriarchal plot. These incidents correspond to their authors' own struggles to influence England's predominant social narrative, which its authors—from judges and M.P.'s to social scientists—defended against these intrusions with a range of legalistic tactics. When Tonna, Gaskell, or Eliot presents a female character testifying before a court, a clear parallel exists between the inconsequentiality or misprision of her language by the hostile arbiters of the law and the tendency of these writers to have their social criticism ignored, dismissed, or coopted by interpretations that served ruling-class interests.

Further, these novels, spanning a period that saw both changes in English jurisprudence that were disadvantageous to women and the beginnings of a concerted feminist assault on women's legal handicaps, reflect a range of opinion on the role of legislation as an effective vehicle of social reform. What they share is the sense that in the eyes of the law, women's speech without patriarchal sanction is rendered illegitimate and female speakers without the paterfamilias are whores. Like shadows lurking behind witnessing women stand other female characters whose stories cannot be entered into the legal record because their transgressions against the patriarchal order have made them criminals—prostitutes, infanticides, adulteresses. Yet they may be the very characters who possess the truth, the crucial bit of evidence to solve the plot's mystery. Gaskell's and Eliot's treatments of the "illegitimate," and therefore illegible, characters reflect their differing judgments of the legitimacy of patriarchal authority and the means for its reform.[2]

Both literally and metaphorically, nineteenth-century law figured as the enemy of women's personal freedom. What I wish to focus on here is the fact that for Tonna, Gaskell, and Eliot, the legal system constituted the quintessential symbol of a more generalized resistance to their public speech. Each writer had experienced women's legal disabilities. Through the early decades of the century the painful bridle remained the legal punishment for scolds in the Cheshire towns surrounding Gaskell's Manchester.[3] Much has been made of William Gaskell's generosity in forgoing his right to Elizabeth's earnings as a writer, but that is because his behavior was the exception, not the rule.[4] Charlotte Elizabeth Tonna, who separated from her husband to escape his beatings, was sued by him for the profits from her earliest writings and subsequently published under her Christian name alone in order to avoid further legal entanglements. "George Eliot" did not escape the lot endured by "Polly Lewes" as the lover of a man legally bound to another woman; even Gaskell wished that *Adam Bede*, which she greatly admired, had not been written by a woman living outside the law.[5] Law enforced each writer's submission to a hostile social order.

Tonna, who died in 1846, did not live to see the sustained and vocal challenge to women's legal oppression launched in the 1850s, but Gaskell and Eliot were lukewarm in their support. Caroline Norton's *English Laws for Women in the Nineteenth Century* (1854), which first overcame public silence on the brutal consequences of married women's status as nonentities in common law, was followed in the same year by Barbara Bodichon's *Brief Summary in Plain Language of the Most Important Laws Concerning Women*, a work paving the way for her petition for a Married Women's Property Act in 1856. Joining more enthusiastic supporters, including Elizabeth Barrett Browning and Jane Welsh Carlyle, both Gaskell and Eliot signed the petition reluctantly. Though they supported the principle articulated in the act, they remained unconvinced that legislation would provide any genuine reform, for unless individual men were converted to the justice of their cause, the law would be ignored.[6] This skepticism over the petition's influence may have been borne out in such incidents as a meeting of the progressive Law Amendment Society called to discuss Bodichon's petition, where the "'large number of ladies who were present at the meeting . . . , though directly interested in the matter under discussion, were forbidden by etiquette from taking part in the proceedings."[7] This ironic situation was a commonplace for female political writers, widely read, yet forbidden to speak in public. Seven female delegates sent to London to address the 1840 World Anti-Slavery Convention were placed behind curtains while the subject of their admission was debated by the male delegates, who decided to allow them to remain, provided they refrained from participating in the Convention's proceedings.[8] Thirteen years later, when the much admired Harriet Beecher Stowe was invited to abolitionist society meetings throughout Scotland and England, she sat demurely in a gallery while her husband spoke on her behalf.[9] Indeed, when a Married Women's Property Act was first read in Parliament on May 14, 1857, it was met by laughter and trivialized in the press.[10]

These events merely recapitulated in a broad public arena what went on daily in English courts of law. In 1836, defense counsel was granted the privilege of addressing the jury as well as cross-examining witnesses. Although this change in criminal trial practice was intended to aid defendants whose knowledge of law and rhetorical skills were seen as no match against those of prosecution—a goal it partially achieved [11]—it effectively eliminated the only occasion in which women spoke in court in their own defense.[12] Harriet Taylor Mill took up a related issue in the "Enfranchisement of Women" when she pointed out that women, unlike foreigners, were denied trial by a jury of their peers.[13]

It was precisely her exclusion from the institutional powers of authorizing or rejecting testimony that so galled Caroline Norton in the suit brought by her husband against Lord Melbourne for Unlawful Congress with Caroline. Although Melbourne was the defendant, the verdict hinged on the allegedly guilty behavior of Caroline Norton. Sir William Follet, representing George Norton, called domestic servants to testify concerning the minute details of Caroline Norton's private life, and encouraged the jury to interpret that evidence according to his purely speculative, and unabashedly purient suggestions:

> From Mrs. Norton's conduct, you, gentlemen [of the jury], must infer what else took place. She goes to her room; prepares herself to receive Lord Melbourne; dresses, arranges her hair, and gets the room ready before he comes. While he was in the house she frequently goes into her bed-room whilst he was there. Her hair is disordered, she goes again to her bedroom to set it to rights. Having arranged her hair she comes down again to Lord Melbourne . . . I ask you as men of the world, with a knowledge of the feelings of your brother men, I ask you what must be the meaning of the visits of Lord Melbourne to this young and beautiful woman?[14]

Caroline Norton becomes a character in Follet's titillating melodrama which, like pornographic representations of women, forms a conspiratorial and voyeuristic relationship between the author and audience that Norton herself could not challenge. Indeed, Lord Melbourne's defense likewise depended on the jury's acceptance of another equally fanciful construction of Caroline Norton. Claiming that Norton and her husband lived on affectionate terms throughout the period in question, the Attorney General, representing Melbourne, concluded:

> Why, they [the jury] all knew that after a woman had surrendered her person to her paramour, she would look upon her husband with loathing—that she would enter his bed with abhorrence, and that it would be impossible for her to meet him without exhibiting to him her loathing, and convincing himself of her guilt.[15]

In either case, the jury was asked to bring the power of the state to sanction a version of Caroline Norton's behavior constructed of patriarchal clichés.

Although Melbourne was acquitted, Norton's legal problems with her husband were far from over, and in 1853, he revived the Melbourne scandal as grounds for exempting him from payment of his wife's debts. In this trial, George Norton called Caroline into the witness stand, where she was humiliated. In her *Letter to the Queen on Lord Chancellor Cranworth's Marriage and Divorce Bill* (1855), Norton described that experience in grotesque and surreal terms which, as we shall see, parallel those used by Tonna and Gaskell to narrate their heroines' examinations:

> I felt giddy; the faces of the people grew indistinct; my sentences became a confused alternation of angry loudness, and husky attempts to speak. I saw nothing—but the husband of whose mercenary nature Lord Melbourne himself had warned me I judged too leniently; nothing but *the Gnome*,— proceeding *again* to dig away, for the sake of money, what remnant of peace, happiness, and reputation, might have rested on the future years of my life. Turning up as he dug—dead sorrows, and buried shames, and miserable recollections—and careless who was hurt by them, as long as he evaded payment of a disputed annuity and stamped his own signature as worthless![16]

Here patriarchal and legal power were quite literally synonymous, rendering Norton helpless to defend herself. As Mary Poovey has pointed out, Norton had to author her own account of the trial in order to legitimate her testimony.

> On that day, when in cold blood, for the sake of money, Mr Norton repeated that which he knew to be false . . . in that little court where I stood apparently helpless, mortified, and degraded—in that bitterest of many bitter hours in my life,—I judged and sentenced him. I annulled the skill of his Tory lawyer's suggestion to a Tory judge. I over-ruled the decision of Lord Abinger in that obscure and forgotten cause, which upheld him against justice. I sentenced Mr Norton to be known.[17]

As author, Caroline Norton attempts to do what can only be done in the Wonderland of literature—to assume the power of representation and judgment: "I sentenced Mr Norton to be known." Yet this gesture can hardly be seen as any real compensation for Norton's defeat at the hands of her husband. The powers and limitations of women's fictional witness are taken up by Norton's contemporaries: Tonna, Gaskell, and Eliot.

In *Helen Fleetwood*, Tonna casts her attack on the dominant social discourse in religious terms, contrasting spiritual testimony with its debased counterpart in legal proceedings. Witnesses who testify to social injustice are presented as beleaguered prophets, their critics as hypocritical pharisees. However, gender is vitally important to Tonna's argument, for only males can attain the status of pharisees—M.P.'s, judges, millowners—inextricably linking the sins of classism and sexism. The novel's principal characters are the Green family—consisting of four orphaned children and their widowed grandmother—and their orphaned cousin, Helen Fleetwood. Victims of both economic and civil laws, Mrs. Green and Helen nevertheless become prophets of social reform by virtue of their biblically privileged status as widow and orphan.[18] However, it is not the patriarchal legal system that heeds them. Tonna exposes social authorities as censors of dissident female voices and appeals to divine authority to feminize the social discourse.

Well before the novel's trial scene, when Helen will appear like Christ before the high priest, Tonna introduces the sexual injustice of conventional patriarchal social relations that the legal system should redress. Alarmed by the children's declining health and spirits after several weeks of mill work, the widow Green goes to the foreman to inform him of the immoral conditions of the factory, but he dismisses her as a troublesome crank. Like the importunate widow of scripture, she takes her cause to the millowner. "Mr. Z." listens patiently to Mrs. Green's petition until he notices that his daughter Amelia is listening as well and casting compassionate looks at the speaker. With that, he sends Amelia from the room, and angrily reprimands Mrs. Green "for introducing such improper subjects in the presence of a young lady, whose ears ought not to have been assailed by discourse so unfit for a delicate mind" (560). Feminine propriety serves to exclude the disruptive prophet lest she make converts among her sisters.

The same misogynous principles by which Mrs. Green is censored are shown to pervade the discourse of the legal system, nullifying the voice of the widow and the orphan. Tonna's attack on the inherent exclusivity—and misogyny—of the dominant social discourse, its resistance to marginalized female prophets, culminates in the novel's trial scene. Helen Fleetwood and Mary Green are harassed in the factory where they work for defending Katy, a younger Irish girl, from the abuse of the other workers. The overlooker, who intervenes to break up a scuffle after Mary pushes Katy's persecutors away, takes this chance to punish the innocent Helen for the subversive influence of her pious behavior, striking her cruelly. Mr. Barlow, the Rector, visits the Greens and discovers Helen's injury. His indignation against the factory system aroused, he insists that they seek justice through the legal system. Barlow reports the incident to a factory inspector, appointed by Parliament to investigate such abuses, and a hearing is scheduled. However, despite the support of a clergyman and an inspector, Helen cannot overcome an entire social structure erected against her. Her powerlessness is manifested by her ineffectual testimony and that of the other girls who testify on her behalf.

The magistrate questions Helen's cousin Mary Green first, but when she tries to explain the history of Katy's persecution that led up to her action, he interupts with a warning that she confine herself to the "facts" of this case. The rules of this investigation allow more freedom to the accused than to the victim, permitting the overlooker John Roy to question Mary, but not the victim her oppressor. Because Mary proves Roy's verbal equal and thwarts his attempts to confuse and contradict her, the magistrate dismisses her as "saucy." Next, Katy herself is called to testify. Her innocent use of Bible language the magistrate ignorantly attributes to the wholesome influence of the factory rather than to widow Green who has actually taught it to her. The overlooker manages to provoke Katy by maligning Mary's character, and the court laughs at her stereotypical Irish temper. When the magistrate demands a translation of her ejaculation in Irish, she gladly responds:

> "It was the verse of a psalm that my father used to say out of the Irish Bible when Helen Fleetwood's character was to be taken away. The English is 'The lying lips shall be put to silence that cruelly, disdainfully, and spitefully speak against the righteous.'" (588)

" 'Are we to have we no decent witnesses . . . ?' " the magistrate inquires. Marginalized by race, class, and sex, Katy is rendered incomprehensible in the legal discourse, as her Irish speech illustrates. However, as Paul writes in Galatians, she is the overlooker's and magistrate's equal in Christ, and her "Bible language" carries divine authority.

Helen Fleetwood testifies last. Her emaciated condition makes her appear "almost heavenly," thinks her cousin Richard, and she "modestly, but clearly and distinctly" delivers her testimony. She is indeed the most effective prophet. One magistrate acknowledges that she has established Mary's innocence, and the overlooker's attempt to discredit Helen backfires. He hopes that by revealing her dependency on the Greens he will reveal her selfish motives in defending Mary. But thanks to her reliance on God, Helen enjoys a radical independence. " 'If by any dispensation of God' " Helen tells the court

> "I was deprived of my best and only friends on earth, I have still one to go to who has said, "Him that cometh unto me I will in no wise cast out.' "
> "That is to say, I suppose, you would turn preacher." [Roy retorts.]
> Here a murmur of "shame!" was distinctly heard; and one of the gentlemen on the bench said, rather warmly, "Enough of this; it will not shake the clear testimony of the young person before us.' " (589)

Nevertheless, though the magistrates recognize the authority of Helen's language—as Pilate respected Jesus—the limitations of the legal system prevent them from responding to it. They will not undergo the radical change of heart, replacing the law with the spirit; they will not repent of the injustice on which their own authority depends. Roy is made to pay a small fine, and the girls' persecution at the factory continues. The factory system claims its victims as always: Mrs. Green goes to the workhouse, and Helen Fleetwood dies of illnesses contracted in the mill. Rejected by men, Helen and Mrs. Green are, however, not diminished as prophets whose testimony is authorized by the word of God. As social prophet, Tonna likewise appeals to a higher authority, witnessing for justice and calling on her readers to repent. The reader is free to respond with a hard heart, as a pharisee, or with a heartfelt repentance, as one of the saved. Regardless of her readers' response, Tonna can remain confident of her own legitimacy by remembering the persecutions endured by prophets before her.

Elizabeth Gaskell, whose first novel *Mary Barton* was greatly influenced by *Helen Fleetwood*,[19] took some courage from a prophetic model of authorial legitimacy, declaring that, as "God will cause the errors [of *Mary Barton*] to be temporary[,] the truth to be eternal, . . . I try not to mind too much what people say either in praise or blame."[20] However, Gaskell sees patriarchal constructions of truth as posing far greater barriers to women's witness than even Tonna allows. Critiques of classism and sexism intersect in *Helen Fleetwood*'s single plot, but Gaskell aims to underscore the unspeakable nature of women's true complaint. While she combines class and sexual exploitation in the novel's dominant plot—Mary Barton's renunciation of Harry Carson in favor of the working-class Jem Wilson, culminating in the trial scene—Gaskell constructs a parallel subplot in which Mary's aunt Esther undergoes her own trial. She is driven outside the law into prostitution, judged guilty by her brother-in-law, John Barton, without an opportunity to defend herself, and condemned to die. Read together, these plots represent patriarchal law as destroying what it cannot appropriate, and women's testimony as fundamentally out of order.

As in *Helen Fleetwood*, a trial scene shows the legal discourse to be structurally incapable of admitting female difference. Deemed relevant to a male audience only when the fate of another male is at stake, a woman's voice—Mary's—is wholly appropriated by a discourse she cannot control, presenting her as a spectacle for the masculine gaze. Never suspecting that Mary holds the very piece of evidence that could acquit Jem—the gun wadding that implicates her father, John Barton—the prosecutor calls her to tell her love story, the sordid flirtation with Harry Carson that provokes Jem to murder. A crowd presses into the courtroom to see the spectacle of her testimony. A beam of "mellow sunlight streams down . . . on her head, and [falls] on the rich treasure of her golden hair," while her face, like Helen Fleetwood's, is "deadly white" (305). As spectacle she possesses "a higher and stranger kind of beauty" than ordinary women, specifically the picturesque beauty one observer associates with "Guido's picture of 'Beatrice Cenci'" (305). Mr. Carson waits anxiously, with "a kind of interest and yet repugnance," to see Mary, "the fatal Helen" (304).

Though Mary imagines herself "bear[ing] witness" to the truth, in fact she has been produced merely to deliver the lines already written for her. Thus, her testimony threatens to alienate Mary from reality and her own sense of identity.

> With all the court reeling before her . . . she heard a voice speak, and answered the simple inquiry (something about her name) mechanically, as if in a dream. So she went on for two or three more questions, with a strange wonder in her brain, as to the reality of the terrible circumstances in which she was placed. (305)

Alice in Wonderland could reduce the court to a pack of cards and awake, but Mary is trapped in this nightmare, "conscious that all was real, that hundreds were looking at her, that true-sounding words were being extracted from her . . . by the pert young barrister who was delighted to have the examination of this witness" (305–06). When that "monkeyfied man" demands to know her preferred lover, Mary is shocked that he "should dare so lightly to ask of her heart's secrets . . . to ask her to tell . . . what woman usually whispers with blushes and tears" (306). Meanwhile, she keeps "the tremendous secret [of her father's guilt] imprisoned within her" (306). Gaskell exposes the real coercion of this supposed dialogue, going so far as to describe the questioning in terms that suggest rape.

In self-defense, Mary tells an alternative love story, confessing her love for Jem. But this is also her story, whose central character is neither Carson nor Wilson, but her mother. Turning away from her inquisitor toward the judge, Mary tries to explain that her relationship with Carson was nothing more than the vain fancies of a motherless girl.

> For, you see, sir, mother died before I was thirteen, before I could know right from wrong about some things; and I was giddy and vain, and ready to listen to any praise of my good looks; and this poor young Mr. Carson fell in with me, and told me he loved me; and I was foolish enough to think he meant marriage: *a mother is a pitiful loss to a girl, sir* . . . [my emphasis] (306–7).

Of course, Mary looks to the wrong judge. Just as Jem has no interest in Esther's "confession," but only in her knowlege of his rival, so Mary's audience, perhaps inclined to pity the prisoner, hears only the confirmation of Jem's guilt. Played false by a vain and giddy girl, Jem must have been driven to an act of passion.

What is worse, Mary's enforced testimony is a wholly unnecessary performance intended to gratify the court's appetite for spectacle, and particularly, the desire of Jem's barrister to orchestrate the most dramatic presentation of his own "forensic eloquence" (311). He knows, as we readers do, that Mary has already been the mediatrix of Jem's salvation, finding the one man who can provide Jem with an alibi, Will Wilson; in the chapters leading up to the trial we have read the story, that none of the legal authorities will ask to hear, of Mary's heroic pursuit of Will, catching up with him just as his ship is about to set sail from Liverpool. Rather than cross-examine Mary, enabling her to record her heroism into the official account of the trial, Jem's barrister imagines the sentimental version of the story, which he will read into the transcript: " 'a gallant tar brought back from the pathless ocean by a girl's noble daring' " (311). Mary's only escape from these patriarchal appropriations is, predictably, madness.

> . . . she caught sight of something,—or some one,—who, even in that state, had power to arrest her attention, and throwing up her arms with wild energy, she shrieked aloud:
> "Oh, Jem! Jem! you're saved; and I *am* mad—" and was instantly seized with convulsions. With much commiseration she was taken out of court, while the attention of many was diverted from her, by the fierce energy with which a sailor forced his way over rails and seats, against turnkeys and policemen. (310)

Mary may risk life and limb to save Jem, but only Will, vaulting over the barriers separating accuser from accused, can provide Jem with a story.

Will is confident "that his tale, or part of a tale, would be heard by judge and jury," and when the prosecution attempts an *ad hominem* attack, asking Will how much he has been paid to lie on Jem's behalf, he can prove the authenticity of his story. Pointing to his ship's pilot in the back of the courtroom, Will asks, "Would somebody with a wig on please to ask him how much he can say for me?" (313). Like Alice in the Looking Glass World, Will has the power to reduce authority to empty fiction: "somebody with a wig on." Mary is absent when the jury returns a verdict of "not guilty."

In a sense, the jury has never heard the principal witnesses. John Barton, the murderer, and Esther, his unwitting accuser, the father and the fallen woman, peer silently from between the lines of testimony. Esther is the source of the "tremendous secret" of the father's guilt; she is the mysterious informer, who tells Jem of Mary's attachment to Carson;[21] she even witnesses the confrontation between Jem and Carson. She should be testifying here, not Mary; but her voice, the voice of the other, is inadmissible, anathema to the foregone conclusions dictated by the dominant discourse. But more importantly, another trial has been narrated in these chapters in which Mary's testimony is perfectly relevant—Esther's trial.

Esther unintentionally bears witness to the wrongs of women by telling her life story, an act she construes as an admission of guilt. Her unsympathetic and self-absorbed audience, Jem Wilson, does nothing to mitigate her sense of shame, but the reader sees in Esther's "confession" to abandonment, poverty, and prostitution, a vindication of a victimized woman.[22] Mary, who might read this story properly and speak in Esther's defense, can never hear it because Esther herself is convinced that it is a "discourse unfit for delicate ears." Esther and Mary are alienated from one another in a fashion analogous to the way in which one generation of female writers has historically been denied access to its precursors. The recovery of literary mothers demands a recognition of their "impropriety" that marks the female reader as fallen herself, and renders her own writing inscrutable to her proper female readers.[23] The law aims to prevent the emergence of a "feminist reader [who] takes the part of the woman writer against patriarchal misreadings."[24]

Gaskell's novels progressively reveal the importance of a female interpretive community. A dissenting minister and a young middle-class woman both speak in defense of the fallen woman in Ruth (1853), but her persecutor, the pharisaical Mr. Bradshaw, is converted only when Ruth dies. Ruth herself assumes the mantle of divine authority in condemning her seducer, Bellingham. Yet, because he recognizes no authority beyond his own desires—particularly when invoked by a desirable female—he remains unconverted. The vocal and persuasive middle-class heroine of North and South (1854–55), having suffered the mortification of ad feminam attacks on her modesty when she acts on moral principle and literally throws herself between the millowner, Thornton, and an angry mob of striking workers, lapses into obedient silence as Thornton's wife. In the Life of Charlotte Brontë

(1857) Gaskell mounted a defense of a sister author against patriarchal mis-readings, making herself the target of all those readers who insisted Brontë behave as a proper lady. Her 1859 story "Lois the Witch" directly pits a vir-tuous young daughter of a parson (the counterpart of Gaskell's middle-class female readers) against the law in Puritan New England. Lois is unable to defend herself against a bogus witchcraft charge and is executed. With an increasing sense of urgency, Gaskell remained committed in her fiction to voicing women's illegal language: "I'm speaking like a woman;" her charac-ter Sylvia exclaims, "like a woman as finds out she's been cheated by men as she trusted, and as has no help for it. It's me as has been wronged, and as has to bear it" (*Sylvia's Lovers*, 443–44).

George Eliot's first novel, *Adam Bede*, discloses the patriarchal connection be-tween sexual and textual legitimacy that Tonna and Gaskell had implied, but places the blame on women who succumb to the same discursive vices that result in "silly novels." Hetty Sorrel typifies the woman victimized by social and fictional convention. She is seduced by the aristocrat Arthur Donni-thorne, thinking that her role in this fairytale romance will bring her new freedom when in fact she becomes part of an all too common tragedy. In man's court of law, with limited and ineffectual counsel, she is too terri-fied to defend herself and is condemned by her own silence (481). Though Donnithorne brings the bit of text, the reprieve, that will save Hetty from the gallows, Dinah must teach her to "unseal [her] closed lips" (497), to tell her story. The poignant story Hetty tells Dinah makes clear her guilt, but it is also an eloquent testimony to the tragic vulnerability of both women and children in a society ruled by Donnithorne's law.

> "I came to a place where there was lots of chips and turf, and I sat down on the trunk of a tree to think what I should do. And all of a sudden I saw a hole under the nut-tree, like a little grave. And it darted to me like lightening—I'd lay the baby there, and cover it with the grass and the chips. I couldn't kill it any other way. And I'd done it in a minute; and, O, it cried so, Dinah—I *couldn't* cover it quite up—I thought perhaps somebody 'ud come and take care of it, and then it wouldn't die . . . And I made myself a bed, ever so far behind, where nobody could find me; and I was so tired and weak, I went to sleep . . . But oh, the baby's crying kept waking me . . . Dinah, do you think God will take away that crying and the place in the wood, now I've told everything?"
>
> "Let us pray, poor sinner: let us fall on our knees again, and pray to the God of all mercy." (499–500)

The child-like simplicity of Hetty's language—its plain description, repeti-tion, and naive sincerity—would have no chance of influencing speakers of the legal discourse; in a court of law it would be as unintelligible as Katy's Irish in *Helen Fleetwood*. Unlike Katy, Hetty cannot ennoble her language with scripture, but Dinah must pray for her, and thus help her, inarticulate as she is, to gain access to the authoritative discourse.

But even Dinah's power is an "extraordinary calling," unavailable to women as a class. Rather than unite Dinah to the evangelical brother, Seth, who would defy male authority in order to guarantee Dinah's right to preach, George Eliot yokes her to Adam, who quietly affirms patriarchal control. Dinah stands silently while her husband explains that she gave up preaching so as to set an example for those women who attempt to preach, even without Dinah's gift. Though the precise nature of Adam's power remains obscure in this novel, it seems the forerunner of the transcendent, wordless law that dominates George Eliot's characters by the time she writes *Felix Holt* (1866).

More than any of Eliot's novels, *Felix Holt* directly concerns the law. Its elaborately researched inheritance plot, criticized as an artistic failure,[25] features the lawyer Jermyn as its heartless villain, and an adulteress, Mrs. Transome, as its victim. The heroine, Esther Lyon, is discovered to be the legitimate heir to the Transome estate, but she eventually renounces her claim in order to marry the reform-minded artisan, Felix Holt, and become an obedient medium for the transcendent laws of a providential history. Eliot sets this plot against the backdrop of the election riots of 1832, one of which Felix tries to quell, thereby implying that Esther's action is a middle-class, private, feminine manifestation of Felix's spiritualized understanding of political reform. But Esther's and Felix's roles are hardly equivalent, as we shall see.

At the same time Eliot was exhibiting such anxiety over her legal expertise, she was devising a mythology intended to transcend entirely the limitations of human law—and language. It is less the case that George Eliot loses faith in women's ability to penetrate social discourse than that she comes to deny the desirability of any social discourse—any privileging of language over action—at all. Unfortunately, the mythology she creates serves to legitimize traditional gender roles, as did Feuerbach's and Comte's.[26] Felix has visions of the transcendent law that would reform human hearts, inclining people to cooperation rather than conflict. Although these visions may flourish under the benevolent influence of women, such influence is not strictly necessary, and Esther's principal duty is to recognize the legitimacy of Felix's "law." "He [Felix] was like no one else to her," Esther muses; "he had seemed to bring at once a law, and the love that gave strength to obey the law" (369). Esther Lyon, rather than transcending law, actually enforces its judgment against the outlawed Mrs. Transome. Esther becomes, not the defiant mother of illegitimate speech—and Mrs. Transome's daughter-in-law—but the silent mother of Felix Holt's son. Thus, *Felix Holt* represents a cycle in feminist thinking familiar to contemporary theorists: in an attempt to escape a repressive ideology—as Tonna and Gaskell identified it—Eliot comes, unwittingly perhaps, to reinscribe its structures.

The novel that became *Felix Holt* may have begun as a treatment of female marginality and silence, the tragedy of Mrs. Transome. Mrs. Transome's story, a significant subplot in the completed novel, tells the dismal fate of a woman married to an imbecile, deserted by her cruel lover—the family lawyer, Jermyn—and tyrannized over by their son, whose illegitimacy is a secret enforcing her isolation and silence. George Eliot suppressed this plot and muted its potential denunciation of patriarchy when she turned to history and the election riots of 1832. This shift in focus cannot be construed as a displacement of feminist concerns onto class struggle as, for example, in Charlotte Brontë's *Shirley*. The tragedy of Mrs. Transome serves not as an indictment of female exploitation, but as a cautionary tale, warning Esther of the desolation awaiting women who transgressed against the patriarchal law in search of pleasure, power, or love.

Again, it is a trial scene that makes clear the nature of women's public speech and social role. Esther will testify on behalf of Felix Holt when he is wrongly accused of a murder that takes place during an election riot he in fact tried to defuse. Namesake of the queen who successfully pleaded the Israelites' cause before the Persian king, that favorite subject of biographical sketches by evangelical women writers, this English Esther should possess great charisma and oratorical power. George Eliot's "sweet-voiced Queen Esther" (160) of Malthouse Yard shares more than a name with the biblical queen. She too is an orphan brought from her native land (in this case France), to be raised by a foster father. As Queen Esther pleaded for her people, she too will plead before the law of the land to save an innocent man—only to have him rule over her as her husband.

In describing Esther's testimony, George Eliot reveals her characteristic scorn for the legal discourse, limited as she sees it by self-interest. She begins by undercutting the validity of testimony: "man cannot be defined as an evidence-giving animal" (563), tempted as he is by "private motive," comments the narrator. The prosecution's witnesses give damning testimony against Felix, and though the narrator attributes to Felix "the sublime delight of truthful speech" in delivering his defense, he manages only to cheer himself without influencing his judges. From all indications Harold Transome is correct in deeming Felix's brilliant peroration an abysmal mistake. The jury will misunderstand it and the judge resent it, he tells Esther, and his assessment is borne out. For his part, Harold manages only slightly better in his attempt to impress the judge and jury, and when the questioning turns to his own political activities, Harold's temper gets the better of his oratory.

As in the trial scenes in George Eliot's earlier novels, testimony that might reveal the ambiguous complexities of reality proves to be irrelevant to the legal proceedings, a judgment having been reached even before the trial has begun. With a sinking sense of the futility of this word game as a means for discovering the truth, Esther is inspired to speak.

The description of Esther's thoughts leading up to this decision reveals the extent of George Eliot's commitment to the myth of woman as oracle for a transcendent law.

> When a woman feels purely and nobly, that ardour of hers which breaks through formulas too rigorously urged on men by daily practical needs, makes one of her most precious influences: she is the added impulse that shatters the stiffening crust of cautious experience. Her inspired ignorance gives a sublimity to actions so incongruously simple that otherwise they would make men smile. Some of that ardour which has flashed out and illuminated all poetry and history was burning to-day in the bosom of sweet Esther Lyon. (571)

Unfortunately, despite Eliot's clear attempt to celebrate women's contributions to the pursuit of truth, one might also read this passage as suggesting that, thanks to her own marginality, ignorance, and impracticality, a woman can offer an original perspective. Recalling George Eliot's own cutting remarks in "Silly Novels" on the inspiration of idiots who have only their passionate intensity to recommend them, the reliability of this perspective seems dubious.[27] Nevertheless, George Eliot wishes here to confer upon such inspiration the sublimity of great poetry and epic actions.

Superficially, Esther's testimony itself follows the model of the female witnesses in Helen Fleetwood. Unlike Gaskell's Mary Barton, she is unselfconscious of herself as spectacle, of her own beauty as well as of the chance that she might look ridiculous. Her speech is sincere and plain: "her clear voice sounded as it might have done if she had been making a confession of faith" (572), and in a sense, she is. She testifies to the nobility of Felix's sentiments, concluding with her confession of faith in Felix: "he could never have had any intention that was not brave and good" (573). Esther's audience is entranced by her "naive and beautiful" action. She has been transformed from a beautiful "toy or ornament" (573) by serving as the medium for some transcendent force. "Some hand had touched the chords, and there came forth music that brought tears" (573). And, still true to the earlier model, the "acting out of that strong impulse . . . exhaust[s] her energy" (573), so that Esther returns to her place in a daze.

Yet, despite the narrator's sound and fury in extolling Esther's action, the content of her testimony signifies virtually nothing in terms of the verdict she meant to influence. Rather, it is the essentially chivalrous desire to please a " 'modest, brave, beautiful woman' " (576) like Esther that moves a man like Sir Maximus Debarry to exert his influence on Felix's behalf. As Harold later tells Esther, " 'I think your speaking for him helped a great deal. You made all the men wish what you wished' " (589). This seems a rather sad anticlimax to so "sublime" a speech. Esther, the "essentially feminine" character, has been robbed of her voice to become an icon whose power depends wholly on her status as an object of desire. Woman is either the medium of a quasi-divine redemptive force, or she is a vessel of sexual power that makes men willing to relinquish their political power.

Esther's dramatic testimony at the trial seems to lead almost without interruption to her union with Felix: " 'I am weak,' " she confesses to Felix in her final dialogue, " 'my husband must be greater and nobler than I am' " (603). The utopian scene of Esther's future provided in the epilogue, which begins with her marriage and ends with the information that she has borne her husband "a young Felix," thus ensuring the continuation of the patriarchy, confirms the wisdom of the heroine's submission to destiny. "I will only say that Esther has never repented," the narrator concludes.

However, in the penultimate chapter, George Eliot returns to the tragedy of Mrs. Transome. The conclusion of this plot deals one last blow to the adulteress's attempt to escape patriarchal control. As ineluctable as the force of history, with which it is perhaps synonymous, patriarchal authority reasserts itself. When the lawyer Jermyn, the father of the illegitimate child, returns to the world of Transome Court, it is to destroy both mother and child. Mrs. Transome allowed herself to become the victim of his law by failing to renounce her desires as Esther has done. Unknowingly, Harold too has sold his soul to this incarnation of self-interest and exploitation by adopting Jermyn's own unscrupulous behavior, thereby following in his father's footsteps.

Esther alone has the power to rescue Mrs. Transome from despair and restore the son to his mother. Isolated from her husband, her former lover, and now her son, Mrs. Transome still remains impenitent, absorbed by self-pity and frustration. Then she thinks of Esther.

> The proud woman yearned for the caressing pity that must dwell in that young bosom . . . She had never yet in her life asked for compassion—had never thrown herself in faith on an unproffered love . . . And she might have gone on pacing the corridor like an uneasy spirit without a goal, if Esther's thought, leaping towards her, had not saved her from the need to ask admission . . . (596)

Esther immediately intuits Mrs. Transome's need and her sympathy goes out to her. But no implicit vindication of Mrs. Transome's rebellion can be found in the ensuing exchange, a significant contrast to the effect of Hetty's confession to Dinah.

Rather, Esther's role apparently requires that she justify the laws of men to women. When Mrs. Transome tells Esther that all men are "selfish and cruel," and that all they "care for is their own pleasure and their own pride," her words fall on Esther "with a painful jar." "Not at all," she replies (597). Esther's sympathy is tinged with horror as she contemplates "the dreary waste of years empty of sweet trust and affection" (597) suggested by Mrs. Transome's bitterness and Esther's vague understanding of her past. Nevertheless, she tends to her with a daughter's tenderness, and exerts her sexual power over Harold in order to restore the son's affection to his mother. Having acted the part of angel of mercy, Esther is then free to join Felix as his heroine. The law of transcendent historical forces—silent, ineluctable patriarchal order—overwhelms the illegitimate woman's voice.

Notes

I wish to thank John Beattie and John Langbein for their advice on researching this article, and my colleagues Catherine McClenehan, Claudia Johnson, Michael Gillespie, John Boly, and Russell Reising for their comments on various drafts.

1. I have used the following editions of these novels: Charlotte Elizabeth Tonna, *Works*, intro. by H. B. Stowe (New York, M. W. Dodd 1852); Elizabeth Gaskell, *Mary Barton* (London, Everyman 1971) (1848); George Eliot, *Adam Bede* (Baltimore, Penguin 1980) (1859) and George Eliot, *Felix Holt* (Baltimore, Penguin 1973) (1866). Page references are given in parentheses in the text.

2. The intersections between legal and literary discourses have become the site of some of the most important interdisciplinary work currently being done in the humanities. Legal scholars, such as Clare Dalton and Lincoln B. Faller, have applied methods of literary analysis to documents ranging from contracts to criminals' confessions, while literary critics, most notably Stanley Fish, have drawn parallels between methods of legal and literary interpretation, or mined court records for evidence of the essential artfulness of even these ostensibly straightforward documents. *See* Sanford Levinson and Steven Mailloux, eds., *Interpreting Law and Literature* (1988); Lincoln B. Faller, *Turned to Account: The Forms and Functions of Criminal Biography in Late Seventeenth- and Early Eighteenth-Century England* (1987). Literary historians interested in how women have been represented, both as political entities and as fictional characters, have found this interdisciplinary tack to be especially fruitful. Margaret Anne Doody, *see* " 'Those Eyes Are Made So Killing': Eighteenth-Century Murderesses and the Law," 46 (1) *Princeton U. Libr. Chron.* 49–80 (1984), and John Zomchick, among others, have done fine work on the interrelationships during the eighteenth century between the ways women were represented in drama and the novel and the way prosecutors, judges, and the press

described female criminals or victims of crime. This work has been possible because of the extensive body of scholarship on eighteenth-century legal history, particularly that of John Langbein and John Beattie. However, relatively little work has been done on this subject in the nineteenth century.

Catherine L. McClenahan has argued that in William Blake's *Jerusalem*, written during one of England's most legally and socially repressive periods, "Man" names that which has the authority to make and enforce law and "Woman" is that which is, or ought to be, subject to the law. Thus Woman's legitimate voice should be only a male-authorized echo; her other option is to be (an) outlaw, by presuming to voice possibilities denied or forbidden by Albion's laws; *see* Catherine L. McClenahan, "'Outlaws of the World': Female Will in Blake's *Jerusalem*" (unpublished paper delivered at the annual convention of the Modern Language Association, Washington, D.C., 1989). Susan Sage Heinzelman has drawn connections between the gendered judgments against the eighteenth-century parricide Mary Blandy and the nineteenth-century matricide Mary Lamb in "Women's Petty Treason: Feminism, Representation, and the Law" 20(2) *Journal of Narrative Technique* (Spring 1990) 89–106. Mary Poovey analyzes literary convention in Caroline Norton's accounts of her legal wranglings with her husband in *Uneven Developments: The Ideological Work of Gender in Mid-Victorian England* 51–88 (1988).

3. A bridle was a harness placed around the head, with a sharp-edged bit fastened in the victim's mouth, which lacerated her tongue if she attempted to speak. Probably the last public use of the bridle was in 1824, when the mayor of Chester ordered Ann Runcom, who had abused church wardens, to be placed in the device; *see Bygone Cheshire* (William Andrews ed., Chester, Phillipson and Golder 1895).

4. Winifred Gérin, *Elizabeth Gaskell* 261 (1980).

5. When Elizabeth Gaskell heard the rumor that *Adam Bede*, which she sincerely praised in a letter to "Gilbert Eliot," had been written by Marian Evans, she wrote to George Smith: "It is a noble grand book, whoever wrote it,—but Miss Evans' life liken at the best construction, does so jar against the beautiful book that one cannot help hoping against hope. But two people have directly assured me they have seen the assertion of her authorship in her own handwriting . . . Oh do say Miss Evans did *not* write it—" (August 4 [1859]. *The Letters of Mrs. Gaskell* 566–67 (J.A.V. Chapple & Arthur Pollard eds., 1966). For examples of Eliot's ostracism from her family and society, *see* Jennifer Uglow, *George Eliot*, 69–70, 144–145 (1987), and Gordon S. Haight, *George Eliot* 231–33, 336–37, 393–95 (1968).

6. Hester Burton, *Barbara Bodichon, 1827–1891*, at 65 (1949).

7. *Id.* at 68–71.

8. *Id.* at 65.

9. Joanna Johnston, *Runaway to Heaven: The Story of Harriet Beecher Stowe* 275 (1963).

10. Burton, *supra* note 6, at 65–66.

11. *See* the 1836 Trials for Felony Act in J. H. Baker, *An Introduction to English Legal History* 279 (2nd ed., 1979). George Eliot approved of this change, referring in *Adam Bede* to

defense counsel's summing up as "a favour not granted to criminals in those stern times" (481).

12. See further, Doody, supra note 2.

13. Harriet Taylor Mill, "The Emancipation of Women" in Essays on Sex Equality 197 (Alice S. Rossi ed., 1970).

14. Extraordinary Trial! Norton v. Viscount Melbourne for Criminal Consort 11–12 (London: William Marshall, 1836).

15. Id. at 33.

16. Caroline Norton, Letter to the Queen on Lord Cranworth's Marriage and Divorce Bill 85–86 (4th ed., London, privately published, 1854), quoted in Poovey, supra note 2, at 66.

17. Norton, supra note 16, at 136, quoted in Poovey, supra note 16, at 67.

18. Catherine Gallagher interprets the "feminization" of working-class characters as a way of insuring their dependence in a paternalistic view of social reform. Catherine Gallagher, The Industrial Reformation of English Fiction: Social Discourse and Narrative Form, 1832–1867, at 128–29 (1985).

19. Monica Correa Fryckstedt, "The Early Industrial Novel: Mary Barton and Its Predecessors," 63 Bull. of the John Rylands U. Libr. of Manchester 11–30 (1980).

20. Letters of Mrs. Gaskell, supra note 5, at 39, to Miss Lamont, January 5 [1849].

21. See Gaskell, Mary Barton, supra note 1, at 217 & 307–8.

22. In this exchange Gaskell upsets the hierarchy between confessor and the confessing described by Michel Foucault in The History of Sexuality: Volume I, at 61–62 (Robert Hurley trans., 1978).

23. Elaine Showalter, A Literature of Their Own: British Women Novelists from Brontë to Lessing 7 (1977).

24. Patrocinio P. Schweickart, "Reading Ourselves: Towards a Feminist Theory of Reading," in Gender and Reading: Essays on Readers, Texts, and Contexts 46 (Elizabeth A. Flynn & Patrocinio P. Schweickart eds., 1986).

25. Fred C. Thomson, "The Genesis of Felix Holt," PMLA (Dec. 1959), 576–84.

26. See Suzanne Graver's detailed discussion of the contradictions that the thought of Comte, Feuerbach, and Herbert Spencer produced in George Eliot's feminism in Suzanne Graver, George Eliot and Community: A Study in Social Theory and Fictional Form (1984). See especially id. at 168–76.

27. Eliot comments of "oracular" novelists that "there seems to be a notion abroad among women, rather akin to the superstition that the speech and actions of idiots are inspired, and that the human being most entirely exhausted of common sense is the fittest vehicle of revelation." The Essays of George Eliot 310 (Thomas Pinney ed., 1963). Suzanne Graver comments on this point: "Esther's power, derived from her 'inspired ignorance' and 'incongruously simple' testimony, speaks only in the most minimal way to the daylight realities presented throughout the novel." Graver, supra note 26, at 145.

REPRESENTING THE LESBIAN IN
LAW AND LITERATURE

Anne B. Goldstein

▼

Introduction

This essay addresses the question "what is involved in representing a lesbian?" in two contexts, law and literature. Its premise is that the work of novelists is enough like the work of lawyers that useful insights can be drawn in at least one direction. That is, lawyers can learn how to represent lesbian clients better by studying books with lesbian characters. This is a preliminary, anecdotal, and impressionistic effort. I do not pretend to have canvassed either all of the reported cases in which one of the parties was identified as a lesbian (either by herself, by another party, or by the court),[1] or all of the books with lesbian characters.[2] For the "law" side of this project, I am relying upon seven years' experience as a litigator and eight years' further reading and reflection about the problems and strategies of representing lesbians. For the "literature" side, I am relying upon my own haphazard reading and upon several more systematic surveys of the field.[3]

The essay begins by exploring the general problem of representing lesbian clients. Then, after a broadbrush survey of lesbian literature, with particular attention to the problems of character construction and presentation, it explores ways images of lesbians from literature have been used, and ways they could be used, to represent the lesbian clients in two paradigmatic cases.

Lesbian Litigation

The work of a lawyer is, in some respects, like the work of a novelist. Litigation is a storytelling contest. To win, a lawyer must tell a compelling story. The story is not fiction, because the lawyer is obligated to present the truth, but truth is a conclusion. Every one of us experiences the world differently. From our particular vantage points, we see and hear what others do not, and we miss some of what they perceive. Shaped by our own histories and hopes, we make our own inferences. We accent. We discount. Six witnesses to the same event will swear to six different versions of it, and none will be lying. The lawyer's job is to take these various, conflicting, accounts and by selection and emphasis construct a version that will convince the finder of fact.[4] The lawyer is a technician of the truth.

The lawyer needs convincing characters and a strong plot for her story as much as any novelist does. The lawyer wants, generally speaking, to show her client to be at least appealing if not attractive and to portray her client's actions as understandably motivated and justifiable. She does not begin with a blank page. A good place for her to begin is with the client's history, personality, and appearance, and the details of the case itself; a good way to begin is by comprehending and refining the client's own self-understanding and self-presentation. These are only beginnings.

Presenting a believable version of any client's character involves imagination, construction, and presentation. The version must be robust enough to survive the opponent's inevitable challenge. Familiar stereotypes, when they fit, tend to be believable. The lawyer can use a suitable stereotype as a template. But for some clients no favorable stereotype seems to be available. Another way of saying this is: it is not at all clear what, if any, image of these clients would be favorable.

The challenging part of creating an image for a client usually begins with the craft of constructing it from evidence and presenting it clearly and persuasively. But for some clients, the challenging part of creating an image begins earlier, with imagining the client's character.

Not all lesbian clients are hard to imagine positively, of course. If the woman has been entirely circumspect about her personal life, and if the case itself has nothing whatever to do with that part of her experience and being, it may be both possible and desirable to preserve the tribunal's implicit assumption that she is heterosexual.[5] But if the client has proclaimed herself a lesbian or is likely to be perceived as one, or if the case itself is intertwined with the idea of lesbianism, the issue cannot be avoided.[6] Any attempt to avoid the issue in such cases will only make the client vulnerable to innuendos she cannot challenge. When the decisionmaker's response to a case depends at least in part upon the meaning it gives to "being a lesbian," the stigma must be confronted; it must be understood; it must be mastered.

This is not an easy job. Our culture is rich with mutually inconsistent but generally unfavorable stereotypes of lesbians. Lesbians are predatory, possessive, promiscuous, jealous, sadistic, masochistic, unnatural, unhealthy, bitter, man-hating, masculine, aggressive, frustrated, cold, over-sexed. Creating a favorable image for a lesbian client requires challenging these stereotypes—certainly not merely selecting from among them.

Fortunately, the lawyer need not struggle alone with this problem. Help is available from the client herself, who will have had to confront this problem in her daily life; moreover, the lesbian community can be a rich resource of self-conscious attempts to understand and represent lesbianism in positive ways. One excellent source of help can be contemporary lesbian novels. Ever since The Well of Loneliness,[7] lesbian novels have been argumentatively engaged in portraying, explaining, justifying, and apologizing for the lesbian.[8]

I am not recommending these books because I think they provide accurate pictures of lesbian life, nor because they bring the full resources of modern literature to bear upon the issues they consider. All too often, they do neither. Nevertheless, they can be valuable tools for a lawyer who is representing a lesbian client. Read carefully, these books illuminate the problems of creating sympathetic lesbian characters. The strengths and weaknesses of each novel's strategies are displayed in its text.

Lesbian Literature in a Nutshell

Although some women have probably felt affection or sexual desire for other women in other societies and at other times, the construction of these feelings and their physical expression into "lesbianism" did not occur until the late 1800s in Western Europe.[9] Before the early twentieth century, women in England, Europe, and North America were encouraged to form emotional attachments with one another; a woman's doing so was considered welcome evidence of her capacity to love a husband and children.[10] That two women might be lovers was often considered literally impossible;[11] even when the possibility was acknowledged, such lovemaking was often considered inherently unthreatening to heterosexuality because two women could not impair one another's virginity, could not produce a child, and could arouse but not satisfy one another.[12] In any event, even when acts of lovemaking between women were condemned and punished, the behavior was not seen as a sign that the women involved were somehow essentially different from other women.

The idea that some women's sexuality made them essentially different from other women emerged from the new discipline of sexology at the end of the nineteenth century, just as the women's movement was developing a critique of incest, rape, and sexual abuse of children and just as some middle-class women were finding it possible to live independently.[13] The sexologists depicted the lesbian as a masculine woman, from birth more like a man than a woman in her tastes, inclinations, activities, and desires.[14] Havelock Ellis called her a "congenital invert," meaning that from birth her interests were the opposite of what they should have been. Clearly, this concept depended upon seeing the sexes as "opposite," with complementary but entirely different qualities. It depended as well upon a normative view of the true woman as one who knew, accepted, even welcomed, her place in the domestic sphere.

According to the early sexologists, the congenital invert had an "unnatural" interest in physical activity, intellectual rigor, and other women. But not in other women like herself: just like a real man, this pseudo-man was interested in "normal women." Every lesbian couple was thus composed of one real lesbian and one pseudo-lesbian, a normal woman whose naive trust and affectionate openness were being exploited by her lover. The real lesbian might be pitied because her congenital abnormality denied her a woman's true fulfillment, loving a man and bearing him children. The pseudo-lesbian, however, was much more to be pitied. Although capable of living a normal life, she was denied one by her thrall to her lover's sterile (if enticing) sexual wiles.[15]

The concept of the invert had an obvious place in the struggle over whether women should be allowed to engage in such "masculine" pursuits as higher education, athletics, voting, holding public office, and working for wages outside the home. It lent scientific respectability to the political position that women should do none of these things but instead should be subject to the control of men, by asserting that autonomy was pathological in women. It undermined women's solidarity by making them uncomfortable with their affection for one another. It was used to stigmatize the unmarried women who led the women's movement as unhealthy, bitter, frustrated, and dangerous spinsters, and to undermine support for feminist reforms.[16]

Women responded to these assaults in a variety of ways. One of those ways was the invention of the lesbian novel.

The Well of Loneliness

Radcliffe Hall invented the lesbian novel in response to the concept of the congenital invert, which she accepted for literary purposes if not in her own life, and the stereotype of the spinster, which she rejected.[17] In The Well of Loneliness, she portrayed independent single women as self-sacrificing, brave, and noble. She hoped that the book would combat the prejudice against them.[18]

Hall's heroine in The Well of Loneliness, Stephen Gordon, was so closely modeled on the sexologists' ideas [19] that Havelock Ellis endorsed the book as presenting "in a completely faithful and uncompromising form, one particular aspect of sexual life as it exists among us to-day." [20] Stephen's early interests in masculine pursuits are encouraged by her father, who recognizes that she is an invert, although he tries to protect her by never sharing this insight with anyone.[21] After her father's death, Stephen falls in love with a married woman and, when the affair becomes known, Stephen is forced by her mother to leave her ancestral estate. The First World War interrupts Stephen's exploration of the homosexual subculture of Paris; she joins the ambulance corps and meets Mary Llewellyn. Mary was as closely modeled on the pseudo-lesbian as Stephen was on the congenital invert. A penniless orphan, she is younger and smaller than Stephen, and described as feminine. During the war, Stephen and Mary drive ambulances together and fall in love. After the war, at Mary's request, they set up housekeeping together in Paris, but Stephen's scruples keep their relationship chaste until Mary, in frustration, threatens to leave.[22] Even then, before she will make love with Mary, Stephen feels bound by honor to warn her that, "Our love may be faithful even unto death and beyond—yet the world will call it unclean." [23] They live together for some years, until Martin Hallam, an old beau of Stephen's, falls in love with Mary and convinces Stephen that Mary would be better off with a real man. Ever noble, Stephen pretends to be having an affair in order to drive Mary away from her and into Martin's arms.

The Well of Loneliness was the first, and probably remains the best known, lesbian novel.[24] It would be an exaggeration to say that every subsequent lesbian novel has been formed in response to it. But many have been. The Well of Loneliness establishes three questions for the lesbian protagonist to answer (or for the author to answer on her behalf): First, who am I (and how did I get this way)? Second, who will love me (given that those I love are forbidden to me)? Third, even if I can find a woman who will love me, how will we live in a world that forbids our love and limits our vocational opportunities? These remain the three characteristic questions of the lesbian novel.[25]

The first question—Who am I and how did I get this way?—provides the ground for The Well of Loneliness. The answer that Stephen was just born that way, a scientifically recognizable and naturally occurring type of human being, is central to the novel's portrayal of her as a tragic figure. Stephen could not choose to be other than she was, a man trapped in a woman's body and circumstances. No matter how honorably she acted, she was wrong, from birth and by definition. The second question—Who will love me?—sets the plot in motion. Stephen spends two-thirds of the book looking for such a person. Yet even when Stephen finds Mary, who feels that she has been waiting all her life for Stephen,[26] the novel's answer to the third question dooms their love. Although Stephen's wealth supports them in comfort, and she earns additional income as an author, society has no place for them. Mary has no family; Stephen's mother permits Stephen to visit only if she comes alone. Respectable homes are closed to them, and the Parisian demimonde where they are welcome is presented as decadent and unfulfilling.[27] Stephen thinks herself strong enough to survive this, but fears that Mary will not be. It is this weight of social disapproval that Stephen means to spare Mary when she drives her into Martin's arms.

These days, lesbians are portrayed as women rather than as men born into the wrong bodies. Concern about the causes and development of lesbianism also seems outdated, perhaps because the respectable scientific opinion now is that it is merely one normal variation among many human possibilities.[28] Those novels that even bother to provide an explanation for their characters' lesbianism tend to rely on psychology rather than biology.[29] Nevertheless, from the 1950s to the present, lesbian novels have tended to have characters that Radcliffe Hall and Havelock Ellis would find familiar. These novels either have protagonists who are really interested only in relationships with other women ("true lesbians") or portray couples where one member is a "true lesbian," while the other is capable of satisfying relationships with men (a "pseudo-lesbian").

It is hard for an author writing about such a couple to keep the true-lesbian character from seeming predatory, because by loving the pseudo-lesbian she is depriving her of other, better opportunities.[30] Stephen's self-sacrificing nobility is one solution, but it is self-defeating. To prove the purity of her love, Stephen has to renounce Mary. This ending promoted Radcliffe Hall's argumentative program; Stephen's suffering was necessary to the plea for tolerance with which the novel ends. But whatever its artistic or argumentative function, Stephen's renunciation of Mary has depressed generations of the novel's readers.[31] Indeed, its critics have sometimes tried to show that a more optimistic message is hidden within the novel[32] or to explain that its portrayal of lesbians is factually inaccurate.[33]

Perhaps the same energy that motivates critics of The Well of Loneliness to rewrite it also animates lesbian novelists. Whether its tragic ending is inevitable is a puzzle that lesbian novels have sought to unravel for decades. Their solutions to the puzzle are diverse, but their strategies fall into a few recognizable patterns. All of them depend upon varying at least one of the key elements of The Well of Loneliness while leaving the others more or less constant.

The key elements of The Well of Loneliness seem to be these. First, the protagonist is a true lesbian, attracted only to other women. Second, the protagonist is stronger and more powerful than the woman to whom she is attracted. Third, the woman to whom she is attracted is a pseudo-lesbian, that is, she is capable of a satisfying relationship with a man. Fourth, society offers two women no opportunities for a full, rich, satisfying, open life together. Finally, the protagonist cannot be happy unless she is in a committed, coupled, relationship with another woman.

Rewriting The Well of Loneliness

Although a few exceptions can be found in which the story is told from Mary Llewelyn's perspective—that is, by a protagonist attracted to both men and women[34]—the first element of The Well of Loneliness is not usually varied. Whether or not she is troubled by her answer, and whether or not she wonders how it came to be thus, the protagonist's answer to the question "Who am I?" is usually "I am a lesbian."

In contrast, many novels abandon the second element, making the true lesbian no stronger than her beloved in order to equalize power between the members of the couple.[35] This is perhaps the most frequently used strategy for undermining the inevitability of Stephen's tragedy. A common device for accomplishing it is to make the true lesbian younger, smaller, less sophisticated, less wealthy, or less self-confident than her lover. A true lesbian who is less powerful than her pseudo-lesbian beloved does not bear Stephen's full responsibility for the relationship, and therefore need not renounce it. The Price of Salt[36] is a classic illustration of this approach. In order to show that neither member of the couple is the other's victim, the book portrays each as an autonomous actor whose occupation and circumstances make her relatively independent of society and of her lover.[37]

In The Price of Salt, the true lesbian is Therese, an orphan in her early twenties working behind the counter of a New York City department store while trying to become an apprentice stage designer. Therese falls in love at her first sight of Carol, a wealthy married woman in her mid-thirties, and pursues her without entirely understanding what she wants. Carol, a pseudo-lesbian[38] who is divorcing her husband and has recently had a brief affair with a girlhood friend, understands but waits through two-thirds of the book before taking Therese to bed. The novel is so successful in disempowering Therese that Carol herself is in danger of seeming predatory. A good part of the last third of the book is therefore spent diminishing Carol's self-confidence and letting Therese mature a little. By the end of the novel, Therese is entering the bohemian and tolerant world of the theater; Carol has a job as a buyer for a furniture store. The book ends with them planning to move together into a two-bedroom apartment in Manhattan.

The Color Purple,[39] which certainly has a larger agenda than rewriting The Well of Loneliness, nevertheless takes the strategy of disempowering the true lesbian to perhaps its furthest possible extreme. Celie, the novel's heroine, is in some respects a classic true lesbian: the only person she is ever sexually attracted to is Shug Avery, her husband's mistress, whom she loves even before first sight (when she sees her photograph).[40] Celie is also the most powerless person in the book. She is raped by her stepfather; her babies are taken away from her; she is married against her will to a man who treats her like a slave and even brings his sick mistress home for her to nurse. For a long time, Celie endures these outrages passively; even when she begins to act independently, she never becomes particularly bold. It is simply not possible to see Celie as predatory, or even seductive. Yet Shug Avery (who is beautiful, powerful, and clearly portrayed as being primarily attracted to men) comes to love Celie, and eventually to choose her over everyone else. Unlike Carol in The Price of Salt, Shug runs no risk of being seen as predatory, either. She is, very clearly, just about the best thing that ever happened to Celie.

Another commonly used way to undermine the inevitability of Stephen's tragedy is to vary the third element of The Well of Loneliness by showing that, whatever her sexual preferences, the woman the true lesbian loves has no realistic hope of a satisfying relationship with a man. There are two ways to do this. One is to present men as so awful that a woman is rationally preferable. The other is to reimagine the couple as composed of two true lesbians.

The Color Purple is almost an example of the first of these devices: Celie is badly abused by men, but since she has already been established as a true lesbian she does not need any additional excuse for preferring a woman lover. Fried Green Tomatoes at the Whistle Stop Cafe[41] therefore provides a clearer example of this device, because here it is used to justify the choice made by a pseudo-lesbian. The relationship between Idgie Threadgoode and Ruth Jamison, the proprietors of the eponymous cafe, is one important strand in this novel's recounting of seventy years' history of the black and white communities in Whistle Stop, Alabama. Idgie is a true lesbian who refuses even to wear women's clothing after age ten or eleven. She falls in love with Ruth when she is sixteen and Ruth about twenty-two, the summer that Ruth stays in Idgie's home while working with Idgie's mother's church. To Idgie's distress, Ruth leaves at the end of the summer to get married. Ruth's husband, Frank Bennett, is the villain of the novel; a seducer of innocent girls and member of the Ku Klux Klan, he rapes Ruth on their wedding night, beats her, runs around, and generally makes her life miserable. In contrast, Idgie, to whom Ruth eventually returns, is brave, funny, loyal, gentle, generous, wise, and completely without race prejudice.

The other way to vary The Well of Loneliness's third element is to reimagine the lesbian couple as composed of two true lesbians. Patience and Sarah[42] is remarkably successful at this. The novel is set in the early 1800s in New England. Patience is a middle-class Quaker spinster in her late twenties; Sarah is six years younger, the tallest daughter of a poor farmer who, because he has no sons, has raised her to do men's work. Neither woman is sexually attracted to men. They meet, fall in love, and plan to homestead on the frontier together. But when their families intervene, Sarah goes away alone, dressed as a boy, to discover the limits of that impersonation and the dangers of the road. Upon her return, Sarah reconciles with Patience and they become lovers. When their lovemaking is interrupted by Patience's sister-in-law, they are compelled to leave their community together. Patience's brother buys out her share in their farm, and she uses the money to buy a new farm in a distant community where, as the novel makes clear, she will live out her life with Sarah.

The novel alternates Patience's first-person narration of the story with Sarah's. This lets us in on both characters' internal lives in order to show us that each woman is moving autonomously toward the other, that their love is mutual, and that their sexual relationship is equally desired and equally important to them both. Moreover, the women are mutually dependent in other ways. Sarah could no more survive without Patience's domestic skills than Patience could survive without Sarah to farm their land. The narration thus works together with the plot to make clear that neither woman is taking advantage of the other.

The fourth element of The Well of Loneliness is Stephen's belief that society offers two women no opportunities for a full and open life together. In a sense, all of the novels that end with a lesbian couple living together are challenging Stephen's view of society, although almost all of them do place the couple in some sheltered nook where the ordinary rules are relaxed.[43] Interestingly, the few novels that take on the issue directly reach equivocal results. Two notable examples are This is Not For You[44] and Cactus.[45]

The final element of The Well of Loneliness is that the true lesbian finds happiness impossible alone. The final way to undermine Stephen's tragedy, therefore, is to teach the heroine other ways to be happy. Rubyfruit Jungle[46] and Unusual Company[47] are two good examples of this strategy, because in them the protagonists' development of autonomy is much more important than their romantic success or lack of it.

Because the lesbian novelist must find a way to reimagine the lesbian heroine and her world in order to rewrite The Well of Loneliness, the novelists' strategies can be useful to a lawyer faced with the analogous problem of reimagining a lesbian client and persuading her world to make room for her.

Using Lesbian Novels to Represent Lesbian Clients

I will use two cases as examples in order to suggest the lineaments of a literary approach to the lawyer's problem of understanding how to represent a lesbian client. The first example is the famous case of Sharon Kowalski and Karen Thompson, which I know about primarily from published reports.[48] It involves a woman, Karen Thompson, who successfully recast the meaning of "lesbian lover," turning her relationship with Sharon Kowalski into a reason for the court to make her Sharon's guardian rather than a reason to let Sharon's father prevent her from visiting Sharon.[49] Sharon's severe injuries involved the courts in what had been until then a merely private dilemma, roughly corresponding to the lesbian novel's second question, "Who will love me?" Karen's lawyer's task was to establish Karen's relationship with Sharon as deserving of recognition and protection, even over Sharon's parents' strenuous objections. To accomplish it, the lawyer had to solve much the same problem as a novelist trying to rewrite The Well of Loneliness: she had to show that her client was not predatory, not decadent, not unnatural, in insisting upon her love rather than nobly renouncing it.

The second example is a case I handled early in my career, involving a woman who almost lost her job for "being a lesbian." It illustrates both the dilemma of "lesbian identity," which roughly corresponds to the lesbian novel's first question, "Who am I?" and the use of strategies taken from novels primarily concerned with the third question, "How will we live?"

Karen Thompson and Sharon Kowalski

Karen Thompson and Sharon Kowalski are perhaps the most famous lesbian couple in the United States. They are famous because, after Sharon was so severely brain-damaged in an automobile collision that she became paralyzed and unable to speak,[50] Karen insisted on the importance, continuity, and permanence of their relationship.

They are famous because Karen refused to go away when Sharon's parents asked her to; Karen instead hired a lawyer and fought to become Sharon's guardian. And when she lost that fight,[51] Karen didn't give up; she fought for the right to visit Sharon over the objection of the guardian the court had chosen, Sharon's father. And when she lost that fight,[52] Karen didn't give up; she fought to have Sharon's competence reexamined, to have experts determine whether Sharon was able to decide for herself who she wanted to have visit her.[53]

Karen Thompson and Sharon Kowalski are famous because, in order to raise money for the legal battles, Karen named them and their love lesbian, and made their story public in such an affecting way that, on Sharon's thirty-second birthday in 1989, National Free Sharon Kowalski Day was celebrated with parades and vigils in twenty-one United States cities.[54] They are famous because two weeks after Sharon was moved from a nursing home to a rehabilitation facility for evaluation and treatment, and three and one-half years after Karen had last been allowed to visit her, Sharon asked to see Karen.[55] They are famous because, finally, eight years after Sharon's accident, the Minnesota Court of Appeals named Karen to be Sharon's guardian, ruling that "Sharon . . . has clearly chosen to return home with [Karen] if possible" and that "[Karen] Thompson and Sharon [Kowalski] are a family of affinity, which ought to be accorded respect."[56]

Sharon Kowalski and Karen Thompson are famous because their story is so arresting; it makes good copy. And so many useful morals can be drawn from it: the importance of committed but unmarried couples exchanging durable powers of attorney;[57] the necessity of legalizing gay marriages;[58] the possibility of women triumphing over adversity;[59] the importance of disabled persons having a voice in their own destinies.[60]

But notice this: the now-dominant version of the story—in which Karen has been steadfastly, faithfully, and courageously keeping the vow she made to Sharon when, in 1979, they secretly exchanged rings and promised to share their lives—was not the only possible interpretation of the evidence. Indeed, trial judges twice rejected it in favor of Sharon's father's competing version of the story. In Donald Kowalski's version, Sharon was not a lesbian and Karen was not her lover.[61] Karen alone was a lesbian, with a predatory, aggressive, possessive, and unnatural interest in Sharon that exposed his gravely disabled daughter to possible sexual abuse.[62]

Sharon's car crashed in November 1983. After Sharon's accident, once it became clear she had been gravely injured, both Karen Thompson and Donald Kowalski sought to become her guardian. The judge believed that Sharon and Karen had a "significant relationship," and therefore, although he named her father as Sharon's guardian, the judge at first required Donald Kowalski to let Karen visit.[63] Unfortunately, Karen's relationship with Sharon's parents was, in the court's delicate words, "difficult," and it "deteriorated."[64] Time and again, they fought in court over access to Sharon's medical and financial records and to Sharon herself. Finally, the judge decided that only one of them could be in control, and, in July 1985, he picked Sharon's father.[65] When he did so, the judge surely knew that Donald Kowalski would use his power to move Sharon three hundred miles away from Karen's home and not let Karen visit. Even after Donald Kowalski had barred Karen from seeing Sharon, the judge backed him up. And, both times, the Court of Appeals of Minnesota backed up the trial judge.[66]

In fact, although Karen's version of the story is undoubtedly the one that, by helping her raise money for legal expenses, enabled her to succeed in court, it has never been entirely the source of that success. The trial judge finally let Karen visit Sharon not because he believed that they were "spouses in every respect but the legal"[67] and that therefore Karen had a right to visit, but instead because he became convinced that Sharon was capable of knowing and expressing her own mind in this matter.[68] Similarly, Karen has succeeded in becoming Sharon's guardian at last because the Minnesota Appeals Court has become convinced that Sharon is capable of choosing her own guardian, and that Karen is extremely caring and devoted to Sharon,[69] and because it rejected the competing version offered by two of Sharon's childhood friends (her father having given up[70]) that Karen is "possessive, manipulative and domineering."[71]

Thus, whatever else it is, the Sharon Kowalski case is an example of two sides to a legal dispute explicitly contesting the character of a self-professed lesbian and the nature of a lesbian relationship. Moreover, whether or not the two sides were consciously aware of this or not, the competing versions of Karen's character, and of the relationship between Karen and Sharon, that each offered the court would be familiar to anyone conversant with the conventions of lesbian novels.

Donald Kowalski's version of Karen's actions and motivations (a version later pressed on the court by Sharon's old friends) draws on the concept of the invert and the stereotype of the spinster that were developed in the early years of this century. Now that North American women have won the rights to vote, to hold office, to go to college, to work for wages, to compete at the marathon distance in the Olympics, and to do many other things formerly denied them as well, it might seem that the concept of the "congenital invert" has become as obsolete as its name. Not so. The idea has survived the incidental specifics of its origin because it responds to anxieties prevalent among both men and women in times of changing expectations.

When Donald Kowalski portrayed Karen as an unhealthily domineering masculine woman who had to be prevented from preying upon his naive, innocent, and normal daughter, he was casting Karen as a congenital invert. In certain respects, she fit this stereotype, being a college professor of physical education—that is, both an athlete and an intellectual. Moreover, she was nine years older than Sharon, had been her teacher, and had even encouraged Sharon to coach track and then to teach physical education at the high school level.

Karen Thompson's response to Donald Kowalski's version of the story can be seen as going through two phases. In the first phase, Karen offered the court a competing version of her relationship with Sharon. In her book, Karen emphasized that it was Sharon who had pursued her. Sharon sought her out and asked to help coach the track team; Sharon visited her at home and in Ohio when she went there to finish her degree; Sharon rode a motorcycle. Sharon pushed Karen to declare her love, and, after they exchanged rings, it was Sharon who took the sexual initiative.[72] Without access to transcripts of the court proceedings, it is difficult to tell whether Karen was trying to show that Sharon was the true lesbian—the Therese to her Carol[73]—or that, like Patience and Sarah,[74] she and Sharon were mutually attracted true lesbians.

Either way, the story did not at first work for Karen. I can think of two possible reasons to account for its failure. First, it may not have been believed. Karen's version fit the evidence before the court no better than Donald Kowalski's did. After all, Karen was nine years older than Sharon, had supported her from time to time, and was the sole owner of their house. Moreover, the persuasiveness of The Price of Salt and Patience and Sarah depend upon their presenting the interior reflections of both members of each couple. For Karen's version to be persuasive, Sharon would have had to be able to second it. She either could not, or was not permitted to do so.[75] Inevitably, Sharon's present vulnerability would be read back into the past, undermining Karen's story.

The second possibility that occurs to me is that Karen's version was believed,[76] but that it did not prove enough. In effect, Karen's story was that she was Sharon's spouse, and should therefore be treated by the court as her natural guardian.[77] But Donald Kowalski was Sharon's father, an equally natural choice as a guardian, as the Minnesota Court of Appeals pointed out in denying Karen's first appeal.[78]

But Karen's response to Donald Kowalski's version of her relationship with Sharon never depended entirely upon proof about Karen's worth. When Donald Kowalski was made Sharon's guardian, Karen retained new counsel[79] and her case entered its second phase. Now, Karen relied not only on her own fitness as Sharon's guardian, but also on Sharon's right to make her own decisions. Perhaps recognizing that her earlier defeat hinged on the court's inability to see Sharon as autonomous, Karen pressed to have Sharon's competence independently and professionally evaluated.[80] If Donald Kowalski had won because he was Sharon's father, then let the court consider the risk that his exertion of patriarchal authority was unnecessarily infantilizing Sharon.[81]

It is this second strategy that seems to have brought Karen success. Thanks to Karen's efforts, Sharon was moved from the nursing home where Donald Kowalski had been keeping her to a rehabilitation facility.[82] Soon afterwards, she asked to see Karen. Since then, Karen has visited "three or more days per week, actively working with her in therapy and daily care."[83]

In December 1990, Karen again sought to be Sharon's guardian, with the support of the entire medical and allied health-professional treatment team caring for Sharon.[84] Surprisingly, although Karen's petition was formally unopposed, the trial judge nevertheless chose to appoint a "neutral third party" as Sharon's guardian instead. His reasons illustrate the extreme difficulty of imagining a lesbian couple in positive ways. Although the judge had by now become entirely convinced both that Sharon "had a loving, intimate relationship with Karen Thompson" before her accident and that Karen had since demonstrated "constant commitment and devotion" to Sharon's welfare,[85] he clearly remained troubled by an issue that both Havelock Ellis and Radcliffe Hall would have recognized: whether, and to what extent, the relationship was truly voluntary on Sharon's part.

First, although the trial judge did not find these concerns to be factually based, his opinion did note that "the evidence is contradictory as to whether [their] relationship was intact or in the process of breaking up at the time of the accident,"[86] and that "[d]espite her energetic commitment to Sharon, Ms. Thompson is described by some witnesses as possessive, authoritative, inflexible, and committed to her own political agenda."[87] Apparently, the judge could neither believe these claims nor entirely dismiss them. On appeal, however, the Minnesota Court of Appeals rejected the first of these contentions implicitly,[88] and the second explicitly.[89]

Second, although the trial judge believed Sharon to be capable of deciding with whom she wants to spend time, he did not believe that she had the capacity to choose her own guardian. Because Sharon "does not remember events subsequent to her accident," "has significant short-term memory loss," "has severe impairment of attention and concentration," and "is selective and inconsistent in the ways she interacts with her environment and other people," the trial judge concluded that Sharon's consistent and reliable requests, made over the past two years, to live in St. Cloud with Karen "are not tantamount to a preference of who should be her guardian."[90] On appeal, however, because the entire treatment and evaluation team working with Sharon had testified that Sharon was capable of expressing a reliable preference for her guardian, the Minnesota Court of Appeals concluded that "in the absence of contradictory evidence about Sharon's decision-making capacity from a professional or anyone in daily contact with her, the trial court's conclusion was clearly erroneous."[91]

Third, although the trial judge recognized that Karen had expressed a continuing desire to make peace with Sharon's family,[92] while they remained so implacably opposed to Karen that all Sharon's blood relatives said they would refuse to visit her if she lived with Karen—or even in the same town,[93] he seemed to blame the breach on Karen.[94] The core of this judgment seemed to be the judge's feeling that Sharon's family's repugnance was natural: Karen should never have told them that she was Sharon's lover. She brought this on herself.[95] Analogizing Sharon to a child claimed by warring parents, the judge concluded that only a neutral guardian could assure Sharon access to both sides of her family: her blood relations and "her family of affinity, the petitioner Karen Thompson."[96] The Court of Appeals saw this situation very differently: "It is not the court's role to accommodate one side's threatened intransigence, where to do so would deprive the ward of an otherwise suitable and preferred guardian."[97]

Finally, the trial judge concluded that Karen had invaded Sharon's privacy when Karen revealed Sharon's sexual orientation to her parents and to the public. He seemed unable to appreciate the link between the courts' earlier failure to recognize and respect Karen's bond with Sharon as important and legitimate—a failure he deplored[98]—and Karen's need to publicize the case in order to raise money for legal fees. The trial court opinion constructs a hypothetical pre-accident Sharon, whose hypothetical preferences the trial judge saw as more legitimate than the real Sharon's real decisions. Even public appearances to which Sharon consented seemed coerced to him.[99] Indeed, the judge suggested that Sharon might have a cause of action against Karen for involuntarily "outing" her, and that this possibility created a conflict of interest which, alone, would preclude Karen from serving as Sharon's guardian.[100] Here, too, the Court of Appeals saw things differently, concluding that "[t]he record does not support the trial court's concern on any of these issues."[101]

Karen Thompson's success in this case derives from her ability to challenge the stereotype within which her opponents attempted to confine her. By emphasizing and supporting Sharon's autonomy, individuality, and choice, Karen both undermined the basis for Donald Kowalski's version of her as a predatory, domineering invert and created conditions that finally permitted Sharon to be heard speaking for herself. Whether or not Karen's new lawyers learned it from the book, they succeeded because they adopted the narrative strategy of *Patience and Sarah* to tell Karen's and Sharon's story.

Mary Carmichael and Virginia

I once represented a young woman threatened with losing her job because she had told two or three people at work that she was a lesbian. I cannot tell you my client's name. Like all of the details of the case, that is a confidence I am bound to keep. But the story is easier to tell if I have a name to call her, so let it be Mary Carmichael.

One of the people Mary had told that she was a lesbian was an adolescent girl working as her after-school assistant. The girl's name is a secret, too; for these purposes, let us call her Virginia W. Virginia was puzzled by Mary's confidences and discussed the matter with her parents. They called the police. The police questioned Virginia at some length, trying to establish whether Mary had touched or otherwise molested her. She had not, but the police did discover that Mary had shown Virginia some "pictures of lesbians."

Virginia was considerably shaken by her interview with the police. She retired to her room to cry for several days, and her parents could not learn anything coherent about what had, or had not, happened. They were livid. They went to Mary's employer and demanded her discharge. Mary had always been a good worker, and her immediate supervisor wanted to keep her on. Mary's employer, however, was worried that her continued employment might bring the entire institution into disrepute. He suspended Mary and told her to get a lawyer.

Mary was bewildered by the storm around her. As it was to Karen Thompson, the idea of "being a lesbian" was new to Mary Carmichael. She was utterly unprepared for the response her announcement had received. She felt strongly that she had done nothing wrong. She was unwilling to resign quietly, even if challenging her discharge meant that she would become infamous in her small community, even if it meant that her widowed mother would learn her secret. It was up to me to control the meaning of her "lesbianism," if I could.

From the beginning, my goal was to convince everyone that my client had "done nothing": nothing bad, that is, nothing for which she should lose her job. At my first meeting with Mary, I learned that she had never been to bed with another woman, never kissed another woman, never even been in love with another woman. I therefore suggested to her that one way out of her difficulties might begin with a recantation. Surely Mary would not be lying if she said that she was not a lesbian. Surely it would not be unreasonable to define the term "lesbian" to include only those women who had actually had a sexual relationship with another woman, and not those, like Mary, who merely thought that they would like to.

I was thinking of Mary's case as a version of Lillian Hellman's "The Children's Hour."[102] In that play, school children convince their elders (almost inadvertently) that two women teachers are lovers although, in fact, they are not. Vague accusations are repeated, eventually acquiring a momentum all their own. The play ends tragically.[103] Virginia's reaction to Mary, Virginia's parents' reaction to their daughter, the police reaction to Virginia, and Mary's employer's reaction to everyone else, seemed similarly excessive. As in Hellman's play, everyone seemed to be responding to their own fears rather than to actual events. I was looking for a way to stop the hysteria, to bring things back to the ground.

But Mary was unwilling to recant. Perhaps she thought she would not be believed, but the reason she articulated was a different one. She had recently made friends with a group of women who identified themselves as lesbians and she had become convinced that she, too, was "a lesbian." She was sure, and, moreover, she felt good about it. She did not want to injure herself by denying what to her was an important and precious part of her identity.

What does it mean to identify oneself as a lesbian? What was it that Mary was so sure of? In Nora D. Randall's short story "Great Explanations," the heroine compares telling her parents that she's gay when she is, in fact, a "single lesbian," to "Edward VIII announcing that he was going to abdicate the throne because he was sexually attracted to foreign divorcées."[104]

Yet Randall's heroine did tell her parents, and Mary Carmichael did proclaim, and then refuse to deny, that she was "a lesbian." Mary identified herself as a lesbian because she considered her desires and inclinations to be at least as important as her actions. Her project, in short, was to understand herself as an active sexual being, as a person who might initiate as well as respond. Her desires mattered enough to be named and acknowledged because she intended that her actions would proceed from them, and that she would be responsible for both desires and actions. Her desires mattered enough that she refused to deny them, even conditionally or instrumentally. She was glad that she had come to understand herself and she was determined to make a place for herself in the world. This goal, in her view, was worth some risks.

Mary Carmichael was a lesbian, therefore, because she said so. Because she had said so, we had to contend with whatever expectations Mary's employers and Virginia's parents had: probably, judging by their reactions, that lesbians were unnatural, lascivious, and predatory. I needed to convince them that Mary had "done nothing," although she had undeniably befriended Virginia and confided in her. What could make it clear that Mary had done no wrong?

The police, Virginia's parents, and Mary's employer all kept coming back to the one concrete instance of misbehavior that their investigation had turned up: Mary had showed pictures of lesbians to an adolescent girl. None of them had seen the pictures; they could imagine them well enough. In fact, the pictures were of Mary's new friends, fully clothed, standing and sitting in someone's living room, smiling near a picnic table in some park. Mary had called them pictures "of lesbians" rather than "of my friends," because she wanted to emphasize that lesbians look, and indeed are, pretty much like everyone else. She had underestimated the difficulty of her point, the pornographic resonance of the phrase "pictures of lesbians."

The job of representing Mary turned out to involve little more than calming everyone down and getting them to look more closely at the evidence. In the end, I convinced them that Mary had done "nothing" because there was "nothing" in the pictures. The main issue for Mary's employer and for Virginia's parents was never whether or not Mary was a lesbian. They just wanted to know whether she had attempted to seduce the teenager working as her assistant. Virginia's parents' wrath, and Mary's employer's institutional concerns, were allayed once the true nature of the pictures was clear to them.[105] Mary was reinstated at work. There was no scandal.[106]

I was successful, I think, because I was able to get everyone to distinguish between the idea of "a lesbian" and the idea of "sex." I was not denying that lesbians have sex, or even that Mary herself did. I was just focusing attention elsewhere, to the fact that lesbians also have picnics. Many recent lesbian novels are similarly focused.[107] Taking their heroines' identities as lesbians for granted, and assuming their right to love, these novels address whatever comes next. Their lesbian characters live in and interact with the larger human community, and are presented as fundamentally like, rather than unlike, other women. These novels are attempting precisely what Mary Carmichael was attempting when she showed Virginia pictures of a picnic and called them "pictures of lesbians."

In contrast, the strategy I first proposed—the one Mary had rejected— was unlikely ever to have been successful. However impetuous Mary had been in disclosing a self-identification formed solely on the basis of desire, her sexual experience or lack of it was really beside the point. Our culture takes such desires very seriously indeed. Although "The Children's Hour" makes clear that Martha and Karen were never lovers, at the end of the play Martha finds herself guilty of the crime of loving Karen "the way they said," and executes herself for it.[108] There is a small subgenre among lesbian novels where the protagonist is clearly marked as a lesbian although she eschews, or renounces, sex altogether.[109] Even Nora D. Randall's quip does not suggest that her heroine was not "really" a lesbian—merely that she took unnecessary risks in admitting it.

Nevertheless, such desires no longer merit the death penalty. Mary Carmichael was entirely in tune with her times when she refused to try to purchase respectability with celibacy. Giving up sex is essentially an old-fashioned approach, in both life and literature. Most modern lesbian novels do not present their protagonists as celibate. Yet there is a curious reticence in their treatment of lesbian sexuality. Even when the novels contain a fair number of sexual encounters, they tend to be implied rather than described. And when the encounters are described, they tend not to be very convincing.[110] Sex is often written about in "vague, generalized, detached, and repetitive" metaphoric terms that lack concrete references, or imply a diffuse sensuality produced without specific touching. These descriptions obscure what the parties might actually be doing[111] in favor of evocations of the characters' emotional entanglements and their increasingly insistent desires.

Many people believe that maintaining silence about their own sexual inclinations, experiences, and actions is submission to societal constraints that they could challenge and perhaps overthrow by speaking. Mary Carmichael herself seemed to believe this. Foucault has taught us, however, that when we talk about sex the discourse itself shapes our experience. Thus, talking about sex is as much a way of submitting to social construction and control over our experiences and practices as it is a way of liberating ourselves from external constraints.[112]

One might ordinarily assume that lesbian novels are engaged in the project of liberating lesbians by breaking an enforced silence. In fact, however, although this is true about some aspects of lesbian existence, it is not generally true of lesbian sexuality. Perhaps this descriptive obscurity is a flaw in these novels, but perhaps not. Perhaps the novelists' strategies and my own were similar because our goals were similar: to deflect attention away from an area of vulnerability to something "more relevant." Whatever the strength of the strategy in novels, it worked for Mary Carmichael: she got her job back. And having been successful with the strategy once, I have used it again here in telling Mary's story: you will notice that I was careful to explain, early on, that Mary had never had a woman lover.[113]

Notes

© Anne B. Goldstein, 1994. An earlier version of this article was presented at the 1991 Orgain Symposium, "Feminist Practice," at the University of Texas School of Law, and has been published as "Representing Lesbians," 1 Tex. J. of Women and the Law 301 (1992). I am indebted to Mona Ammon, Pat Dickson, Nikki Fuller, Jack Getman,

Cathy Jones, Don Korobkin, Lorena Sol, Zipporah Wiseman, and especially Kathleen Lachance, for help with this article in its various stages of development. The errors of fact, judgment, and sensibility are entirely my own.

1. See Rhonda R. Rivera, "Queer Law: Sexual Orientation Law in the Mid-Eighties" (pts. I & II), 10 U. Dayton L. Rev. 459 (1985), 11 U. Dayton L. Rev. 275 (1986); Rhonda R. Rivera, "Recent Developments in Sexual Preference Law," 30 Drake L. Rev. 311 (1980–81); Rhonda R. Rivera, "Our Straight-Laced Judges: The Legal Position of Homosexual Persons in the United States," 30 Hastings L.J. 799 (1979).

2. This would be a truly daunting task. The standard bibliographical references are Jeannette Foster, Sex Variant Women in Literature (2d ed. 1975) (photo. reprint 1956); Barbara Grier, The Lesbian in Literature (3d ed. 1981); Miriam Saphira, The New Lesbian Literature, 1980–1988 (1988).

3. There are now many such studies; I have relied principally upon Jane Rule, Lesbian Images (1975); Lillian Faderman, Surpassing the Love of Men: Romantic Friendship and Love between Women from the Renaissance to the Present (1981); Lesbian Texts and Contexts: Radical Revisions (Karla Jay & Joanne Glasgow eds., 1990); Bonnie Zimmerman, The Safe Sea of Women: Lesbian Fiction 1969–1989 (1990); Paulina Palmer, "Contemporary Lesbian Feminist Fiction: Texts for Everywoman," in Plotting Change: Contemporary Women's Fiction 43, 43–62 (Linda Anderson ed., 1990).

4. This is a technical term. In a jury trial, it refers to the jury.

5. This course of action is never cost-free nor risk-free. It forsakes some opportunities to share humanizing details of the client's life, and risks exposing her to unanswerable and damaging innuendo. Nevertheless, the dangers of identifying the client as a lesbian may seem too great to risk "unnecessarily."

6. Perhaps the client is challenging the army's right to discharge her and refuse to let her reenlist after she has proclaimed herself "a lesbian" to her commanding officer. See, e.g., benShalom v. Secretary of Army, 489 F. Supp. 964 (E.D. Wis., 1980) (ordering reinstatement); benShalom v. Marsh, 690 F. Supp. 774 (E.D. Wis., 1988) (ordering reenlistment), cert. denied, 110 S. Ct. 1296 (1990). Or someone may be claiming that because she is a lesbian she is an unfit mother. Some states will never give custody to a homosexual parent, see Jacobsen v. Jacobsen, 314 N.W.2d 78 (N.D. 1981) (custody changed because mother is lesbian); Roe v. Roe, 324 S.E.2d 691 (Va. 1985) (award of custody to actively homosexual father error of law); others have held that a parent's sexual orientation is relevant to custody determination only if it is adversely affecting the child, see, e.g., Bezio v. Patenaude, 410 N.E.2d 1207 (Mass. 1980) (mother's lesbianism alone insufficient to deny her return of custody); Schuster v. Schuster, 585 P.2d 130 (Wash. 1979) (lesbian cohabitation in violation of prior custody decrees insufficient to warrant change of custody). See generally "Developments in the Law—Sexual Orientation and the Law," 102 Harv. L. Rev. 1508, 1630–40 (1989).

7. Radcliffe Hall, The Well of Loneliness (Anchor Books 1990) (1928).

8. Interestingly, writers of lesbian short stories often set themselves more ambitious agendas, but a discussion of these works is beyond the scope of this article.

9. See Ann Ferguson, "Is There a Lesbian Culture?" in *Lesbian Philosophies and Cultures* 63, 63–84 (Jeffner Allen ed., 1990); Diana Richardson, "The Dilemma of Essentiality in Homosexual Theory," in *Origins of Sexuality and Homosexuality* 79, 79–90 (John P. DeCecco & Michael G. Shively eds., 1985). Interestingly, the construction of love between men into "homosexuality" occurred at approximately the same time, although for different reasons. See Anne Goldstein, "History, Homosexuality and Political Values: Searching for the Hidden Determinants of *Bowers v. Hardwick*," 97 Yale L.J. 1073, 1086–89 (1988).

10. Faderman, *supra* note 3, at 65–102.

11. Lillian Faderman, *Scotch Verdict* (1983).

12. Faderman, *supra* note 3, at 23–37.

13. Sheila Jeffreys, *The Spinster and Her Enemies: Feminism and Sexuality 1880–1930* (1985).

14. Havelock Ellis described the "congenital invert" as a woman whose "female garments . . . usually show some traits of masculine simplicity," and whose "brusque energetic movements, the attitude of the arms, the direct speech, the inflections of the voice, the masculine straightforwardness and sense of honor, and especially the attitude towards men, free from any suggestion of either shyness or audacity," suggests her "underlying psychic abnormality." According to Ellis, congenital inverts smoked both cigarettes and cigars, had "a dislike and sometimes incapacity for needlework and other domestic occupations" and "some capacity for athletics." *Id.* at 106 (quoting 2 Havelock Ellis, *Sexual Inversion, Studies in the Psychology of Sex* 250 (F. A. Davis 1927) (1897).

15. *Id.* at 102–27; Esther Newton, "The Mythic Mannish Lesbian: Radcliffe Hall and the New Woman," in *The Lesbian Issue: Essays from Signs* 16–17 (Estelle B. Freedman et al. eds., 1985).

16. Jeffreys, *supra* note 13.

17. See Una, Lady Troubridge, *The Life of Radcliffe Hall* (1st Am. ed. 1963).

18. *Id.* at 81–82.

19. Stephen Gordon may have been modeled on Case 31 in Richard von Krafft-Ebbing, *Psychopathia Sexualis* (Philadelphia, London, F. A. Davis Co. 1892). See Rebecca O'Rourke, *Reflecting on The Well of Loneliness* 3–4 (1989).

20. Havelock Ellis, Commentary to *The Well of Loneliness*, *supra* note 7.

21. From the novelist's point of view, this was a mistake; Book One is full of Stephen's father's missed opportunities, culminating in his unsuccessful deathbed attempt to explain Stephen to her mother. Hall, *supra* note 7, at 118.

22. Stephen's scruples are explicitly based on the sexologists' models: she sees herself as "marked and blemished," like Cain, able to offer Mary love but neither protection nor respectability. *Id.* at 296–313.

23. *Id.* at 301. Mary responds: "What do I care for the world's opinion? What do I care for anything but you, and you just as you are—as you are, I love you!" *Id.* at 312.

24. See, e.g., Rule, *supra* note 3, at 50; O'Rourke, *supra* note 19, at 114–17; Zimmerman, *supra* note 3, at 7.

25. Bonnie Zimmerman identifies three similar questions about "the lesbian self," "the lesbian couple," and "the lesbian community." Zimmerman, *supra* note 3.

26. Hall, *supra* note 7, at 294 (she makes this declaration to Stephen the evening after Stephen is awarded the Croix de Guerre).

27. *Id.* at 333–91.

28. In 1973, the American Psychiatric Association removed homosexuality from its list of mental disorders because "homosexuality *per se* does not constitute any form of mental disease." *Resolution of the American Psychiatric Association*, December 14, 1973. In 1975, the American Psychological Association and the American Public Health Association each passed similar resolutions. *Resolution of the Council of Representatives of the American Psychological Association* (1975); *Resolution No. 7514 of the American Public Health Association* (1975).

29. The variety of psychological explanations offered reflects the self-contradictory diversity of theory that gave the etiology question such a bad name in the first place.

30. *See* Zimmerman, *supra* note 3, at 97.

31. O'Rourke, *supra* note 19, at 90–142.

32. *Id.* at 78–81.

33. Rule, *supra* note 3, at 60.

34. Letting the reader enter the pseudo-lesbian's consciousness would provide an opportunity to learn firsthand whether or not advantage is being taken of her. This strategy is used surprisingly infrequently, considering the volume of writing asserting that lesbianism is a choice which virtually any woman could make. *See, e.g.*, Jill Johnston, *Lesbian Nation: The Feminist Solution* (1974); Adrienne Rich, "Compulsory Heterosexuality," in *Powers of Desire: The Politics of Sexuality* 177, 177–205 (Ann Snitow et al. eds., 1983). Perhaps authors find it difficult to show that a protagonist who could choose to love either women or men is being neither decadent nor perverted when she chooses a woman.

Ann Cameron's novel, *The Journey* (1986), which does use this strategy, solves the problem by making every male character either unavailable or brutal. The novel is set in Canada in the late 1800s and tells the story of Anne and Sarah. Anne is a true lesbian, a tough orphan some eight or ten years younger than Sarah. She is only fourteen when she meets Sarah, a prostitute who has just been tarred and feathered by the same mob that lynched her pimp and lover, the gambler Keno. The two women join forces, first to operate a laundry, then to travel west with a wagon train, and finally to raise a brood of children on the Pacific coast. The text makes clear both that Sarah begins to feel a protective love for Anne almost immediately, and that Sarah remains sexually attracted to men. Sarah, who has had at least one woman lover in the past, avoids appearing predatory by waiting until Anne has grown up (and the book is almost over) before making love to her.

35. E.g., Suniti Namjoshi, *The Conversations of Cow* (1985) (exploring the assumption, implicit in most of the works under discussion, that if two women are lovers and their power is not equal, one is taking advantage of the other). This delightfully entertaining book tells the simple story of Suniti, a lesbian professor of English literature in Toronto, and Cow, a Brahmin lesbian cow goddess named Bhadravati (B for short).

The writing is so spare that a plot summary would be nearly as long as the book itself. Cow transforms herself into a human being of either sex, transforms Suniti into a variety of animals, and even gives her the experience of being "by herself" by splitting her into two identical women, S1 and S2. The transformations are often used to explore power dynamics between the couple. The novel is structured like an Indian myth exploring the meaning of gender, roles, and love.

36. Claire Morgan, *The Price of Salt* (Naiad Press rev. ed. 1984) (1952).

37. This strategy is so powerful that it is used even in books where both women are portrayed as attracted to men. *See* Jane Rule, *Desert of the Heart* (Talonbooks 1977) (1964 U.S. ed.). Ann is an orphan of twenty-five, working in a gambling casino in Reno, Nevada, and drawing cartoons for newspapers and magazines in her free time. Ann may be a pseudo-lesbian; it is hard to interpret the novel's insistence that she "could not marry [Bill,] a man she loved." *Id.* at 38. Instead, Ann chooses Evelyn, a pseudo-lesbian college English professor fifteen years her senior, in town only long enough to get divorced. After they have known each other for two weeks, Ann makes the first move. Evelyn rejects her out of "guilt and goodness," id. at 124, but relents a week later; further on in the book, Evelyn temporarily renounces Ann again, and for approximately the same reasons. The book ends with the couple planning to live together in the San Francisco Bay Area, where Evelyn teaches; Ann can live on her inheritance, draw her cartoons at home, and sell them by mail.

38. The novel emphasizes that Carol finds lovemaking with a woman no more "pleasant" than with a man, and that Carol's divorce was not precipitated by her attraction to women. Morgan, *supra* note 36, at 184, 188.

39. Alice Walker, *The Color Purple* (1982).

40. *Id.* at 16.

41. Fannie Flagg, *Fried Green Tomatoes at the Whistle Stop Cafe* (1988).

42. Isabel Miller, *Patience and Sarah* (Fawcett Crest, 1973) (1972 hardcover edition, which reprinted a self-published version titled *A Place for Us*).

43. *But see* Maureen Brady, *Folly* (1982) (offering an interesting counterexample). The novel's main characters, Folly and Martha, work in a mill together and live in adjacent mobile homes. They love each other as friends for years, but their sexual attraction develops while they are in the midst of leading a wildcat strike. Although their union comrades seem oblivious when Folly and Martha become lovers, a sub-plot does show Folly dealing with the reaction of her teenage daughter, Mary Lou, to her mother's lesbianism. *Folly* is one of the few novels of which I am aware which does not insulate its lesbian couple from societal disapproval by giving them wealth or privilege, by isolating them physically, or by situating them within a lesbian community that is presented, as Bonnie Zimmerman accurately observed, as a "safe sea of women." *See* Zimmerman, *supra* note 3. *See also* Edith Forbes, *Alma Rose* (1993) (story set in small Western town; protagonist and her two lovers are the only lesbians).

44. Jane Rule, *This is Not for You* (Naiad Press, 1982) (1970). *This is Not For You* reinterprets Stephen's nobility as guilt, self-denial, and self-hatred by showing that her fear

of society was irrational. The novel's protagonist, Kate, is a true lesbian who has refused to make a life with Esther, a college classmate who loves her. Time and again, Kate rejects Esther, driving her first to sex with men, then to a loveless marriage, and finally into a cloistered order. Kate herself eventually becomes a sort of secular nun, living celibately in Greece and administering a relief agency. The novel is in the form of a long autobiographical letter from Kate, written on the occasion of Esther's taking her final vows; the letter, like Kate's life, is "not" for Esther. Kate believes that she is protecting Esther, but the novel has a different point of view. A subplot, in which a true lesbian named Sandy achieves a happy and satisfying long-term relationship with another woman, makes it abundantly clear that Kate's self-denial is idiosyncratic and self-imposed rather than tragically inevitable.

45. Anna Wilson, *Cactus* (1980). *Cactus* gives full weight to Stephen's concern about social disapproval and isolation, but shows that times change. The novel tells a double story of two couples, a generation apart. Eleanor and Beatrice work in the same office and are best friends. During a seaside holiday, they become lovers. Eleanor wants to make their relationship permanent, but Beatrice finds this impossible because "you can't live a secret, because out in the open you find you're living something else. . . . [T]here really is no way of explaining it— . . . it's so totally inexplicable to the rest of the world that it doesn't exist." *Id.* at 11. So Beatrice marries and has two daughters; Eleanor remains single, supports her mother, and saves her money. After her mother dies, Eleanor buys a fruit shop in a small rural village and moves there. Eleanor has reached her mid-fifties when Ann and Dee, a lesbian couple in their late twenties, move to the village from London in order to "make a tangible commitment" to their relationship. *Id.* at 24. Ann works on her sculpture at home while Dee takes a job as Eleanor's assistant. The developing friendship between Eleanor and the younger couple causes Eleanor to reflect on what might have been with Beatrice, and starts Ann and Dee thinking about the ways a lesbian relationship could seem possible now but have seemed impossible a generation before. Then Beatrice, who has been finding her role as wife less engaging and fulfilling since her children have grown, unexpectedly arrives to visit Eleanor for a few days. Beatrice seems to be considering staying, but in the end she returns to her respectable husband Tim. Eleanor, grieving, withdraws from Ann and Dee. They, in turn, find village life unbearable without her friendship, and the book ends with their return to London's lesbian "ghetto."

46. Rita M. Brown, *Rubyfruit Jungle* (1973). *Rubyfruit Jungle* is much more the story of Molly Bolt's development than it is about her search for a mate. Molly falls in love several times, gets her heart broken, and bounces right back. For Molly, there is no important difference between real and pseudo-lesbians. As she says to one of her lovers, who is attempting to establish herself as a pseudo-lesbian to Molly's true lesbian, "We don't look like men, but when women make love it's commonly labeled lesbianism so you'd better learn not to cringe when you hear the word." *Id.* at 92. For Molly, the important distinction is between women with the courage to go after what they want, and women who lack that courage. Although the book ends with

Molly alone and out of work, the ending is happy because Molly has kept her courage intact.

47. Margaret Erhart, *Unusual Company* (1987). *Unusual Company* is the story of Franny's development. When the novel begins, Franny is twenty-two, a shy college student still living at home. She meets the thirty-year-old Claire in a New York City bookstore and begins slowly to get to know her. They are frightened of each other and of intimacy. Before they become lovers, Claire tells Franny,

> If you expect me to seduce you, throw you down, smother you with kisses, leap all over your body, you'll be disappointed. . . . If you want me, you're going to have to come half-way to get me. Otherwise on your part it's just you wanting the idea of me, isn't it? It's a put-on boldness, nothing to do with you."

Id. at 36.

This could be the story of two shy, powerless, true lesbians finding love together, but it takes another turn. Several months after they become lovers, Claire goes to the Caroline Islands to spend two years in an ashram and Franny buys a car and sets out across the country. From then on, the novel is the story of Franny's working through her grief over Claire's rejection. She meets, and loves, a series of women. Unlike Molly Bolt in *Rubyfruit Jungle*, whose affairs end when her lover's courage fails, Franny just moves on. The women she loves are confident and autonomous; none of them seems to be hoping for or expecting true love. By the end of the novel, Claire has returned, and Franny has rejected her. Franny, now twenty-seven, has grown two inches and learned "to make love to other women from a large place in me instead of in order to win them." *Id.* at 222.

48. On March 6, 1991, I attended a talk given by Karen Thompson at Smith College in Northampton, Mass. After the conclusion of the talk, I was able to speak with Ms. Thompson briefly. We also spoke briefly by telephone on March 17, 1991.

49. *In re Guardianship of Kowalski*, 478 N.W.2d 790 (Minn. App. 1991) (ordering that Karen Thompson be appointed Sharon Kowalski's guardian).

50. According to the most recent trial court decision in the case, as a result of severe closed-head injuries, Sharon Kowalski "suffers from 'traumatic encephalopathy,' which is considerable brain damage manifesting in memory loss, cognitive dysfunction, spasticity, lack of coordination, and motor problems that affect her posture, balance, arms, legs, and trunk." *In re Sharon Kowalski*, No. 11146, at 3–4 (Minn. Dist. Ct. April 23, 1991).

51. *In re Kowalski*, 382 N.W.2d 861 (Minn. Ct. App.), *cert. denied*, 106 S. Ct. 1467 (1986).

52. *In re Kowalski*, 392 N.W.2d 310 (Minn. Ct. App. 1986).

53. Joyce Murdoch, "Transfer Ordered for Disabled Woman; Minnesota Court Ruling May Open Door for Visits by Lover," *Washington Post*, December 15, 1988, at A21. After a six-day evaluation of Sharon at the nursing home where she had been living for the past three years, a team of evaluators recommended to the court that Sharon be transferred to a long-term rehabilitation facility to improve her commu-

nication skills, so that she could reliably express her wishes concerning visitation. They found Sharon's mental abilities "adequate but untested," because of her poor communication skills.

54. Nadine Brozan, "Gay Groups are Rallied to Aid 2 Women's Fight," *New York Times*, August 7, 1988, at A26.

55. Joyce Murdoch, "Minn. Woman Allowed to See Disabled Lover; Visit with Judge's Approval Is Latest Chapter in Lesbian Rights Case," *Washington Post*, February 6, 1989, at A18.

56. In re Guardianship of Kowalski, 478 N.W.2d 790, 793, 797 (Minn. App. 1991).

57. "Developments in the Law—Sexual Orientation and the Law," 102 *Harv. L. Rev.* 1508, 1623 n.136 (1989) ("Had the ward executed a durable power of attorney prior to her accident, the court might well have recognized her partner's right to legal guardianship."); Rhonda R. Rivera, "Lawyers, Clients, and AIDS: Some Notes from the Trenches," 49 *Ohio St. L.J.* 884, 896 (1989).

The book Karen wrote to help gather support for her legal battle appends forms to be used in creating a durable power of attorney. Karen Thompson & Julie Andreze-jewski, *Why Can't Sharon Kowalski Come Home?* at app. B (1988).

58. Thomas B. Stoddard, "Gay Marriages: Make Them Legal," *New York Times*, March 4, 1989, at 27.

59. When they received Women of Courage Awards from the National Organiza-tion for Women last July, N.O.W. President Molly Yard said, "Such a demonstration of guts. The letters I get from so many women who feel they're being totally screwed by the legal system—Sharon and Karen give them hope." Sally Ann Stewart, "NOW Salutes Couple's Five Year Legal Battle," *U.S.A. Today* (final edition), July 2, 1990, at 3A.

60. Brozan, *supra* note 54.

61. The Kowalskis emphasized that Sharon had closed the joint bank account she had maintained with Karen, and had told her sister that she was considering moving to Colorado because Karen was "very possessive." They didn't believe that Sharon and Karen had been lovers, because Sharon had told them nothing of the sort. In re Kowalski, 382 N.W.2d 861, 863 (Minn. Ct. App.), cert. denied, 106 S. Ct. 1467 (1986).

62. David Behrens, "The Case of Sharon Kowalski," *Newsday*, August 5, 1988, § 2, at 2 (Nassau & Suffolk ed.); Brozan, *supra* note 54.

63. In re Kowalski, 382 N.W.2d at 863.

64. Id. In her book, Karen tells this story in some detail. Thompson & Andreze-jewski, *supra* note 57, at 7–164.

65. In re Kowalski, 382 N.W.2d at 863–64.

66. The court noted that there was conflicting evidence about the nature of their relationship before Sharon's accident, and that although Sharon enjoyed Karen's visits she always became depressed after Karen left. In re Kowalski, 382 N.W.2d at 863, 865; In re Kowalski, 392 N.W.2d 310, 313–14 (1986).

67. Stoddard, *supra* note 58.

68. See In re Guardianship of Kowalski, 478 N.W.2d 790, 793 (Minn. App. 1991).

69. Id. at 795. This conclusion was based upon the testimony of all of the "approximately 16 medical witnesses . . . who had treated Sharon and had firsthand knowledge of her condition and care." Id. at 793.

70. Id. at 791–92; see also Wire Dispatches and Staff Report, "Nurses Testify in Lesbian-Lover Case," Washington Times, Dec. 6, 1990, at B-5.

71. Associated Press, "Lesbian's Plea to End Guardianship Battle," Chicago Tribune, Dec. 9, 1990, at C-12.

72. Thompson & Andrezejewski, supra note 57, at 10–16.

73. Morgan, supra note 36.

74. Miller, supra note 42.

75. The court found that Sharon's "ability to respond or communicate had been inconsistent and, at times, unreliable." In re Sharon Kowalski, 382 N.W.2d 861, 865 (Minn. Ct. App.), cert. denied, 106 S. Ct. 1467 (1986). Karen, in her book, insists (as she apparently did, from the beginning, in court) that Sharon's consistent and reliably expressed desires to be with Karen were being ignored. Thompson & Andrezejewski, supra note 57, at 109–15, 152–53.

76. The trial court did find that Karen had a "significant relationship" with Sharon. In re Sharon Kowalski, 382 N.W.2d 861, 863 (Minn. Ct. App.), cert. denied, 106 S. Ct. 1467 (1986).

77. Id. at 864.

78. Id. at 865.

79. Thompson & Andrezejewski, supra note 57, at 168.

80. Murdoch, supra note 55.

81. Donald Kowalski indisputably presented his daughter as reduced to helpless, sexless infancy, at least to the press. He was quoted as saying, "What the hell difference does it make if she's gay or lesbian or straight or anything because she's laying there in diapers? . . . Let the poor kid rest in peace." Joyce Murdoch, "Fighting for Control of a Loved One; Guardianship Dispute Pits Disabled Woman's Partner, Family," Washington Post (final edition), August 5, 1988, at A1.

82. Id.

83. In re Guardianship of Kowalski, 478 N.W.2d 790, 794 (Minn. App. 1991). Karen's renewed attention to Sharon and involvement in her care has brought Sharon many benefits. For example, during Sharon's three-year stay in the nursing home she had curled into fetal position and, not being regularly exercised, developed contractures. After Sharon was moved, her contractures were surgically released to permit her to be able to learn to use her limbs again. Karen Thompson, Talk at Smith College (March 6, 1991); accord, In re Sharon Kowalski, No. 11146, at 4 (Minn. Dist. Ct. April 23, 1991).

84. In re Guardianship of Kowalski, 478 N.W.2d, at 791.

85. In re Sharon Kowalski, No. 11146, at 10.

86. Id. (emphasis added).

87. Id. at 11 (emphasis added).

88. The court found, "At the time of the accident, Sharon was sharing a home in St. Cloud with her lesbian partner, appellant Karen Thompson. They had exchanged

rings, named each other as insurance beneficiaries, and had been living as a couple for four years." In re Guardianship of Kowalski, 478 N.W.2d, at 793–94.

89. "[T]he medical witnesses were asked how Thompson interacted with the staff and whether she was troublesome or overbearing in her demands for Sharon. No witness responded that Thompson caused trouble, but rather each said she is highly cooperative and exceptionally attentive to what treatments and activities are in Sharon's best interests. The court-appointed social worker also testified that Thompson was attentive to Sharon's needs, and would be a forceful advocate for Sharon's rehabilitation." Id. at 794.

90. In re Sharon Kowalski, No. 11146, at 3–6 (Minn. Dist. Ct. April 23, 1991).

91. In re Guardianship of Kowalski, 478 N.W.2d, at 793.

92. In re Sharon Kowalski, No. 11146, at 14.

93. Id.

94. For example, the judge found that "Karen Thompson has demonstrated a lack of understanding of Sharon's consanguineous family and the family's Minnesota Iron Range cultural background [which] is injurious to Sharon's social and emotional wellbeing." Id. at 16. This was tantamount to holding Karen responsible for Sharon's family's intolerance.

95. Id. at 11–12.

96. In re Sharon Kowalski, No. 11146 (Minn. Dist. Ct., April 23, 1991).

97. In re Guardianship of Kowalski, 478 N.W.2d 790, 795 (Minn. App. 1991).

98. In re Sharon Kowalski, No. 11146, at 8.

99. This is the crucial paragraph:

> Sharon has appeared at several public events since her accident, events whose themes have been celebration of gay and lesbian pride or recognition of Sharon as a woman of courage in the struggle for gay and lesbian rights. While present stimulation helps her, and while the testimony is undisputed that Sharon assented to such appearances, it is by no means certain that Sharon made [them] of her own free will, but rather to please [Karen] who was present whenever the questions of attendance were put to Sharon. Free speech presumes sound memory of recent past and distant past and reasonable perception of the present. Since there is no dispute that Sharon's short-term memory is very poor and her life consists of the present and her premorbid past, averment of free choice by Sharon is highly questionable, particularly in light of her lack of political activism and undisputed reluctance to reveal her sexual orientation before her accident.

Id. at 6.

100. Id. at 5–6.

101. In re Guardianship of Kowalski, 478 N.W.2d 790, 795 (Minn. App. 1991). "[W]hile the extent to which Sharon had publicly acknowledged her sexual preference at the time of the accident is unclear, this is no longer relevant. Since the accident, Sharon's doctors and therapists testified that Sharon has voluntarily told them of her relationship with Thompson. Moreover, Sharon's doctor testified that it was in Sharon's best interest for Thompson to reveal the nature of their relationship promptly after the

accident because it is crucial for doctors to understand who their patient was prior to the accident, including that patient's sexuality." Id. The Court of Appeals also noted that all firsthand observers agreed Sharon had consented to, and enjoyed, her public appearances. Finally, the court rejected the suggestion that Karen had any conflicts of interest disqualifying her from being Sharon's guardian. Id.

102. Lillian Hellman, "The Children's Hour," in Plays By and About Women, 19, 19–96 (Victoria Sullivan & James Hatch eds. 1974).

103. At the play's end Karen has broken her engagement and faces a bleak and penurious future; Martha has killed herself.

104. Nora D. Randall, "Great Explanations," in Dykewords: An Anthology of Lesbian Writing 135, 139 (The Lesbian Writing and Publishing Collective eds., 1990).

105. Virginia found a different after-school job. I assured her parents, in good conscience, that Mary was romantically interested only in "adults like herself" (she was about twenty) and not in "children" like their sixteen-year-old daughter. This was certainly true. Mary understood that there are worse risks than rejection, and that however shy she felt with her peers or confident with someone younger, even a "mature" high school student was too young for her.

106. Mary did confide in her mother, against the possibility that the story would get in the local press. She said it brought them closer together.

107. Some examples, more or less randomly chosen, are: Jan Clausen, Sinking, Stealing (1985); Anna Livia, Relatively Norma (1982); Renee, Willy Nilly (1990).

108. Hellman, supra note 102, at 89–90.

109. E.g., Radcliffe Hall, The Unlit Lamp (Dial Press, 1981) (1924). Two women spend years planning to go away together, but never do. Kate, the lesbian heroine of Jane Rule's This is Not For You, supra note 44, never sleeps with the one woman she loves, Esther, and eventually stops having sex with anyone at all.

110. Zimmerman, supra note 3, at 96.

111. Id. at 99–103. This may reflect a more general poverty of language to describe lesbian sexual experience. See Marilyn Frye, "Lesbian 'Sex,'" in Lesbian Philosophies and Cultures 305, 305–15 (Jeffner Allen ed. 1990).

112. See Michel Foucault, The History of Sexuality, Vol. I: An Introduction (Robert Hurley trans., 1980).

113. Interestingly, when Lillian Hellman dramatized the true story of Miss Pirie and Miss Woods (recounted in Faderman, supra note 11) in "The Children's Hour," one of the changes she made was to make it clear that the women were not lovers. Faderman, after much study, couldn't be sure whether they had been or not.

NOTES ON EDITORS AND CONTRIBUTORS

▼

Susan Sage Heinzelman is Senior Lecturer in the English Department at the University of Texas at Austin. She is the author of several articles that investigate the relationship between feminist, literary, and legal theory. Her essay in this anthology is part of a larger project on the relationship between eighteenth-century evidentiary theory and women's writing titled *Legal Facts and Feminist Fictions: Laws of Evidence and Women's Writing, 1688–1760*.

Zipporah Batshaw Wiseman is Thomas H. Law Professor of Law at the University of Texas at Austin. She teaches commercial law, courses on women and law, and feminist jurisprudence. She has published articles on commercial law and the history of the Uniform Commercial Code and is working on a biography of Soia Mentschikoff. She organized, with Susan Sage Heinzelman, the conference that was the genesis of this anthology.

Kathyrn Abrams is Professor of Law and Associate Professor of Ethics and Public Life at Cornell University. She teaches gender discrimination, voting rights, and local government. She is the author of many articles on a broad range of subjects from legal interpretation to issues of gender, race, and narrative in the law.

Linda Brodkey is Associate Professor of English and Director of the Writing Program at the University of California at San Diego. She has published many articles on composition theory and pedagogy and is the author of *Academic Writing as Social Practice* (1987).

Rita Copeland is Associate Professor of English at the University of Minnesota. She is the author of *Rhetoric, Hermeneutics, and Translation in the Middle Ages: Academic Traditions and Vernacular Texts* (1991) and of many articles on medieval literary theory. Her current research concerns Lollard textuality, critical theory, and political dissent in the late Middle Ages.

Elizabeth Cullingford is Professor of English at the University of Texas at Austin. She is the author of *Yeats, Ireland and Fascism* (1981) and editor of *Yeats's Poems, 1919–1935: A Casebook* (1984). She has recently published *Gender and History in Yeats's Love Poetry* (1993).

Margaret Anne Doody is Andrew W. Mellon Professor of Humanities and Professor of English at Vanderbilt University, where she is Director of the Comparative Literature Program. She has authored several books on subjects ranging from Augustan poetry to the fiction of Samuel Richardson. She also published the first critical biography of the novelist Frances Burney, titled *Frances Burney: The Life in the Works* (1987).

Susan B. Estrich is the Robert Kingsley Professor of Law and Political Science at the University of Southern California, where she teaches criminal law. She is the author of *Real Rape* (1987), which examines the discontinuities between the contemporary law of rape and women's lives. She was campaign manager for the Dukakis-Bentsen presidential campaign and currently hosts a radio talk show in Los Angeles.

Michelle Fine is Professor of Education at the University of Pennsylvania. She has authored books and articles on educational policy, pedagogy, and feminist research. Her most recent study is titled *Beyond Silenced Voices: Class, Race, and Gender in United States Schools* (1993).

Anne B. Goldstein is Professor of Law at Western New England College School of Law, where she teaches family law, conflict of laws, trusts and estates, and criminal law. She practiced civil rights law in Boston before she became a teacher of law. She is the author of "History, Homosexuality, and Political Values: Searching for the Hidden Determinants of *Bowers v. Hardwick*" (97 *Yale L.J.* 1073 [1988]).

Angela P. Harris is Acting Professor of Law at the University of California at Berkeley. She teaches courses in criminal law, civil rights, and contemporary American legal theory. She is interested in the relationship among race, gender, and class in legal theory and in social life.

Christine L. Krueger is Associate Professor of English at Marquette University. She is the author of *The Reader's Repentance: Women Preachers, Women Writers, and Nineteenth-Century Social Discourse* (1992).

Martha Minow is Professor of Law at Harvard University. In addition to her leading articles in feminist theory, she writes and lectures extensively on other areas of difference. She is the author, most recently, of *Making All* the *Difference* (1990), which examines issues of exclusion and inclusion in American law.

Carol Sanger is Professor of Law at Santa Clara University, where she teaches family law, contracts, and feminist jurisprudence. She has written several articles on the family formation and is the author of *Separating from Children: Literary and Legal Responses to Maternal-Child Separations* (forthcoming).

Judy Scales-Trent is Professor of Law at SUNY-Buffalo, where she teaches constitutional law, law and literature, and legal and policy issues affecting women of color. She practiced at the Equal Employment Opportunity Commission before she became a teacher of law. She is the author of several articles on race and legal pedagogy.

Library of Congress Cataloging-in-Publication Data

Representing women : law, literature, and feminism / Susan Sage
Heinzelman and Zipporah Batshaw Wiseman, editors.

p.   cm.

Includes bibliographical references and index.

ISBN 0-8223-1481-9 (cloth : acid-free paper).—

ISBN 0-8223-1495-9 (paper : acid-free paper)

1. Women—Legal status, laws, etc.   2. Feminist jurisprudence.

3. Women in literature.   4. Women—Social conditions.

I. Heinzelman, Susan Sage.   II. Wiseman, Zipporah Batshaw.

K349.R47   1994

305.42—dc20   94-6023   CIP